INTERNATIONAL CAPITAL MARKETS STATISTICS

This special historical edition provides a unique set of statistics on euro-bond and foreign bond issues since 1950, and medium-term syndicated bank loan operations since 1972. In the electronic edition, statistics are provided as **MONTHLY SERIES** and include a number of detailed breakdowns aggregated by borrowing country, by currency of issue or market, and by type of instrument.

Diskettes come with STATVIEW, a modern publication programme for statistical information developed by and for the Netherlands Central Bureau of Statistics. STATVIEW allows easy data handling and extraction to your own computer. STATVIEW allows you to download massive tables of OECD data and to tailor them easily and rapidly for your own needs. Tables can be exported in standard file formats and instructions can be safeguarded for repeated operations. STATVIEW also allows you to view the selected data in simplified analytical graph form. Technical documentation provides information on STATVIEW and a comprehensive description of the underlying data.
STATVIEW is suitable for use on IBM compatible PCs running MS-DOS or Microsoft Windows version 3.1 or higher.

Monthly updates of the historical edition are also available on diskette under the title OECD *Financial Statistics Monthly -- Part 1 - Section 1: International Markets*.

1996 Subscription: FF 2 700 £ 300 US$ 490 DM 820
Historical data available separately at: FF 800 £ 90 US$ 145 DM 240

Please return the order form below to OECD in Paris, one of the OECD Publications Centres in Bonn, Mexico, Tokyo or Washington, or the OECD Distributor in your country (see list at the end of this book).

OECD Publications
2, Rue André-Pascal
75775 Paris Cedex 16, France

———————— ORDER FORM ————————

❏ I wish to subscribe to the *OECD Financial Statistics Monthly- Part 1-Section 1: International Markets* on diskette, **at the price of: FF 2 700 £ 300 US$ 490 DM 820**
❏ I wish to order *International Capital Markets Statistics 1950-1995* on diskette at the price of:
FF 800 £ 90 US$ 145 DM 240

❏ Payment is enclosed
❏ Charge my card VISA/MASTERCARD/EUROCARD *(You will be invoiced in French Francs)*
Card No.:..Expiration Date:..........................Signature:...........................

Send to *(Please print)*:

Name:...

Address:..

Country:......................................Tel. No. ....Fax No.:...........................

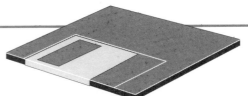

STATISTIQUES DES MARCHÉS INTERNATIONAUX DES CAPITAUX

Cette édition historique spéciale présente un ensemble unique de statistiques sur les euro-obligations et les émissions étrangères depuis 1950, ainsi que sur les crédits consortiaux à moyen terme depuis 1972. La publication électronique contient des **SÉRIES MENSUELLES**, de même qu'une décomposition détaillée des statistiques regroupées par pays emprunteurs, par devise d'émission ou marché, et par type d'instrument financier.

Les disquettes sont livrées avec le programme STATVIEW, un programme moderne de publications d'informations statistiques, mis au point par le Bureau central des statistiques des Pays-Bas. STATVIEW permet un traitement aisé des données et leur extraction vers votre propre ordinateur. STATVIEW vous permet de télécharger des tableaux importants de données de l'OCDE et de les façonner très rapidement et en toute facilité selon vos besoins. Les tableaux peuvent être exportés dans des formats standards et les instructions peuvent être sauvegardées pour des opérations répétitives. STATVIEW vous permet également de visualiser les informations choisies sous une forme graphique simple. Vous trouverez des informations détaillées sur STATVIEW dans la documentation technique ainsi qu'une description complète des données.

STATVIEW peut être utilisé sur un PC compatible IBM, fonctionnant sous MS-DOS, ou Microsoft Windows, version 3.1 ou supérieure.

Des mises à jour mensuelles de l'édition historique sont également disponibles sur disquette sous le titre *Statistiques financières mensuelles de l'OCDE -- partie I -- Section 1 : Marchés internationaux.*

Abonnement 1996 : FF 2 700 £ 300 US$ 490 DM 820

Données historiques disponibles séparément : FF 800 £ 90 US$ 145 DM 240

Vous pouvez renvoyer le bon de commande ci-dessous aux Éditions de l'OCDE à Paris, à l'un des Centres de publications et d'information à Bonn, Mexico, Tokyo, ou Washington, ou au distributeur de l'OCDE dans votre pays (c.f. liste à la fin ce cet ouvrage.)

OCDE Publications
2, Rue André-Pascal, 75775 Paris Cedex 16, France

– – – – – – – Bon de Commande – – – – – – –

❏ Je souhaite m'abonner aux *Statistiques financières mensuelles de l'OCDE - Partie 1 - Section 1: Marchés internationaux* sous forme de disquette, au prix de : **FF 2 700 £ 300 US$ 490 DM 820**

❏ Je souhaite recevoir *Statistiques des marchés internationaux des capitaux 1950-1995* sous forme de disquette au prix de : **FF 800 £ 90 US$ 145 DM 240**

❏ Règlement joint

❏ Débitez ma carte VISA/MASTERCARD/EUROCARD *(Vous serez facturé en francs français)*

N° de carte :..................................Date d'expiration:....................Signature:.........................

Adresse d'expédition *(Prière d'écrire en majuscules)*:

Nom :..

Adresse :...

Pays :...Tél. N°:......................Fax N°:..................................

BANK PROFITABILITY
Financial Statements
of Banks
[1979–1994]*

The data, provided on 3 1/2" double-sided, double-density diskettes formatted on both sides, suitable for IBM or IBM-compatible microcomputers, are supplied in a compressed format specific to OECD. The diskettes include a simple program for transferring data into DIF, SYLK, or LOTUS.WKS formats. Data can therefore be readily used with such software packages as LOTUS 1-2-3, QUATTRO-PRO, EXCEL and the MS-DOS operating system.

Full technical documentation, including a detailed section on "Definitions", accompanies each data package.

The price for the 1996 edition of this annual diskette has been fixed at:

FF 1 100   US$ 200   £ 120   DM 335

with discounts for academic circles and government agencies. Subscribers wishing to redistribute the statistics shall be required to complete a special contract.

Orders or enquiries should be sent to OECD Publications in Paris, one of OECD's Centres in Bonn, Tokyo or Washington, or the OECD Distributor in your country.

OECD Publications
2, rue André-Pascal, 75775 Paris Cedex 16, France
Fax: (33)1-49.10.42.76

* Includes also statistics on Iceland and Mexico, published for the first time.

BANK PROFITABILITY

◆

RENTABILITÉ DES BANQUES

FINANCIAL
STATEMENTS OF BANKS
COMPTES DES BANQUES
1985-1994

ORGANISATION FOR ECONOMIC CO-OPERATION AND DEVELOPMENT
ORGANISATION DE COOPÉRATION ET DE DÉVELOPPEMENT ÉCONOMIQUES

ORGANISATION FOR ECONOMIC CO-OPERATION AND DEVELOPMENT

ORGANISATION DE COOPÉRATION ET DE DÉVELOPPEMENT ÉCONOMIQUES

Pursuant to Article 1 of the Convention signed in Paris on 14th December 1960, and which came into force on 30th September 1961, the Organisation for Economic Co-operation and Development (OECD) shall promote policies designed:

- to achieve the highest sustainable economic growth and employment and a rising standard of living in Member countries, while maintaining financial stability, and thus to contribute to the development of the world economy;
- to contribute to sound economic expansion in Member as well as non-member countries in the process of economic development; and
- to contribute to the expansion of world trade on a multilateral, non-discriminatory basis in accordance with international obligations.

The original Member countries of the OECD are Austria, Belgium, Canada, Denmark, France, Germany, Greece, Iceland, Ireland, Italy, Luxembourg, the Netherlands, Norway, Portugal, Spain, Sweden, Switzerland, Turkey, the United Kingdom and the United States. The following countries became Members subsequently through accession at the dates indicated hereafter: Japan (28th April 1964), Finland (28th January 1969), Australia (7th June 1971), New Zealand (29th May 1973), Mexico (18th May 1994) and the Czech Republic (21st December 1995). The Commission of the European Communities takes part in the work of the OECD (Article 13 of the OECD Convention).

En vertu de l'article 1er de la Convention signée le 14 décembre 1960, à Paris, et entrée en vigueur le 30 septembre 1961, l'Organisation de Coopération et de Développement Économiques (OCDE) a pour objectif de promouvoir des politiques visant :

- à réaliser la plus forte expansion de l'économie et de l'emploi et une progression du niveau de vie dans les pays Membres, tout en maintenant la stabilité financière, et à contribuer ainsi au développement de l'économie mondiale ;
- à contribuer à une saine expansion économique dans les pays Membres, ainsi que les pays non membres, en voie de développement économique ;
- à contribuer à l'expansion du commerce mondial sur une base multilatérale et non discriminatoire conformément aux obligations internationales.

Les pays Membres originaires de l'OCDE sont : l'Allemagne, l'Autriche, la Belgique, le Canada, le Danemark, l'Espagne, les États-Unis, la France, la Grèce, l'Irlande, l'Islande, l'Italie, le Luxembourg, la Norvège, les Pays-Bas, le Portugal, le Royaume-Uni, la Suède, la Suisse et la Turquie. Les pays suivants sont ultérieurement devenus Membres par adhésion aux dates indiquées ci-après : le Japon (28 avril 1964), la Finlande (28 janvier 1969), l'Australie (7 juin 1971), la Nouvelle-Zélande (29 mai 1973), le Mexique (18 mai 1994) et la République tchèque (21 décembre 1995). La Commission des Communautés européennes participe aux travaux de l'OCDE (article 13 de la Convention de l'OCDE).

FOREWORD

This publication provides data on financial statements of banks for the period 1985-1994, and updates the statistics published in *Bank Profitability, Financial Statements of Banks 1984-93 (*OECD, Paris, 1995). The coverage of banks in these statistics is not the same in each country, though the objective is to include all institutions which conduct ordinary banking business, namely institutions which primarily take deposits from the public at large and provide finance for a wide range of purposes. Some supplementary information on the number of reporting banks, their branches and staff is also included.

The institutional coverage of the tables has been largely dictated by the availability of data on income and expenditure accounts of banks. As a result of the reporting methods which are being used in OECD countries, the tables are not integrated in the system of national accounts and are, therefore, not compatible with the *Financial Accounts of OECD Countries*. International comparisons in the field of income and expenditure accounts of banks are particularly difficult due to considerable differences in OECD countries as regards structural and regulatory features of national banking systems, accounting rules and practices, and reporting methods.

The preparation of this publication could not have been accomplished without the assistance of the members of the OECD Group of Financial Statisticians and the national administrations which they represent. It is published, on the Group's recommendation, on the responsibility of the Secretary-General of the OECD.

AVANT-PROPOS

Cet ouvrage présente les données relatives aux comptes de résultats et aux bilans des banques pour la période 1985-94, et met à jour les statistiques publiées dans *Rentabilité des banques, Comptes des banques 1984-1993* (OCDE, Paris, 1995). La couverture des banques figurant dans ces statistiques n'est pas la même dans chaque pays, bien que l'objectif reste d'inclure toutes les institutions qui effectuent des opérations courantes de banque, c'est-à-dire qui reçoivent des dépôts du public et offrent des concours financiers à des fins très étendues. Des informations complémentaires sur le nombre de banques, celui de leurs succursales et de leurs salariés figurent également dans cet ouvrage.

La couverture institutionnelle des tableaux a été largement dictée par la disponibillité des données sur les comptes de revenus et de dépenses des banques. Du fait des modes de communication des données en vigueur dans les pays de l'OCDE, ces tableaux ne sont pas intégrés dans le Système de comptabilité nationale et ne sont donc pas compatibles avec les *Comptes financiers des pays de l'OCDE*. Les comparaisons internationales dans le domaine des comptes de revenus et de dépenses des banques sont particulièrement délicates étant donné les différences importantes qui existent entre les pays de l'OCDE en ce qui concerne la structure du système bancaire et la réglementation des banques, les règles et pratiques comptables et le système de communication des données.

Cette publication n'aurait pu être réalisée sans l'aide des membres du Groupe de statisticiens financiers de l'OCDE et des administrations nationales qu'ils représentent. Cet ouvrage est publié, sur la recommandation du Groupe, sous la responsabilité du Secrétaire général de l'OCDE.

CONTENTS

CONVENTIONAL SIGNS

N.A.	*Not available*
-	*Nil or negligible*
..	*Not applicable or breakdown not available*
·	*Decimal point*

TABLE DES MATIERES

SIGNES CONVENTIONNELS

N.A. *Non disponible*
- *Nul ou négligeable*
.. *Non approprié ou*
   ventilation non disponible
· *Point decimal (sépare*
   les unités des décimale)

INTRODUCTION

National data on **income and expenditure accounts of banks** are grouped and, where necessary, re-classified to fit as far as possible into the following standard framework of presentation:

Income statement

1. Interest income

2. Interest expenses

3. Net interest income (item 1 minus item 2)

4. Non-interest income (net)

5. Gross income (item 3 plus item 4)

6. Operating expenses

7. Net income (item 5 minus item 6)

8. Provisions (net)

9. Profit before tax (item 7 minus item 8)

10. Income tax

11. Profit after tax (item 9 minus item 10)

12. Distributed profit

13. Retained profit (item 11 minus item 12)

Memorandum items

14. Staff costs (included in item 6)

15. Net provisions on loans (included in item 8)

16. Net provisions on securities (included in item 8)

Interest income (item 1) generally includes income on interest-bearing assets, fee income related to lending operations, and dividend income on shares and participations. In some cases it may also include income on bonds calculated as the difference between the book value and the redemption value of bonds.

Interest expenses (item 2) generally includes interest paid on liabilities, fee expenses related to borrowing operations and may include in some cases the difference between the issue price on debt instruments and their par value.

Non-interest income (net) (item 4) is generally the net result of a number of different income and expense items (other than those included in items 1 and 2) such as the following: commissions received and paid in connection with payments services, securities transactions and related services (new issues, trading, portfolio management, safe-custody) and foreign exchange transactions in the banks' own name and on behalf of clients. Other income and expenses resulting from special transactions which do not represent ordinary and regular banking business may also be included. Realised losses and gains on foreign-exchange operations and securities transactions are generally included as well.

Operating expenses (item 6) usually include all expenses relating to the ordinary and regular banking business other than those included in items 2 and 4, particularly salaries and other employee benefits, including transfers to pension reserves (staff costs), and expenses for property and equipment and related depreciation expenses. Taxes other than income or corporate taxes are also included.

Provisions (net) (item 8) generally include, in part or in full, charges for value adjustments in respect of loans, credits and securities, book gains from such adjustments, losses on loans and transfers to and from reserves for possible losses on such assets. Realised gains or losses from foreign exchange transactions and securities transactions are, however, generally included under *Non-interest income (net)* (item 4).

Any deviation from this standard presentation and classification of income and expenditure account items is generally indicated in the methodological country notes.

National data on **balance sheets of banks** are grouped and, where necessary, re-classified in order to fit as far as possible into the following standard framework of presentations:

Balance sheet

Assets

17.   Cash and balance with Central bank

18.   Interbank deposits

19.   Loans

20.   Securities

21.   Other assets

Liabilities

22.   Capital and reserves

23.   Borrowing from Central bank

24.   Interbank deposits

25.   Non-bank deposits

26.   Bonds

27.   Other liabilities

Balance sheet total

28.   End-year total (sum of items 17 to 21 or 22 to 27)

29.   Average total

Memorandum items

30.   Short-term securities (included in item 20)

31.   Bonds (included in item 20)

32.   Shares and participations (included in item 20)

33.   Claims on non-residents (included in items 18 to 21)

34.   Liabilities to non-residents (included in items 24 to 27)

Short-term securities (item 30) are, following the definition used in the European System of Integrated Accounts (paragraph 539), securities with an original maturity of usually up to 12 months, but with a maximum maturity of two years.

Bonds (item 31), are, following the definition of the European System of Integrated Accounts (paragraph 542), fixed or variable-interest rate securities with an original maturity of several years.

In countries in which there is re-discounting of commercial bills with the central bank, the volume of re-discounted bills is usually included on each side of the balance sheet, under *Loans* (item 19) on the assets side and under *Borrowing from central bank* (item 23) on the liabilities side.

The following **supplementary information** is provided:

35.   Number of institutions (covered by the data)

36.   Number of branches (covered by the data)

37.   Number of staff ('000) (of the institutions covered by the data)

In order to facilitate the interpretation and analysis of the data included in the present publication and to enable the user of the data to judge how cautiously the figures should be used for comparative purposes, the notes which give detailed information on the following:

- Institutional coverage, and the relative importance of the institutions covered as compared with the whole financial system;

- Geographical coverage and degree of consolidation indicating whether domestic or foreign financial or non-financial subsidiaries of the reporting banks are covered by the data and whether branches and/or subsidiaries of foreign banks are included;

- Summary description of activities of banks indicating in particular whether the banks carry out important service activities producing fee income such as a wide range of securities-related activities and foreign exchange trading;

- Income statement reconciliation table giving detailed information on the way in which the income statement data shown in the present publication are derived from generally more detailed national data;

- Balance sheet reconciliation table giving detailed information on the way in which the balance sheet data shown in the present publication are derived from more detailed national balance sheet data;

- Explanations on some items of the income statement and balance sheet in cases in which national data cannot entirely be fitted into the standard framework. The income statement item *Provisions (net)* (item 8) receives special attention in the commentary;

- Sources of data on income statements and balance sheets of banks with indication of method of compilation.

INTRODUCTION

Les données communiquées par les pays concernant **les comptes de résultats des banques** sont groupées après, le cas échéant, reclassement pour cadrer, autant que possible, avec le modèle de présentation ci-après :

Compte de resultats

1. Produits financiers,

2. Frais financiers

3. Produits financiers nets (poste 1 moins poste 2)

4. Produits non financiers (nets)

5. Résultat brut (poste 3 plus poste 4)

6. Frais d'exploitation

7. Résultat net (poste 5 moins poste 6)

8. Provisions (nettes)

9. Bénéfices avant impôt (poste 7 moins poste 8)

10. Impôt sur le revenu/les sociétés

11. Bénéfices après impôt (poste 9 moins poste 10)

12. Bénéfices distribués

13. Bénéfices mis en réserve (poste 11 moins poste 12)

Pour mémoire

14. Frais de personnel (comptabilisés au poste 6)

15. Provisions nettes sur prêts (comptabilisées au poste 8)

16. Provisions nettes sur titres (comptabilisées au poste 8)

Le poste *Produits financiers,* (poste 1) comprend, en principe, les revenus procurés par les actifs porteurs d'intérêts, les commissions afférentes aux opérations de prêt, ainsi que les dividendes d'actions et titres de participation. Dans certains cas, il peut comprendre aussi les revenus d'obligations considérés comme étant égaux à la différence entre la valeur comptable et la valeur de remboursement des titres.

Le poste *Frais financiers* (poste 2) comprend, en principe, les intérêts versés sur les emprunts et les commissions versées sur les opérations d'emprunt. Il peut comprendre aussi la différence entre la valeur d'émission des instruments de dette et leur valeur nominale.

Le poste *Produits non financiers (nets)* (poste 4) est normalement le résultat net d'un certain nombre de produits et frais différents (autres que ceux repris aux postes 1 et 2) comme les commissions perçues et versées à l'occasion de diverses opérations -- paiements, opérations sur titres (placement d'émissions, contrepartie, gestion de portefeuille, garde de titres), opérations de change -- effectuées par les banques tant pour leur propre compte que pour celui de leurs clients. Figurent aussi à ce poste, les produits et les charges résultant d'opérations exceptionnelles et non des activités courantes des banques. Les gains et pertes de change et les plus-values et moins-values sur la réalisation de titres de placement y figurent également.

Le poste *Frais d'exploitation* (poste 6) comprend, normalement, toutes les charges afférentes aux activités courantes des banques (à l'exclusion de celles reprises aux postes 2 et 4), en particulier les salaires et autres avantages perçus par les salariés, y compris les dotations au fonds de pension (frais de personnel) et les charges afférentes aux terrains et immeubles et aux matériels, mobilier et installations ainsi que les amortissements. Sont aussi comptabilisés à ce poste les impôts autres que l'impôt sur le revenu ou les sociétés.

Le poste *Provisions (nettes)* (poste 8) comprend, en principe, en partie ou en totalité, les charges pour ajustement de la valeur comptable des prêts, crédits et titres de placement, les plus-values comptables découlant de cet ajustement, les pertes sur prêts, les dotations aux provisions pour pertes sur ces éléments d'actif et les reprises de provisions. En revanche, les gains ou pertes de change et les plus-values ou moins-values sur la réalisation de titres de placement figurent normalement au poste *Produits non financiers (nets)* (poste 4).

Toute différence de présentation avec le présent modèle des éléments du compte de résultats est en principe indiquée dans les notes méthodologiques par pays.

Les données communiquées par les pays concernant **les bilans des banques** sont groupées après, le cas échéant, reclassement pour cadrer, autant que possible, avec le modèle de présentation ci-après :

Bilan

Actif

17.   Caisse et soldes auprès de la Banque centrale

18.   Dépôts interbancaires

19.   Prêts

20. Valeurs mobilières

21. Autres actifs

Passif

22. Capital et réserves

23. Emprunts auprès de la Banque centrale

24. Dépôts interbancaires

25. Dépôts non bancaires

26. Obligations

27. Autres engagements

Total du bilan

28. Total en fin d'exercice (somme des postes 17 à 21 ou 22 à 27)

29. Total moyen

Pour mémoire

30. Titres à court terme (comptabilisés au poste 20)

31. Obligations (comptabilisées au poste 20)

32. Actions et participations (comptabilisées au poste 20)

33. Créances sur des non résidents (comptabilisées aux postes 18 à 21)

34. Engagements envers des non résidents (comptabilisés aux postes 24 à 27)

Le poste *Titres à court terme* (poste 30) comprend, selon la définition du Système européen de comptes économiques intégrés (paragraphe 539), les titres dont l'échéance initiale est normalement de 12 mois, deux ans maximum.

Le poste *Obligations* (poste 31) comprend, selon la définition du Système européen de comptes économiques intégrés (paragraphe 542), les titres à revenu fixe ou variable initialement à plusieurs années d'échéance.

Dans les pays où existe la possibilité de réescompter des effets de commerce auprès de la Banque centrale, le montant des effets réescomptés figure habituellement à la fois à l'actif du bilan poste *Prêts* (poste 19) et au passif poste *Emprunts auprès de la Banque centrale* (poste 23).

On trouvera également les **renseignements complémentaires** suivants:

35.   Nombre d'institutions (prises en compte)

36.   Nombre de succursales (prises en compte)

37.   Nombre de salariés (en milliers) (des institutions prises en compte)

Pour faciliter l'interprétation et l'analyse des données reprises dans la présente publication et pour inciter l'utilisateur à être prudent dans l'utilisation des statistiques à des fins de comparaisons internationales, les notes apportent des précisions sur les points suivants :

- Les institutions sur lesquelles portent les statistiques et leur importance par rapport à l'ensemble du système financier.

- Le champ géographique et le degré de consolidation des opérations de ces institutions. Il sera précisé si sont comprises dans les données les filiales financières ou non financières, domestiques ou étrangères, des banques déclarantes ainsi que les succursales/filiales des banques étrangères.

- Une description succincte des activités des banques . Il sera indiqué, en particulier, si les banques se livrent à des activités de service génératrices de commissions, telles que des activités se rapportant aux valeurs mobilières et au commerce de devises.

- Un tableau de concordance des comptes de résultats qui donne des renseignements précis sur la façon dont les informations relatives aux comptes de résultats publiées dans cette publication ont été obtenues à partir de sources nationales, en général plus détaillées.

- Un tableau de concordance des bilans qui donne des renseignements précis sur la façon dont les bilans reproduits dans cette publication ont été construits à partir des bilans, plus détaillés, publiés dans le pays.

- Des explications sur certains postes des comptes de résultats et des bilans des banques, lorsqu'il n'est pas possible de faire parfaitement cadrer les données nationales avec la présentation type retenue. Le poste du compte de résultats *Provisions (nettes)* (poste 8), notamment, donne lieu à des commentaires.

- Les sources des données concernant les comptes de résultats et les bilans des banques ainsi que le mode de collecte.

FINANCIAL STATEMENTS OF BANKS 1985-94

COMPTES DES BANQUES 1985-94

AUSTRALIA

All banks

Million Australian dollars

AUSTRALIE

Ensemble des banques

Millions de dollars australiens

	1986	1987	1988	1989	1990	1991	1992	1993	1994	
INCOME STATEMENT										**COMPTE DE RESULTATS**
1. Interest income	21114	25061	27384	37341	48101	42744	33653	29136	28844	1. Produits financiers
2. Interest expenses	15770	18869	19173	27691	37442	31712	23306	18300	16909	2. Frais financiers
3. Net interest income	5344	6192	8211	9650	10659	11032	10347	10836	11935	3. Produits financiers nets
4. Non-interest income (net)	3420	4658	5327	5948	7129	10075	8111	7762	8409	4. Produits non financiers (nets)
5. Gross income	8764	10850	13538	15598	17788	21107	18458	18598	20344	5. Résultat brut
6. Operating expenses	6430	7238	8770	10144	11748	12672	13635	12409	12854	6. Frais d'exploitation
7. Net income	2334	3612	4768	5454	6040	8435	4823	6189	7490	7. Résultat net
8. Provisions (net)	461	803	1052	1709	3402	5117	4900	2560	1437	8. Provisions (nettes)
9. Profit before tax	1873	2809	3716	3745	2638	3318	-77	3629	6053	9. Bénéfices avant impôt
10. Income tax	658	1198	1703	1446	1079	1500	336	1440	1703	10. Impôt
11. Profit after tax	1215	1611	2013	2299	1559	1818	-413	2189	4350	11. Bénéfices après impôt
12. Distributed profit	571	579	1220	2102	1742	1390	1627	2101	2790	12. Bénéfices distribués
13. Retained profit	644	1032	793	197	-183	428	-2040	88	1560	13. Bénéfices mis en réserve
Memoranda										*Pour mémoire*
14. *Staff costs*	::	::	::	::	::	::	::	::	::	14. *Frais de personnel*
15. *Provisions on loans*	::	::	::	::	::	::	::	::	::	15. *Provisions sur prêts*
16. *Provisions on securities*	::	::	::	::	::	::	::	::	::	16. *Provisions sur titres*
BALANCE SHEET										**BILAN**
Assets										**Actif**
17. Cash & balance with Central bank	4639	4633	4714	4376	4197	3919	4215	4363	4768	17. Caisse & solde auprès de la Banque centrale
18. Interbank deposits	18751	18121	19191	31833	34483	32884	34770	28707	24597	18. Dépôts interbancaires
19. Loans (1)	116315	137164	161963	206300	239051	249425	256501	271828	284599	19. Prêts (1)
20. Securities (1)	33487	37877	46875	49597	30852	35460	40438	37524	38298	20. Valeurs mobilières (1)
21. Other assets (1)	37892	49876	68955	82233	109737	111918	118047	118955	113827	21. Autres actifs (1)
Liabilities										**Passif**
22. Capital & reserves	12766	15796	22953	28363	39300	43289	45221	46779	48803	22. Capital et réserves
23. Borrowing from Central bank	::	::	::	::	::	::	::	::	::	23. Emprunts auprès de la Banque centrale
24. Interbank deposits	24152	25528	26175	38352	36263	36914	42222	35436	33052	24. Dépôts interbancaires
25. Non-bank deposits (1)	::	::	::	::	228711	232934	245237	260154	269323	25. Dépôts non bancaires (1)
26. Bonds	::	::	::	::	::	::	::	::	::	26. Obligations
27. Other liabilities (1)	174166	206348	252568	307624	114046	120471	121294	119008	114911	27. Autres engagements (1)
Balance sheet total										**Total du bilan**
28. End-year total	211085	247673	301697	374339	418322	433608	453971	461377	466089	28. En fin d'exercice
29. Average total	184463	229379	274685	338018	396331	425965	443790	457674	463733	29. Moyen
Memoranda										*Pour mémoire*
30. *Short-term securities*	2874	6405	7712	8958	5919	10780	10212	9412	11262	30. *Titres à court terme*
31. *Bonds*	18288	18802	19443	14369	17160	14159	16024	15621	15674	31. *Obligations*
32. *Shares and participations (1)*	8047	8929	13508	14219	:	:	:	:	:	32. *Actions et participations (1)*
33. *Claims on non-residents*	:	:	:	:	:	:	:	:	:	33. *Créances sur des non résidents*
34. *Liabilities to non-residents*	:	:	:	:	:	:	:	:	:	34. *Engagements envers des non résidents*
SUPPLEMENTARY INFORMATION										**RENSEIGNEMENTS COMPLEMENTAIRES**
35. Number of institutions	31	32	32	32	32	29	28	29	29	35. Nombre d'institutions
36. Number of branches	15462	14981	14381	15009	14617	14203	13491	13338	12832	36. Nombre de succursales
37. Number of employees (x 1000)	NA	NA	NA	NA	NA	NA	NA	NA	NA	37. Nombre de salariés (x 1000)

AUSTRALIA

All banks

AUSTRALIE

Ensemble des banques

Per cent	1986	1987	1988	1989	1990	1991	1992	1993	1994	Pourcentage
INCOME STATEMENT ANALYSIS										**ANALYSE DU COMPTE DE RESULTATS**
% of average balance sheet total										**% du total moyen du bilan**
38. Interest income	11.45	10.93	9.97	11.05	12.14	10.03	7.58	6.37	6.22	38. Produits financiers
39. Interest expenses	8.55	8.23	6.98	8.19	9.45	7.44	5.25	4.00	3.65	39. Frais financiers
40. Net interest income	2.90	2.70	2.99	2.85	2.69	2.59	2.33	2.37	2.57	40. Produits financiers nets
41. Non-interest income (net)	1.85	2.03	1.94	1.76	1.80	2.37	1.83	1.70	1.81	41. Produits non financiers (nets)
42. Gross income	4.75	4.73	4.93	4.61	4.49	4.96	4.16	4.06	4.39	42. Résultat brut
43. Operating expenses	3.49	3.16	3.19	3.00	2.96	2.97	3.07	2.71	2.77	43. Frais d'exploitation
44. Net income	1.27	1.57	1.74	1.61	1.52	1.98	1.09	1.35	1.62	44. Résultat net
45. Provisions (net)	0.25	0.35	0.38	0.51	0.86	1.20	1.10	0.56	0.31	45. Provisions (nettes)
46. Profit before tax	1.02	1.22	1.35	1.11	0.67	0.78	-0.02	0.79	1.31	46. Bénéfices avant impôt
47. Income tax	0.36	0.52	0.62	0.43	0.27	0.35	0.08	0.31	0.37	47. Impôt
48. Profit after tax	0.66	0.70	0.73	0.68	0.39	0.43	-0.09	0.48	0.94	48. Bénéfices après impôt
49. Distributed profit	0.31	0.25	0.44	0.62	0.44	0.33	0.37	0.46	0.60	49. Bénéfices distribués
50. Retained profit	0.35	0.45	0.29	0.06	-0.05	0.10	-0.46	0.02	0.34	50. Bénéfices mis en réserve
51. Staff costs	:	:	:	:	:	:	:	:	:	51. Frais de personnel
52. Provisions on loans	:	:	:	:	:	:	:	:	:	52. Provisions sur prêts
53. Provisions on securities	:	:	:	:	:	:	:	:	:	53. Provisions sur titres
% of gross income										**% du total du résultat brut**
54. Net interest income	60.98	57.07	60.65	61.87	59.92	52.27	56.06	58.26	58.67	54. Produits financiers nets
55. Non-interest income (net)	39.02	42.93	39.35	38.13	40.08	47.73	43.94	41.74	41.33	55. Produits non financiers (nets)
56. Operating expenses	73.37	66.71	64.78	65.03	66.04	60.04	73.87	66.72	63.18	56. Frais d'exploitation
57. Net income	26.63	33.29	35.22	34.97	33.96	39.96	26.13	33.28	36.82	57. Résultat net
58. Provisions (net)	5.26	7.40	7.77	10.96	19.13	24.24	26.55	13.76	7.06	58. Provisions (nettes)
59. Profit before tax	21.37	25.89	27.45	24.01	14.83	15.72	-0.42	19.51	29.75	59. Bénéfices avant impôt
60. Income tax	7.51	11.04	12.58	9.27	6.07	7.11	1.82	7.74	8.37	60. Impôt
61. Profit after tax	13.86	14.85	14.87	14.74	8.76	8.61	-2.24	11.77	21.38	61. Bénéfices après impôt
62. Staff costs	:	:	:	:	:	:	:	:	:	62. Frais de personnel
% of net income										**% du total du résultat net**
63. Provisions (net)	19.75	22.23	22.06	31.33	56.32	60.66	101.60	41.36	19.19	63. Provisions (nettes)
64. Profit before tax	80.25	77.77	77.94	68.67	43.68	39.34	-1.60	58.64	80.81	64. Bénéfices avant impôt
65. Income tax	28.19	33.17	35.72	26.51	17.86	17.78	6.97	23.27	22.74	65. Impôt
66. Profit after tax	52.06	44.60	42.22	42.15	25.81	21.55	-8.56	35.37	58.08	66. Bénéfices après impôt

AUSTRALIA

All banks

Per cent

BALANCE SHEET ANALYSIS

% of year-end balance sheet total

	1986	1987	1988	1989	1990	1991	1992	1993	1994
Assets									
67. Cash & balance with Central bank	2.20	1.87	1.56	1.17	1.00	0.90	0.93	0.95	1.02
68. Interbank deposits	8.88	7.32	6.36	8.50	8.24	7.58	7.66	6.22	5.28
69. Loans (1)	55.10	55.38	53.68	55.11	57.15	57.52	56.50	58.92	61.06
70. Securities (1)	15.86	15.29	15.54	13.25	7.38	8.18	8.91	8.13	8.22
71. Other assets (1)	17.95	20.14	22.86	21.97	26.23	25.81	26.00	25.78	24.42
Liabilities									
72. Capital & reserves	6.05	6.38	7.61	7.58	9.39	9.98	9.96	10.14	10.47
73. Borrowing from Central bank	..	..	..	..	..	..	..	..	..
74. Interbank deposits	11.44	10.31	8.68	10.25	8.67	8.51	9.30	7.68	7.09
75. Non-bank deposits (1)	..	..	..	..	54.67	53.72	54.02	56.39	57.78
76. Bonds	..	..	..	..	..	..	..	..	..
77. Other liabilities (1)	82.51	83.31	83.72	82.18	27.26	27.78	26.72	25.79	24.65
Memoranda									
78. Short-term securities	*1.36*	*2.59*	*2.56*	*2.39*	*1.41*	*2.49*	*2.25*	*2.04*	*2.42*
79. Bonds	*8.66*	*7.59*	*6.44*	*3.84*	*4.10*	*3.27*	*3.53*	*3.39*	*3.36*
80. Shares and participations (1)	*3.81*	*3.61*	*4.48*	*3.80*	*..*	*..*	*..*	*..*	*..*
81. Claims on non-residents	*..*	*..*	*..*	*..*	*..*	*..*	*..*	*..*	*..*
82. Liabilities to non-residents	*..*	*..*	*..*	*..*	*..*	*..*	*..*	*..*	*..*

1. Change in methodology.

Change in methodology:

• Introduction of revised statistical collection in 1990 resulted in reclassification of shares and participations from "Securities" (item 20 or item 70) to "Loans" (item 19 or item 69) and "Other assets" (item 21 or item 71).

• As from 1990, "Shares and participations" (item 32 or item 80) are not separately available following the introduction of revised statistical collection.

• Until 1990, "Non-bank deposits" (item 25 or item 75) were included under "Other liabilities" (item 27 or item 77). This item includes a small proportion of deposits from other banks.

AUSTRALIE

Ensemble des banques

Pourcentage

ANALYSE DU BILAN

% du total du bilan en fin d'exercice

Actif
67. Caisse & solde auprès de la Banque centrale
68. Dépôts interbancaires
69. Prêts (1)
70. Valeurs mobilières (1)
71. Autres actifs (1)

Passif
72. Capital et réserves
73. Emprunts auprès de la Banque centrale
74. Dépôts interbancaires
75. Dépôts non bancaires (1)
76. Obligations
77. Autres engagements (1)

Pour mémoire
78. Titres à court terme
79. Obligations
80. Actions et participations (1)
81. Créances sur des non résidents
82. Engagements envers des non résidents

1. Changement méthodologique.

Changement méthodologique :

• La reclassification des actions et participations du poste 20 (ou poste 70) "Titres" au poste 19 (ou poste 69) "Prêts" et 21 (ou poste 71) "Autres actifs" est consécutive à l'introduction en 1990 d'une révision de la collecte statistique.

• A partir de 1990, les "Actions et participations" (poste 32 ou poste 80) ne sont plus disponibles séparément suite à l'introduction d'une révision de la collecte statistique.

• Jusqu'en 1990, les "Dépôts non bancaires" (poste 25 ou poste 75) étaient inclus sous "Autres engagements" (poste 27 ou poste 77). Ce poste inclut une petite partie des dépôts des autres banques.

AUSTRIA / AUTRICHE

All banks / Ensemble des banques

Million schillings / Millions de schillings

	English	French	1987	1988	1989	1990	1991	1992	1993	1994
INCOME STATEMENT		**COMPTE DE RESULTATS**								
1.	Interest income	Produits financiers	215539	229896	275916	327360	347980	355738	332995	315878
2.	Interest expenses	Frais financiers	156960	166908	210562	256357	271594	273939	241563	221898
3.	Net interest income	Produits financiers nets	58579	62988	65354	71003	76386	81799	91432	93980
4.	Non-interest income (net)	Produits non financiers (nets)	14353	17415	25226	31767	36158	41005	35430	37905
5.	Gross income	Résultat brut	72932	80403	90580	102770	112544	122804	126862	131885
6.	Operating expenses	Frais d'exploitation	51111	55047	59340	66661	73061	78573	80545	85851
7.	Net income	Résultat net	21821	25356	31240	36109	39483	44231	46317	46034
8.	Provisions (net)	Provisions (nettes)			14813	20032	22077	29108	25284	25287
9.	Profit before tax	Bénéfices avant impôt	21821	25356	16427	16077	17406	15123	21033	20747
10.	Income tax	Impôt	2934	3103	3157	3032	2911	2600	2725	2434
11.	Profit after tax	Bénéfices après impôt	18887	22253	13270	13045	14495	12523	18308	18313
12.	Distributed profit	Bénéfices distribués	..	..	..	..	..	..	..	..
13.	Retained profit	Bénéfices mis en réserve	..	..	..	..	..	..	..	..
	Memoranda	*Pour mémoire*								
14.	Staff costs	Frais de personnel	30098	32181	34696	39547	43379	46817	47343	50668
15.	Provisions on loans	Provisions sur prêts	..	..	6566	8050	11875	17857	19344	18167
16.	Provisions on securities	Provisions sur titres	..	..	5789	7348	3206	3749	1107	4741
BALANCE SHEET		**BILAN**								
Assets		**Actif**								
17.	Cash & balance with Central bank	Caisse & solde auprès de la Banque centrale	63737	67199	76883	73166	68441	83827	86601	93228
18.	Interbank deposits	Dépôts interbancaires	1220499	1231639	1223461	1235092	1242533	1303640	1437018	1472119
19.	Loans	Prêts	1561331	1710902	1884902	2048063	2213849	2379219	2467115	2562296
20.	Securities	Valeurs mobilières	388599	424417	445993	468099	492964	476684	539811	638953
21.	Other assets	Autres actifs	184965	183171	199619	216056	258405	297082	296131	312130
Liabilities		**Passif**								
22.	Capital & reserves	Capital et réserves	119054	141636	163595	186199	202114	220564	241649	263679
23.	Borrowing from Central bank	Emprunts auprès de la Banque centrale	2298	2792	1144	1533	1103	557	598	1378
24.	Interbank deposits	Dépôts interbancaires	1254249	1287885	1286495	1280553	1315567	1359228	1418268	1472380
25.	Non-bank deposits	Dépôts non bancaires	1373945	1452911	1569986	1725712	1876343	2029440	2144613	2272048
26.	Bonds	Obligations	517067	593320	659477	692662	705669	737231	815018	847944
27.	Other liabilities	Autres engagements	152517	138785	150162	153816	175396	193432	206529	221298
Balance sheet total		**Total du bilan**								
28.	End-year total	En fin d'exercice	3419130	3617329	3830858	4040476	4276192	4540452	4826676	5078727
29.	Average total	Moyen	3334251	3543249	3769759	4012331	4228420	4414568	4335612	4946920
	Memoranda	*Pour mémoire*								
30.	Short-term securities	Titres à court terme	10145	8439	5951	6807	6088	5468	5516	13496
31.	Bonds	Obligations	305492	334051	348443	352728	366784	361695	408885	493859
32.	Shares and participations	Actions et participations	51819	62326	76772	93973	112789	127830	133843	139862
33.	Claims on non-residents	Créances sur des non résidents	751664	816929	842640	843875	846806	915883	1012407	1039462
34.	Liabilities to non-residents	Engagements envers des non résidents	790712	877311	926274	932278	958893	1045004	1084039	1110421
SUPPLEMENTARY INFORMATION		**RENSEIGNEMENTS COMPLEMENTAIRES**								
35.	Number of institutions	Nombre d'institutions	1252	1250	1240	1210	1165	1104	1063	1053
36.	Number of branches	Nombre de succursales	4203	4295	4373	4497	4594	4667	4691	4683
37.	Number of employees (x 1000)	Nombre de salariés (x 1000)	68.6	70.2	66.6	68.5	69.9	70.0	68.9	71.2

AUSTRIA

All banks

AUTRICHE

Ensemble des banques

Per cent / *Pourcentage*

INCOME STATEMENT ANALYSIS / **ANALYSE DU COMPTE DE RESULTATS**

	1987	1988	1989	1990	1991	1992	1993	1994	
% of average balance sheet total									**% du total moyen du bilan**
38. Interest income	6.46	6.49	7.32	8.16	8.23	8.06	7.68	6.39	38. Produits financiers
39. Interest expenses	4.71	4.71	5.59	6.39	6.42	6.21	5.57	4.49	39. Frais financiers
40. Net interest income	1.76	1.78	1.73	1.77	1.81	1.85	2.11	1.90	40. Produits financiers nets
41. Non-interest income (net)	0.43	0.49	0.67	0.79	0.86	0.93	0.82	0.77	41. Produits non financiers (nets)
42. Gross income	2.19	2.27	2.40	2.56	2.66	2.78	2.93	2.67	42. Résultat brut
43. Operating expenses	1.53	1.55	1.57	1.66	1.73	1.78	1.86	1.74	43. Frais d'exploitation
44. Net income	0.65	0.72	0.83	0.90	0.93	1.00	1.07	0.93	44. Résultat net
45. Provisions (net)	..	..	0.39	0.50	0.52	0.66	0.58	0.51	45. Provisions (nettes)
46. Profit before tax	0.65	0.72	0.44	0.40	0.41	0.34	0.49	0.42	46. Bénéfices avant impôt
47. Income tax	0.09	0.09	0.08	0.08	0.07	0.06	0.06	0.05	47. Impôt
48. Profit after tax	0.57	0.63	0.35	0.33	0.34	0.28	0.42	0.37	48. Bénéfices après impôt
49. Distributed profit	..	..	..	..	..	..	..	..	49. Bénéfices distribués
50. Retained profit	..	..	..	..	..	..	..	..	50. Bénéfices mis en réserve
51. Staff costs	0.90	0.91	0.92	0.99	1.03	1.06	1.09	1.02	51. Frais de personnel
52. Provisions on loans	..	..	0.17	0.20	0.28	0.40	0.45	0.37	52. Provisions sur prêts
53. Provisions on securities	..	..	0.15	0.18	0.08	0.08	0.03	0.10	53. Provisions sur titres
% of gross income									**% du total du résultat brut**
54. Net interest income	80.32	78.34	72.15	69.09	67.87	66.61	72.07	71.26	54. Produits financiers nets
55. Non-interest income (net)	19.68	21.66	27.85	30.91	32.13	33.39	27.93	28.74	55. Produits non financiers (nets)
56. Operating expenses	70.08	68.46	65.51	64.86	64.92	63.98	63.49	65.10	56. Frais d'exploitation
57. Net income	29.92	31.54	34.49	35.14	35.08	36.02	36.51	34.90	57. Résultat net
58. Provisions (net)	..	..	16.35	19.49	19.62	23.70	19.93	19.17	58. Provisions (nettes)
59. Profit before tax	29.92	31.54	18.14	15.64	15.47	12.31	16.58	15.73	59. Bénéfices avant impôt
60. Income tax	4.02	3.86	3.49	2.95	2.59	2.12	2.15	1.85	60. Impôt
61. Profit after tax	25.90	27.68	14.65	12.69	12.88	10.20	14.43	13.89	61. Bénéfices après impôt
62. Staff costs	41.27	40.02	38.30	38.48	38.54	38.12	37.32	38.42	62. Frais de personnel
% of net income									**% du total du résultat net**
63. Provisions (net)	100.00	100.00	47.42	55.48	55.92	65.81	54.59	54.93	63. Provisions (nettes)
64. Profit before tax	..	..	52.58	44.52	44.08	34.19	45.41	45.07	64. Bénéfices avant impôt
65. Income tax	13.45	12.24	10.11	8.40	7.37	5.88	5.88	5.29	65. Impôt
66. Profit after tax	86.55	87.76	42.48	36.13	36.71	28.31	39.53	39.78	66. Bénéfices après impôt

AUSTRIA

All banks

AUTRICHE

Ensemble des banques

Per cent / *Pourcentage*

BALANCE SHEET ANALYSIS / **ANALYSE DU BILAN**

	1987	1988	1989	1990	1991	1992	1993	1994	
% of year-end balance sheet total									**% du total du bilan en fin d'exercice**
Assets									**Actif**
67. Cash & balance with Central bank	1.86	1.86	2.01	1.81	1.60	1.85	1.79	1.84	67. Caisse & solde auprès de la Banque centrale
68. Interbank deposits	35.70	34.05	31.94	30.57	29.06	28.71	29.77	28.99	68. Dépôts interbancaires
69. Loans	45.66	47.30	49.20	50.69	51.77	52.40	51.11	50.45	69. Prêts
70. Securities	11.37	11.73	11.64	11.59	11.53	10.50	11.18	12.58	70. Valeurs mobilières
71. Other assets	5.41	5.06	5.21	5.35	6.04	6.54	6.14	6.15	71. Autres actifs
Liabilities									**Passif**
72. Capital & reserves	3.48	3.92	4.27	4.61	4.73	4.86	5.01	5.19	72. Capital et réserves
73. Borrowing from Central bank	0.07	0.08	0.03	0.04	0.03	0.01	0.01	0.03	73. Emprunts auprès de la Banque centrale
74. Interbank deposits	36.68	35.60	33.58	31.69	30.76	29.94	29.38	28.99	74. Dépôts interbancaires
75. Non-bank deposits	40.18	40.17	40.98	42.71	43.88	44.70	44.43	44.74	75. Dépôts non bancaires
76. Bonds	15.12	16.40	17.21	17.14	16.50	16.24	16.89	16.70	76. Obligations
77. Other liabilities	4.46	3.84	3.92	3.81	4.10	4.26	4.28	4.36	77. Autres engagements
Memoranda									*Pour mémoire*
78. Short-term securities	0.30	0.23	0.16	0.17	0.14	0.12	0.11	0.27	78. Titres à court terme
79. Bonds	8.93	9.23	9.10	8.73	8.58	7.97	8.47	9.72	79. Obligations
80. Shares and participations	1.52	1.72	2.00	2.33	2.64	2.82	2.77	2.75	80. Actions et participations
81. Claims on non-residents	21.98	22.58	21.98	20.89	19.80	20.17	20.98	20.47	81. Créances sur des non résidents
82. Liabilities to non-residents	23.13	24.25	24.18	23.07	22.42	23.02	22.46	21.86	82. Engagements envers des non résidents

Notes

• Average balance sheet totals (item 29) are based on twelve end-month data.

Notes

• La moyenne du total des actifs/passifs (poste 29) est basée sur douze données de fin de mois.

BELGIUM

All banks

Million Belgian francs

BELGIQUE

Ensemble des banques

Millions de francs belges

	1985	1986	1987	1988	1989	1990	1991	1992	1993	1994
INCOME STATEMENT — COMPTE DE RESULTATS										
1. Interest income — Produits financiers	1231991	1160123	1173311	1329265	1682787	1895521	1952442	2005480	2360986	2191851
2. Interest expenses — Frais financiers	1018885	922014	934572	1080027	1416434	1624356	1672337	1705669	2080214	1880681
3. Net interest income — Produits financiers nets	213106	238109	238739	249238	266353	271165	280105	299811	280772	311170
4. Non-interest income (net) — Produits non financiers (nets)	48229	57522	65196	80695	78157	61232	73190	82626	141190	97870
5. Gross income — Résultat brut	261335	295631	303935	329933	344510	332397	353295	382437	421962	409040
6. Operating expenses — Frais d'exploitation	178207	194854	210043	212760	230194	240333	242262	255658	285403	291423
7. Net income — Résultat net	83128	100777	93892	117173	114316	92064	111033	126779	136559	117617
8. Provisions (net) — Provisions (nettes)	39439	47377	46225	67740	78687	39603	58965	75207	54543	34275
9. Profit before tax — Bénéfices avant impôt	43689	53400	47667	49433	35629	52461	52068	51572	82016	83342
10. Income tax — Impôt	18938	22710	19544	14125	13666	12569	13611	17336	24812	26907
11. Profit after tax — Bénéfices après impôt	24751	30690	28123	35308	21963	39892	38457	34236	57204	56435
12. Distributed profit (1) — Bénéfices distribués (1)	..	..	..	..	..	..	..	..	26412	28606
13. Retained profit (1) — Bénéfices mis en réserve (1)	..	..	..	..	..	..	..	..	31498	25263
Memoranda — Pour mémoire										
14. Staff costs (2) — Frais de personnel (2)	93137	99379	103765	107866	114791	121940	125381	131918	173714	177194
15. Provisions on loans — Provisions sur prêts	700	527	1033	1398	1720	656	1086	1496	2882	2032
16. Provisions on securities (3) — Provisions sur titres (3)	..	..	..	..	..	..	..	..	2490	3417
BALANCE SHEET — BILAN										
Assets — Actif										
17. Cash & balance with Central bank — Caisse & solde auprès de la Banque centrale	31063	33425	35130	35067	41994	37856	55718	42907	39916	42867
18. Interbank deposits — Dépôts interbancaires	4176638	4295333	4730700	5353508	5582422	6005165	6060663	6378056	6703817	6447806
19. Loans — Prêts	4307745	4400342	4703861	5221802	6018525	6380491	6733063	7129799	8464451	9052110
20. Securities — Valeurs mobilières	3772183	4365333	4702079	4960616	5128815	5355436	5373426	5987508	6475602	6833915
21. Other assets — Autres actifs	554689	565304	600657	746342	835262	916069	939793	907116	1025264	997676
Liabilities — Passif										
22. Capital & reserves — Capital et réserves	326316	381841	424299	502301	594211	632723	722028	809018	859376	944769
23. Borrowing from Central bank (3)(4) — Emprunts auprès de la Banque centrale (3)(4)	-	-	-	-	500	3000	4703	4710	1459	3010
24. Interbank deposits — Dépôts interbancaires	5938444	6131388	6593756	7325812	7697079	8018769	7595140	7980658	8106757	7691612
25. Non-bank deposits — Dépôts non bancaires	3812928	4276816	4790737	5365347	5962446	6366836	6807430	7410378	7780741	8117304
26. Bonds (5) — Obligations (5)	2119372	2182203	2204040	2271121	2316290	2632235	2929716	3066669	4017143	4173026
27. Other liabilities — Autres engagements	645258	687489	759595	852754	1034492	1041454	1103646	1173953	1943574	2444653
Balance sheet total — Total du bilan										
28. End-year total — En fin d'exercice	12842318	13659737	14772427	16317335	17605018	18695017	19162663	20445386	22709050	23374374
29. Average total — Moyen	12393347	13251028	14216082	15544881	16961177	18150018	18928840	19804025	22276405	23411724
Memoranda — Pour mémoire										
30. Short-term securities (2) — Titres à court terme (2)	711112	915191	976889	911849	1013808	1073607	850297	872936	1150415	1505064
31. Bonds (2) — Obligations (2)	1953569	2167577	2272611	2512578	2520453	2693915	2876444	3201526	4962859	4998351
32. Shares and participations (2) — Actions et participations (2)	48516	53546	79937	104694	122660	114820	128649	127618	362328	330500
33. Claims on non-residents (2) — Créances sur des non résidents (2)	4842845	4974640	5180066	5962069	6316380	6454242	6607820	6876595	8798061	8789130
34. Liabilities to non-residents (2) — Engagements envers des non résidents (2)	5696467	5884085	6129864	7067369	7545517	7708313	7506927	7806888	9533425	9847159
SUPPLEMENTARY INFORMATION — RENSEIGNEMENTS COMPLEMENTAIRES										
35. Number of institutions — Nombre d'institutions	120	123	124	122	120	115	119	121	133	130
36. Number of branches (2) — Nombre de succursales (2)	24937	24456	23435	22231	19211	18389	17078	16405	17757	17040
37. Number of employees (x 1000) — Nombre de salariés (x 1000)	71.1	73.0	75.5	76.0	79.0	79.0	77.0	76.0	76.3	76.3

BELGIUM

All banks

BELGIQUE

Ensemble des banques

Per cent / *Pourcentage*

INCOME STATEMENT ANALYSIS / **ANALYSE DU COMPTE DE RESULTATS**

% of average balance sheet total / % du total moyen du bilan

#	Item	1985	1986	1987	1988	1989	1990	1991	1992	1993	1994	Poste
38.	Interest income	9.94	8.75	8.25	8.55	9.92	10.44	10.31	10.13	10.60	9.36	Produits financiers
39.	Interest expenses	8.22	6.96	6.57	6.95	8.35	8.95	8.83	8.61	9.34	8.03	Frais financiers
40.	Net interest income	1.72	1.80	1.68	1.60	1.57	1.49	1.48	1.51	1.26	1.33	Produits financiers nets
41.	Non-interest income (net)	0.39	0.43	0.46	0.52	0.46	0.34	0.39	0.42	0.63	0.42	Produits non financiers (nets)
42.	Gross income	2.11	2.23	2.14	2.12	2.03	1.83	1.87	1.93	1.89	1.75	Résultat brut
43.	Operating expenses	1.44	1.47	1.48	1.37	1.36	1.32	1.28	1.29	1.28	1.24	Frais d'exploitation
44.	Net income	0.67	0.76	0.66	0.75	0.67	0.51	0.59	0.64	0.61	0.50	Résultat net
45.	Provisions (net)	0.32	0.36	0.33	0.44	0.46	0.22	0.31	0.38	0.24	0.15	Provisions (nettes)
46.	Profit before tax	0.35	0.40	0.34	0.32	0.21	0.29	0.28	0.26	0.37	0.36	Bénéfices avant impôt
47.	Income tax	0.15	0.17	0.14	0.09	0.08	0.07	0.07	0.09	0.11	0.11	Impôt
48.	Profit after tax	0.20	0.23	0.20	0.23	0.13	0.22	0.20	0.17	0.26	0.24	Bénéfices après impôt
49.	Distributed profit (1)	..	..	..	..	..	..	..	..	0.15	0.15	Bénéfices distribués (1)
50.	Retained profit (1)	..	..	..	..	..	..	..	..	0.17	0.13	Bénéfices mis en réserve (1)
51.	Staff costs (2)	0.75	0.75	0.73	0.69	0.68	0.67	0.66	0.67	0.78	0.76	Frais de personnel (2)
52.	Provisions on loans	..	..	..	..	..	..	..	..	..	..	Provisions sur prêts
53.	Provisions on securities	0.01	0.00	0.01	0.01	0.01	0.00	0.01	0.01	0.01	0.01	Provisions sur titres

% of gross income / % du total du résultat brut

#	Item	1985	1986	1987	1988	1989	1990	1991	1992	1993	1994	Poste
54.	Net interest income	81.55	80.54	78.55	75.54	77.31	81.58	79.28	78.39	66.54	76.07	Produits financiers nets
55.	Non-interest income (net)	18.45	19.46	21.45	24.46	22.69	18.42	20.72	21.61	33.46	23.93	Produits non financiers (nets)
56.	Operating expenses	68.19	65.91	69.11	64.49	66.82	72.30	68.57	66.85	67.64	71.25	Frais d'exploitation
57.	Net income	31.81	34.09	30.89	35.51	33.18	27.70	31.43	33.15	32.36	28.75	Résultat net
58.	Provisions (net)	15.09	16.03	15.21	20.53	22.84	11.91	16.69	19.67	12.93	8.38	Provisions (nettes)
59.	Profit before tax	16.72	18.06	15.68	14.98	10.34	15.78	14.74	13.49	19.44	20.38	Bénéfices avant impôt
60.	Income tax	7.25	7.68	6.43	4.28	3.97	3.78	3.85	4.53	5.88	6.58	Impôt
61.	Profit after tax	9.47	10.38	9.25	10.70	6.38	12.00	10.89	8.95	13.56	13.80	Bénéfices après impôt
62.	Staff costs (2)	35.64	33.62	34.14	32.69	33.32	36.69	35.49	34.49	41.17	43.32	Frais de personnel (2)

% of net income / % du total du résultat net

#	Item	1985	1986	1987	1988	1989	1990	1991	1992	1993	1994	Poste
63.	Provisions (net)	47.44	47.01	49.23	57.81	68.83	43.02	53.11	59.32	39.94	29.14	Provisions (nettes)
64.	Profit before tax	52.56	52.99	50.77	42.19	31.17	56.98	46.89	40.68	60.06	70.86	Bénéfices avant impôt
65.	Income tax	22.78	22.53	20.82	12.05	11.95	13.65	12.26	13.67	18.17	22.88	Impôt
66.	Profit after tax	29.77	30.45	29.95	30.13	19.21	43.33	34.64	27.00	41.89	47.98	Bénéfices après impôt

BELGIUM

All banks

Per cent

BALANCE SHEET ANALYSIS

% of year-end balance sheet total

BELGIQUE

Ensemble des banques

Pourcentage

ANALYSE DU BILAN

% du total du bilan en fin d'exercice

	1985	1986	1987	1988	1989	1990	1991	1992	1993	1994	
Assets											**Actif**
67. Cash & balance with Central bank	0.24	0.24	0.24	0.21	0.24	0.20	0.29	0.21	0.18	0.18	67. Caisse & solde auprès de la Banque centrale
68. Interbank deposits	32.52	31.45	32.02	32.81	31.71	32.12	31.63	31.20	29.52	27.58	68. Dépôts interbancaires
69. Loans	33.54	32.21	31.84	32.00	34.19	34.13	35.14	34.87	37.27	38.73	69. Prêts
70. Securities	29.37	31.96	31.83	30.40	29.12	28.65	28.04	29.29	28.52	29.24	70. Valeurs mobilières
71. Other assets	4.32	4.14	4.07	4.57	4.74	4.90	4.90	4.44	4.51	4.27	71. Autres actifs
Liabilities											**Passif**
72. Capital & reserves	2.54	2.80	2.87	3.08	3.38	3.38	3.77	3.96	3.78	4.04	72. Capital et réserves
73. Borrowing from Central bank (3)(4)	-	-	-	-	-	0.02	0.02	0.02	0.01	0.01	73. Emprunts auprès de la Banque centrale (3)(4)
74. Interbank deposits	46.24	44.89	44.64	44.90	43.72	42.89	39.64	39.03	35.70	32.91	74. Dépôts interbancaires
75. Non-bank deposits	29.69	31.31	32.43	32.88	33.87	34.06	35.52	36.24	34.26	34.73	75. Dépôts non bancaires
76. Bonds (5)	16.50	15.98	14.92	13.92	13.16	14.08	15.29	15.00	17.69	17.85	76. Obligations (5)
77. Other liabilities	5.02	5.03	5.14	5.23	5.88	5.57	5.76	5.74	8.56	10.46	77. Autres engagements
Memoranda											*Pour mémoire*
78. Short-term securities (2)	5.54	6.70	6.61	5.59	5.76	5.74	4.44	4.27	5.07	6.44	78. Titres à court terme (2)
79. Bonds (2)	15.21	15.87	15.38	15.40	14.32	14.41	15.01	15.66	21.85	21.38	79. Obligations (2)
80. Shares and participations (2)	0.38	0.39	0.54	0.64	0.70	0.61	0.67	0.62	1.60	1.41	80. Actions et participations (2)
81. Claims on non-residents (2)	37.71	36.42	35.07	36.54	35.88	34.52	34.48	33.63	38.74	37.60	81. Créances sur des non résidents (2)
82. Liabilities to non-residents (2)	44.36	43.08	41.50	43.31	42.86	41.23	39.17	38.18	41.98	42.13	82. Engagements envers des non résidents (2)

1. Data available beginning 1993 and only for credit institutions governed by Belgian law.

2. Up to 1992, includes Commercial banks and Savings banks only.

3. Up to 1992, includes Savings banks only.

4. Up to 1992, for Commercial banks, included under "Interbank deposits" (item 24 or item 74).

5. Including CD's.

Notes

- All banks includes all Belgian credit institutions.
- Beginning 1993, average balance sheet totals (item 29) are the average of monthly data within the calendar year.

1. Les données ne sont disponibles qu'à partir de 1993 et seulement pour les institutions de crédit régies par la législation belge.

2. Jusqu'à 1992, sont incluses les Banques commerciales et les Caisses d'épargne uniquement.

3. Jusqu'à 1992, sont incluses les Caisses d'épargne uniquement.

4. Jusqu'à 1992, pour les Banques commerciales, inclus sous "Dépôts interbancaires" (poste 24 ou poste 74).

5. Y compris les certificats de dépôt.

Notes

- L'ensemble des banques comprend toutes les institutions de crédit belges.
- A partir de 1993, la moyenne du total des actifs/passifs (poste 29) est la moyenne des données mensuelles de l'anée.

CANADA

Commercial banks (consolidated world-wide)

CANADA

Banques commerciales (consolidées sur une base mondiale)

Million Canadian dollars / *Millions de dollars canadiens*

		1985	1986	1987	1988	1989	1990	1991	1992	1993	1994	
INCOME STATEMENT												**COMPTE DE RESULTATS**
1.	Interest income	38809	37719	35560	40482	49671	54109	51530	44115	41878	44623	1. Produits financiers
2.	Interest expenses	28719	26758	24210	27110	35516	40006	35688	27324	24122	25588	2. Frais financiers
3.	Net interest income	10090	10961	11350	13372	14155	14103	15842	16791	17756	19035	3. Produits financiers nets
4.	Non-interest income (net)	3135	3601	4491	5044	5831	6321	6821	7533	8419	15566	4. Produits non financiers (nets)
5.	Gross income	13225	14562	15841	18416	19986	20424	22663	24324	26175	34601	5. Résultat brut
6.	Operating expenses	7915	8576	9108	10362	11798	12996	14063	15367	16713	18493	6. Frais d'exploitation
7.	Net income	5310	5986	6733	8054	8188	7428	8600	8957	9462	16108	7. Résultat net
8.	Provisions (net)	2340	2996	2771	2520	5108	1692	2704	6035	4780	3469	8. Provisions (nettes)
9.	Profit before tax	2970	2990	3962	5534	3080	5736	5896	2922	4682	12639	9. Bénéfices avant impôt
10.	Income tax	861	854	1440	2230	1106	2127	2086	969	1666	2744	10. Impôt
11.	Profit after tax	2109	2136	2522	3304	1974	3609	3810	1953	3016	9895	11. Bénéfices après impôt
12.	Distributed profit	..	..	..	..	..	..	..	..	..	..	12. Bénéfices distribués
13.	Retained profit	..	..	..	..	..	..	..	..	..	..	13. Bénéfices mis en réserve
Memoranda												*Pour mémoire*
14.	Staff costs	4761	4942	5186	5980	6785	7433	7970	8502	9250	10269	14. Frais de personnel
15.	Provisions on loans	2340	2996	2771	2520	5108	1692	2704	6035	4780	3469	15. Provisions sur prêts
16.	Provisions on securities	..	..	..	..	..	..	..	..	..	..	16. Provisions sur titres
BALANCE SHEET												**BILAN**
Assets												**Actif**
17.	Cash & balance with Central bank	5928	6419	6913	6834	6446	5653	6113	5897	5179	4433	17. Caisse & solde auprès de la Banque centrale
18.	Interbank deposits	47183	50221	42233	34129	33346	32947	33609	36007	38148	53801	18. Dépôts interbancaires
19.	Loans	289770	289762	307519	320722	351748	375601	393693	421772	457155	501495	19. Prêts
20.	Securities	40212	43867	38711	43971	46347	49147	68855	89920	115151	135128	20. Valeurs mobilières
21.	Other assets	11857	12772	15329	17093	18914	20289	19457	22444	27208	28653	21. Autres actifs
Liabilities												**Passif**
22.	Capital & reserves	18383	20966	20648	22830	24926	27326	31066	31899	35352	38635	22. Capital et réserves
23.	Borrowing from Central bank	2368	71	376	342	261	38	53	6	311	61	23. Emprunts auprès de la Banque centrale
24.	Interbank deposits	89920	80609	73953	56068	54211	60214	60955	81352	81890	97693	24. Dépôts interbancaires
25.	Non-bank deposits	265050	280380	292328	311483	339626	354773	381258	405925	445195	481651	25. Dépôts non bancaires
26.	Bonds	5921	6986	5579	7862	8270	9212	10817	12376	15309	16208	26. Obligations
27.	Other liabilities	13308	14029	17821	24164	29507	32074	37578	44482	64784	89262	27. Autres engagements
Balance sheet total												**Total du bilan**
28.	End-year total	394950	403041	410705	422749	456801	483637	521727	576040	642841	723510	28. En fin d'exercice
29.	Average total	380142	398996	406873	416727	439775	470219	502682	548883	609440	683176	29. Moyen
Memoranda												*Pour mémoire*
30.	Short-term securities	..	..	..	..	..	..	..	..	..	..	30. Titres à court terme
31.	Bonds	..	..	..	..	..	..	..	..	..	..	31. Obligations
32.	Shares and participations	..	..	..	..	..	..	..	..	..	..	32. Actions et participations
33.	Claims on non-residents	..	..	..	..	..	..	..	..	..	..	33. Créances sur des non résidents
34.	Liabilities to non-residents	..	..	..	..	..	..	..	..	..	..	34. Engagements envers des non résidents
SUPPLEMENTARY INFORMATION												**RENSEIGNEMENTS COMPLEMENTAIRES**
35.	Number of institutions	NA	NA	11	10	10	10	10	10	11	11	35. Nombre d'institutions
36.	Number of branches	NA	NA	NA	NA	NA	NA	NA	NA	NA	NA	36. Nombre de succursales
37.	Number of employees (x 1000)	NA	NA	NA	NA	NA	NA	NA	NA	NA	NA	37. Nombre de salariés (x 1000)

CANADA

Commercial banks (consolidated world-wide)

Per cent

INCOME STATEMENT ANALYSIS

	1985	1986	1987	1988	1989	1990	1991	1992	1993	1994
% of average balance sheet total										
38. Interest income	10.21	9.45	8.74	9.71	11.29	11.51	10.25	8.04	6.87	6.53
39. Interest expenses	7.55	6.71	5.95	6.51	8.08	8.51	7.10	4.98	3.96	3.75
40. Net interest income	2.65	2.75	2.79	3.21	3.22	3.00	3.15	3.06	2.91	2.79
41. Non-interest income (net)	0.82	0.90	1.10	1.21	1.33	1.34	1.36	1.37	1.38	2.28
42. Gross income	3.48	3.65	3.89	4.42	4.54	4.34	4.51	4.43	4.29	5.06
43. Operating expenses	2.08	2.15	2.24	2.49	2.68	2.76	2.80	2.80	2.74	2.71
44. Net income	1.40	1.50	1.65	1.93	1.86	1.58	1.71	1.63	1.55	2.36
45. Provisions (net)	0.62	0.75	0.68	0.60	1.16	0.36	0.54	1.10	0.78	0.51
46. Profit before tax	0.78	0.75	0.97	1.33	0.70	1.22	1.17	0.53	0.77	1.85
47. Income tax	0.23	0.21	0.35	0.54	0.25	0.45	0.41	0.18	0.27	0.40
48. Profit after tax	0.55	0.54	0.62	0.79	0.45	0.77	0.76	0.36	0.49	1.45
49. Distributed profit	..	..	..	..	..			..	..	..
50. Retained profit	..	..	..	..	..			..	..	..
51. Staff costs	1.25	1.24	1.27	1.43	1.54	1.58	1.59	1.55	1.52	1.50
52. Provisions on loans	0.62	0.75	0.68	0.60	1.16	0.36	0.54	1.10	0.78	0.51
53. Provisions on securities	..	..	..	..	..			..	..	..
% of gross income										
54. Net interest income	76.29	75.27	71.65	72.61	70.82	69.05	69.90	69.03	67.84	55.01
55. Non-interest income (net)	23.71	24.73	28.35	27.39	29.18	30.95	30.10	30.97	32.16	44.99
56. Operating expenses	59.85	58.89	57.50	56.27	59.03	63.63	62.05	63.18	63.85	53.45
57. Net income	40.15	41.11	42.50	43.73	40.97	36.37	37.95	36.82	36.15	46.55
58. Provisions (net)	17.69	20.57	17.49	13.68	25.56	8.28	11.93	24.81	18.26	10.03
59. Profit before tax	22.46	20.53	25.01	30.05	15.41	28.08	26.02	12.01	17.89	36.53
60. Income tax	6.51	5.86	9.09	12.11	5.53	10.41	9.20	3.98	6.36	7.93
61. Profit after tax	15.95	14.67	15.92	17.94	9.88	17.67	16.81	8.03	11.52	28.60
62. Staff costs	36.00	33.94	32.74	32.47	33.95	36.39	35.17	34.95	35.34	29.68
% of net income										
63. Provisions (net)	44.07	50.05	41.16	31.29	62.38	22.78	31.44	67.38	50.52	21.54
64. Profit before tax	55.93	49.95	58.84	68.71	37.62	77.22	68.56	32.62	49.48	78.46
65. Income tax	16.21	14.27	21.39	27.69	13.51	28.63	24.26	10.82	17.61	17.04
66. Profit after tax	39.72	35.68	37.46	41.02	24.11	48.59	44.30	21.80	31.87	61.43

CANADA

Banques commerciales (consolidées sur une base mondiale)

Pourcentage

ANALYSE DU COMPTE DE RESULTATS

% du total moyen du bilan
38. Produits financiers
39. Frais financiers
40. Produits financiers nets
41. Produits non financiers (nets)
42. Résultat brut
43. Frais d'exploitation
44. Résultat net
45. Provisions (nettes)
46. Bénéfices avant impôt
47. Impôt
48. Bénéfices après impôt
49. Bénéfices distribués
50. Bénéfices mis en réserve
51. Frais de personnel
52. Provisions sur prêts
53. Provisions sur titres

% du total du résultat brut
54. Produits financiers nets
55. Produits non financiers (nets)
56. Frais d'exploitation
57. Résultat net
58. Provisions (nettes)
59. Bénéfices avant impôt
60. Impôt
61. Bénéfices après impôt
62. Frais de personnel

% du total du résultat net
63. Provisions (nettes)
64. Bénéfices avant impôt
65. Impôt
66. Bénéfices après impôt

CANADA

Commercial banks (consolidated world-wide)

Per cent	1985	1986	1987	1988	1989	1990	1991	1992	1993	1994
BALANCE SHEET ANALYSIS										
% of year-end balance sheet total										
Assets										
67. Cash & balance with Central bank	1.50	1.59	1.68	1.62	1.41	1.17	1.17	1.02	0.81	0.61
68. Interbank deposits	11.95	12.46	10.28	8.07	7.30	6.81	6.44	6.25	5.93	7.44
69. Loans	73.37	71.89	74.88	75.87	77.00	77.66	75.46	73.22	71.11	69.31
70. Securities	10.18	10.88	9.43	10.40	10.15	10.16	13.20	15.61	17.91	18.68
71. Other assets	3.00	3.17	3.73	4.04	4.14	4.20	3.73	3.90	4.23	3.96
Liabilities										
72. Capital & reserves	4.65	5.20	5.03	5.40	5.46	5.65	5.95	5.54	5.50	5.34
73. Borrowing from Central bank	0.60	0.02	0.09	0.08	0.06	0.01	0.01	0.00	0.05	0.01
74. Interbank deposits	22.77	20.00	18.01	13.26	11.87	12.45	11.68	14.12	12.74	13.50
75. Non-bank deposits	67.11	69.57	71.18	73.68	74.35	73.36	73.08	70.47	69.25	66.57
76. Bonds	1.50	1.73	1.36	1.86	1.81	1.90	2.07	2.15	2.38	2.24
77. Other liabilities	3.37	3.48	4.34	5.72	6.46	6.63	7.20	7.72	10.08	12.34
Memoranda										
78. Short-term securities	..	..	..	..	..	..	..	..	..	..
79. Bonds	..	..	..	..	..	..	..	..	..	..
80. Shares and participations	..	..	..	..	..	..	..	..	..	..
81. Claims on non-residents	..	..	..	..	..	..	..	..	..	..
82. Liabilities to non-residents	..	..	..	..	..	..	..	..	..	..

CANADA

Banques commerciales (consolidées sur une base mondiale)

Pourcentage

ANALYSE DU BILAN

% du total du bilan en fin d'exercice

Actif
67. Caisse & solde auprès de la Banque centrale
68. Dépôts interbancaires
69. Prêts
70. Valeurs mobilières
71. Autres actifs

Passif
72. Capital et réserves
73. Emprunts auprès de la Banque centrale
74. Dépôts interbancaires
75. Dépôts non bancaires
76. Obligations
77. Autres engagements

Pour mémoire
78. Titres à court terme
79. Obligations
80. Actions et participations
81. Créances sur des non résidents
82. Engagements envers des non résidents

Notes

- Data relate to Canadian bank groups reporting on a consolidated world-wide basis.
- The reporting period is the fiscal year ending 31st October.

Notes

- Les données se rapportent au groupe de banques canadiennes qui consolident leurs comptes à l'échelle mondiale.
- La période couverte est l'exercice financier qui se termine le 31 octobre.

CANADA

Foreign commercial banks

Million Canadian dollars

CANADA

Banques commerciales étrangères

Millions de dollars canadiens

	1985	1986	1987	1988	1989	1990	1991	1992	1993	1994	
INCOME STATEMENT											**COMPTE DE RESULTATS**
1. Interest income	2416	2366	2845	3391	4003	4945	4669	3792	3515	3608	1. Produits financiers
2. Interest expenses	1985	1911	2247	2671	3250	4030	3664	2908	2628	2580	2. Frais financiers
3. Net interest income	431	455	598	720	753	915	1005	884	887	1028	3. Produits financiers nets
4. Non-interest income (net)	163	223	278	331	378	511	775	787	884	935	4. Produits non financiers (nets)
5. Gross income	594	678	876	1051	1131	1426	1780	1671	1771	1963	5. Résultat brut
6. Operating expenses	346	402	590	657	626	865	1143	1168	1273	1311	6. Frais d'exploitation
7. Net income	248	276	286	394	505	561	637	503	498	652	7. Résultat net
8. Provisions (net)	50	146	216	95	106	288	524	1102	628	451	8. Provisions (nettes)
9. Profit before tax	198	130	70	299	399	273	113	-599	-130	201	9. Bénéfices avant impôt
10. Income tax	92	60	78	140	164	112	53	-212	13	150	10. Impôt
11. Profit after tax	106	70	-8	159	235	161	60	-387	-143	51	11. Bénéfices après impôt
12. Distributed profit	..	..	..	..	..	..	..	..	..	..	12. Bénéfices distribués
13. Retained profit	..	..	..	..	..	..	..	..	..	..	13. Bénéfices mis en réserve
Memoranda											*Pour mémoire*
14. *Staff costs*	*163*	*185*	*289*	*320*	*308*	*376*	*426*	*434*	*478*	*515*	14. *Frais de personnel*
15. *Provisions on loans*	*50*	*146*	*216*	*95*	*106*	*288*	*524*	*1102*	*628*	*451*	15. *Provisions sur prêts*
16. *Provisions on securities*	*..*	*..*	*..*	*..*	*..*	*..*	*..*	*..*	*..*	*..*	16. *Provisions sur titres*
BALANCE SHEET											**BILAN**
Assets											*Actif*
17. Cash & balance with Central bank	21	117	185	234	267	123	146	103	162	204	17. Caisse & solde auprès de la Banque centrale
18. Interbank deposits	5074	6053	7050	6134	7221	6177	7427	8260	6230	8650	18. Dépôts interbancaires
19. Loans	17085	24098	25327	28207	31037	33987	34140	36285	37245	39464	19. Prêts
20. Securities	2168	2850	4442	4920	4664	5932	7071	9221	12474	11170	20. Valeurs mobilières
21. Other assets	724	914	1008	1029	1167	1507	1303	1736	2722	2053	21. Autres actifs
Liabilities											*Passif*
22. Capital & reserves	1857	2586	2816	3107	3416	3973	3952	3697	3830	4012	22. Capital et réserves
23. Borrowing from Central bank	-	6	60	-	-	-	-	-	-	-	23. Emprunts auprès de la Banque centrale
24. Interbank deposits	7491	8966	10940	12185	13080	15281	15530	17049	15202	18419	24. Dépôts interbancaires
25. Non-bank deposits	14713	20730	22219	22752	24545	23863	24857	27680	30565	30942	25. Dépôts non bancaires
26. Bonds	44	91	99	192	292	557	873	1147	1155	1272	26. Obligations
27. Other liabilities	967	1653	1878	2288	3023	4052	4875	6032	8081	6896	27. Autres engagements
Balance sheet total											*Total du bilan*
28. End-year total	25072	34032	38012	40524	44356	47726	50087	55605	58833	61541	28. En fin d'exercice
29. Average total	23593	29552	36022	39268	42440	46041	48906	52846	57219	60187	29. Moyen
Memoranda											*Pour mémoire*
30. *Short-term securities*	*..*	*..*	*..*	*..*	*..*	*..*	*..*	*..*	*..*	*..*	30. *Titres à court terme*
31. *Bonds*	*..*	*..*	*..*	*..*	*..*	*..*	*..*	*..*	*..*	*..*	31. *Obligations*
32. *Shares and participations*	*..*	*..*	*..*	*..*	*..*	*..*	*..*	*..*	*..*	*..*	32. *Actions et participations*
33. *Claims on non-residents*	*..*	*..*	*..*	*..*	*..*	*..*	*..*	*..*	*..*	*..*	33. *Créances sur des non résidents*
34. *Liabilities to non-residents*	*..*	*..*	*..*	*..*	*..*	*..*	*..*	*..*	*..*	*..*	34. *Engagements envers des non résidents*
SUPPLEMENTARY INFORMATION											**RENSEIGNEMENTS COMPLÉMENTAIRES**
35. Number of institutions	NA	NA	58	57	57	56	56	56	56	53	35. Nombre d'institutions
36. Number of branches	NA	NA	NA	NA	NA	NA	NA	NA	NA	NA	36. Nombre de succursales
37. Number of employees (x 1000)	NA	NA	NA	NA	NA	NA	NA	NA	NA	NA	37. Nombre de salariés (x 1000)

CANADA

Foreign commercial banks

Per cent

INCOME STATEMENT ANALYSIS

	1985	1986	1987	1988	1989	1990	1991	1992	1993	1994
% of average balance sheet total										
38. Interest income	10.24	8.01	7.90	8.64	9.43	10.74	9.55	7.18	6.14	5.99
39. Interest expenses	8.41	6.47	6.24	6.80	7.66	8.75	7.49	5.50	4.59	4.29
40. Net interest income	1.83	1.54	1.66	1.83	1.77	1.99	2.05	1.67	1.55	1.71
41. Non-interest income (net)	0.69	0.75	0.77	0.84	0.89	1.11	1.58	1.49	1.54	1.55
42. Gross income	2.52	2.29	2.43	2.68	2.66	3.10	3.64	3.16	3.10	3.26
43. Operating expenses	1.47	1.36	1.64	1.67	1.48	1.88	2.34	2.21	2.22	2.18
44. Net income	1.05	0.93	0.79	1.00	1.19	1.22	1.30	0.95	0.87	1.08
45. Provisions (net)	0.21	0.49	0.60	0.24	0.25	0.63	1.07	2.09	1.10	0.75
46. Profit before tax	0.84	0.44	0.19	0.76	0.94	0.59	0.23	-1.13	-0.23	0.33
47. Income tax	0.39	0.20	0.22	0.36	0.39	0.24	0.11	-0.40	0.02	0.25
48. Profit after tax	0.45	0.24	-0.02	0.40	0.55	0.35	0.12	-0.73	-0.25	0.08
49. Distributed profit	:	:	:	:	:	:	:	:	:	:
50. Retained profit	:	:	:	:	:	:	:	:	:	:
51. Staff costs	0.69	0.63	0.80	0.81	0.73	0.82	0.87	0.82	0.84	0.86
52. Provisions on loans	0.21	0.49	0.60	0.24	0.25	0.63	1.07	2.09	1.10	0.75
53. Provisions on securities	:	:	:	:	:	:	:	:	:	:
% of gross income										
54. Net interest income	72.56	67.11	68.26	68.51	66.58	64.17	56.46	52.90	50.08	52.37
55. Non-interest income (net)	27.44	32.89	31.74	31.49	33.42	35.83	43.54	47.10	49.92	47.63
56. Operating expenses	58.25	59.29	67.35	62.51	55.35	60.66	64.21	69.90	71.88	66.79
57. Net income	41.75	40.71	32.65	37.49	44.65	39.34	35.79	30.10	28.12	33.21
58. Provisions (net)	8.42	21.53	24.66	9.04	9.37	20.20	29.44	65.95	35.46	22.98
59. Profit before tax	33.33	19.17	7.99	28.45	35.28	19.14	6.35	-35.85	-7.34	10.24
60. Income tax	15.49	8.85	8.90	13.32	14.50	7.85	2.98	-12.69	0.73	7.64
61. Profit after tax	17.85	10.32	-0.91	15.13	20.78	11.29	3.37	-23.16	-8.07	2.60
62. Staff costs	27.44	27.29	32.99	30.45	27.23	26.37	23.93	25.97	26.99	26.24
% of net income										
63. Provisions (net)	20.16	52.90	75.52	24.11	20.99	51.34	82.26	:	:	69.17
64. Profit before tax	79.84	47.10	24.48	75.89	79.01	48.66	17.74	:	:	30.83
65. Income tax	37.10	21.74	27.27	35.53	32.48	19.96	8.32	:	:	23.01
66. Profit after tax	42.74	25.36	-2.80	40.36	46.53	28.70	9.42	:	:	7.82

CANADA

Banques commerciales étrangères

Pourcentage

ANALYSE DU COMPTE DE RESULTATS

% du total moyen du bilan
38. Produits financiers
39. Frais financiers
40. Produits financiers nets
41. Produits non financiers (nets)
42. Résultat brut
43. Frais d'exploitation
44. Résultat net
45. Provisions (nettes)
46. Bénéfices avant impôt
47. Impôt
48. Bénéfices après impôt
49. Bénéfices distribués
50. Bénéfices mis en réserve
51. Frais de personnel
52. Provisions sur prêts
53. Provisions sur titres

% du total du résultat brut
54. Produits financiers nets
55. Produits non financiers (nets)
56. Frais d'exploitation
57. Résultat net
58. Provisions (nettes)
59. Bénéfices avant impôt
60. Impôt
61. Bénéfices après impôt
62. Frais de personnel

% du total du résultat net
63. Provisions (nettes)
64. Bénéfices avant impôt
65. Impôt
66. Bénéfices après impôt

CANADA

Foreign commercial banks

Per cent

BALANCE SHEET ANALYSIS

% of year-end balance sheet total

	1985	1986	1987	1988	1989	1990	1991	1992	1993	1994
Assets										
67. Cash & balance with Central bank	0.08	0.34	0.49	0.58	0.60	0.26	0.29	0.19	0.28	0.33
68. Interbank deposits	20.24	17.79	18.55	15.14	16.28	12.94	14.83	14.85	10.59	14.06
69. Loans	68.14	70.81	66.63	69.61	69.97	71.21	68.16	65.25	63.31	64.13
70. Securities	8.65	8.37	11.69	12.14	10.51	12.43	14.12	16.58	21.20	18.15
71. Other assets	2.89	2.69	2.65	2.54	2.63	3.16	2.60	3.12	4.63	3.34
Liabilities										
72. Capital & reserves	7.41	7.60	7.41	7.67	7.70	8.32	7.89	6.65	6.51	6.52
73. Borrowing from Central bank	-	0.02	0.16	-	-	-	-	-	-	-
74. Interbank deposits	29.88	26.35	28.78	30.07	29.49	32.02	31.01	30.66	25.84	29.93
75. Non-bank deposits	58.68	60.91	58.45	56.14	55.34	50.00	49.63	49.78	51.95	50.28
76. Bonds	0.18	0.27	0.26	0.47	0.66	1.17	1.74	2.06	1.96	2.07
77. Other liabilities	3.86	4.86	4.94	5.65	6.82	8.49	9.73	10.85	13.74	11.21
Memoranda										
78. Short-term securities	:	:	:	:	:	:	:	:	:	:
79. Bonds	:	:	:	:	:	:	:	:	:	:
80. Shares and participations	:	:	:	:	:	:	:	:	:	:
81. Claims on non-residents	:	:	:	:	:	:	:	:	:	:
82. Liabilities to non-residents	:	:	:	:	:	:	:	:	:	:

Notes

- The reporting period is the fiscal year ending 31st October.

CANADA

Banques commerciales étrangères

Pourcentage

ANALYSE DU BILAN

% du total du bilan en fin d'exercice

Actif

- 67. Caisse & solde auprès de la Banque centrale
- 68. Dépôts interbancaires
- 69. Prêts
- 70. Valeurs mobilières
- 71. Autres actifs

Passif

- 72. Capital et réserves
- 73. Emprunts auprès de la Banque centrale
- 74. Dépôts interbancaires
- 75. Dépôts non bancaires
- 76. Obligations
- 77. Autres engagements

Pour mémoire

- 78. Titres à court terme
- 79. Obligations
- 80. Actions et participations
- 81. Créances sur des non résidents
- 82. Engagements envers des non résidents

Notes

- La période couverte est l'exercice financier qui se termine le 31 octobre.

DENMARK

Commercial banks and savings banks

DANEMARK

Banques commerciales et caisses d'épargne

Million Danish kroner / *Millions de couronnes danoises*

		1985	1986	1987	1988	1989	1990	1991 (1)	1992	1993	1994		
INCOME STATEMENT													**COMPTE DE RESULTATS**
1.	Interest income	57628	60547	66452	68776	87280	103599	100453	98915	96366	77135	1.	Produits financiers
2.	Interest expenses	39156	40002	43458	44703	61504	75254	66050	64453	59298	39070	2.	Frais financiers
3.	Net interest income	18472	20545	22994	24073	25776	28345	34403	34462	37068	38065	3.	Produits financiers nets
4.	Non-interest income (net)	25248	-3668	4205	13784	7170	4016	5728	-3984	9435	-5450	4.	Produits non financiers (nets)
5.	Gross income	43720	16877	27199	37857	32946	32361	40131	30478	46503	32615	5.	Résultat brut
6.	Operating expenses	15106	16686	18686	20135	21383	22200	25112	24800	23759	23650	6.	Frais d'exploitation
7.	Net income	28614	191	8513	17722	11563	10161	15019	5678	22744	8965	7.	Résultat net
8.	Provisions (net)	5928	3084	5662	9416	8777	13111	15113	17331	16651	8924	8.	Provisions (nettes)
9.	Profit before tax	22686	-2893	2851	8306	2786	-2950	-94	-11653	6093	41	9.	Bénéfices avant impôt
10.	Income tax	10657	-251	1067	2572	522	-238	331	189	2114	361	10.	Impôt
11.	Profit after tax	12029	-2642	1784	5734	2264	-2712	-425	-11842	3979	-320	11.	Bénéfices après impôt
12.	Distributed profit	1150	1242	1245	1274	1666	1320	1861	959	1141	1209	12.	Bénéfices distribués
13.	Retained profit	10879	-3884	539	4460	598	-4032	-2286	-12801	2838	-1529	13.	Bénéfices mis en réserve
Memoranda													*Pour mémoire*
14.	Staff costs	9593	10446	11776	12682	13340	13814	15165	15141	14497	14627	14.	Frais de personnel
15.	Provisions on loans	3985	2019	4303	8043	7388	11408	13592	15826	15108	7382	15.	Provisions sur prêts
16.	Provisions on securities	..	..	..	..	..	..	..	..	..	..	16.	Provisions sur titres
BALANCE SHEET													**BILAN**
Assets													**Actif**
17.	Cash & balance with Central bank	38627	21640	11618	16180	17005	14341	19979	20858	37790	34464	17.	Caisse & solde auprès de la Banque centrale
18.	Interbank deposits	123235	107838	141350	169575	171700	170112	189185	160419	252109	183329	18.	Dépôts interbancaires
19.	Loans	269248	341748	390488	410545	456793	495821	508427	479976	478311	433769	19.	Prêts
20.	Securities	210632	207587	171418	200753	230152	212776	244309	227649	231968	251488	20.	Valeurs mobilières
21.	Other assets	123818	142785	155521	175828	184476	228538	47885	48069	41620	42668	21.	Autres actifs
Liabilities													**Passif**
22.	Capital & reserves	66424	70790	74779	87933	92470	88199	67564	55379	57424	62246	22.	Capital et réserves
23.	Borrowing from Central bank	23177	45170	18178	3513	19844	4880	19339	34573	83646	64046	23.	Emprunts auprès de la Banque centrale
24.	Interbank deposits	177718	162959	201379	233807	271829	292874	313462	242967	249313	204647	24.	Dépôts interbancaires
25.	Non-bank deposits	369105	406369	424496	471360	496049	526552	503260	499060	558750	537310	25.	Dépôts non bancaires
26.	Bonds							42821	32761	22524	14051	26.	Obligations
27.	Other liabilities	129136	136310	151563	176268	179934	209083	63339	72231	70141	63418	27.	Autres engagements
Balance sheet total													**Total du bilan**
28.	End-year total	765560	821598	870395	972881	1060126	1121588	1009785	936971	1041798	945718	28.	En fin d'exercice
29.	Average total	609853	781707	805018	867164	1010504	1084007	1016200	967878	989385	993758	29.	Moyen
Memoranda													*Pour mémoire*
30.	Short-term securities	12394	11712	21118	34208	21240	23713	48935	73969	51710	67767	30.	Titres à court terme
31.	Bonds	173747	165718	121559	132322	165343	147593	159252	120665	142582	146079	31.	Obligations
32.	Shares and participations	19525	22633	21721	27553	36782	34341	36122	33015	37676	37642	32.	Actions et participations
33.	Claims on non-residents	166477	167628	209273	276874	324297	365812	..	..	..	..	33.	Créances sur des non résidents
34.	Liabilities to non-residents	208806	212624	251325	329555	386679	420807	..	..	..	..	34.	Engagements envers des non résidents
SUPPLEMENTARY INFORMATION													**RENSEIGNEMENTS COMPLEMENTAIRES**
35.	Number of institutions	217	216	214	206	199	189	119	113	112	113	35.	Nombre d'institutions
36.	Number of branches	3331	3302	3264	3159	3059	2884	2652	2467	2340	2245	36.	Nombre de succursales
37.	Number of employees (x 1000)	52	55	57	56	56	55	56	52	50	49	37.	Nombre de salariés (x 1000)

DENMARK

Commercial banks and savings banks

DANEMARK

Banques commerciales et caisses d'épargne

Per cent / *Pourcentage*

INCOME STATEMENT ANALYSIS / **ANALYSE DU COMPTE DE RESULTATS**

		1985	1986	1987	1988	1989	1990	1991 (1)	1992	1993	1994		
% of average balance sheet total													**% du total moyen du bilan**
38. Interest income		9.45	7.75	8.25	7.93	8.64	9.56	9.89	10.22	9.74	7.76	38.	Produits financiers
39. Interest expenses		6.42	5.12	5.40	5.16	6.09	6.94	6.50	6.66	5.99	3.93	39.	Frais financiers
40. Net interest income		3.03	2.63	2.86	2.78	2.55	2.61	3.39	3.56	3.75	3.83	40.	Produits financiers nets
41. Non-interest income (net)		4.14	-0.47	0.52	1.59	0.71	0.37	0.56	-0.41	0.95	-0.55	41.	Produits non financiers (nets)
42. Gross income		7.17	2.16	3.38	4.37	3.26	2.99	3.95	3.15	4.70	3.28	42.	Résultat brut
43. Operating expenses		2.48	2.13	2.32	2.32	2.12	2.05	2.47	2.56	2.40	2.38	43.	Frais d'exploitation
44. Net income		4.69	0.02	1.06	2.04	1.14	0.94	1.48	0.59	2.30	0.90	44.	Résultat net
45. Provisions (net)		0.97	0.39	0.70	1.09	0.87	1.21	1.49	1.79	1.68	0.90	45.	Provisions (nettes)
46. Profit before tax		3.72	-0.37	0.35	0.96	0.28	-0.27	-0.01	-1.20	0.62	0.00	46.	Bénéfices avant impôt
47. Income tax		1.75	-0.03	0.13	0.30	0.05	-0.02	0.03	0.02	0.21	0.04	47.	Impôt
48. Profit after tax		1.97	-0.34	0.22	0.66	0.22	-0.25	-0.04	-1.22	0.40	-0.03	48.	Bénéfices après impôt
49. Distributed profit		0.19	0.16	0.15	0.15	0.16	0.12	0.18	0.10	0.12	0.12	49.	Bénéfices distribués
50. Retained profit		1.78	-0.50	0.07	0.51	0.06	-0.37	-0.22	-1.32	0.29	-0.15	50.	Bénéfices mis en réserve
51. Staff costs		1.57	1.34	1.46	1.46	1.32	1.27	1.49	1.56	1.47	1.47	51.	Frais de personnel
52. Provisions on loans		0.65	0.26	0.53	0.93	0.73	1.05	1.34	1.64	1.53	0.74	52.	Provisions sur prêts
53. Provisions on securities		..	..	..	..	..	..	..	..	..	..	53.	Provisions sur titres
% of gross income													**% du total du résultat brut**
54. Net interest income		42.25	121.73	84.54	63.59	78.24	87.59	85.73	113.07	79.71	116.71	54.	Produits financiers nets
55. Non-interest income (net)		57.75	-21.73	15.46	36.41	21.76	12.41	14.27	-13.07	20.29	-16.71	55.	Produits non financiers (nets)
56. Operating expenses		34.55	98.87	68.70	53.19	64.90	68.60	62.58	81.37	51.09	72.51	56.	Frais d'exploitation
57. Net income		65.45	1.13	31.30	46.81	35.10	31.40	37.42	18.63	48.91	27.49	57.	Résultat net
58. Provisions (net)		13.56	18.27	20.82	24.87	26.64	40.51	37.66	56.86	35.81	27.36	58.	Provisions (nettes)
59. Profit before tax		51.89	-17.14	10.48	21.94	8.46	-9.12	-0.23	-38.23	13.10	0.13	59.	Bénéfices avant impôt
60. Income tax		24.38	-1.49	3.92	6.79	1.58	-0.74	0.82	0.62	4.55	1.11	60.	Impôt
61. Profit after tax		27.51	-15.65	6.56	15.15	6.87	-8.38	-1.06	-38.85	8.56	-0.98	61.	Bénéfices après impôt
62. Staff costs		21.94	61.89	43.30	33.50	40.49	42.69	37.79	49.68	31.17	44.85	62.	Frais de personnel
% of net income													**% du total du résultat net**
63. Provisions (net)		20.72	..	66.51	53.13	75.91	129.03	100.63	..	73.21	99.54	63.	Provisions (nettes)
64. Profit before tax		79.28	..	33.49	46.87	24.09	-29.03	-0.63	..	26.79	0.46	64.	Bénéfices avant impôt
65. Income tax		37.24	..	12.53	14.51	4.51	-2.34	2.20	..	9.29	4.03	65.	Impôt
66. Profit after tax		42.04	..	20.96	32.36	19.58	-26.69	-2.83	..	17.49	-3.57	66.	Bénéfices après impôt

DENMARK

Commercial banks and savings banks

DANEMARK

Banques commerciales et caisses d'épargne

Per cent / Pour cent	1985	1986	1987	1988	1989	1990	1991 (1)	1992	1993	1994	
BALANCE SHEET ANALYSIS											**ANALYSE DU BILAN**
% of year-end balance sheet total											**% du total du bilan en fin d'exercice**
Assets											**Actif**
67. Cash & balance with Central bank	5.05	2.63	1.33	1.66	1.60	1.28	1.98	2.23	3.63	3.64	67. Caisse & solde auprès de la Banque centrale
68. Interbank deposits	16.10	13.13	16.24	17.43	16.20	15.17	18.74	17.12	24.20	19.39	68. Dépôts interbancaires
69. Loans	35.17	41.60	44.86	42.20	43.09	44.21	50.35	51.23	45.91	45.87	69. Prêts
70. Securities	27.51	25.27	19.69	20.63	21.71	18.97	24.19	24.30	22.27	26.59	70. Valeurs mobilières
71. Other assets	16.17	17.38	17.87	18.07	17.40	20.38	4.74	5.13	4.00	4.51	71. Autres actifs
Liabilities											**Passif**
72. Capital & reserves	8.68	8.62	8.59	9.04	8.72	7.86	6.69	5.91	5.51	6.58	72. Capital et réserves
73. Borrowing from Central bank	3.03	5.50	2.09	0.36	1.87	0.44	1.92	3.69	8.03	6.77	73. Emprunts auprès de la Banque centrale
74. Interbank deposits	23.21	19.83	23.14	24.03	25.64	26.11	31.04	25.93	23.93	21.64	74. Dépôts interbancaires
75. Non-bank deposits	48.21	49.46	48.77	48.45	46.79	46.95	49.84	53.26	53.63		75. Dépôts non bancaires
76. Bonds							4.24	3.50	2.16		76. Obligations
77. Other liabilities	16.87	16.59	17.41	18.12	16.97	18.64	6.27	7.71	6.73	6.71	77. Autres engagements
Memoranda											*Pour mémoire*
78. Short-term securities	1.62	1.43	2.43	3.52	2.00	2.11	4.85	7.89	4.96	7.17	78. Titres à court terme
79. Bonds	22.70	20.17	13.97	13.60	15.60	13.16	15.77	12.88	13.69	15.45	79. Obligations
80. Shares and participations	2.55	2.75	2.50	2.83	3.47	3.06	3.58	3.52	3.62	3.98	80. Actions et participations
81. Claims on non-residents	21.75	20.40	24.04	28.46	30.59	32.62	:	:	:	:	81. Créances sur des non résidents
82. Liabilities to non-residents	27.27	25.88	28.87	33.87	36.47	37.52	:	:	:	:	82. Engagements envers des non résidents

1. Break in series.

1. Rupture dans les séries.

Notes

• "Non-interest income (net)" (item 4) includes value adjustments on foreign currency assets and liabilities and on securities.

• Until 1993, average balance sheet totals (item 29) are based on twelve end-month data.

Notes

• Les "Produits non financiers (net)" (poste 4) contiennent des ajustements en valeurs concernant les actifs/passifs en monnaies étrangères et les valeurs mobilières.

• Jusqu'à 1993, la moyenne du total des actifs/passifs (poste 29) est basée sur douze données de fin de mois.

FINLAND

All banks

Million markkaa

FINLANDE

Ensemble des banques

Millions de markkas

	1985	1986	1987	1988	1989	1990	1991	1992	1993	1994	
INCOME STATEMENT											**COMPTE DE RESULTATS**
1. Interest income	26513	26760	32567	43193	60507	74459	77567	72766	57372	41211	1. Produits financiers
2. Interest expenses	19483	19540	23530	32492	48838	60676	65331	63567	44912	29470	2. Frais financiers
3. Net interest income	7030	7220	9037	10701	11669	13783	12236	9199	12460	11741	3. Produits financiers nets
4. Non-interest income (net)	5835	6603	8018	12112	10977	11750	13228	13589	17181	10348	4. Produits non financiers (nets)
5. Gross income	12865	13823	17055	22813	22646	25533	25464	22788	29641	22089	5. Résultat brut
6. Operating expenses	10177	11314	13712	16790	19199	20807	31372	43397	40444	30900	6. Frais d'exploitation
7. Net income	2688	2509	3343	6023	3447	4726	-5908	-20609	-10803	-8811	7. Résultat net
8. Provisions (net)	1558	1116	1922	2980	1618	1890	-53	-442	-42	-240	8. Provisions (nettes)
9. Profit before tax	1130	1393	1421	3043	1829	2836	-5855	-20167	-10761	-8571	9. Bénéfices avant impôt
10. Income tax	359	316	332	457	602	961	475	263	179	163	10. Impôt
11. Profit after tax	771	1077	1089	2586	1227	1875	-6330	-20430	-10940	-8734	11. Bénéfices après impôt
12. Distributed profit	677	835	896	1052	1177	727	273	58	77	65	12. Bénéfices distribués
13. Retained profit	94	242	193	1534	50	1148	-6603	-20488	-11017	-8799	13. Bénéfices mis en réserve
Memoranda											*Pour mémoire*
14. Staff costs	*5130*	*5450*	*6509*	*7357*	*8014*	*8015*	*8438*	*7947*	*7117*	*3869*	*14. Frais de personnel*
15. Provisions on loans	*1023*	*1106*	*1546*	*2084*	*2231*	*2192*	*-10*	*-259*	*92*	*-203*	*15. Provisions sur prêts*
16. Provisions on securities	*..*	*..*	*376*	*675*	*-623*	*-973*	*-43*	*-182*	*-134*	*-37*	*16. Provisions sur titres*
BALANCE SHEET											**BILAN**
Assets											**Actif**
17. Cash & balance with Central bank	14257	12367	15567	24465	32085	24491	19090	26007	13416	11814	17. Caisse & solde auprès de la Banque centrale
18. Interbank deposits	13562	19865	17692	22749	24534	24072	22011	25911	51076	20044	18. Dépôts interbancaires
19. Loans	199393	232398	277749	367326	444797	483139	490581	464070	399735	348145	19. Prêts
20. Securities	30104	45230	62843	77809	89223	95149	130734	125917	155032	158305	20. Valeurs mobilières
21. Other assets	54745	72137	78623	91617	91812	107152	107975	118736	134830	142477	21. Autres actifs
Liabilities											**Passif**
22. Capital & reserves	20059	23075	27045	39098	45677	50563	53350	41264	37874	33999	22. Capital et réserves
23. Borrowing from Central bank	7144	11477	2711	4813	3871	3918	5804	8019	5732	881	23. Emprunts auprès de la Banque centrale
24. Interbank deposits	11527	16293	13656	16480	18075	17363	18828	22158	17046	19613	24. Dépôts interbancaires
25. Non-bank deposits	200859	222640	264361	328332	347022	378838	390247	393512	372121	360365	25. Dépôts non bancaires
26. Bonds	7164	12731	17404	29922	44580	62675	78444	75613	65159	63193	26. Obligations
27. Other liabilities	65308	95781	127297	165321	223226	220646	223718	220075	256157	202734	27. Autres engagements
Balance sheet total											**Total du bilan**
28. End-year total	312061	381997	452474	583966	682451	734003	770391	760641	754089	680785	28. En fin d'exercice
29. Average total	290447	347030	417236	518221	633209	708228	752198	765517	757366	717437	29. Moyen
Memoranda											*Pour mémoire*
30. Short-term securities (1)	*25165*	*2688*	*18505*	*28582*	*30029*	*36176*	*50621*	*47230*	*66606*	*85634*	*30. Titres à court terme (1)*
31. Bonds	*..*	*36457*	*36675*	*38546*	*42763*	*42423*	*55802*	*64888*	*74528*	*58112*	*31. Obligations*
32. Shares and participations	*4939*	*6085*	*7663*	*10681*	*16431*	*16550*	*24311*	*13799*	*13898*	*14559*	*32. Actions et participations*
33. Claims on non-residents	*42239*	*69528*	*76255*	*88306*	*94136*	*102036*	*103688*	*116390*	*128716*	*107683*	*33. Créances sur des non résidents*
34. Liabilities to non-residents	*71030*	*98424*	*130202*	*158315*	*176339*	*218019*	*221916*	*212036*	*185571*	*145536*	*34. Engagements envers des non résidents*
SUPPLEMENTARY INFORMATION											**RENSEIGNEMENTS COMPLEMENTAIRES**
35. Number of institutions	635	621	610	589	553	523	438	370	358	357	35. Nombre d'institutions
36. Number of branches	2934	2924	2938	2956	2977	2821	2662	2393	2200	1828	36. Nombre de succursales
37. Number of employees (x 1000)	42.9	44.4	45.5	47.4	48.6	46.1	42.8	38.9	36.0	34.1	37. Nombre de salariés (x 1000)

FINLAND

All banks

Per cent

INCOME STATEMENT ANALYSIS

FINLANDE

Ensemble des banques

Pourcentage

ANALYSE DU COMPTE DE RESULTATS

		1985	1986	1987	1988	1989	1990	1991	1992	1993	1994		
% of average balance sheet total													**% du total moyen du bilan**
38.	Interest income	9.13	7.71	7.81	8.33	9.56	10.51	10.31	9.51	7.58	5.74	38.	Produits financiers
39.	Interest expenses	6.71	5.63	5.64	6.27	7.71	8.57	8.69	8.30	5.93	4.11	39.	Frais financiers
40.	Net interest income	2.42	2.08	2.17	2.06	1.84	1.95	1.63	1.20	1.65	1.64	40.	Produits financiers nets
41.	Non-interest income (net)	2.01	1.90	1.92	2.34	1.73	1.66	1.76	1.78	2.27	1.44	41.	Produits non financiers (nets)
42.	Gross income	4.43	3.98	4.09	4.40	3.58	3.61	3.39	2.98	3.91	3.08	42.	Résultat brut
43.	Operating expenses	3.50	3.26	3.29	3.24	3.03	2.94	4.17	5.67	5.34	4.31	43.	Frais d'exploitation
44.	Net income	0.93	0.72	0.80	1.16	0.54	0.67	-0.79	-2.69	-1.43	-1.23	44.	Résultat net
45.	Provisions (net)	0.54	0.32	0.46	0.58	0.26	0.27	-0.01	-0.06	-0.01	-0.03	45.	Provisions (nettes)
46.	Profit before tax	0.39	0.40	0.34	0.59	0.29	0.40	-0.78	-2.63	-1.42	-1.19	46.	Bénéfices avant impôt
47.	Income tax	0.12	0.09	0.08	0.09	0.10	0.14	0.06	0.03	0.02	0.02	47.	Impôt
48.	Profit after tax	0.27	0.31	0.26	0.50	0.19	0.26	-0.84	-2.67	-1.44	-1.22	48.	Bénéfices après impôt
49.	Distributed profit	0.23	0.24	0.21	0.20	0.19	0.10	0.04	0.01	0.01	0.01	49.	Bénéfices distribués
50.	Retained profit	0.03	0.07	0.05	0.30	0.01	0.16	-0.88	-2.68	-1.45	-1.23	50.	Bénéfices mis en réserve
51.	Staff costs	1.77	1.57	1.56	1.42	1.27	1.13	1.12	1.04	0.94	0.54	51.	Frais de personnel
52.	Provisions on loans	0.35	0.32	0.37	0.40	0.35	0.31	0.00	-0.03	0.01	-0.03	52.	Provisions sur prêts
53.	Provisions on securities	..	..	0.09	0.13	-0.10	-0.14	-0.01	-0.02	-0.02	-0.01	53.	Provisions sur titres
% of gross income													**% du total du résultat brut**
54.	Net interest income	54.64	52.23	52.99	46.91	51.53	53.98	48.05	40.37	42.04	53.15	54.	Produits financiers nets
55.	Non-interest income (net)	45.36	47.77	47.01	53.09	48.47	46.02	51.95	59.63	57.96	46.85	55.	Produits non financiers (nets)
56.	Operating expenses	79.11	81.85	80.40	73.60	84.78	81.49	123.20	190.44	136.45	139.89	56.	Frais d'exploitation
57.	Net income	20.89	18.15	19.60	26.40	15.22	18.51	-23.20	-90.44	-36.45	-39.89	57.	Résultat net
58.	Provisions (net)	12.11	8.07	11.27	13.06	7.14	7.40	-0.21	-1.94	-0.14	-1.09	58.	Provisions (nettes)
59.	Profit before tax	8.78	10.08	8.33	13.34	8.08	11.11	-22.99	-88.50	-36.30	-38.80	59.	Bénéfices avant impôt
60.	Income tax	2.79	2.29	1.95	2.00	2.66	3.76	1.87	1.15	0.60	0.74	60.	Impôt
61.	Profit after tax	5.99	7.79	6.39	11.34	5.42	7.34	-24.86	-89.65	-36.91	-39.54	61.	Bénéfices après impôt
62.	Staff costs	39.88	39.43	38.16	32.25	35.39	31.39	33.14	34.87	24.01	17.52	62.	Frais de personnel
% of net income													**% du total du résultat net**
63.	Provisions (net)	57.96	44.48	57.49	49.48	46.94	39.99	0.90	2.14	0.39	2.72	63.	Provisions (nettes)
64.	Profit before tax	42.04	55.52	42.51	50.52	53.06	60.01	99.10	97.86	99.61	97.28	64.	Bénéfices avant impôt
65.	Income tax	13.36	12.59	9.93	7.59	17.46	20.33	-8.04	-1.28	-1.66	-1.85	65.	Impôt
66.	Profit after tax	28.68	42.93	32.58	42.94	35.60	39.67	107.14	99.13	101.27	99.13	66.	Bénéfices après impôt

FINLAND

All banks

Per cent

BALANCE SHEET ANALYSIS

	1985	1986	1987	1988	1989	1990	1991	1992	1993	1994
% of year-end balance sheet total										
Assets										
67. Cash & balance with Central bank	4.57	3.24	3.44	4.19	4.70	3.34	2.48	3.42	1.78	1.74
68. Interbank deposits	4.35	5.20	3.91	3.90	3.59	3.28	2.86	3.41	6.77	2.94
69. Loans	63.90	60.84	61.38	62.90	65.18	65.82	63.68	61.01	53.01	51.14
70. Securities	9.65	11.84	13.89	13.32	13.07	12.96	16.97	16.55	20.56	23.25
71. Other assets	17.54	18.88	17.38	15.69	13.45	14.60	14.02	15.61	17.88	20.93
Liabilities										
72. Capital & reserves	6.43	6.04	5.98	6.70	6.69	6.89	6.93	5.42	5.02	4.99
73. Borrowing from Central bank	2.29	3.00	0.60	0.82	0.57	0.53	0.75	1.05	0.76	0.13
74. Interbank deposits	3.69	4.27	3.02	2.82	2.65	2.37	2.44	2.91	2.26	2.88
75. Non-bank deposits	64.37	58.28	58.43	56.22	50.85	51.61	50.66	51.73	49.35	52.93
76. Bonds	2.30	3.33	3.85	5.12	6.53	8.54	10.18	9.94	8.64	9.28
77. Other liabilities	20.93	25.07	28.13	28.31	32.71	30.06	29.04	28.93	33.97	29.78
Memoranda										
78. Short-term securities (1)	*..*	*0.70*	*4.09*	*4.89*	*4.40*	*4.93*	*6.57*	*6.21*	*8.83*	*12.58*
79. Bonds	*8.06*	*9.54*	*8.11*	*6.60*	*6.27*	*5.78*	*7.24*	*8.53*	*9.88*	*8.54*
80. Shares and participations	*1.58*	*1.59*	*1.69*	*1.83*	*2.41*	*2.25*	*3.16*	*1.81*	*1.84*	*2.14*
81. Claims on non-residents	*13.54*	*18.20*	*16.85*	*15.12*	*13.79*	*13.90*	*13.46*	*15.30*	*17.07*	*15.82*
82. Liabilities to non-residents	*22.76*	*25.77*	*28.78*	*27.11*	*25.84*	*29.70*	*28.81*	*27.88*	*24.61*	*21.38*

1. Until 1986, included under "Bonds" (item 31 or item 79).

Notes

- All banks include Commercial banks, Post office banks, Foreign commercial banks, Savings banks and Co-operative banks.

Change in methodology:

- As from 1984, foreign branches of Finnish commercial banks are also included in the data.

FINLANDE

Ensemble des banques

Pourcentage

ANALYSE DU BILAN

% du total du bilan en fin d'exercice

Actif

67. Caisse & solde auprès de la Banque centrale
68. Dépôts interbancaires
69. Prêts
70. Valeurs mobilières
71. Autres actifs

Passif

72. Capital et réserves
73. Emprunts auprès de la Banque centrale
74. Dépôts interbancaires
75. Dépôts non bancaires
76. Obligations
77. Autres engagements

Pour mémoire

78. Titres à court terme (1)
79. Obligations
80. Actions et participations
81. Créances sur des non résidents
82. Engagements envers des non résidents

1 Jusqu'à 1986, inclus sous "Obligations" (poste 31 ou poste 79).

Notes

- L'Ensemble des banques comprend les Banques commerciales, la Banque postale, les Banques commerciales étrangères, les Caisses d'épargne et les Banques mutualistes.

Changement méthodologique :

- Depuis 1984, les données comprennent les chiffres relatifs aux succursales étrangères des banques commerciales finlandaises.

40

Commercial banks

Million markkaa

#		1985	1986	1987	1988	1989	1990	1991	1992	1993	1994	
	INCOME STATEMENT											**COMPTE DE RESULTATS**
1.	Interest income	14335	14165	18048	28941	41113	51091	52508	49389	38713	29219	Produits financiers
2.	Interest expenses	11605	11682	14349	23252	35004	43382	46022	43463	31396	22152	Frais financiers
3.	Net interest income	2730	2483	3699	5689	6109	7709	6486	5926	7317	7067	Produits financiers nets
4.	Non-interest income (net)	3719	4053	4589	7703	7679	8060	8645	7221	7686	7486	Produits non financiers (nets)
5.	Gross income	6449	6536	8288	13392	13788	15769	15131	13147	15003	14553	Résultat brut
6.	Operating expenses	4638	5055	6103	9951	11300	12589	20804	22942	24234	20658	Frais d'exploitation
7.	Net income	1811	1481	2185	3441	2488	3180	-5673	-9795	-9231	-6105	Résultat net
8.	Provisions (net)	939	401	1131	1407	1024	924	-54	-59	20	-250	Provisions (nettes)
9.	Profit before tax	872	1080	1054	2034	1464	2256	-5619	-9736	-9251	-5855	Bénéfices avant impôt
10.	Income tax	250	182	189	326	421	735	272	127	39	18	Impôt
11.	Profit after tax	622	898	865	1708	1043	1521	-5891	-9863	-9290	-5873	Bénéfices après impôt
12.	Distributed profit	616	761	812	991	1111	665	223	30	57	63	Bénéfices distribués
13.	Retained profit	6	137	53	717	-68	856	-6114	-9893	-9347	-5936	Bénéfices mis en réserve
	Memoranda											*Pour mémoire*
14.	*Staff costs*	*2250*	*2318*	*2772*	*3997*	*4500*	*4501*	*5013*	*4559*	*4108*	*1522*	*Frais de personnel*
15.	*Provisions on loans*	*546*	*487*	*871*	*1354*	*1355*	*1225*	*-465*	*-46*	*43*	*-211*	*Provisions sur prêts*
16.	*Provisions on securities*	*..*	*..*	*258*	*52*	*-330*	*-950*	*411*	*-12*	*-23*	*-39*	*Provisions sur titres*
	BALANCE SHEET											**BILAN**
	Assets											**Actif**
17.	Cash & balance with Central bank	6216	5397	7147	13457	16228	12485	10489	11440	9296	7947	Caisse & solde auprès de la Banque centrale
18.	Interbank deposits	1565	2292	4255	7586	8034	6464	3232	8236	4573	4170	Dépôts interbancaires
19.	Loans	103700	121845	149775	235294	289508	321154	327169	308638	293033	245139	Prêts
20.	Securities	22119	33069	37963	64450	72232	77896	111357	109499	137389	143269	Valeurs mobilières
21.	Other assets	40456	53995	56944	74991	74888	85839	80049	84579	100224	97814	Autres actifs
	Liabilities											**Passif**
22.	Capital & reserves	13257	15072	17490	28065	32255	36206	39140	27247	26411	24374	Capital et réserves
23.	Borrowing from Central bank	5769	9511	856	3283	2001	2292	4013	5436	5416	605	Emprunts auprès de la Banque centrale
24.	Interbank deposits	11364	15929	12744	16142	17207	17139	18706	22060	16456	19589	Dépôts interbancaires
25.	Non-bank deposits	98347	111246	137585	204387	212448	241785	245335	250665	266582	249732	Dépôts non bancaires
26.	Bonds	5128	7007	8784	25529	37690	54424	63503	57863	48379	49753	Obligations
27.	Other liabilities	40191	57833	78625	118372	159289	151992	161599	159121	181271	154286	Autres engagements
	Balance sheet total											**Total du bilan**
28.	End-year total	174056	216598	256084	395778	460890	503838	532296	522392	544515	498339	En fin d'exercice
29.	Average total	160765	195327	236341	353724	428334	482364	518067	527344	533454	521427	Moyen
	Memoranda											*Pour mémoire*
30.	*Short-term securities (1)*	*..*	*954*	*7227*	*24184*	*25650*	*31939*	*43075*	*39169*	*57799*	*73528*	*Titres à court terme (1)*
31.	*Bonds*	*18677*	*28261*	*25810*	*32844*	*36928*	*35860*	*50301*	*59575*	*68817*	*58112*	*Obligations*
32.	*Shares and participations*	*3442*	*3854*	*4926*	*7422*	*9654*	*10097*	*17981*	*10755*	*10773*	*11629*	*Actions et participations*
33.	*Claims on non-residents*	*35588*	*61473*	*66516*	*87112*	*92621*	*101667*	*102735*	*114403*	*127282*	*103937*	*Créances sur des non résidents*
34.	*Liabilities to non-residents*	*58491*	*84898*	*111453*	*154544*	*172104*	*215469*	*218400*	*205809*	*182759*	*142186*	*Engagements envers des non résidents*
	SUPPLEMENTARY INFORMATION											**RENSEIGNEMENTS COMPLEMENTAIRES**
35.	Number of institutions	7	6	6	7	10	10	12	10	10	10	Nombre d'institutions
36.	Number of branches	959	930	937	1004	1010	1037	948	860	1114	909	Nombre de succursales
37.	Number of employees (x 1000)	17.5	18.5	18.8	26.2	26.9	26.5	24.2	22.3	20.1	23.1	Nombre de salariés (x 1000)

FINLAND

Commercial banks

FINLANDE

Banques commerciales

Per cent — *Pourcentage*

INCOME STATEMENT ANALYSIS — **ANALYSE DU COMPTE DE RESULTATS**

	1985	1986	1987	1988	1989	1990	1991	1992	1993	1994		
% of average balance sheet total												**% du total moyen du bilan**
38. Interest income	8.92	7.25	7.64	8.18	9.60	10.59	10.14	9.37	7.26	5.60	38.	Produits financiers
39. Interest expenses	7.22	5.98	6.07	6.57	8.17	8.99	8.88	8.24	5.89	4.25	39.	Frais financiers
40. Net interest income	1.70	1.27	1.57	1.61	1.43	1.60	1.25	1.12	1.37	1.36	40.	Produits financiers nets
41. Non-interest income (net)	2.31	2.07	1.94	2.18	1.79	1.67	1.67	1.37	1.44	1.44	41.	Produits non financiers (nets)
42. Gross income	4.01	3.35	3.51	3.79	3.22	3.27	2.92	2.49	2.81	2.79	42.	Résultat brut
43. Operating expenses	2.88	2.59	2.58	2.81	2.64	2.61	4.02	4.35	4.54	3.96	43.	Frais d'exploitation
44. Net income	1.13	0.76	0.92	0.97	0.58	0.66	-1.10	-1.86	-1.73	-1.17	44.	Résultat net
45. Provisions (net)	0.58	0.21	0.48	0.40	0.24	0.19	-0.01	-0.01		-0.05	45.	Provisions (nettes)
46. Profit before tax	0.54	0.55	0.45	0.58	0.34	0.47	-1.08	-1.85	-1.73	-1.12	46.	Bénéfices avant impôt
47. Income tax	0.16	0.09	0.08	0.09	0.10	0.15	0.05	0.02	0.01	0.00	47.	Impôt
48. Profit after tax	0.39	0.46	0.37	0.48	0.24	0.32	-1.14	-1.87	-1.74	-1.13	48.	Bénéfices après impôt
49. Distributed profit	0.38	0.39	0.34	0.28	0.26	0.14	0.04	0.01	0.01	0.01	49.	Bénéfices distribués
50. Retained profit	0.00	0.07	0.02	0.20	-0.02	0.18	-1.18	-1.88	-1.75	-1.14	50.	Bénéfices mis en réserve
51. Staff costs	1.40	1.19	1.17	1.13	1.05	0.93	0.97	0.86	0.77	0.29	51.	Frais de personnel
52. Provisions on loans	0.34	0.25	0.37	0.38	0.32	0.25	-0.09	-0.01	0.01	-0.04	52.	Provisions sur prêts
53. Provisions on securities	..	..	0.11	0.01	-0.08	-0.20	0.08	.	.	-0.01	53.	Provisions sur titres
% of gross income												**% du total du résultat brut**
54. Net interest income	42.33	37.99	44.63	42.48	44.31	48.89	42.87	45.07	48.77	48.56	54.	Produits financiers nets
55. Non-interest income (net)	57.67	62.01	55.37	57.52	55.69	51.11	57.13	54.93	51.23	51.44	55.	Produits non financiers (nets)
56. Operating expenses	71.92	77.34	73.64	74.31	81.96	79.83	137.49	174.50	161.53	141.95	56.	Frais d'exploitation
57. Net income	28.08	22.66	26.36	25.69	18.04	20.17	-37.49	-74.50	-61.53	-41.95	57.	Résultat net
58. Provisions (net)	14.56	6.14	13.65	10.51	7.43	5.86	-0.36	-0.45	0.13	-1.72	58.	Provisions (nettes)
59. Profit before tax	13.52	16.52	12.72	15.19	10.62	14.31	-37.14	-74.05	-61.66	-40.23	59.	Bénéfices avant impôt
60. Income tax	3.88	2.78	2.28	2.43	3.05	4.66	1.80	0.97	0.26	0.12	60.	Impôt
61. Profit after tax	9.64	13.74	10.44	12.75	7.56	9.65	-38.93	-75.02	-61.92	-40.36	61.	Bénéfices après impôt
62. Staff costs	34.89	35.47	33.45	29.85	32.64	28.54	33.13	34.68	27.38	10.46	62.	Frais de personnel
% of net income												**% du total du résultat net**
63. Provisions (net)	51.85	27.08	51.76	40.89	41.16	29.06	0.95	0.60	-0.22	4.10	63.	Provisions (nettes)
64. Profit before tax	48.15	72.92	48.24	59.11	58.84	70.94	99.05	99.40	100.22	95.90	64.	Bénéfices avant impôt
65. Income tax	13.80	12.29	8.65	9.47	16.92	23.11	-4.79	-1.30	-0.42	-0.29	65.	Impôt
66. Profit after tax	34.35	60.63	39.59	49.64	41.92	47.83	103.84	100.69	100.64	96.20	66.	Bénéfices après impôt

FINLAND

Commercial banks

Per cent

BALANCE SHEET ANALYSIS

% of year-end balance sheet total

	1985	1986	1987	1988	1989	1990	1991	1992	1993	1994
Assets										
67. Cash & balance with Central bank	3.57	2.49	2.79	3.40	3.52	2.48	1.97	2.19	1.71	1.59
68. Interbank deposits	0.90	1.06	1.66	1.92	1.74	1.28	0.61	1.58	0.84	0.84
69. Loans	59.58	56.25	58.49	59.45	62.81	63.74	61.46	59.08	53.82	49.19
70. Securities	12.71	15.27	14.82	16.28	15.67	15.46	20.92	20.96	25.23	28.75
71. Other assets	23.24	24.93	22.24	18.95	16.25	17.04	15.04	16.19	18.41	19.63
Liabilities										
72. Capital & reserves	7.62	6.96	6.83	7.09	7.00	7.19	7.35	5.22	4.85	4.89
73. Borrowing from Central bank	3.31	4.39	0.33	0.83	0.43	0.45	0.75	1.04	0.99	0.12
74. Interbank deposits	6.53	7.35	4.98	4.08	3.73	3.40	3.51	4.22	3.02	3.93
75. Non-bank deposits	56.50	51.36	53.73	51.64	46.10	47.99	46.09	47.98	48.96	50.11
76. Bonds	2.95	3.24	3.43	6.45	8.18	10.80	11.93	11.08	8.88	9.98
77. Other liabilities	23.09	26.70	30.70	29.91	34.56	30.17	30.36	30.46	33.29	30.96
Memoranda										
78. Short-term securities (1)	*..*	*0.44*	*2.82*	*6.11*	*5.57*	*6.34*	*8.09*	*7.50*	*10.61*	*14.75*
79. Bonds	*10.73*	*13.05*	*10.08*	*8.30*	*8.01*	*7.12*	*9.45*	*11.40*	*12.64*	*11.66*
80. Shares and participations	*1.98*	*1.78*	*1.92*	*1.88*	*2.09*	*2.00*	*3.38*	*2.06*	*1.98*	*2.33*
81. Claims on non-residents	*20.45*	*28.38*	*25.97*	*22.01*	*20.10*	*20.18*	*19.30*	*21.90*	*23.38*	*20.86*
82. Liabilities to non-residents	*33.60*	*39.20*	*43.52*	*39.05*	*37.34*	*42.77*	*41.03*	*39.40*	*33.56*	*28.53*

1. Until 1986, included under "Bonds" (item 31 or item 79).

Change in methodology:

• As from 1984, foreign branches of Finnish commercial banks are also included in the data.

• As from 1988, data include the Post office bank (Postipankki) classified thereafter under Commercial banks.

FINLANDE

Banques commerciales

Pourcentage

ANALYSE DU BILAN

% du total du bilan en fin d'exercice

Actif
67. Caisse & solde auprès de la Banque centrale
68. Dépôts interbancaires
69. Prêts
70. Valeurs mobilières
71. Autres actifs

Passif
72. Capital et réserves
73. Emprunts auprès de la Banque centrale
74. Dépôts interbancaires
75. Dépôts non bancaires
76. Obligations
77. Autres engagements

Pour mémoire
78. Titres à court terme (1)
79. Obligations
80. Actions et participations
81. Créances sur des non résidents
82. Engagements envers des non résidents

1. Jusqu'à 1986, inclus sous "Obligations" (poste 31 ou poste 79).

Changement méthodologique :

• Depuis 1984, les données comprennent les chiffres relatifs aux succursales étrangères des banques commerciales finlandaises.

• Depuis 1988, la Banque postale (Postipankki) est classée dans les données concernant les Banques commerciales.

43

FINLAND

Post office bank

Million markkaa

FINLANDE

Banque postale

Millions de markkaa

			1985	1986	1987	
INCOME STATEMENT						**COMPTE DE RESULTATS**
1.	Interest income		3434	3715	4151	1. Produits financiers
2.	Interest expenses		2256	2468	2942	2. Frais financiers
3.	Net interest income		1178	1247	1209	3. Produits financiers nets
4.	Non-interest income (net)		549	630	1030	4. Produits non financiers (nets)
5.	Gross income		1727	1877	2239	5. Résultat brut
6.	Operating expenses		1493	1554	1993	6. Frais d'exploitation
7.	Net income		234	323	246	7. Résultat net
8.	Provisions (net)		152	217	129	8. Provisions (nettes)
9.	Profit before tax		82	106	117	9. Bénéfices avant impôt
10.	Income tax		32	46	47	10. Impôt
11.	Profit after tax		50	60	70	11. Bénéfices après impôt
12.	Distributed profit		25	30	35	12. Bénéfices distribués
13.	Retained profit		25	30	35	13. Bénéfices mis en réserve
Memoranda						***Pour mémoire***
14.	*Staff costs*		*758*	*706*	*977*	*14. Frais de personnel*
15.	*Provisions on loans*		*126*	*203*	*183*	*15. Provisions sur prêts*
16.	*Provisions on securities*		*..*	*..*	*-42*	*16. Provisions sur titres*
BALANCE SHEET						**BILAN**
Assets						**Actif**
17.	Cash & balance with Central bank		2143	1536	1992	17. Caisse & solde auprès de la Banque centrale
18.	Interbank deposits		2072	6308	1321	18. Dépôts interbancaires
19.	Loans		22319	26606	27829	19. Prêts
20.	Securities		4168	6705	15077	20. Valeurs mobilières
21.	Other assets		5274	7774	9366	21. Autres actifs
Liabilities						**Passif**
22.	Capital & reserves		1716	1980	2154	22. Capital et réserves
23.	Borrowing from Central bank		337	755	472	23. Emprunts auprès de la Banque centrale
24.	Interbank deposits		148	109	106	24. Dépôts interbancaires
25.	Non-bank deposits		24434	24935	27030	25. Dépôts non bancaires
26.	Bonds		1209	4360	6714	26. Obligations
27.	Other liabilities		8132	16790	19109	27. Autres engagements
Balance sheet total						**Total du bilan**
28.	End-year total		35976	48929	55585	28. En fin d'exercice
29.	Average total		33859	42453	52257	29. Moyen
Memoranda						***Pour mémoire***
30.	*Short-term securities (1)*		*..*	*1504*	*7990*	*30. Titres à court terme (1)*
31.	*Bonds*		*3865*	*4687*	*6548*	*31. Obligations*
32.	*Shares and participations*		*303*	*514*	*539*	*32. Actions et participations*
33.	*Claims on non-residents*		*5812*	*7295*	*8994*	*33. Créances sur des non résidents*
34.	*Liabilities to non-residents*		*9281*	*12194*	*15790*	*34. Engagements envers des non résidents*
SUPPLEMENTARY INFORMATION						**RENSEIGNEMENTS COMPLEMENTAIRES**
35.	Number of institutions		1	1	1	35. Nombre d'institutions
36.	Number of branches		47	49	56	36. Nombre de succursales
37.	Number of employees (x 1000)		5.9	6.0	6.1	37. Nombre de salariés (x 1000)

FINLAND

Post office bank

Per cent

FINLANDE

Banque postale

Pourcentage

INCOME STATEMENT ANALYSIS

ANALYSE DU COMPTE DE RESULTATS

	1985	1986	1987		
% of average balance sheet total				**% du total moyen du bilan**	
38. Interest income	10.14	8.75	7.94	38. Produits financiers	
39. Interest expenses	6.66	5.81	5.63	39. Frais financiers	
40. Net interest income	3.48	2.94	2.31	40. Produits financiers nets	
41. Non-interest income (net)	1.62	1.48	1.97	41. Produits non financiers (nets)	
42. Gross income	5.10	4.42	4.28	42. Résultat brut	
43. Operating expenses	4.41	3.66	3.81	43. Frais d'exploitation	
44. Net income	0.69	0.76	0.47	44. Résultat net	
45. Provisions (net)	0.45	0.51	0.25	45. Provisions (nettes)	
46. Profit before tax	0.24	0.25	0.22	46. Bénéfices avant impôt	
47. Income tax	0.09	0.11	0.09	47. Impôt	
48. Profit after tax	0.15	0.14	0.13	48. Bénéfices après impôt	
49. Distributed profit	0.07	0.07	0.07	49. Bénéfices distribués	
50. Retained profit	0.07	0.07	0.07	50. Bénéfices mis en réserve	
51. Staff costs	2.24	1.66	1.87	51. Frais de personnel	
52. Provisions on loans	0.37	0.48	0.35	52. Provisions sur prêts	
53. Provisions on securities	:	:	-0.08	53. Provisions sur titres	
% of gross income				**% du total du résultat brut**	
54. Net interest income	68.21	66.44	54.00	54. Produits financiers nets	
55. Non-interest income (net)	31.79	33.56	46.00	55. Produits non financiers (nets)	
56. Operating expenses	86.45	82.79	89.01	56. Frais d'exploitation	
57. Net income	13.55	17.21	10.99	57. Résultat net	
58. Provisions (net)	8.80	11.56	5.76	58. Provisions (nettes)	
59. Profit before tax	4.75	5.65	5.23	59. Bénéfices avant impôt	
60. Income tax	1.85	2.45	2.10	60. Impôt	
61. Profit after tax	2.90	3.20	3.13	61. Bénéfices après impôt	
62. Staff costs	43.89	37.61	43.64	62. Frais de personnel	
% of net income				**% du total du résultat net**	
63. Provisions (net)	64.96	67.18	52.44	63. Provisions (nettes)	
64. Profit before tax	35.04	32.82	47.56	64. Bénéfices avant impôt	
65. Income tax	13.68	14.24	19.11	65. Impôt	
66. Profit after tax	21.37	18.58	28.46	66. Bénéfices après impôt	

FINLAND

Post office bank

FINLANDE

Banque postale

Per cent	1985	1986	1987	Pourcentage
BALANCE SHEET ANALYSIS				**ANALYSE DU BILAN**
% of year-end balance sheet total				**% du total du bilan en fin d'exercice**
Assets				**Actif**
67. Cash & balance with Central bank	5.96	3.14	3.58	67. Caisse & solde auprès de la Banque centrale
68. Interbank deposits	5.76	12.89	2.38	68. Dépôts interbancaires
69. Loans	62.04	54.38	50.07	69. Prêts
70. Securities	11.59	13.70	27.12	70. Valeurs mobilières
71. Other assets	14.66	15.89	16.85	71. Autres actifs
Liabilities				**Passif**
72. Capital & reserves	4.77	4.05	3.88	72. Capital et réserves
73. Borrowing from Central bank	0.94	1.54	0.85	73. Emprunts auprès de la Banque centrale
74. Interbank deposits	0.41	0.22	0.19	74. Dépôts interbancaires
75. Non-bank deposits	67.92	50.96	48.63	75. Dépôts non bancaires
76. Bonds	3.36	8.91	12.08	76. Obligations
77. Other liabilities	22.60	34.32	34.38	77. Autres engagements
Memoranda				*Pour mémoire*
78. Short-term securities (1)	*..*	*3.07*	*14.37*	*78. Titres à court terme (1)*
79. Bonds	*10.74*	*9.58*	*11.78*	*79. Obligations*
80. Shares and participations	*0.84*	*1.05*	*0.97*	*80. Actions et participations*
81. Claims on non-residents	*16.16*	*14.91*	*16.18*	*81. Créances sur des non résidents*
82. Liabilities to non-residents	*25.80*	*24.92*	*28.41*	*82. Engagements envers des non résidents*

1. Until 1986, included under "Bonds" (item 31 or 79).

1. Jusqu'à 1986, inclus sous "Obligations" (poste 31 ou poste 79).

Change in methodology:

• As from 1988, the Post office bank (Postipankki) is included under Commercial banks.

Changement méthodologique :

• Depuis 1988, la Banque postale (Postipankki) est classée dans les données concernant les Banques commerciales.

46

FINLAND

Foreign commercial banks

FINLANDE

Banques commerciales étrangères

Million markkaa / *Millions de markkas*

	English	Français	1985	1986	1987	1988	1989	1990	1991	1992	1993	1994
	INCOME STATEMENT	**COMPTE DE RESULTATS**										
1.	Interest income	Produits financiers	196	182	488	744	1121	984	1526	1554	1190	718
2.	Interest expenses	Frais financiers	175	163	459	715	1086	923	1507	1506	1137	666
3.	Net interest income	Produits financiers nets	21	19	29	29	35	61	19	48	53	52
4.	Non-interest income (net)	Produits non financiers (nets)	30	27	37	37	40	38	36	83	74	38
5.	Gross income	Résultat brut	51	46	66	66	75	99	55	131	127	90
6.	Operating expenses	Frais d'exploitation	33	37	63	70	126	95	133	149	92	110
7.	Net income	Résultat net	18	9	3	-4	-51	4	-78	-18	35	-20
8.	Provisions (net)	Provisions (nettes)	5	4	11	-3	3		5	41	-5	-11
9.	Profit before tax	Bénéfices avant impôt	13	5	-8	-1	-54	4	-83	-59	40	-9
10.	Income tax	Impôt	4	2		3	2	4	1	3	9	4
11.	Profit after tax	Bénéfices après impôt	9	3	-8	-4	-56	0	-84	-62	31	-13
12.	Distributed profit	Bénéfices distribués	4	6								
13.	Retained profit	Bénéfices mis en réserve	5	-3	-8	-4	-56	0	-84	-62	31	-13
	Memoranda	*Pour mémoire*										
14.	*Staff costs*	*Frais de personnel*	*18*	*20*	*34*	*39*	*37*	*37*	*47*	*38*	*39*	*40*
15.	*Provisions on loans*	*Provisions sur prêts*	*3*	*3*	*3*	*1*	*1*	*2*	*5*	*3*	*-5*	*1*
16.	*Provisions on securities*	*Provisions sur titres*	*..*	*..*	*8*	*3*	*2*	*-2*		*38*		*-12*
	BALANCE SHEET	**BILAN**										
	Assets	**Actif**										
17.	Cash & balance with Central bank	Caisse & solde auprès de la Banque centrale	358	21	126	176	154	36	108	108	43	86
18.	Interbank deposits	Dépôts interbancaires	309	528	171	323	81	297	314	33	4	104
19.	Loans	Prêts	579	887	586	447	1458	792	1771	1899	380	354
20.	Securities	Valeurs mobilières	20	305	3292	3315	2637	2896	4528	4787	4430	6682
21.	Other assets	Autres actifs	768	423	803	950	488	356	463	871	1331	5161
	Liabilities	**Passif**										
22.	Capital & reserves	Capital et réserves	122	122	211	243	240	186	254	120	150	13
23.	Borrowing from Central bank	Emprunts auprès de la Banque centrale	38	21		1			99	1		103
24.	Interbank deposits	Dépôts interbancaires	3	183	794	244	608	51	50		506	10
25.	Non-bank deposits	Dépôts non bancaires	1664	1380	2542	2910	1966	2267	2642	287	1458	3216
26.	Bonds	Obligations										
27.	Other liabilities	Autres engagements	207	458	1431	1813	2004	1873	4139	7290	4074	9045
	Balance sheet total	**Total du bilan**										
28.	End-year total	En fin d'exercice	2034	2164	4978	5211	4818	4377	7184	7698	6188	12387
29.	Average total	Moyen	2310	2099	3571	5095	5015	4598	5781	7441	6943	9288
	Memoranda	*Pour mémoire*										
30.	*Short-term securities (1)*	*Titres à court terme (1)*	*..*	*230*	*3094*	*3152*	*2304*	*2747*	*4298*	*4300*	*3556*	*6680*
31.	*Bonds*	*Obligations*	*15*	*70*	*186*	*150*	*319*	*136*	*216*	*479*	*866*	
32.	*Shares and participations*	*Actions et participations*	*5*	*5*	*12*	*13*	*14*	*13*	*14*	*8*	*8*	*2*
33.	*Claims on non-residents*	*Créances sur des non résidents*	*757*	*680*	*604*	*745*	*714*	*237*	*918*	*1940*	*1331*	*3722*
34.	*Liabilities to non-residents*	*Engagements envers des non résidents*	*1629*	*1332*	*2828*	*2860*	*1917*	*2229*	*2517*	*4875*	*1458*	*3333*
	SUPPLEMENTARY INFORMATION	**RENSEIGNEMENTS COMPLEMENTAIRES**										
35.	Number of institutions	Nombre d'institutions	3	3	4	4	4	4	5	4	4	4
36.	Number of branches	Nombre de succursales										
37.	Number of employees	Nombre de salariés	103	98	169	156	154	137	144	99	98	175

FINLAND

Foreign commercial banks

Per cent

FINLANDE

Banques commerciales étrangères

Pourcentage

	1985	1986	1987	1988	1989	1990	1991	1992	1993	1994		
INCOME STATEMENT ANALYSIS												**ANALYSE DU COMPTE DE RESULTATS**
% of average balance sheet total												**% du total moyen du bilan**
38. Interest income	8.49	8.67	13.67	14.60	22.36	21.40	26.40	20.88	17.14	7.73	38.	Produits financiers
39. Interest expenses	7.58	7.77	12.85	14.03	21.66	20.08	26.07	20.24	16.38	7.17	39.	Frais financiers
40. Net interest income	0.91	0.91	0.81	0.57	0.70	1.33	0.33	0.65	0.76	0.56	40.	Produits financiers nets
41. Non-interest income (net)	1.30	1.29	1.04	0.73	0.80	0.83	0.62	1.12	1.07	0.41	41.	Produits non financiers (nets)
42. Gross income	2.21	2.19	1.85	1.30	1.50	2.15	0.95	1.76	1.83	0.97	42.	Résultat brut
43. Operating expenses	1.43	1.76	1.76	1.37	2.51	2.07	2.30	2.00	1.33	1.18	43.	Frais d'exploitation
44. Net income	0.78	0.43	0.08	-0.08	-1.02	0.09	-1.35	-0.24	0.50	-0.22	44.	Résultat net
45. Provisions (net)	0.22	0.19	0.31	-0.06	0.06		0.09	0.55	-0.07	-0.12	45.	Provisions (nettes)
46. Profit before tax	0.56	0.24	-0.22	-0.02	-1.08	0.09	-1.44	-0.79	0.58	-0.10	46.	Bénéfices avant impôt
47. Income tax	0.17	0.10		0.06	0.04	0.09	0.02	0.04	0.13	0.04	47.	Impôt
48. Profit after tax	0.39	0.14	-0.22	-0.08	-1.12	0.00	-1.45	-0.83	0.45	-0.14	48.	Bénéfices après impôt
49. Distributed profit	0.17	0.29									49.	Bénéfices distribués
50. Retained profit	0.22	-0.14	-0.22	-0.08	-1.12	0.00	-1.45	-0.83	0.45	-0.14	50.	Bénéfices mis en réserve
51. Staff costs	0.78	0.95	0.95	0.77	0.74	0.80	0.81	0.51	0.56	0.43	51.	Frais de personnel
52. Provisions on loans	0.13	0.14	0.08	0.02	0.02	0.04	0.09	0.04	-0.07	0.01	52.	Provisions sur prêts
53. Provisions on securities			0.22	0.06	0.04	-0.04		0.51		-0.13	53.	Provisions sur titres
% of gross income												**% du total du résultat brut**
54. Net interest income	41.18	41.30	43.94	43.94	46.67	61.62	34.55	36.64	41.73	57.78	54.	Produits financiers nets
55. Non-interest income (net)	58.82	58.70	56.06	56.06	53.33	38.38	65.45	63.36	58.27	42.22	55.	Produits non financiers (nets)
56. Operating expenses	64.71	80.43	95.45	106.06	168.00	95.96	241.82	113.74	72.44	122.22	56.	Frais d'exploitation
57. Net income	35.29	19.57	4.55	-6.06	-68.00	4.04	-141.82	-13.74	27.56	-22.22	57.	Résultat net
58. Provisions (net)	9.80	8.70	16.67	-4.55	4.00		9.09	31.30	-3.94	-12.22	58.	Provisions (nettes)
59. Profit before tax	25.49	10.87	-12.12	-1.52	-72.00	4.04	-150.91	-45.04	31.50	-10.00	59.	Bénéfices avant impôt
60. Income tax	7.84	4.35		4.55	2.67	4.04	1.82	2.29	7.09	4.44	60.	Impôt
61. Profit after tax	17.65	6.52	-12.12	-6.06	-74.67	0.00	-152.73	-47.33	24.41	-14.44	61.	Bénéfices après impôt
62. Staff costs	35.29	43.48	51.52	59.09	49.33	37.37	85.45	29.01	30.71	44.44	62.	Frais de personnel
% of net income												**% du total du résultat net**
63. Provisions (net)	27.78	44.44	:	:	:	:	:	:	:	55.00	63.	Provisions (nettes)
64. Profit before tax	72.22	55.56	:	:	:	:	:	:	:	45.00	64.	Bénéfices avant impôt
65. Income tax	22.22	22.22	:	:	:	:	:	:	:	-20.00	65.	Impôt
66. Profit after tax	50.00	33.33	:	:	:	:	:	:	:	65.00	66.	Bénéfices après impôt

FINLAND

Foreign commercial banks

Per cent

BALANCE SHEET ANALYSIS

	1985	1986	1987	1988	1989	1990	1991	1992	1993	1994
% of year-end balance sheet total										
Assets										
67. Cash & balance with Central bank	17.60	0.97	2.53	3.38	3.20	0.82	1.50	1.40	0.69	0.69
68. Interbank deposits	15.19	24.40	3.44	6.20	1.68	6.79	4.37	0.43	0.06	0.84
69. Loans	28.47	40.99	11.77	8.58	30.26	18.09	24.65	24.67	6.14	2.86
70. Securities	0.98	14.09	66.13	63.62	54.73	66.16	63.03	62.18	71.59	53.94
71. Other assets	37.76	19.55	16.13	18.23	10.13	8.13	6.44	11.31	21.51	41.66
Liabilities										
72. Capital & reserves	6.00	5.64	4.24	4.66	4.98	4.25	3.54	1.56	2.42	0.10
73. Borrowing from Central bank	1.87	0.97	-	0.02	-	-	1.38	0.01	-	0.83
74. Interbank deposits	0.15	8.46	15.95	4.68	12.62	1.17	0.70	-	8.18	0.08
75. Non-bank deposits	81.81	63.77	51.06	55.84	40.81	51.79	36.78	3.73	23.56	25.96
76. Bonds	-	-	-	-	-	-	-	-	-	-
77. Other liabilities	10.18	21.16	28.75	34.79	41.59	42.79	57.61	94.70	65.84	73.02
Memoranda										
78. Short-term securities (1)	*..*	*10.63*	*62.15*	*60.49*	*47.82*	*62.76*	*59.83*	*55.86*	*57.47*	*53.93*
79. Bonds	*0.74*	*3.23*	*3.74*	*2.88*	*6.62*	*3.11*	*3.01*	*6.22*	*13.99*	*-*
80. Shares and participations	*0.25*	*0.23*	*0.24*	*0.25*	*0.29*	*0.30*	*0.19*	*0.10*	*0.13*	*0.02*
81. Claims on non-residents	*37.22*	*31.42*	*12.13*	*14.30*	*14.82*	*5.41*	*12.78*	*25.20*	*21.51*	*30.05*
82. Liabilities to non-residents	*80.09*	*61.55*	*56.81*	*54.88*	*39.79*	*50.93*	*35.04*	*63.33*	*23.56*	*26.91*

1. Until 1986, included under "Bonds" (item 31 or item 79).

FINLANDE

Banques commerciales étrangères

Pourcentage

ANALYSE DU BILAN

% du total du bilan en fin d'exercice

Actif
67. Caisse & solde auprès de la Banque centrale
68. Dépôts interbancaires
69. Prêts
70. Valeurs mobilières
71. Autres actifs

Passif
72. Capital et réserves
73. Emprunts auprès de la Banque centrale
74. Dépôts interbancaires
75. Dépôts non bancaires
76. Obligations
77. Autres engagements

Pour mémoire
78. Titres à court terme (1)
79. Obligations
80. Actions et participations
81. Créances sur des non résidents
82. Engagements envers des non résidents

1. Jusqu'à 1986, inclus sous "Obligations" (poste 31 ou poste 79).

FINLAND

Savings banks

Million markkaa

FINLANDE

Caisses d'épargne

Millions de markkaa

	1985	1986	1987	1988	1989	1990	1991	1992	1993	1994 (1)	
INCOME STATEMENT											**COMPTE DE RÉSULTATS**
1. Interest income	4498	4575	5171	7171	9967	12042	12413	10426	7610	2672	1. Produits financiers
2. Interest expenses	2886	2739	3022	4572	7041	9119	9888	10008	6198	2397	2. Frais financiers
3. Net interest income	1612	1836	2149	2599	2926	2923	2525	418	1412	275	3. Produits financiers nets
4. Non-interest income (net)	902	1098	1412	3051	1865	2128	2401	3188	7416	757	4. Produits non financiers (nets)
5. Gross income	2514	2934	3561	5650	4791	5051	4926	3606	8828	1032	5. Résultat brut
6. Operating expenses	2220	2579	3087	3777	4337	4298	5760	14489	8391	2235	6. Frais d'exploitation
7. Net income	294	355	474	1873	454	753	-834	-10883	437	-1203	7. Résultat net
8. Provisions (net)	211	248	332	1028	234	508	-319	-370	17	9	8. Provisions (nettes)
9. Profit before tax	83	107	142	845	220	245	-515	-10513	420	-1212	9. Bénéfices avant impôt
10. Income tax	38	47	51	68	100	97	50	16	7	13	10. Impôt
11. Profit after tax	45	60	91	777	120	148	-565	-10529	413	-1225	11. Bénéfices après impôt
12. Distributed profit	-	-	-	-	-	-	-	-	-	-	12. Bénéfices distribués
13. Retained profit	45	60	91	777	120	148	-565	-10529	413	-1225	13. Bénéfices mis en réserve
Memoranda											*Pour mémoire*
14. Staff costs	*1177*	*1336*	*1556*	*1873*	*1830*	*1830*	*1714*	*1644*	*1456*	*672*	*14. Frais de personnel*
15. Provisions on loans	*172*	*210*	*253*	*399*	*494*	*523*	*94*	*-262*	*15*	*16*	*15. Provisions sur prêts*
16. Provisions on securities	*..*	*..*	*77*	*425*	*-263*	*-23*	*-413*	*-108*	*2*	*-7*	*16. Provisions sur titres*
BALANCE SHEET											**BILAN**
Assets											**Actif**
17. Cash & balance with Central bank	3025	2930	3486	5960	9169	6279	4459	9577	838	818	17. Caisse & solde auprès de la Banque centrale
18. Interbank deposits	5160	5519	6020	8182	8564	9134	9109	7771	32505	1692	18. Dépôts interbancaires
19. Loans	37006	42263	51152	69181	83957	85554	82047	73871	17398	18110	19. Prêts
20. Securities	2083	2579	3650	5603	9777	8780	8228	4910	6692	5163	20. Valeurs mobilières
21. Other assets	5124	6184	7077	10031	9786	12072	16181	17890	16571	18487	21. Autres actifs
Liabilities											**Passif**
22. Capital & reserves	2546	2980	3706	6317	8144	7891	7227	6178	3085	1487	22. Capital et réserves
23. Borrowing from Central bank	599	736	855	1028	1178	1107	1150	2108	316	173	23. Emprunts auprès de la Banque centrale
24. Interbank deposits	2	2	2	84	250	173	72	96	84	14	24. Dépôts interbancaires
25. Non-bank deposits	41562	45933	52440	65717	71340	68107	70422	66714	14568	16173	25. Dépôts non bancaires
26. Bonds	612	709	835	1891	3238	2229	5516	7912	7240	5181	26. Obligations
27. Other liabilities	7077	9115	13547	23920	37103	42312	35637	31011	48711	21242	27. Autres engagements
Balance sheet total											**Total du bilan**
28. End-year total	52398	59475	71385	98957	121253	121819	120024	114019	74004	44270	28. En fin d'exercice
29. Average total	49231	55937	65430	85171	110105	121536	120922	117022	94012	59137	29. Moyen
Memoranda											*Pour mémoire*
30. Short-term securities (2)	*1394*	*1725*	*169*	*953*	*1946*	*1329*	*1810*	*2236*	*3915*	*4140*	*30. Titres à court terme (2)*
31. Bonds	*689*	*854*	*2210*	*2861*	*2611*	*2420*	*1742*	*1291*	*1458*	*-*	*31. Obligations*
32. Shares and participations	*2*	*6*	*1271*	*1789*	*5220*	*5031*	*4676*	*1383*	*1319*	*1023*	*32. Actions et participations*
33. Claims on non-residents	*-*	*-*	*92*	*394*	*742*	*54*	*28*	*39*	*98*	*19*	*33. Créances sur des non résidents*
34. Liabilities to non-residents	*1629*	*-*	*129*	*911*	*2318*	*321*	*4*	*1334*	*181*	*14*	*34. Engagements envers des non résidents*
SUPPLEMENTARY INFORMATION											**RENSEIGNEMENTS COMPLÉMENTAIRES**
35. Number of institutions	254	241	230	211	178	150	86	39	41	41	35. Nombre d'institutions
36. Number of branches	1076	1091	1093	1102	1130	984	967	845	173	233	36. Nombre de succursales
37. Number of employees (x 1000)	10.7	10.9	11.2	11.7	11.9	10.1	9.5	7.8	7.2	1.7	37. Nombre de salariés (x 1000)

FINLAND

Savings banks

INCOME STATEMENT ANALYSIS

Per cent	1985	1986	1987	1988	1989	1990	1991	1992	1993	1994 (1)
% of average balance sheet total										
38. Interest income	9.14	8.18	7.90	8.42	9.05	9.91	10.27	8.91	8.09	4.52
39. Interest expenses	5.86	4.90	4.62	5.37	6.39	7.50	8.18	8.55	6.59	4.05
40. Net interest income	3.27	3.28	3.28	3.05	2.66	2.41	2.09	0.36	1.50	0.47
41. Non-interest income (net)	1.83	1.96	2.16	3.58	1.69	1.75	1.99	2.72	7.89	1.28
42. Gross income	5.11	5.25	5.44	6.63	4.35	4.16	4.07	3.08	9.39	1.75
43. Operating expenses	4.51	4.61	4.72	4.43	3.94	3.54	4.76	12.38	8.93	3.78
44. Net income	0.60	0.63	0.72	2.20	0.41	0.62	-0.69	-9.30	0.46	-2.03
45. Provisions (net)	0.43	0.44	0.51	1.21	0.21	0.42	-0.26	-0.32	0.02	0.02
46. Profit before tax	0.17	0.19	0.22	0.99	0.20	0.20	-0.43	-8.98	0.45	-2.05
47. Income tax	0.08	0.08	0.08	0.08	0.09	0.08	0.04	0.01	0.01	0.02
48. Profit after tax	0.09	0.11	0.14	0.91	0.11	0.12	-0.47	-9.00	0.44	-2.07
49. Distributed profit										
50. Retained profit	0.09	0.11	0.14	0.91	0.11	0.12	-0.47	-9.00	0.44	-2.07
51. Staff costs	2.39	2.39	2.38	2.20	1.66	1.51	1.42	1.40	1.55	1.14
52. Provisions on loans	0.35	0.38	0.39	0.47	0.45	0.43	0.08	-0.22	0.02	0.03
53. Provisions on securities	..	..	0.12	0.50	-0.24	-0.02	-0.34	-0.09	-	-0.01
% of gross income										
54. Net interest income	64.12	62.58	60.35	46.00	61.07	57.87	51.26	..	15.99	..
55. Non-interest income (net)	35.88	37.42	39.65	54.00	38.93	42.13	48.74	..	84.01	..
56. Operating expenses	88.31	87.90	86.69	66.85	90.52	85.09	116.93	..	95.05	..
57. Net income	11.69	12.10	13.31	33.15	9.48	14.91	-16.93	..	4.95	..
58. Provisions (net)	8.39	8.45	9.32	18.19	4.88	10.06	-6.48	..	0.19	..
59. Profit before tax	3.30	3.65	3.99	14.96	4.59	4.85	-10.45	..	4.76	..
60. Income tax	1.51	1.60	1.43	1.20	2.09	1.92	1.02	..	0.08	..
61. Profit after tax	1.79	2.04	2.56	13.75	2.50	2.93	-11.47	..	4.68	..
62. Staff costs	46.82	45.54	43.70	33.15	38.20	36.23	34.79	..	16.49	..
% of net income										
63. Provisions (net)	71.77	69.86	70.04	54.89	51.54	67.46	..	..	3.89	..
64. Profit before tax	28.23	30.14	29.96	45.11	48.46	32.54	..	..	96.11	..
65. Income tax	12.93	13.24	10.76	3.63	22.03	12.88	..	..	1.60	..
66. Profit after tax	15.31	16.90	19.20	41.48	26.43	19.65	..	..	94.51	..

FINLANDE

Caisses d'épargne

Pourcentage

ANALYSE DU COMPTE DE RESULTATS

% du total moyen du bilan
38. Produits financiers
39. Frais financiers
40. Produits financiers nets
41. Produits non financiers (nets)
42. Résultat brut
43. Frais d'exploitation
44. Résultat net
45. Provisions (nettes)
46. Bénéfices avant impôt
47. Impôt
48. Bénéfices après impôt
49. Bénéfices distribués
50. Bénéfices mis en réserve
51. Frais de personnel
52. Provisions sur prêts
53. Provisions sur titres

% du total du résultat brut
54. Produits financiers nets
55. Produits non financiers (nets)
56. Frais d'exploitation
57. Résultat net
58. Provisions (nettes)
59. Bénéfices avant impôt
60. Impôt
61. Bénéfices après impôt
62. Frais de personnel

% du total du résultat net
63. Provisions (nettes)
64. Bénéfices avant impôt
65. Impôt
66. Bénéfices après impôt

FINLAND

Savings banks

Per cent

BALANCE SHEET ANALYSIS

% of year-end balance sheet total

FINLANDE

Caisses d'épargne

Pourcentage

ANALYSE DU BILAN

% du total du bilan en fin d'exercice

	1985	1986	1987	1988	1989	1990	1991	1992	1993	1994 (1)		
Assets												**Actif**
67. Cash & balance with Central bank	5.77	4.93	4.88	6.02	7.56	5.15	3.72	8.40	1.13	1.85	67.	Caisse & solde auprès de la Banque centrale
68. Interbank deposits	9.85	9.28	8.43	8.27	7.06	7.50	7.59	6.82	43.92	3.82	68.	Dépôts interbancaires
69. Loans	70.62	71.06	71.66	69.91	69.24	70.23	68.36	64.79	23.51	40.91	69.	Prêts
70. Securities	3.98	4.34	5.11	5.66	8.06	7.21	6.86	4.31	9.04	11.66	70.	Valeurs mobilières
71. Other assets	9.78	10.40	9.91	10.14	8.07	9.91	13.48	15.69	22.39	41.76	71.	Autres actifs
Liabilities												**Passif**
72. Capital & reserves	4.86	5.01	5.19	6.38	6.72	6.48	6.02	5.42	4.17	3.36	72.	Capital et réserves
73. Borrowing from Central bank	1.14	1.24	1.20	1.04	0.97	0.91	0.96	1.85	0.43	0.39	73.	Emprunts auprès de la Banque centrale
74. Interbank deposits	0.00	0.00	0.00	0.08	0.21	0.14	0.06	0.08	0.11	0.03	74.	Dépôts interbancaires
75. Non-bank deposits	79.32	77.23	73.46	66.41	58.84	55.91	58.67	58.51	19.69	36.53	75.	Dépôts non bancaires
76. Bonds	1.17	1.19	1.17	1.91	2.67	1.83	4.60	6.94	9.78	11.70	76.	Obligations
77. Other liabilities	13.51	15.33	18.98	24.17	30.60	34.73	29.69	27.20	65.82	47.98	77.	Autres engagements
Memoranda												***Pour mémoire***
78. *Short-term securities (2)*	*..*	*..*	*0.24*	*0.96*	*1.60*	*1.09*	*1.51*	*1.96*	*5.29*	*9.35*	*78.*	*Titres à court terme (2)*
79. *Bonds*	*2.66*	*2.90*	*3.10*	*2.89*	*2.15*	*1.99*	*1.45*	*1.13*	*1.97*	*-*	*79.*	*Obligations*
80. *Shares and participations*	*1.31*	*1.44*	*1.78*	*1.81*	*4.31*	*4.13*	*3.90*	*1.21*	*1.78*	*2.31*	*80.*	*Actions et participations*
81. *Claims on non-residents*	*0.00*	*0.01*	*0.13*	*0.40*	*0.61*	*0.04*	*0.02*	*0.03*	*0.13*	*0.04*	*81.*	*Créances sur des non résidents*
82. *Liabilities to non-residents*	*3.11*	*-*	*0.18*	*0.92*	*1.91*	*0.26*	*0.00*	*1.17*	*0.24*	*0.03*	*82.*	*Engagements envers des non résidents*

1. Break in series. Change in the composition of "Savings banks".

2. Until 1987, included under "Bonds" (item 31 or item 79).

1. Rupture dans les séries. Changement dans la composition des "Caisses d'épargne"

2. Jusqu'à 1987, inclus sous "Obligations" (poste 31 ou poste 79).

FINLAND

Co-operative banks

FINLANDE

Banques mutualistes

Million markkaa / *Millions de markkas*

	Item / Poste	1985	1986	1987	1988	1989	1990	1991	1992	1993	1994
	INCOME STATEMENT / COMPTE DE RESULTATS										
1.	Interest income / Produits financiers	4050	4123	4709	6337	8306	10342	11120	11397	9859	8602
2.	Interest expenses / Frais financiers	2561	2488	2758	3953	5707	7252	7914	8590	6181	4255
3.	Net interest income / Produits financiers nets	1489	1635	1951	2384	2599	3090	3206	2807	3678	4347
4.	Non-interest income (net) / Produits non financiers (nets)	635	795	950	1321	1393	1524	2146	3097	2005	2067
5.	Gross income / Résultat brut	2124	2430	2901	3705	3992	4614	5352	5904	5683	6414
6.	Operating expenses / Frais d'exploitation	1793	2089	2466	2992	3436	3825	4675	5817	7727	7897
7.	Net income / Résultat net	331	341	435	713	556	789	677	87	-2044	-1483
8.	Provisions (net) / Provisions (nettes)	251	246	319	548	357	458	315	-54	-74	12
9.	Profit before tax / Bénéfices avant impôt	80	95	116	165	199	331	362	141	-1970	-1495
10.	Income tax / Impôt	35	39	45	60	79	125	152	117	124	128
11.	Profit after tax / Bénéfices après impôt	45	56	71	105	120	206	210	24	-2094	-1623
12.	Distributed profit / Bénéfices distribués	32	38	49	61	66	62	50	28	20	2
13.	Retained profit / Bénéfices mis en réserve	13	18	22	44	54	144	160	-4	-2114	-1625
	Memoranda / Pour mémoire										
14.	*Staff costs / Frais de personnel*	*927*	*1070*	*1170*	*1448*	*1647*	*1647*	*1664*	*1706*	*1514*	*1635*
15.	*Provisions on loans / Provisions sur prêts*	*176*	*203*	*236*	*330*	*381*	*442*	*356*	*46*	*39*	*-9*
16.	*Provisions on securities / Provisions sur titres*	*..*	*..*	*75*	*195*	*-32*	*2*	*-41*	*-100*	*-113*	*21*
	BALANCE SHEET / BILAN										
	Assets / Actif										
17.	Cash & balance with Central bank / Caisse & solde auprès de la Banque centrale	2515	2483	2816	4872	6534	5691	4034	4882	3239	2963
18.	Interbank deposits / Dépôts interbancaires	4456	5218	5925	6658	7855	8177	9356	9871	13994	14078
19.	Loans / Prêts	35789	40797	48407	62404	69874	75639	79594	79662	88924	84542
20.	Securities / Valeurs mobilières	1714	2572	2861	4441	4577	5577	6621	6721	6521	3191
21.	Other assets / Autres actifs	3123	3761	4433	5645	6650	8885	11282	15396	16704	21015
	Liabilities / Passif										
22.	Capital & reserves / Capital et réserves	2418	2921	3484	4473	5038	6280	6729	7719	8228	8125
23.	Borrowing from Central bank / Emprunts auprès de la Banque centrale	401	454	528	501	692	519	542	474	-	-
24.	Interbank deposits / Dépôts interbancaires	10	70	10	10	10	-	-	2	-	-
25.	Non-bank deposits / Dépôts non bancaires	34852	39146	44764	55318	61268	66679	71848	75846	89513	91244
26.	Bonds / Obligations	215	655	1071	2502	3652	6022	9425	9838	9540	8259
27.	Other liabilities / Autres engagements	9701	11585	14585	21216	24830	24469	22343	22653	22101	18161
	Balance sheet total / Total du bilan										
28.	End-year total / En fin d'exercice	47597	54831	64442	84020	95490	103969	110887	116532	129382	125789
29.	Average total / Moyen	44282	51214	59637	74231	89755	99730	107428	113710	122957	127586
	Memoranda / Pour mémoire										
30.	*Short-term securities (1) / Titres à court terme (1)*	*1214*	*..*	*25*	*293*	*129*	*161*	*1438*	*1525*	*1336*	*1286*
31.	*Bonds / Obligations*	*500*	*1714*	*1921*	*2691*	*2905*	*4007*	*3543*	*3543*	*3387*	*-*
32.	*Shares and participations / Actions et participations*	*80*	*858*	*915*	*1457*	*1543*	*1409*	*1640*	*1653*	*1798*	*1905*
33.	*Claims on non-residents / Créances sur des non résidents*	*-*	*74*	*49*	*55*	*59*	*78*	*7*	*8*	*5*	*5*
34.	*Liabilities to non-residents / Engagements envers des non résidents*	*-*	*-*	*2*	*-*	*-*	*-*	*995*	*18*	*1173*	*3*
	SUPPLEMENTARY INFORMATION / RENSEIGNEMENTS COMPLEMENTAIRES										
35.	Number of institutions / Nombre d'institutions	370	370	369	367	361	359	335	317	303	302
36.	Number of branches / Nombre de succursales	852	854	852	850	837	800	747	688	913	686
37.	Number of employees (x 1000) / Nombre de salariés (x 1000)	8.7	9.0	9.2	9.4	9.6	9.3	9.0	8.7	8.6	9.1

Per cent	1985	1986	1987	1988	1989	1990	1991	1992	1993	1994	Pourcentage	
INCOME STATEMENT ANALYSIS											**ANALYSE DU COMPTE DE RESULTATS**	
% of average balance sheet total											**% du total moyen du bilan**	
38. Interest income	9.15	8.05	7.90	8.54	9.25	10.37	10.35	10.02	8.02	6.74	38. Produits financiers	
39. Interest expenses	5.78	4.86	4.62	5.33	6.36	7.27	7.37	7.55	5.03	3.34	39. Frais financiers	
40. Net interest income	3.36	3.19	3.27	3.21	2.90	3.10	2.98	2.47	2.99	3.41	40. Produits financiers nets	
41. Non-interest income (net)	1.43	1.55	1.59	1.78	1.55	1.53	2.00	2.72	1.63	1.62	41. Produits non financiers (nets)	
42. Gross income	4.80	4.74	4.86	4.99	4.45	4.63	4.98	5.19	4.62	5.03	42. Résultat brut	
43. Operating expenses	4.05	4.08	4.14	4.03	3.83	3.84	4.35	5.12	6.28	6.19	43. Frais d'exploitation	
44. Net income	0.75	0.67	0.73	0.96	0.62	0.79	0.63	0.08	-1.66	-1.16	44. Résultat net	
45. Provisions (net)	0.57	0.48	0.53	0.74	0.40	0.46	0.29	-0.05	-0.06	0.01	45. Provisions (nettes)	
46. Profit before tax	0.18	0.19	0.19	0.22	0.22	0.33	0.34	0.12	-1.60	-1.17	46. Bénéfices avant impôt	
47. Income tax	0.08	0.08	0.08	0.08	0.09	0.13	0.14	0.10	0.10	0.10	47. Impôt	
48. Profit after tax	0.10	0.11	0.12	0.14	0.13	0.21	0.20	0.02	-1.70	-1.27	48. Bénéfices après impôt	
49. Distributed profit	0.07	0.07	0.08	0.08	0.07	0.06	0.05	0.02	0.02	0.00	49. Bénéfices distribués	
50. Retained profit	0.03	0.04	0.04	0.06	0.06	0.14	0.15	-	-1.72	-1.27	50. Bénéfices mis en réserve	
51. Staff costs	2.09	2.09	1.96	1.95	1.83	1.65	1.55	1.50	1.23	1.28	51. Frais de personnel	
52. Provisions on loans	0.40	0.40	0.40	0.44	0.42	0.44	0.33	0.04	0.03	-0.01	52. Provisions sur prêts	
53. Provisions on securities	..	..	0.13	0.26	-0.04	0.00	-0.04	-0.09	-0.09	0.02	53. Provisions sur titres	
% of gross income											**% du total du résultat brut**	
54. Net interest income	70.10	67.28	67.25	64.35	65.11	66.97	59.90	47.54	64.72	67.77	54. Produits financiers nets	
55. Non-interest income (net)	29.90	32.72	32.75	35.65	34.89	33.03	40.10	52.46	35.28	32.23	55. Produits non financiers (nets)	
56. Operating expenses	84.42	85.97	85.01	80.76	86.07	82.90	87.35	98.53	135.97	123.12	56. Frais d'exploitation	
57. Net income	15.58	14.03	14.99	19.24	13.93	17.10	12.65	1.47	-35.97	-23.12	57. Résultat net	
58. Provisions (net)	11.82	10.12	11.00	14.79	8.94	9.93	5.89	-0.91	-1.30	0.19	58. Provisions (nettes)	
59. Profit before tax	3.77	3.91	4.00	4.45	4.98	7.17	6.76	2.39	-34.66	-23.31	59. Bénéfices avant impôt	
60. Income tax	1.65	1.60	1.55	1.62	1.98	2.71	2.84	1.98	2.18	2.00	60. Impôt	
61. Profit after tax	2.12	2.30	2.45	2.83	3.01	4.46	3.92	0.41	-36.85	-25.30	61. Bénéfices après impôt	
62. Staff costs	43.64	44.03	40.33	39.08	41.26	35.70	31.09	28.90	26.64	25.49	62. Frais de personnel	
% of net income											**% du total du résultat net**	
63. Provisions (net)	75.83	72.14	73.33	76.86	64.21	58.05	46.53	-62.07	3.62	-0.81	63. Provisions (nettes)	
64. Profit before tax	24.17	27.86	26.67	23.14	35.79	41.95	53.47	162.07	96.38	100.81	64. Bénéfices avant impôt	
65. Income tax	10.57	11.44	10.34	8.42	14.21	15.84	22.45	134.48	-6.07	-8.63	65. Impôt	
66. Profit after tax	13.60	16.42	16.32	14.73	21.58	26.11	31.02	27.59	102.45	109.44	66. Bénéfices après impôt	

FINLAND

Co-operative banks

FINLANDE

Banques mutualistes

Per cent / *Pourcentage*

BALANCE SHEET ANALYSIS / **ANALYSE DU BILAN**

% of year-end balance sheet total / % du total du bilan en fin d'exercice

	1985	1986	1987	1988	1989	1990	1991	1992	1993	1994	
Assets											**Actif**
67. Cash & balance with Central bank	5.28	4.53	4.37	5.80	6.84	5.47	3.64	4.19	2.50	2.36	67. Caisse & solde auprès de la Banque centrale
68. Interbank deposits	9.36	9.52	9.19	7.92	8.23	7.86	8.44	8.47	10.82	11.19	68. Dépôts interbancaires
69. Loans	75.19	74.40	75.12	74.27	73.17	72.75	71.78	68.36	68.73	67.21	69. Prêts
70. Securities	3.60	4.69	4.44	5.29	4.79	5.36	5.97	5.77	5.04	2.54	70. Valeurs mobilières
71. Other assets	6.56	6.86	6.88	6.72	6.96	8.55	10.17	13.21	12.91	16.71	71. Autres actifs
Liabilities											**Passif**
72. Capital & reserves	5.08	5.33	5.41	5.32	5.28	6.04	6.07	6.62	6.36	6.46	72. Capital et réserves
73. Borrowing from Central bank	0.84	0.83	0.82	0.60	0.72	0.50	0.49	0.41	-	-	73. Emprunts auprès de la Banque centrale
74. Interbank deposits	0.02	0.13	0.02	0.01	0.01	-	-	-	-	-	74. Dépôts interbancaires
75. Non-bank deposits	73.22	71.39	69.46	65.84	64.16	64.13	64.79	65.09	69.19	72.54	75. Dépôts non bancaires
76. Bonds	0.45	1.19	1.66	2.98	3.82	5.79	8.50	8.44	7.37	6.57	76. Obligations
77. Other liabilities	20.38	21.13	22.63	25.25	26.00	23.53	20.15	19.44	17.08	14.44	77. Autres engagements
Memoranda											***Pour mémoire***
78. Short-term securities (1)	*2.55*	*3.13*	*0.04*	*0.35*	*0.14*	*0.15*	*1.30*	*1.31*	*1.03*	*1.02*	*78. Titres à court terme (1)*
79. Bonds			*2.98*	*3.20*	*3.04*	*3.85*	*3.20*	*3.04*	*2.62*	*-*	*79. Obligations*
80. Shares and participations	*1.05*	*1.56*	*1.42*	*1.73*	*1.62*	*1.36*	*1.48*	*1.42*	*1.39*	*1.51*	*80. Actions et participations*
81. Claims on non-residents	*0.17*	*0.13*	*0.08*	*0.07*	*0.06*	*0.08*	*0.01*	*0.01*	*-*	*-*	*81. Créances sur des non résidents*
82. Liabilities to non-residents	*-*	*-*	*-*	*-*	*-*	*-*	*0.90*	*0.02*	*0.91*	*-*	*82. Engagements envers des non résidents*

1. Until 1986, included under "Bonds" (item 31 or item 79).

1. Jusqu'à 1986, inclus sous "Obligations" (poste 31 ou poste 79).

FRANCE

All banks

FRANCE

Ensemble des banques

Million French francs — *Millions de francs français*

	1988	1989	1990	1991	1992	1993	1994	
INCOME STATEMENT								**COMPTE DE RESULTATS**
1. Interest income	1024255	1203030	1354016	1397529	1366318	1425991	1206329	1. Produits financiers
2. Interest expenses	774949	948273	1091208	1126018	1102977	1193519	979138	2. Frais financiers
3. Net interest income	249306	254757	262808	271511	263341	232472	227191	3. Produits financiers nets
4. Non-interest income (net)	48950	62377	67756	92235	119813	154760	126312	4. Produits non financiers (nets)
5. Gross income	298256	317134	330564	363746	383154	387232	353503	5. Résultat brut
6. Operating expenses	191909	204998	218530	228997	239581	257801	259784	6. Frais d'exploitation
7. Net income	106347	112136	112034	134749	143573	129431	93719	7. Résultat net
8. Provisions (net)	49835	56938	60374	72592	98186	107964	89915	8. Provisions (nettes)
9. Profit before tax	56512	55198	51660	62157	45387	21467	3804	9. Bénéfices avant impôt
10. Income tax	14680	14230	12240	14804	17451	17940	13774	10. Impôt
11. Profit after tax	41832	40968	39420	47353	27936	3527	-9970	11. Bénéfices après impôt
12. Distributed profit	17772	19059	20215	21499	20296	22493	20874	12. Bénéfices distribués
13. Retained profit	24059	21908	19205	25853	7640	-18966	-30844	13. Bénéfices mis en réserve
Memoranda								*Pour mémoire*
14. Staff costs	113058	119257	125812	130362	135394	141658	140589	14. Frais de personnel
15. Provisions on loans	30310	36065	40781	53782	84276	103766	91353	15. Provisions sur prêts
16. Provisions on securities	-4286	3446	8583	1476	14626	10919	10950	16. Provisions sur titres
BALANCE SHEET								**BILAN**
Assets								**Actif**
17. Cash & balance with Central bank	172920	169185	126305	112979	68015	37566	31113	17. Caisse & solde auprès de la Banque centrale
18. Interbank deposits	5269601	5742202	6077862	5945363	6144978	6582695	6166380	18. Dépôts interbancaires
19. Loans	4924195	5534081	6063585	6374522	6605304	6677026	6156189	19. Prêts
20. Securities	954343	1081494	1195292	1729495	2034701	2426133	2404285	20. Valeurs mobilières
21. Other assets	1154354	1358106	1606675	1339189	1428041	940892	868315	21. Autres actifs
Liabilities								**Passif**
22. Capital & reserves	367452	433817	508976	595549	655102	748312	736328	22. Capital et réserves
23. Borrowing from Central bank	188379	199912	246453	203427	201535	35555	20868	23. Emprunts auprès de la Banque centrale
24. Interbank deposits	5628342	6208164	6278748	6219400	6093769	6460470	6086607	24. Dépôts interbancaires
25. Non-bank deposits	2960740	3200707	3415472	3708179	3862696	4267827	4236214	25. Dépôts non bancaires
26. Bonds	2073982	2399780	2922003	3256746	3765388	3991842	3526728	26. Obligations
27. Other liabilities	1256518	1442688	1698067	1518246	1702548	1160305	1019535	27. Autres engagements
Balance sheet total								**Total du bilan**
28. End-year total	12475413	13885068	15069719	15501548	16281038	16664311	15626282	28. En fin d'exercice
29. Average total	11759263	13331073	14340336	15809633	16138135	17522864	17836966	29. Moyen
Memoranda								*Pour mémoire*
30. Short-term securities	..	..	..	..	..	1245397	1262658	30. Titres à court terme
31. Bonds	..	..	..	..	..	502362	428357	31. Obligations
32. Shares and participations	..	..	..	..	..	..	..	32. Actions et participations
33. Claims on non-residents	2922453	3234899	3717170	3727448	4216633	3253328	3128923	33. Créances sur des non résidents
34. Liabilities to non-residents	2879663	3261710	3794796	3902550	4196000	2933944	3063172	34. Engagements envers des non résidents
SUPPLEMENTARY INFORMATION								**RENSEIGNEMENTS COMPLEMENTAIRES**
35. Number of institutions	2050	2021	1981	1823	1701	1635	1618	35. Nombre d'institutions
36. Number of branches	NA	NA	NA	NA	NA	26291	26180	36. Nombre de succursales
37. Number of employees (x 1000)	444.6	443.1	440.0	433.6	425.0	406.1	408.8	37. Nombre de salariés (x 1000)

FRANCE

All banks

FRANCE

Ensemble des banques

	1988	1989	1990	1991	1992	1993	1994		
Per cent								*Pourcentage*	
INCOME STATEMENT ANALYSIS								**ANALYSE DU COMPTE DE RESULTATS**	
% of average balance sheet total								**% du total moyen du bilan**	
38. Interest income	8.71	9.02	9.44	8.84	8.47	8.14	6.76	38. Produits financiers	
39. Interest expenses	6.59	7.11	7.61	7.12	6.83	6.81	5.49	39. Frais financiers	
40. Net interest income	2.12	1.91	1.83	1.72	1.63	1.33	1.27	40. Produits financiers nets	
41. Non-interest income (net)	0.42	0.47	0.47	0.58	0.74	0.88	0.71	41. Produits non financiers (nets)	
42. Gross income	2.54	2.38	2.31	2.30	2.37	2.21	1.98	42. Résultat brut	
43. Operating expenses	1.63	1.54	1.52	1.45	1.48	1.47	1.46	43. Frais d'exploitation	
44. Net income	0.90	0.84	0.78	0.85	0.89	0.74	0.53	44. Résultat net	
45. Provisions (net)	0.42	0.43	0.42	0.46	0.61	0.62	0.50	45. Provisions (nettes)	
46. Profit before tax	0.48	0.41	0.36	0.39	0.28	0.12	0.02	46. Bénéfices avant impôt	
47. Income tax	0.12	0.11	0.09	0.09	0.11	0.10	0.08	47. Impôt	
48. Profit after tax	0.36	0.31	0.27	0.30	0.17	0.02	-0.06	48. Bénéfices après impôt	
49. Distributed profit	0.15	0.14	0.14	0.14	0.13	0.13	0.12	49. Bénéfices distribués	
50. Retained profit	0.20	0.16	0.13	0.16	0.05	-0.11	-0.17	50. Bénéfices mis en réserve	
51. Staff costs	0.96	0.89	0.88	0.82	0.84	0.81	0.79	51. Frais de personnel	
52. Provisions on loans	0.26	0.27	0.28	0.34	0.52	0.59	0.51	52. Provisions sur prêts	
53. Provisions on securities	-0.04	0.03	0.06	0.01	0.09	0.06	0.06	53. Provisions sur titres	
% of gross income								**% du total du résultat brut**	
54. Net interest income	83.59	80.33	79.50	74.64	68.73	60.03	64.27	54. Produits financiers nets	
55. Non-interest income (net)	16.41	19.67	20.50	25.36	31.27	39.97	35.73	55. Produits non financiers (nets)	
56. Operating expenses	64.34	64.64	66.11	62.96	62.53	66.58	73.49	56. Frais d'exploitation	
57. Net income	35.66	35.36	33.89	37.04	37.47	33.42	26.51	57. Résultat net	
58. Provisions (net)	16.71	17.95	18.26	19.96	25.63	27.88	25.44	58. Provisions (nettes)	
59. Profit before tax	18.95	17.41	15.63	17.09	11.85	5.54	1.08	59. Bénéfices avant impôt	
60. Income tax	4.92	4.49	3.70	4.07	4.55	4.63	3.90	60. Impôt	
61. Profit after tax	14.03	12.92	11.93	13.02	7.29	0.91	-2.82	61. Bénéfices après impôt	
62. Staff costs	37.91	37.60	38.06	35.84	35.34	36.58	39.77	62. Frais de personnel	
% of net income								**% du total du résultat net**	
63. Provisions (net)	46.86	50.78	53.89	53.87	68.39	83.41	95.94	63. Provisions (nettes)	
64. Profit before tax	53.14	49.22	46.11	46.13	31.61	16.59	4.06	64. Bénéfices avant impôt	
65. Income tax	13.80	12.69	10.93	10.99	12.15	13.86	14.70	65. Impôt	
66. Profit after tax	39.34	36.53	35.19	35.14	19.46	2.73	-10.64	66. Bénéfices après impôt	

FRANCE

All banks

Per cent

BALANCE SHEET ANALYSIS

	1988	1989	1990	1991	1992	1993	1994
% of year-end balance sheet total							
Assets							
67. Cash & balance with Central bank	1.39	1.22	0.84	0.73	0.42	0.23	0.20
68. Interbank deposits	42.24	41.36	40.33	38.35	37.74	39.50	39.46
69. Loans	39.47	39.86	40.24	41.12	40.57	40.07	39.40
70. Securities	7.65	7.79	7.93	11.16	12.50	14.56	15.39
71. Other assets	9.25	9.78	10.66	8.64	8.77	5.65	5.56
Liabilities							
72. Capital & reserves	2.95	3.12	3.38	3.84	4.02	4.49	4.71
73. Borrowing from Central bank	1.51	1.44	1.64	1.31	1.24	0.21	0.13
74. Interbank deposits	45.12	44.71	41.66	40.12	37.43	38.77	38.95
75. Non-bank deposits	23.73	23.05	22.66	23.92	23.73	25.61	27.11
76. Bonds	16.62	17.28	19.39	21.01	23.13	23.95	22.57
77. Other liabilities	10.07	10.39	11.27	9.79	10.46	6.96	6.52
Memoranda							
78. Short-term securities	..	..	..	..	..	*7.47*	*8.08*
79. Bonds	..	..	..	..	..	*3.01*	*2.74*
80. Shares and participations							
81. Claims on non-residents	*23.43*	*23.30*	*24.67*	*24.05*	*25.90*	*19.52*	*20.02*
82. Liabilities to non-residents	*23.08*	*23.49*	*25.18*	*25.18*	*25.77*	*17.61*	*19.60*

FRANCE

Ensemble des banques

Pourcentage

ANALYSE DU BILAN

% du total du bilan en fin d'exercice

Actif
67. Caisse & solde auprès de la Banque centrale
68. Dépôts interbancaires
69. Prêts
70. Valeurs mobilières
71. Autres actifs

Passif
72. Capital et réserves
73. Emprunts auprès de la Banque centrale
74. Dépôts interbancaires
75. Dépôts non bancaires
76. Obligations
77. Autres engagements

Pour mémoire
78. Titres à court terme
79. Obligations
80. Actions et participations
81. Créances sur des non résidents
82. Engagements envers des non résidents

Notes

• The corporate data -- presented for all financial institutions and for each of the main categories of banks -- cover the activities and results of the foreign branches of banks with headquarters in France. The activity and results of subsidiaries outside France are excluded.

• Foreign-controlled banks operating in France, in the form of branches or subsidiaries, are dealt with in the same way as banks under French control. However, branches of banks with headquarters in another European Union country are excluded.

• Average balance sheet totals (item 29) are based on the average of quarterly totals.

Change in methodology:

• The way information is collected from financial institutions in France changed on 1 January 1993, with alternations to the reporting forms. The series shown has been reworked from 1988 to make it consistent over time, for both balance sheet and income statement.

Notes

• Les données établies sur une base sociale -- ensemble des établissements de crédit et principales catégories juridiques -- incluent l'activité et les résultats des succursales à l'étranger dont le siège est en France. L'activité et les résultats des filiales étrangères sont exclus.

• Les établissements sous contrôle étranger opérant en France, sous la forme de succursales ou de filiales, sont traités dans les mêmes conditions que les banques sous contrôle français. Toutefois, sont exclues de cette présentation les succursales d'établissements dont le siège est implanté dans un autre pays de l'Union européenne.

• La moyenne du total des actifs/passifs (poste 29) est basée sur la moyenne des totaux des situations trimestrielles.

Changement méthodologique :

• La réforme de la collecte de l'information demandée aux établissements de crédit français, qui est entrée en vigueur le 1er janvier 1993, a entraîné la modification des documents comptables. La série présentée a été retraitée depuis 1988 afin d'assurer sa cohérence dans le temps, aussi bien pour le bilan que pour le compte de résultat.

FRANCE

Commercial banks

FRANCE

Banques commerciales

Million French francs / *Millions de francs français*

	1988	1989	1990	1991	1992	1993	1994	
INCOME STATEMENT								**COMPTE DE RESULTATS**
1. Interest income	484464	612946	697833	694273	674894	714849	557519	1. Produits financiers
2. Interest expenses	357886	488878	572077	570991	567793	620942	466848	2. Frais financiers
3. Net interest income	126578	124068	125756	123282	107101	93907	90671	3. Produits financiers nets
4. Non-interest income (net)	28540	38218	39633	56225	77444	98606	72842	4. Produits non financiers (nets)
5. Gross income	155118	162286	165389	179507	184545	192513	163513	5. Résultat brut
6. Operating expenses	103315	109276	115232	120483	126632	139320	139279	6. Frais d'exploitation
7. Net income	51803	53010	50157	59024	57913	53193	24234	7. Résultat net
8. Provisions (net)	29638	35008	34118	38942	52394	56207	43060	8. Provisions (nettes)
9. Profit before tax	22165	18002	16039	20082	5519	-3014	-18826	9. Bénéfices avant impôt
10. Income tax	6792	5612	4285	5290	6587	4548	4142	10. Impôt
11. Profit after tax	15373	12390	11754	14792	-1068	-7562	-22968	11. Bénéfices après impôt
12. Distributed profit	6900	7707	7801	8520	7135	7763	6992	12. Bénéfices distribués
13. Retained profit	8473	4683	3953	6272	-8203	-15325	-29960	13. Bénéfices mis en réserve
Memoranda								*Pour mémoire*
14. Staff costs	66066	69408	72646	74780	77282	80859	79481	14. Frais de personnel
15. Provisions on loans	19927	22330	22011	29833	49574	55413	45962	15. Provisions sur prêts
16. Provisions on securities	-2993	1938	5791	-192	8488	7315	10823	16. Provisions sur titres
BALANCE SHEET								**BILAN**
Assets								**Actif**
17. Cash & balance with Central bank	131182	125075	79476	73546	42517	23418	17707	17. Caisse & solde auprès de la Banque centrale
18. Interbank deposits	2713282	2959361	3199937	3038222	3552598	3711820	3197175	18. Dépôts interbancaires
19. Loans	2322752	2624220	2939519	3092549	3197034	3172440	2571922	19. Prêts
20. Securities	554633	635974	718197	1072814	1348412	1655767	1455233	20. Valeurs mobilières
21. Other assets	681057	803147	956134	776378	863368	628818	548106	21. Autres actifs
Liabilities								**Passif**
22. Capital & reserves	143022	169327	203738	235273	276205	303881	269779	22. Capital et réserves
23. Borrowing from Central bank	166882	174301	199632	182233	178987	27041	17300	23. Emprunts auprès de la Banque centrale
24. Interbank deposits	3082312	3344754	3389267	3217563	3623724	3956838	3442443	24. Dépôts interbancaires
25. Non-bank deposits	1420381	1563196	1656666	1766012	1837436	1998841	1714224	25. Dépôts non bancaires
26. Bonds	911603	1108308	1499625	1807004	2095380	2099763	1692079	26. Obligations
27. Other liabilities	678706	787891	944335	845423	992199	805900	654317	27. Autres engagements
Balance sheet total								**Total du bilan**
28. End-year total	6402906	7147777	7893263	8053509	9003930	9192264	7790142	28. En fin d'exercice
29. Average total	5969210	6993134	7494651	8185218	8579526	10065924	10191644	29. Moyen
Memoranda								*Pour mémoire*
30. Short-term securities	..	..	..	..	..	837888	785426	30. Titres à court terme
31. Bonds	..	..	..	..	..	292936	211908	31. Obligations
32. Shares and participations	..	..	..	..	..	..	..	32. Actions et participations
33. Claims on non-residents	2793077	2935016	3381089	3349161	3775335	2720709	2626942	33. Créances sur des non résidents
34. Liabilities to non-residents	2743653	2982889	3489028	3552549	3668305	2388398	2478113	34. Engagements envers des non résidents
SUPPLEMENTARY INFORMATION								**RENSEIGNEMENTS COMPLEMENTAIRES**
35. Number of institutions	395	407	408	414	409	415	421	35. Nombre d'institutions
36. Number of branches	10293	10367	10166	10177	10081	10451	10131	36. Nombre de succursales
37. Number of employees (x 1000)	248.3	246.9	243.1	238.7	232.3	219.2	218.0	37. Nombre de salariés (x 1000)

FRANCE

Commercial banks

FRANCE

Banques commerciales

Per cent	1988	1989	1990	1991	1992	1993	1994	*Pourcentage*
INCOME STATEMENT ANALYSIS								**ANALYSE DU COMPTE DE RESULTATS**
% of average balance sheet total								**% du total moyen du bilan**
38. Interest income	8.12	8.76	9.31	8.48	7.87	7.10	5.47	38. Produits financiers
39. Interest expenses	6.00	6.99	7.63	6.98	6.62	6.17	4.58	39. Frais financiers
40. Net interest income	2.12	1.77	1.68	1.51	1.25	0.93	0.89	40. Produits financiers nets
41. Non-interest income (net)	0.48	0.55	0.53	0.69	0.90	0.98	0.71	41. Produits non financiers (nets)
42. Gross income	2.60	2.32	2.21	2.19	2.15	1.91	1.60	42. Résultat brut
43. Operating expenses	1.73	1.56	1.54	1.47	1.48	1.38	1.37	43. Frais d'exploitation
44. Net income	0.87	0.76	0.67	0.72	0.68	0.53	0.24	44. Résultat net
45. Provisions (net)	0.50	0.50	0.46	0.48	0.61	0.56	0.42	45. Provisions (nettes)
46. Profit before tax	0.37	0.26	0.21	0.25	0.06	-0.03	-0.18	46. Bénéfices avant impôt
47. Income tax	0.11	0.08	0.06	0.06	0.08	0.05	0.04	47. Impôt
48. Profit after tax	0.26	0.18	0.16	0.18	-0.01	-0.08	-0.23	48. Bénéfices après impôt
49. Distributed profit	0.12	0.11	0.10	0.10	0.08	0.08	0.07	49. Bénéfices distribués
50. Retained profit	0.14	0.07	0.05	0.08	-0.10	-0.15	-0.29	50. Bénéfices mis en réserve
51. Staff costs	1.11	0.99	0.97	0.91	0.90	0.80	0.78	51. Frais de personnel
52. Provisions on loans	0.33	0.32	0.29	0.36	0.58	0.55	0.45	52. Provisions sur prêts
53. Provisions on securities	-0.05	0.03	0.08	.	0.10	0.07	0.11	53. Provisions sur titres
% of gross income								**% du total du résultat brut**
54. Net interest income	81.60	76.45	76.04	68.68	58.04	48.78	55.45	54. Produits financiers nets
55. Non-interest income (net)	18.40	23.55	23.96	31.32	41.96	51.22	44.55	55. Produits non financiers (nets)
56. Operating expenses	66.60	67.34	69.67	67.12	68.62	72.37	85.18	56. Frais d'exploitation
57. Net income	33.40	32.66	30.33	32.88	31.38	27.63	14.82	57. Résultat net
58. Provisions (net)	19.11	21.57	20.63	21.69	28.39	29.20	26.33	58. Provisions (nettes)
59. Profit before tax	14.29	11.09	9.70	11.19	2.99	-1.57	-11.51	59. Bénéfices avant impôt
60. Income tax	4.38	3.46	2.59	2.95	3.57	2.36	2.53	60. Impôt
61. Profit after tax	9.91	7.63	7.11	8.24	-0.58	-3.93	-14.05	61. Bénéfices après impôt
62. Staff costs	42.59	42.77	43.92	41.66	41.88	42.00	48.61	62. Frais de personnel
% of net income								**% du total du résultat net**
63. Provisions (net)	57.21	66.04	68.02	65.98	90.47	105.67	177.68	63. Provisions (nettes)
64. Profit before tax	42.79	33.96	31.98	34.02	9.53	-5.67	-77.68	64. Bénéfices avant impôt
65. Income tax	13.11	10.59	8.54	8.96	11.37	8.55	17.09	65. Impôt
66. Profit after tax	29.68	23.37	23.43	25.06	-1.84	-14.22	-94.78	66. Bénéfices après impôt

FRANCE

Commercial banks

FRANCE

Banques commerciales

Per cent / *Pourcentage*

BALANCE SHEET ANALYSIS / ANALYSE DU BILAN

% of year-end balance sheet total / **% du total du bilan en fin d'exercice**

	1988	1989	1990	1991	1992	1993	1994	
Assets								**Actif**
67. Cash & balance with Central bank	2.05	1.75	1.01	0.91	0.47	0.25	0.23	67. Caisse & solde auprès de la Banque centrale
68. Interbank deposits	42.38	41.40	40.54	37.73	39.46	40.38	41.04	68. Dépôts interbancaires
69. Loans	36.28	36.71	37.24	38.40	35.51	34.51	33.02	69. Prêts
70. Securities	8.66	8.90	9.10	13.32	14.98	18.01	18.68	70. Valeurs mobilières
71. Other assets	10.64	11.24	12.11	9.64	9.59	6.84	7.04	71. Autres actifs
Liabilities								**Passif**
72. Capital & reserves	2.23	2.37	2.58	2.92	3.07	3.31	3.46	72. Capital et réserves
73. Borrowing from Central bank	2.61	2.44	2.53	2.26	1.99	0.29	0.22	73. Emprunts auprès de la Banque centrale
74. Interbank deposits	48.14	46.79	42.94	39.95	40.25	43.05	44.19	74. Dépôts interbancaires
75. Non-bank deposits	22.18	21.87	20.99	21.93	20.41	21.74	22.01	75. Dépôts non bancaires
76. Bonds	14.24	15.51	19.00	22.44	23.27	22.84	21.72	76. Obligations
77. Other liabilities	10.60	11.02	11.96	10.50	11.02	8.77	8.40	77. Autres engagements
Memoranda								*Pour mémoire*
78. Short-term securities	..	..	..	..	..	*9.12*	*10.08*	*78. Titres à court terme*
79. Bonds	..	..	..	..	..	*3.19*	*2.72*	*79. Obligations*
80. Shares and participations	..	..	..	..	..	..	..	*80. Actions et participations*
81. Claims on non-residents	*43.62*	*41.06*	*42.84*	*41.59*	*41.93*	*29.60*	*33.72*	*81. Créances sur des non résidents*
82. Liabilities to non-residents	*42.85*	*41.73*	*44.20*	*44.11*	*42.96*	*25.98*	*31.81*	*82. Engagements envers des non résidents*

Notes

- New series. See notes under All banks.
- Average balance sheet totals (item 29) are based on the average of quarterly totals.

Change in methodology:

- See notes under All banks.

Notes

- Nouvelles séries (voir notes sous Ensemble des banques).
- La moyenne du total des actifs/passifs (poste 29) est basée sur la moyenne des totaux des situations trimestrielles.

Changement méthodologique :

- Voir notes sous Ensemble des banques.

FRANCE

Large commercial banks

FRANCE

Grandes banques commerciales

Million French francs / *Millions de francs français*

	1988	1989	1990	1991	1992	1993	1994	
INCOME STATEMENT								**COMPTE DE RESULTATS**
1. Interest income	371737	453953	523423	557294	582094	564010	460234	1. Produits financiers
2. Interest expenses	274877	356680	421992	446751	460796	473054	368949	2. Frais financiers
3. Net interest income	96860	97273	101431	110543	121298	90956	91285	3. Produits financiers nets
4. Non-interest income (net)	32189	44557	50478	55055	50636	89266	74397	4. Produits non financiers (nets)
5. Gross income	129049	141830	151909	165598	171934	180222	165682	5. Résultat brut
6. Operating expenses	87329	93729	105555	113711	118922	125080	125359	6. Frais d'exploitation
7. Net income	41720	48101	46354	51887	53012	55142	40323	7. Résultat net
8. Provisions (net)	20420	23906	26990	32702	40500	46468	36740	8. Provisions (nettes)
9. Profit before tax	21300	24195	19364	19185	12512	8674	3583	9. Bénéfices avant impôt
10. Income tax	6593	6232	4464	5827	4677	6236	6487	10. Impôt
11. Profit after tax	14707	17963	14900	13358	7835	2438	-2904	11. Bénéfices après impôt
12. Distributed profit	11813	14588	11473	10088	4489	-157	-5973	12. Bénéfices distribués
13. Retained profit	2894	3375	3427	3270	3346	2595	3069	13. Bénéfices mis en réserve
Memoranda								*Pour mémoire*
14. Staff costs	51267	54436	60595	64553	67446	73593	72209	14. Frais de personnel
15. Provisions on loans	..	..	..	..	..	46486	39395	15. Provisions sur prêts
16. Provisions on securities	..	..	..	..	..	-3171	-4542	16. Provisions sur titres
BALANCE SHEET								**BILAN**
Assets								**Actif**
17. Cash & balance with Central bank	88618	80328	60999	62944	42770	34745	29234	17. Caisse & solde auprès de la Banque centrale
18. Interbank deposits	1319089	1359943	1422493	1311688	1625298	1821703	1672483	18. Dépôts interbancaires
19. Loans	1915070	2195698	2520626	2694960	2947556	2972956	2865339	19. Prêts
20. Securities	321767	361489	554970	898305	1061499	1344023	1305815	20. Valeurs mobilières
21. Other assets	604544	720477	804448	669719	742539	577052	533069	21. Autres actifs
Liabilities								**Passif**
22. Capital & reserves	107290	103927	128280	144610	156316	248696	242577	22. Capital et réserves
23. Borrowing from Central bank	130125	141485	169301	149765	138011	42100	25821	23. Emprunts auprès de la Banque centrale
24. Interbank deposits	1689863	1750115	1795833	1749765	1972138	2373656	2298899	24. Dépôts interbancaires
25. Non-bank deposits	1535665	1738573	2162728	1699324	1889242	2012156	2004032	25. Dépôts non bancaires
26. Bonds	288957	322228	367725	1128139	1393178	1263664	1085795	26. Obligations
27. Other liabilities	497189	661607	739669	766015	870778	810206	748816	27. Autres engagements
Balance sheet total								**Total du bilan**
28. End-year total	4249088	4717935	5363536	5637617	6419663	6750478	6405939	28. En fin d'exercice
29. Average total	NA	4483512	5040736	5500577	6028640	6585071	6578209	29. Moyen
Memoranda								*Pour mémoire*
30. Short-term securities	..	..	..	..	..	..	..	30. Titres à court terme
31. Bonds	..	..	..	..	..	..	..	31. Obligations
32. Shares and participations	44824	64294	118523	152262	169317	182215	179527	32. Actions et participations
33. Claims on non-residents	..	..	..	..	..	793522	724175	33. Créances sur des non résidents
34. Liabilities to non-residents	..	..	..	..	..	..	..	34. Engagements envers des non résidents
SUPPLEMENTARY INFORMATION								**RENSEIGNEMENTS COMPLEMENTAIRES**
35. Number of institutions	5	5	5	5	5	5	5	35. Nombre d'institutions
36. Number of branches	NA	NA	NA	NA	NA	NA	NA	36. Nombre de succursales
37. Number of employees (x 1000)	NA	NA	NA	NA	NA	NA	NA	37. Nombre de salariés (x 1000)

FRANCE

Large commercial banks

FRANCE

Grandes banques commerciales

Per cent	1988	1989	1990	1991	1992	1993	1994		Pourcentage
INCOME STATEMENT ANALYSIS									**ANALYSE DU COMPTE DE RESULTATS**
% of average balance sheet total									**% du total moyen du bilan**
38. Interest income	NA	10.12	10.38	10.13	9.66	8.56	7.00		38. Produits financiers
39. Interest expenses	NA	7.96	8.37	8.12	7.64	7.18	5.61		39. Frais financiers
40. Net interest income	NA	2.17	2.01	2.01	2.01	1.38	1.39		40. Produits financiers nets
41. Non-interest income (net)	NA	0.99	1.00	1.00	0.84	1.36	1.13		41. Produits non financiers (nets)
42. Gross income	NA	3.16	3.01	3.01	2.85	2.74	2.52		42. Résultat brut
43. Operating expenses	NA	2.09	2.09	2.07	1.97	1.90	1.91		43. Frais d'exploitation
44. Net income	NA	1.07	0.92	0.94	0.88	0.84	0.61		44. Résultat net
45. Provisions (net)	NA	0.53	0.54	0.59	0.67	0.71	0.56		45. Provisions (nettes)
46. Profit before tax	NA	0.54	0.38	0.35	0.21	0.13	0.05		46. Bénéfices avant impôt
47. Income tax	NA	0.14	0.09	0.11	0.08	0.09	0.10		47. Impôt
48. Profit after tax	NA	0.40	0.30	0.24	0.13	0.04	-0.04		48. Bénéfices après impôt
49. Distributed profit	NA	0.33	0.23	0.18	0.07	0.00	-0.09		49. Bénéfices distribués
50. Retained profit	NA	0.08	0.07	0.06	0.06	0.04	0.05		50. Bénéfices mis en réserve
51. Staff costs	NA	1.21	1.20	1.17	1.12	1.12	1.10		51. Frais de personnel
52. Provisions on loans	..	..	..	..	..	0.71	0.60		52. Provisions sur prêts
53. Provisions on securities	..	..	..	..	..	-0.05	-0.07		53. Provisions sur titres
% of gross income									**% du total du résultat brut**
54. Net interest income	75.06	68.58	66.77	66.75	70.55	50.47	55.10		54. Produits financiers nets
55. Non-interest income (net)	24.94	31.42	33.23	33.25	29.45	49.53	44.90		55. Produits non financiers (nets)
56. Operating expenses	67.67	66.09	69.49	68.67	69.17	69.40	75.66		56. Frais d'exploitation
57. Net income	32.33	33.91	30.51	31.33	30.83	30.60	24.34		57. Résultat net
58. Provisions (net)	15.82	16.86	17.77	19.75	23.56	25.78	22.18		58. Provisions (nettes)
59. Profit before tax	16.51	17.06	12.75	11.59	7.28	4.81	2.16		59. Bénéfices avant impôt
60. Income tax	5.11	4.39	2.94	3.52	2.72	3.46	3.92		60. Impôt
61. Profit after tax	11.40	12.67	9.81	8.07	4.56	1.35	-1.75		61. Bénéfices après impôt
62. Staff costs	39.73	38.38	39.89	38.98	39.23	40.83	43.58		62. Frais de personnel
% of net income									**% du total du résultat net**
63. Provisions (net)	48.95	49.70	58.23	63.03	76.40	84.27	91.11		63. Provisions (nettes)
64. Profit before tax	51.05	50.30	41.77	36.97	23.60	15.73	8.89		64. Bénéfices avant impôt
65. Income tax	15.80	12.96	9.63	11.23	8.82	11.31	16.09		65. Impôt
66. Profit after tax	35.25	37.34	32.14	25.74	14.78	4.42	-7.20		66. Bénéfices après impôt

63

FRANCE

Large commercial banks

Per cent

BALANCE SHEET ANALYSIS

	1988	1989	1990	1991	1992	1993	1994
% of year-end balance sheet total							
Assets							
67. Cash & balance with Central bank	2.09	1.70	1.14	1.12	0.67	0.51	0.46
68. Interbank deposits	31.04	28.82	26.52	23.27	25.32	26.99	26.11
69. Loans	45.07	46.54	47.00	47.80	45.91	44.04	44.73
70. Securities	7.57	7.66	10.35	15.93	16.54	19.91	20.38
71. Other assets	14.23	15.27	15.00	11.88	11.57	8.55	8.32
Liabilities							
72. Capital & reserves	2.53	2.20	2.39	2.57	2.43	3.68	3.79
73. Borrowing from Central bank	3.06	3.00	3.16	2.66	2.15	0.62	0.40
74. Interbank deposits	39.77	37.09	33.48	31.04	30.72	35.16	35.89
75. Non-bank deposits	36.14	36.85	40.32	30.14	29.43	29.81	31.28
76. Bonds	6.80	6.83	6.86	20.01	21.70	18.72	16.95
77. Other liabilities	11.70	14.02	13.79	13.59	13.56	12.00	11.69
Memoranda							
78. Short-term securities	..	..	..	..	..	..	..
79. Bonds	..	..	..	..	..	*11.76*	*11.30*
80. Shares and participations	*1.05*	*1.36*	*2.21*	*2.70*	*2.64*	*2.70*	*2.80*
81. Claims on non-residents	..	..	..	..	..	..	..
82. Liabilities to non-residents	..	..	..	..	..	..	..

Notes

- New series. The consolidated data for Large commercial banks cover all subsidiaries and branches, including non-financial agencies, in France and abroad. Accordingly, they are not comparable with the corporate data for Commercial banks.

Change in methodology:

- See notes under All banks.

FRANCE

Grandes banques commerciales

Pourcentage

ANALYSE DU BILAN

% du total du bilan en fin d'exercice

Actif

67. Caisse & solde auprès de la Banque centrale
68. Dépôts interbancaires
69. Prêts
70. Valeurs mobilières
71. Autres actifs

Passif

72. Capital et réserves
73. Emprunts auprès de la Banque centrale
74. Dépôts interbancaires
75. Dépôts non bancaires
76. Obligations
77. Autres engagements

Pour mémoire

78. Titres à court terme
79. Obligations
80. Actions et participations
81. Créances sur des non résidents
82. Engagements envers des non résidents

Notes

- Nouvelle série. Les données consolidées des Grandes banques commerciales incluent l'ensemble des succursales et filiales, y compris non établissement de crédit, installées en France et à l'étranger. Ces données ne sont donc pas comparables aux données de la catégorie des Banques commerciales.

Changement méthodologique :

- Voir notes sous Ensemble des banques.

FRANCE

Savings banks

Million French francs

FRANCE

Caisses d'épargne

Millions de francs français

		1988	1989	1990	1991	1992	1993	1994
INCOME STATEMENT	**COMPTE DE RESULTATS**							
1. Interest income	1. Produits financiers	55286	60334	64328	70218	63010	61834	61680
2. Interest expenses	2. Frais financiers	43623	45869	48896	52253	41136	41552	43122
3. Net interest income	3. Produits financiers nets	11663	14465	15432	17965	21874	20282	18558
4. Non-interest income (net)	4. Produits non financiers (nets)	3227	2242	2682	3230	3378	6270	4623
5. Gross income	5. Résultat brut	14890	16707	18114	21195	25252	26552	23181
6. Operating expenses	6. Frais d'exploitation	11225	12265	13693	15297	17977	20091	20486
7. Net income	7. Résultat net	3665	4442	4421	5898	7275	6461	2695
8. Provisions (net)	8. Provisions (nettes)	1440	2014	1943	3460	3749	2693	1184
9. Profit before tax	9. Bénéfices avant impôt	2225	2428	2478	2438	3526	3768	1511
10. Income tax	10. Impôt	139	378	523	855	1433	1994	194
11. Profit after tax	11. Bénéfices après impôt	2086	2050	1955	1583	2093	1774	1317
12. Distributed profit	12. Bénéfices distribués	-	-	-	48	-	-	-
13. Retained profit	13. Bénéfices mis en réserve	2085	2051	1955	1535	2092	1775	1317
Memoranda	*Pour mémoire*							
14. Staff costs	14. Frais de personnel	7189	7791	8481	9244	10772	11438	11564
15. Provisions on loans	15. Provisions sur prêts	555	847	1031	1774	2134	1640	1037
16. Provisions on securities	16. Provisions sur titres	77	59	-87	-13	-29	-73	-42
BALANCE SHEET	**BILAN**							
Assets	**Actif**							
17. Cash & balance with Central bank	17. Caisse & solde auprès de la Banque centrale	5272	2648	2691	2947	3078	2615	2749
18. Interbank deposits	18. Dépôts interbancaires	733349	772524	689041	679144	483626	468192	493442
19. Loans	19. Prêts	196214	218861	245482	252711	283909	298700	320726
20. Securities	20. Valeurs mobilières	3469	4852	6086	7753	77318	116768	139982
21. Other assets	21. Autres actifs	33309	36072	36698	39550	54981	42452	47476
Liabilities	**Passif**							
22. Capital & reserves	22. Capital et réserves	20835	23342	25669	27836	37421	41243	43194
23. Borrowing from Central bank	23. Emprunts auprès de la Banque centrale	1080	436	18	24	638	358	116
24. Interbank deposits	24. Dépôts interbancaires	290605	342472	284132	305108	47725	33757	95627
25. Non-bank deposits	25. Dépôts non bancaires	644903	648488	652587	631823	723659	774885	839042
26. Bonds	26. Obligations	1202	1528	2577	1790	44653	61437	9063
27. Other liabilities	27. Autres engagements	12989	18691	15015	15525	48815	17047	17334
Balance sheet total	**Total du bilan**							
28. End-year total	28. En fin d'exercice	971613	1034957	977998	982106	902912	928727	1004376
29. Average total	29. Moyen	946352	1011108	978288	1228899	912780	914881	955025
Memoranda	*Pour mémoire*							
30. Short-term securities	30. Titres à court terme	..	..	..	..	..	78763	99077
31. Bonds	31. Obligations	..	..	..	..	..	3914	4467
32. Shares and participations	32. Actions et participations	..	..	..	..	..	2526	5488
33. Claims on non-residents	33. Créances sur des non résidents	1	1	2	8	17	..	..
34. Liabilities to non-residents	34. Engagements envers des non résidents	3	2	7	221	14	307	301
SUPPLEMENTARY INFORMATION	**RENSEIGNEMENTS COMPLEMENTAIRES**							
35. Number of institutions	35. Nombre d'institutions	280	212	186	36	36	35	35
36. Number of branches	36. Nombre de succursales	4269	4432	4623	4030	4411	4308	4200
37. Number of employees (x 1000)	37. Nombre de salariés (x 1000)	32.8	31.0	32.2	33.6	35.8	35.8	35.7

FRANCE

Savings banks

FRANCE

Caisses d'épargne

Per cent

Pourcentage

	1988	1989	1990	1991	1992	1993	1994		
INCOME STATEMENT ANALYSIS									**ANALYSE DU COMPTE DE RESULTATS**
% of average balance sheet total									**% du total moyen du bilan**
38. Interest income	5.84	5.97	6.58	5.71	6.90	6.76	6.46	38.	Produits financiers
39. Interest expenses	4.61	4.54	5.00	4.25	4.51	4.54	4.52	39.	Frais financiers
40. Net interest income	1.23	1.43	1.58	1.46	2.40	2.22	1.94	40.	Produits financiers nets
41. Non-interest income (net)	0.34	0.22	0.27	0.26	0.37	0.69	0.48	41.	Produits non financiers (nets)
42. Gross income	1.57	1.65	1.85	1.72	2.77	2.90	2.43	42.	Résultat brut
43. Operating expenses	1.19	1.21	1.40	1.24	1.97	2.20	2.15	43.	Frais d'exploitation
44. Net income	0.39	0.44	0.45	0.48	0.80	0.71	0.28	44.	Résultat net
45. Provisions (net)	0.15	0.20	0.20	0.28	0.41	0.29	0.12	45.	Provisions (nettes)
46. Profit before tax	0.24	0.24	0.25	0.20	0.39	0.41	0.16	46.	Bénéfices avant impôt
47. Income tax	0.01	0.04	0.05	0.07	0.16	0.22	0.02	47.	Impôt
48. Profit after tax	0.22	0.20	0.20	0.13	0.23	0.19	0.14	48.	Bénéfices après impôt
49. Distributed profit	-	-	-	-	-	-	-	49.	Bénéfices distribués
50. Retained profit	0.22	0.20	0.20	0.12	0.23	0.19	0.14	50.	Bénéfices mis en réserve
51. Staff costs	0.76	0.77	0.87	0.75	1.18	1.25	1.21	51.	Frais de personnel
52. Provisions on loans	0.06	0.08	0.11	0.14	0.23	0.18	0.11	52.	Provisions sur prêts
53. Provisions on securities	0.01	0.01	-0.01	-	-	-0.01	-	53.	Provisions sur titres
% of gross income									**% du total du résultat brut**
54. Net interest income	78.33	86.58	85.19	84.76	86.62	76.39	80.06	54.	Produits financiers nets
55. Non-interest income (net)	21.67	13.42	14.81	15.24	13.38	23.61	19.94	55.	Produits non financiers (nets)
56. Operating expenses	75.39	73.41	75.59	72.17	71.19	75.67	88.37	56.	Frais d'exploitation
57. Net income	24.61	26.59	24.41	27.83	28.81	24.33	11.63	57.	Résultat net
58. Provisions (net)	9.67	12.05	10.73	16.32	14.85	10.14	5.11	58.	Provisions (nettes)
59. Profit before tax	14.94	14.53	13.68	11.50	13.96	14.19	6.52	59.	Bénéfices avant impôt
60. Income tax	0.93	2.26	2.89	4.03	5.67	7.51	0.84	60.	Impôt
61. Profit after tax	14.01	12.27	10.79	7.47	8.29	6.68	5.68	61.	Bénéfices après impôt
62. Staff costs	48.28	46.63	46.82	43.61	42.66	43.08	49.89	62.	Frais de personnel
% of net income									**% du total du résultat net**
63. Provisions (net)	39.29	45.34	43.95	58.66	51.53	41.68	43.93	63.	Provisions (nettes)
64. Profit before tax	60.71	54.66	56.05	41.34	48.47	58.32	56.07	64.	Bénéfices avant impôt
65. Income tax	3.79	8.51	11.83	14.50	19.70	30.86	7.20	65.	Impôt
66. Profit after tax	56.92	46.15	44.22	26.84	28.77	27.46	48.87	66.	Bénéfices après impôt

66

FRANCE

Savings banks

Caisses d'épargne (FRANCE)

Per cent / *Pourcentage*	1988	1989	1990	1991	1992	1993	1994	
BALANCE SHEET ANALYSIS								**ANALYSE DU BILAN**
% of year-end balance sheet total								**% du total du bilan en fin d'exercice**
Assets								*Actif*
67. Cash & balance with Central bank	0.54	0.26	0.27	0.30	0.34	0.28	0.27	67. Caisse & solde auprès de la Banque centrale
68. Interbank deposits	75.48	74.64	70.31	69.15	53.56	50.41	49.13	68. Dépôts interbancaires
69. Loans	20.19	21.15	25.05	25.73	31.44	32.16	31.93	69. Prêts
70. Securities	0.36	0.47	0.62	0.79	8.56	12.57	13.94	70. Valeurs mobilières
71. Other assets	3.43	3.49	3.74	4.03	6.09	4.57	4.73	71. Autres actifs
Liabilities								*Passif*
72. Capital & reserves	2.14	2.26	2.62	2.83	4.14	4.44	4.30	72. Capital et réserves
73. Borrowing from Central bank	0.11	0.04	-	-	0.07	0.04	0.01	73. Emprunts auprès de la Banque centrale
74. Interbank deposits	29.91	33.09	28.99	31.07	5.29	3.63	9.52	74. Dépôts interbancaires
75. Non-bank deposits	66.37	62.66	66.59	64.33	80.15	83.44	83.54	75. Dépôts non bancaires
76. Bonds	0.12	0.15	0.26	0.18	4.95	6.62	0.90	76. Obligations
77. Other liabilities	1.34	1.81	1.53	1.58	5.41	1.84	1.73	77. Autres engagements
Memoranda								*Pour mémoire*
78. *Short-term securities*	..	..	..	..	..	..	..	78. *Titres à court terme*
79. *Bonds*	..	..	..	..	..	8.48	9.86	79. *Obligations*
80. *Shares and participations*	..	..	..	..	..	0.42	0.44	80. *Actions et participations*
81. *Claims on non-residents*	-	-	-	-	-	0.27	0.55	81. *Créances sur des non résidents*
82. *Liabilities to non-residents*	-	-	-	-	-	0.03	0.03	82. *Engagements envers des non résidents*

Notes
- New series. See notes under All banks.
- Average balance sheet totals (item 29) are based on the average of quarterly totals.

Change in methodology:
- See notes under All banks.

Notes
- Nouvelles séries (voir notes sous Ensemble des banques).
- La moyenne du total des actifs/passifs (poste 29) est basée sur la moyenne des totaux des situations trimestrielles.

Changement méthodologique :
- Voir notes sous Ensemble des banques.

FRANCE

Co-operative banks

Million French francs

FRANCE

Banques mutualistes

Millions de francs français

	1988	1989	1990	1991	1992	1993	1994	
INCOME STATEMENT								**COMPTE DE RESULTATS**
1. Interest income	218036	247073	274830	286644	291920	302760	270776	1. Produits financiers
2. Interest expenses	151408	175858	200247	208426	207707	226057	200337	2. Frais financiers
3. Net interest income	66628	71215	74583	78218	84213	76703	70439	3. Produits financiers nets
4. Non-interest income (net)	5918	7996	9848	14767	17263	26504	28067	4. Produits non financiers (nets)
5. Gross income	72546	79211	84431	92985	101476	103207	98506	5. Résultat brut
6. Operating expenses	50359	53933	57593	60049	62561	65654	66752	6. Frais d'exploitation
7. Net income	22187	25278	26838	32936	38915	37553	31754	7. Résultat net
8. Provisions (net)	12724	15252	16690	19581	24613	22848	18334	8. Provisions (nettes)
9. Profit before tax	9463	10026	10148	13355	14302	14705	13420	9. Bénéfices avant impôt
10. Income tax	3569	3820	3393	4409	5267	6351	5165	10. Impôt
11. Profit after tax	5894	6206	6755	8946	9035	8354	8255	11. Bénéfices après impôt
12. Distributed profit	1462	1790	1807	2176	2555	2420	2647	12. Bénéfices distribués
13. Retained profit	4432	4417	4949	6769	6480	5935	5608	13. Bénéfices mis en réserve
Memoranda								*Pour mémoire*
14. Staff costs	*28957*	*30622*	*32237*	*33296*	*34670*	*35510*	*36093*	*14. Frais de personnel*
15. Provisions on loans	*6291*	*8036*	*10977*	*12935*	*16498*	*20980*	*16542*	*15. Provisions sur prêts*
16. Provisions on securities	*146*	*385*	*919*	*445*	*758*	*573*	*57*	*16. Provisions sur titres*
BALANCE SHEET								**BILAN**
Assets								**Actif**
17. Cash & balance with Central bank	27461	34522	37322	30147	14991	8812	8896	17. Caisse & solde auprès de la Banque centrale
18. Interbank deposits	1229501	1349433	1474238	1504305	1535896	1752636	1821189	18. Dépôts interbancaires
19. Loans	975434	1151635	1285240	1352492	1393626	1396465	1410596	19. Prêts
20. Securities	145002	173034	184344	268052	268265	286928	394792	20. Valeurs mobilières
21. Other assets	247202	321078	392196	291350	298445	162458	171208	21. Autres actifs
Liabilities								**Passif**
22. Capital & reserves	63684	72676	87452	116469	131350	136050	146722	22. Capital et réserves
23. Borrowing from Central bank	9763	14908	22257	17604	20192	741	626	23. Emprunts auprès de la Banque centrale
24. Interbank deposits	1053864	1261548	1339453	1405356	1378176	1452842	1524101	24. Dépôts interbancaires
25. Non-bank deposits	830289	925072	1048224	1183186	1245533	1430879	1566252	25. Dépôts non bancaires
26. Bonds	428625	462660	502812	447746	450986	467123	451641	26. Obligations
27. Other liabilities	238374	292837	373143	275985	284987	119664	117340	27. Autres engagements
Balance sheet total								**Total du bilan**
28. End-year total	2624599	3029702	3373340	3446346	3511224	3607299	3806681	28. En fin d'exercice
29. Average total	2478794	2741006	3110641	3416549	3490033	3628285	3780283	29. Moyen
Memoranda								*Pour mémoire*
30. Short-term securities	*..*	*..*	*..*	*..*	*..*	*150689*	*191706*	*30. Titres à court terme*
31. Bonds	*..*	*..*	*..*	*..*	*..*	*57532*	*63641*	*31. Obligations*
32. Shares and participations	*85798*	*245068*	*264271*	*283446*	*327946*	*303492*	*274762*	*32. Actions et participations*
33. Claims on non-residents	*84674*	*230398*	*251231*	*266061*	*241536*	*167922*	*174386*	*33. Créances sur des non résidents*
34. Liabilities to non-residents								*34. Engagements envers des non résidents*
SUPPLEMENTARY INFORMATION								**RENSEIGNEMENTS COMPLEMENTAIRES**
35. Number of institutions	182	178	176	168	158	150	144	35. Nombre d'institutions
36. Number of branches	11241	11311	11151	11048	10704	9903	10082	36. Nombre de succursales
37. Number of employees (x 1000)	126.2	126.8	126.1	123.4	121.9	115.1	119.9	37. Nombre de salariés (x 1000)

FRANCE

Co-operative banks

FRANCE

Banques mutualistes

Per cent / *Pourcentage*

INCOME STATEMENT ANALYSIS / ANALYSE DU COMPTE DE RESULTATS

	1988	1989	1990	1991	1992	1993	1994		
% of average balance sheet total								**% du total moyen du bilan**	
38. Interest income	8.80	9.01	8.84	8.39	8.36	8.34	7.16	38. Produits financiers	
39. Interest expenses	6.11	6.42	6.44	6.10	5.95	6.23	5.30	39. Frais financiers	
40. Net interest income	2.69	2.60	2.40	2.29	2.41	2.11	1.86	40. Produits financiers nets	
41. Non-interest income (net)	0.24	0.29	0.32	0.43	0.49	0.73	0.74	41. Produits non financiers (nets)	
42. Gross income	2.93	2.89	2.71	2.72	2.91	2.84	2.61	42. Résultat brut	
43. Operating expenses	2.03	1.97	1.85	1.76	1.79	1.81	1.77	43. Frais d'exploitation	
44. Net income	0.90	0.92	0.86	0.96	1.12	1.04	0.84	44. Résultat net	
45. Provisions (net)	0.51	0.56	0.54	0.57	0.71	0.63	0.48	45. Provisions (nettes)	
46. Profit before tax	0.38	0.37	0.33	0.39	0.41	0.41	0.35	46. Bénéfices avant impôt	
47. Income tax	0.14	0.14	0.11	0.13	0.15	0.18	0.14	47. Impôt	
48. Profit after tax	0.24	0.23	0.22	0.26	0.26	0.23	0.22	48. Bénéfices après impôt	
49. Distributed profit	0.06	0.07	0.06	0.06	0.07	0.07	0.07	49. Bénéfices distribués	
50. Retained profit	0.18	0.16	0.16	0.20	0.19	0.16	0.15	50. Bénéfices mis en réserve	
51. Staff costs	1.17	1.12	1.04	0.97	0.99	0.98	0.95	51. Frais de personnel	
52. Provisions on loans	0.25	0.29	0.35	0.38	0.47	0.58	0.44	52. Provisions sur prêts	
53. Provisions on securities	0.01	0.01	0.03	0.01	0.02	0.02	0.00	53. Provisions sur titres	
% of gross income								**% du total du résultat brut**	
54. Net interest income	91.84	89.91	88.34	84.12	82.99	74.32	71.51	54. Produits financiers nets	
55. Non-interest income (net)	8.16	10.09	11.66	15.88	17.01	25.68	28.49	55. Produits non financiers (nets)	
56. Operating expenses	69.42	68.09	68.21	64.58	61.65	63.61	67.76	56. Frais d'exploitation	
57. Net income	30.58	31.91	31.79	35.42	38.35	36.39	32.24	57. Résultat net	
58. Provisions (net)	17.54	19.25	19.77	21.06	24.25	22.14	18.61	58. Provisions (nettes)	
59. Profit before tax	13.04	12.66	12.02	14.36	14.09	14.25	13.62	59. Bénéfices avant impôt	
60. Income tax	4.92	4.82	4.02	4.74	5.19	6.15	5.24	60. Impôt	
61. Profit after tax	8.12	7.83	8.00	9.62	8.90	8.09	8.38	61. Bénéfices après impôt	
62. Staff costs	39.92	38.66	38.18	35.81	34.17	34.41	36.64	62. Frais de personnel	
% of net income								**% du total du résultat net**	
63. Provisions (net)	57.35	60.34	62.19	59.45	63.25	60.84	57.74	63. Provisions (nettes)	
64. Profit before tax	42.65	39.66	37.81	40.55	36.75	39.16	42.26	64. Bénéfices avant impôt	
65. Income tax	16.09	15.11	12.64	13.39	13.53	16.91	16.27	65. Impôt	
66. Profit after tax	26.57	24.55	25.17	27.16	23.22	22.25	26.00	66. Bénéfices après impôt	

FRANCE

Co-operative banks

Per cent

BALANCE SHEET ANALYSIS

% of year-end balance sheet total

	1988	1989	1990	1991	1992	1993	1994
Assets							
67. Cash & balance with Central bank	1.05	1.14	1.11	0.87	0.43	0.24	0.23
68. Interbank deposits	46.85	44.54	43.70	43.65	43.74	48.59	47.84
69. Loans	37.17	38.01	38.10	39.24	39.69	38.71	37.06
70. Securities	5.52	5.71	5.46	7.78	7.64	7.95	10.37
71. Other assets	9.42	10.60	11.63	8.45	8.50	4.50	4.50
Liabilities							
72. Capital & reserves	2.43	2.40	2.59	3.38	3.74	3.77	3.85
73. Borrowing from Central bank	0.37	0.49	0.66	0.51	0.58	0.02	0.02
74. Interbank deposits	40.15	41.64	39.71	40.78	39.25	40.28	40.04
75. Non-bank deposits	31.63	30.53	31.07	34.33	35.47	39.67	41.14
76. Bonds	16.33	15.27	14.91	12.99	12.84	12.95	11.86
77. Other liabilities	9.08	9.67	11.06	8.01	8.12	3.32	3.08
Memoranda							
78. Short-term securities	..	..	..	..	..	..	..
79. Bonds	..	..	..	..	..	*4.18*	*5.04*
80. Shares and participations	..	..	..	..	..	*1.59*	*1.67*
81. Claims on non-residents	*3.27*	*8.09*	*7.83*	*8.22*	*9.34*	*8.41*	*7.22*
82. Liabilities to non-residents	*3.23*	*7.60*	*7.45*	*7.72*	*6.88*	*4.66*	*4.58*

Notes

- New series. See notes under All banks.
- Average balance sheet totals (item 29) are based on the average of quarterly totals.

Change in methodology:

- See notes under All banks.

FRANCE

Banques mutualistes

Pourcentage

ANALYSE DU BILAN

% du total du bilan en fin d'exercice

Actif
67. Caisse & solde auprès de la Banque centrale
68. Dépôts interbancaires
69. Prêts
70. Valeurs mobilières
71. Autres actifs

Passif
72. Capital et réserves
73. Emprunts auprès de la Banque centrale
74. Dépôts interbancaires
75. Dépôts non bancaires
76. Obligations
77. Autres engagements

Pour mémoire
78. Titres à court terme
79. Obligations
80. Actions et participations
81. Créances sur des non résidents
82. Engagements envers des non résidents

Notes

- Nouvelles séries (voir notes sous Ensemble des banques).
- La moyenne du total des actifs/passifs (poste 29) est basée sur la moyenne des totaux des situations trimestrielles.

Changement méthodologique :

- Voir notes sous Ensemble des banques.

FRANCE

Other banks

FRANCE

Autres banques

Million French francs / *Millions de francs français*

	1988	1989	1990	1991	1992	1993	1994	
INCOME STATEMENT								**COMPTE DE RESULTATS**
1. Interest income	266469	282676	317025	346395	336493	346548	316355	1. Produits financiers
2. Interest expenses	222032	237668	269988	294348	286340	304968	268831	2. Frais financiers
3. Net interest income	44437	45008	47037	52047	50153	41580	47524	3. Produits financiers nets
4. Non-interest income (net)	11266	13921	15593	18013	21728	23379	20780	4. Produits non financiers (nets)
5. Gross income	55703	58929	62630	70060	71881	64959	68304	5. Résultat brut
6. Operating expenses	27010	29524	32012	33168	32411	32736	33267	6. Frais d'exploitation
7. Net income	28693	29405	30618	36892	39470	32223	35037	7. Résultat net
8. Provisions (net)	6033	4664	7623	10610	17429	26216	27337	8. Provisions (nettes)
9. Profit before tax	22660	24741	22995	26282	22041	6007	7700	9. Bénéfices avant impôt
10. Income tax	4181	4421	4039	4251	4163	5047	4273	10. Impôt
11. Profit after tax	18479	20320	18955	22031	17878	960	3427	11. Bénéfices après impôt
12. Distributed profit	9410	9563	10607	10754	10606	12311	11235	12. Bénéfices distribués
13. Retained profit	9068	10758	8347	11277	7272	-11351	-7808	13. Bénéfices mis en réserve
Memoranda								*Pour mémoire*
14. Staff costs	*10846*	*11435*	*12448*	*13042*	*12669*	*13851*	*13451*	*14. Frais de personnel*
15. Provisions on loans	*3537*	*4851*	*6762*	*9240*	*16069*	*25733*	*27812*	*15. Provisions sur prêts*
16. Provisions on securities	*-1516*	*1063*	*1960*	*1236*	*5410*	*3104*	*111*	*16. Provisions sur titres*
BALANCE SHEET								**BILAN**
Assets								**Actif**
17. Cash & balance with Central bank	9006	6940	6815	6339	7429	2720	1760	17. Caisse & solde auprès de la Banque centrale
18. Interbank deposits	593469	660884	714646	723692	572857	650046	654574	18. Dépôts interbancaires
19. Loans	1429795	1539365	1593345	1676770	1730736	1809420	1852945	19. Prêts
20. Securities	251240	267634	286665	380876	340706	366670	414278	20. Valeurs mobilières
21. Other assets	192786	197809	221647	231911	211246	107165	101525	21. Autres actifs
Liabilities								**Passif**
22. Capital & reserves	139911	168472	192117	215972	210126	267139	276634	22. Capital et réserves
23. Borrowing from Central bank	10654	10268	24546	3566	1718	7416	2826	23. Emprunts auprès de la Banque centrale
24. Interbank deposits	1201562	1259390	1265896	1291373	1044144	1017032	1024436	24. Dépôts interbancaires
25. Non-bank deposits	65168	63950	57995	127158	56068	63223	116696	25. Dépôts non bancaires
26. Bonds	732552	827283	916988	1000206	1174369	1363518	1373945	26. Obligations
27. Other liabilities	326449	343268	365574	381313	376547	217693	230544	27. Autres engagements
Balance sheet total								**Total du bilan**
28. End-year total	2476295	2672631	2823118	3019588	2862973	2936022	3025082	28. En fin d'exercice
29. Average total	2364906	2585825	2756756	2978968	3155796	2913774	2190013	29. Moyen
Memoranda								*Pour mémoire*
30. Short-term securities	*..*	*..*	*..*	*..*	*..*	*178057*	*196449*	*30. Titres à court terme*
31. Bonds	*..*	*..*	*..*	*..*	*..*	*147980*	*148340*	*31. Obligations*
32. Shares and participations	*..*	*..*	*..*	*..*	*..*	*226601*	*221731*	*32. Actions et participations*
33. Claims on non-residents	*43576*	*54814*	*71808*	*94834*	*113334*	*226601*	*221731*	*33. Créances sur des non résidents*
34. Liabilities to non-residents	*51333*	*48420*	*54531*	*83720*	*86146*	*377318*	*410373*	*34. Engagements envers des non résidents*
SUPPLEMENTARY INFORMATION								**RENSEIGNEMENTS COMPLEMENTAIRES**
35. Number of institutions	1193	1224	1211	1205	1098	1035	1018	35. Nombre d'institutions
36. Number of branches	NA	NA	NA	NA	NA	1629	1767	36. Nombre de succursales
37. Number of employees (x 1000)	37.3	38.3	38.6	37.8	35.0	36.0	35.3	37. Nombre de salariés (x 1000)

FRANCE

Other banks

FRANCE

Autres banques

Per cent

Pourcentage

	1988	1989	1990	1991	1992	1993	1994		
INCOME STATEMENT ANALYSIS									**ANALYSE DU COMPTE DE RESULTATS**
% of average balance sheet total									**% du total moyen du bilan**
38. Interest income	11.27	10.93	11.50	11.63	10.66	11.89	14.45	38.	Produits financiers
39. Interest expenses	9.39	9.19	9.79	9.88	9.07	10.47	12.28	39.	Frais financiers
40. Net interest income	1.88	1.74	1.71	1.75	1.59	1.43	2.17	40.	Produits financiers nets
41. Non-interest income (net)	0.48	0.54	0.57	0.60	0.69	0.80	0.95	41.	Produits non financiers (nets)
42. Gross income	2.36	2.28	2.27	2.35	2.28	2.23	3.12	42.	Résultat brut
43. Operating expenses	1.14	1.14	1.16	1.11	1.03	1.12	1.52	43.	Frais d'exploitation
44. Net income	1.21	1.14	1.11	1.24	1.25	1.11	1.60	44.	Résultat net
45. Provisions (net)	0.26	0.18	0.28	0.36	0.55	0.90	1.25	45.	Provisions (nettes)
46. Profit before tax	0.96	0.96	0.83	0.88	0.70	0.21	0.35	46.	Bénéfices avant impôt
47. Income tax	0.18	0.17	0.15	0.14	0.13	0.17	0.20	47.	Impôt
48. Profit after tax	0.78	0.79	0.69	0.74	0.57	0.03	0.16	48.	Bénéfices après impôt
49. Distributed profit	0.40	0.37	0.38	0.36	0.34	0.42	0.51	49.	Bénéfices distribués
50. Retained profit	0.38	0.42	0.30	0.38	0.23	-0.39	-0.36	50.	Bénéfices mis en réserve
51. Staff costs	0.46	0.44	0.45	0.44	0.40	0.48	0.61	51.	Frais de personnel
52. Provisions on loans	0.15	0.19	0.25	0.31	0.51	0.88	1.27	52.	Provisions sur prêts
53. Provisions on securities	-0.06	0.04	0.07	0.04	0.17	0.11	0.01	53.	Provisions sur titres
% of gross income									**% du total du résultat brut**
54. Net interest income	79.77	76.38	75.10	74.29	69.77	64.01	69.58	54.	Produits financiers nets
55. Non-interest income (net)	20.23	23.62	24.90	25.71	30.23	35.99	30.42	55.	Produits non financiers (nets)
56. Operating expenses	48.49	50.10	51.11	47.34	45.09	50.39	48.70	56.	Frais d'exploitation
57. Net income	51.51	49.90	48.89	52.66	54.91	49.61	51.30	57.	Résultat net
58. Provisions (net)	10.83	7.91	12.17	15.14	24.25	40.36	40.02	58.	Provisions (nettes)
59. Profit before tax	40.68	41.98	36.72	37.51	30.66	9.25	11.27	59.	Bénéfices avant impôt
60. Income tax	7.51	7.50	6.45	6.07	5.79	7.77	6.26	60.	Impôt
61. Profit after tax	33.17	34.48	30.27	31.45	24.87	1.48	5.02	61.	Bénéfices après impôt
62. Staff costs	19.47	19.40	19.88	18.62	17.62	21.32	19.69	62.	Frais de personnel
% of net income									**% du total du résultat net**
63. Provisions (net)	21.03	15.86	24.90	28.76	44.16	81.36	78.02	63.	Provisions (nettes)
64. Profit before tax	78.97	84.14	75.10	71.24	55.84	18.64	21.98	64.	Bénéfices avant impôt
65. Income tax	14.57	15.03	13.19	11.52	10.55	15.66	12.20	65.	Impôt
66. Profit after tax	64.40	69.10	61.91	59.72	45.30	2.98	9.78	66.	Bénéfices après impôt

FRANCE

Other banks

FRANCE

Autres banques

Per cent / *Pourcentage*

BALANCE SHEET ANALYSIS / ANALYSE DU BILAN

% of year-end balance sheet total / % du total du bilan en fin d'exercice

	1988	1989	1990	1991	1992	1993	1994	
Assets								**Actif**
67. Cash & balance with Central bank	0.36	0.26	0.24	0.21	0.26	0.09	0.06	67. Caisse & solde auprès de la Banque centrale
68. Interbank deposits	23.97	24.73	25.31	23.97	20.01	22.14	21.64	68. Dépôts interbancaires
69. Loans	57.74	57.60	56.44	55.53	60.45	61.63	61.25	69. Prêts
70. Securities	10.15	10.01	10.15	12.61	11.90	12.49	13.69	70. Valeurs mobilières
71. Other assets	7.79	7.40	7.85	7.68	7.38	3.65	3.36	71. Autres actifs
Liabilities								**Passif**
72. Capital & reserves	5.65	6.30	6.81	7.15	7.34	9.10	9.14	72. Capital et réserves
73. Borrowing from Central bank	0.43	0.38	0.87	0.12	0.06	0.25	0.09	73. Emprunts auprès de la Banque centrale
74. Interbank deposits	48.52	47.12	44.84	42.77	36.47	34.64	33.86	74. Dépôts interbancaires
75. Non-bank deposits	2.63	2.39	2.05	4.21	1.96	2.15	3.86	75. Dépôts non bancaires
76. Bonds	29.58	30.95	32.48	33.12	41.02	46.44	45.42	76. Obligations
77. Other liabilities	13.18	12.84	12.95	12.63	13.15	7.41	7.62	77. Autres engagements
Memoranda								*Pour mémoire*
78. Short-term securities	..	..	..	..	..	..	..	*78. Titres à court terme*
79. Bonds	..	..	..	..	..	6.06	6.49	*79. Obligations*
80. Shares and participations	..	..	..	..	..	5.04	4.90	*80. Actions et participations*
81. Claims on non-residents	1.76	2.05	2.54	3.14	3.96	7.72	7.33	*81. Créances sur des non résidents*
82. Liabilities to non-residents	2.07	1.81	1.93	2.77	3.01	12.85	13.57	*82. Engagements envers des non résidents*

Notes

- Other banks include mutual credit banks, finance companies and specialised financial institutions.

- New series. See notes under All banks.
- Average balance sheet totals (item 29) are based on the average of quarterly totals.

Change in methodology:

- See notes under All banks.

Notes

- Autres banques comprennent les caisses de crédit municipal, les sociétés financières et les institutions financières spécialisées.

- Nouvelles séries (voir notes sous Ensemble des banques).
- La moyenne du total des actifs/passifs (poste 29) est basée sur la moyenne des totaux des situations trimestrielles.

Changement méthodologique :

- Voir notes sous Ensemble des banques.

GERMANY / ALLEMAGNE

All banks / **Ensemble des banques**

Million DM / *Millions de DM*

	1985	1986	1987	1988	1989	1990	1991	1992	1993 (1)	1994
INCOME STATEMENT / **COMPTE DE RESULTATS**										
1. Interest income / Produits financiers	180527	181159	182155	191817	224774	272413	317946	356962	384049	382080
2. Interest expenses / Frais financiers	120692	116811	117875	125596	157915	201200	236652	266815	276603	260654
3. Net interest income / Produits financiers nets	59835	64348	64280	66221	66859	71213	81294	90147	107446	121426
4. Non-interest income (net) / Produits non financiers (nets)	15515	16335	16131	15442	22957	26055	25789	28250	33327	29282
5. Gross income / Résultat brut	75350	80683	80411	81663	89816	97268	107083	118397	140773	150708
6. Operating expenses / Frais d'exploitation	45627	50530	53176	55598	57993	62987	69779	76406	87828	91434
7. Net income / Résultat net	29723	30153	27235	26065	31823	34281	37304	41991	52945	59274
8. Provisions (net) / Provisions (nettes)	11958	11488	10477	6808	15294	16807	14008	17325	23363	29960
9. Profit before tax / Bénéfices avant impôt	17765	18665	16758	19257	16529	17474	23296	24666	29582	29314
10. Income tax / Impôt	11393	11595	10316	11965	9275	9408	13585	15266	16313	14335
11. Profit after tax / Bénéfices après impôt	6372	7070	6442	7292	7254	8066	9711	9400	13269	14979
12. Distributed profit / Bénéfices distribués	4417	5063	4844	5088	5506	5828	6192	6522	8712	9464
13. Retained profit / Bénéfices mis en réserve	1955	2007	1598	2204	1748	2238	3519	2878	4557	5515
Memoranda / *Pour mémoire*										
14. Staff costs / Frais de personnel	*29379*	*32328*	*34180*	*35770*	*36971*	*40178*	*44264*	*48301*	*53949*	*55650*
15. Provisions on loans / Provisions sur prêts	*11661*	*11142*	*10218*	*6736*	*15093*	*16295*	*13680*	*16900*	*23042*	*28454*
16. Provisions on securities (2) / Provisions sur titres (2)	..	..	..	..	..	..	..	..	..	..
BALANCE SHEET / **BILAN**										
Assets / **Actif**										
17. Cash & balance with Central bank / Caisse & solde auprès de la Banque centrale	69835	71528	75478	76127	85858	92447	93057	101914	95002	77324
18. Interbank deposits / Dépôts interbancaires	541786	641874	703121	773067	855091	942832	957079	1008667	1205859	1239952
19. Loans / Prêts	1525921	1616444	1684653	1802314	1923523	2103045	2369096	2594859	2988906	3197909
20. Securities / Valeurs mobilières	398718	433365	476356	511376	535369	627941	667974	753966	1023748	1158357
21. Other assets / Autres actifs	73062	80010	81740	84842	90902	95027	114479	113267	137687	138124
Liabilities / **Passif**										
22. Capital & reserves / Capital et réserves	92823	105015	113259	119755	133480	146444	161709	187401	217654	246503
23. Borrowing from Central bank / Emprunts auprès de la Banque centrale	87133	81888	71563	125163	153961	164043	186258	152691	231356	198440
24. Interbank deposits / Dépôts interbancaires	568000	640764	694531	758172	798405	914820	964155	1100162	1245884	1428941
25. Non-bank deposits / Dépôts non bancaires	1408483	1532971	1632736	1733511	1843035	2010213	2197726	2354476	2783864	2850359
26. Bonds / Obligations	35817	374807	397643	392924	434797	480036	526178	586482	720182	838650
27. Other liabilities / Autres engagements	94666	107776	111616	118201	127065	145736	165659	191461	252262	248773
Balance sheet total / **Total du bilan**										
28. End-year total / En fin d'exercice	2609322	2843221	3021348	3247726	3490743	3861292	4201685	4572673	5451202	5811666
29. Average total / Moyen	2481800	2695352	2901013	3101033	3318573	3625716	3993446	4359930	5061788	5560841
Memoranda / *Pour mémoire*										
30. Short-term securities / Titres à court terme	*69639*	*64291*	*67080*	*58176*	*51859*	*104948*	*132600*	*134122*	*171279*	*148225*
31. Bonds / Obligations	*287412*	*318939*	*353433*	*394145*	*412249*	*431455*	*432463*	*497933*	*696572*	*831214*
32. Shares and participations / Actions et participations	*41667*	*50135*	*55843*	*59055*	*71261*	*91538*	*102911*	*121911*	*155897*	*178918*
33. Claims on non-residents / Créances sur des non résidents	*298645*	*374699*	*413771*	*494438*	*572825*	*745902*	*687172*	*730577*	*934094*	*928465*
34. Liabilities to non-residents / Engagements envers des non résidents	*249585*	*251922*	*275524*	*328618*	*337417*	*440078*	*423857*	*530575*	*576967*	*693487*
SUPPLEMENTARY INFORMATION / **RENSEIGNEMENTS COMPLEMENTAIRES**										
35. Number of institutions / Nombre d'institutions	4439	4465	4340	4223	4089	3913	3716	3517	3769	3613
36. Number of branches / Nombre de succursales	38867	39812	39744	39679	39651	39576	39228	39295	44922	44436
37. Number of employees (x 1000) / Nombre de salariés (x 1000)	NA	NA	NA	NA	NA	NA	NA	NA	NA	NA

GERMANY

All banks

Per cent

INCOME STATEMENT ANALYSIS

	1985	1986	1987	1988	1989	1990	1991	1992	1993 (1)	1994
% of average balance sheet total										
38. Interest income	7.27	6.72	6.28	6.19	6.77	7.51	7.96	8.19	7.59	6.87
39. Interest expenses	4.86	4.33	4.06	4.05	4.76	5.55	5.93	6.12	5.46	4.69
40. Net interest income	2.41	2.39	2.22	2.14	2.01	1.96	2.04	2.07	2.12	2.18
41. Non-interest income (net)	0.63	0.61	0.56	0.50	0.69	0.72	0.65	0.65	0.66	0.53
42. Gross income	3.04	2.99	2.77	2.63	2.71	2.68	2.68	2.72	2.78	2.71
43. Operating expenses	1.84	1.87	1.83	1.79	1.75	1.74	1.75	1.75	1.74	1.64
44. Net income	1.20	1.12	0.94	0.84	0.96	0.95	0.93	0.96	1.05	1.07
45. Provisions (net)	0.48	0.43	0.36	0.22	0.46	0.46	0.35	0.40	0.46	0.54
46. Profit before tax	0.72	0.69	0.58	0.62	0.50	0.48	0.58	0.57	0.58	0.53
47. Income tax	0.46	0.43	0.36	0.39	0.28	0.26	0.34	0.35	0.32	0.26
48. Profit after tax	0.26	0.26	0.22	0.24	0.22	0.22	0.24	0.22	0.26	0.27
49. Distributed profit	0.18	0.19	0.17	0.16	0.17	0.16	0.16	0.15	0.17	0.17
50. Retained profit	0.08	0.07	0.06	0.07	0.05	0.06	0.09	0.07	0.09	0.10
51. Staff costs	1.18	1.20	1.18	1.15	1.11	1.11	1.11	1.11	1.07	1.00
52. Provisions on loans	0.47	0.41	0.35	0.22	0.45	0.45	0.34	0.39	0.46	0.51
53. Provisions on securities (2)	:	:	:	:	:	:	:	:	:	:
% of gross income										
54. Net interest income	79.41	79.75	79.94	81.09	74.44	73.21	75.92	76.14	76.33	80.57
55. Non-interest income (net)	20.59	20.25	20.06	18.91	25.56	26.79	24.08	23.86	23.67	19.43
56. Operating expenses	60.55	62.63	66.13	68.08	64.57	64.76	65.16	64.53	62.39	60.67
57. Net income	39.45	37.37	33.87	31.92	35.43	35.24	34.84	35.47	37.61	39.33
58. Provisions (net)	15.87	14.24	13.03	8.34	17.03	17.28	13.08	14.63	16.60	19.88
59. Profit before tax	23.58	23.13	20.84	23.58	18.40	17.96	21.76	20.83	21.01	19.45
60. Income tax	15.12	14.37	12.83	14.65	10.33	9.67	12.69	12.89	11.59	9.51
61. Profit after tax	8.46	8.76	8.01	8.93	8.08	8.29	9.07	7.94	9.43	9.94
62. Staff costs	38.99	40.07	42.51	43.80	41.16	41.31	41.34	40.80	38.32	36.93
% of net income										
63. Provisions (net)	40.23	38.10	38.47	26.12	48.06	49.03	37.55	41.26	44.13	50.54
64. Profit before tax	59.77	61.90	61.53	73.88	51.94	50.97	62.45	58.74	55.87	49.46
65. Income tax	38.33	38.45	37.88	45.90	29.15	27.44	36.42	36.36	30.81	24.18
66. Profit after tax	21.44	23.45	23.65	27.98	22.79	23.53	26.03	22.39	25.06	25.27

ALLEMAGNE

Ensemble des banques

Pourcentage

ANALYSE DU COMPTE DE RESULTATS

% du total moyen du bilan
38. Produits financiers
39. Frais financiers
40. Produits financiers nets
41. Produits non financiers (nets)
42. Résultat brut
43. Frais d'exploitation
44. Résultat net
45. Provisions (nettes)
46. Bénéfices avant impôt
47. Impôt
48. Bénéfices après impôt
49. Bénéfices distribués
50. Bénéfices mis en réserve
51. Frais de personnel
52. Provisions sur prêts
53. Provisions sur titres (2)

% du total du résultat brut
54. Produits financiers nets
55. Produits non financiers (nets)
56. Frais d'exploitation
57. Résultat net
58. Provisions (nettes)
59. Bénéfices avant impôt
60. Impôt
61. Bénéfices après impôt
62. Frais de personnel

% du total du résultat net
63. Provisions (nettes)
64. Bénéfices avant impôt
65. Impôt
66. Bénéfices après impôt

GERMANY
All banks

Per cent / *Pourcentage*

BALANCE SHEET ANALYSIS / **ANALYSE DU BILAN**

% of year-end balance sheet total / % du total du bilan en fin d'exercice

	1985	1986	1987	1988	1989	1990	1991	1992	1993 (1)	1994	
Assets											**Actif**
67. Cash & balance with Central bank	2.68	2.52	2.50	2.34	2.46	2.39	2.21	2.23	1.74	1.33	67. Caisse & solde auprès de la Banque centrale
68. Interbank deposits	20.76	22.58	23.27	23.80	24.50	24.42	22.78	22.06	22.12	21.34	68. Dépôts interbancaires
69. Loans	58.48	56.85	55.76	55.49	55.10	54.46	56.38	56.75	54.83	55.03	69. Prêts
70. Securities	15.28	15.24	15.77	15.75	15.34	16.26	15.90	16.49	18.78	19.93	70. Valeurs mobilières
71. Other assets	2.80	2.81	2.71	2.61	2.60	2.46	2.72	2.48	2.53	2.38	71. Autres actifs
Liabilities											**Passif**
72. Capital & reserves	3.56	3.69	3.75	3.69	3.82	3.79	3.85	4.10	3.99	4.24	72. Capital et réserves
73. Borrowing from Central bank	3.34	2.88	2.37	3.85	4.41	4.25	4.43	3.34	4.24	3.41	73. Emprunts auprès de la Banque centrale
74. Interbank deposits	21.77	22.54	22.99	23.34	22.87	23.69	22.95	24.06	22.86	24.59	74. Dépôts interbancaires
75. Non-bank deposits	53.98	53.92	54.04	53.38	52.80	52.06	52.31	51.49	51.07	49.05	75. Dépôts non bancaires
76. Bonds	13.73	13.18	13.16	12.10	12.46	12.43	12.52	12.83	13.21	14.43	76. Obligations
77. Other liabilities	3.63	3.79	3.69	3.64	3.64	3.77	3.94	4.19	4.63	4.28	77. Autres engagements
Memoranda											*Pour mémoire*
78. Short-term securities	2.67	2.26	2.22	1.79	1.49	2.72	3.16	2.93	3.14	2.55	78. Titres à court terme
79. Bonds	11.01	11.22	11.70	12.14	11.81	11.17	10.29	10.89	12.78	14.30	79. Obligations
80. Shares and participations	1.60	1.76	1.85	1.82	2.04	2.37	2.45	2.67	2.86	3.08	80. Actions et participations
81. Claims on non-residents	11.45	13.18	13.69	15.22	16.41	19.32	16.35	15.98	17.14	15.98	81. Créances sur des non résidents
82. Liabilities to non-residents	9.57	8.86	9.12	10.12	9.67	11.40	10.09	11.60	10.58	11.93	82. Engagements envers des non résidents

1. Break in series due to change in methodology.
2. Included under "Provisions on loans" (item 15 or item 52).

Notes

- All banks include Commercial banks, Regional giro institutions, Savings banks, Regional institutions of co-operative banks and Co-operative banks.

- Average balance sheet totals (item 29) are based on twelve end-month data.

Change in methodology:

- As from 1985, all credit co-operatives are included in the data.

- As from 1986, the so-called Instalment sales financing institutions are included in the data.

- As from 1993, data include eastern German credit institutions and are in accordance with the new accounting regulations.

1. Rupture de comparabilité dans les séries dûe aux changements méthodologiques.
2. Inclus sous "Provisions sur prêts" (poste 15 ou poste 52).

Notes

- L'Ensemble des banques comprend les Banques commerciales, les Organismes régionaux de compensation, les Caisses d'épargne, les Institutions régionales des banques mutualistes et les Banques mutualistes.

- La moyenne du total des actifs/passifs (poste 29) est basée sur douze données de fin de mois.

Changement méthodologique :

- Depuis 1985, les données comprennent l'ensemble des banques mutualistes.

- Depuis 1986, les données comprennent les Etablissements de financement des ventes à crédit.

- Depuis 1993, les données comprennent les organismes de crédit d'Allemagne orientale et sont conformes aux nouvelles règles de comptabilité.

GERMANY

Commercial banks

Million DM

ALLEMAGNE

Banques commerciales

Millions de DM

	1985	1986	1987	1988	1989	1990	1991	1992	1993 (1)	1994
INCOME STATEMENT										
1. Interest income	51916	54708	55057	60714	75952	93502	109785	125197	128218	123283
2. Interest expenses	34339	33552	34574	39455	54081	68910	80576	92094	91170	82808
3. Net interest income	17577	21156	20483	21259	21871	24592	29209	33103	37048	40475
4. Non-interest income (net)	7551	8872	8709	9283	12315	13742	12825	14735	16981	13837
5. Gross income	25128	30028	29192	30542	34186	38334	42034	47838	54029	54312
6. Operating expenses	15799	18911	19976	21137	22245	24427	27834	30451	33026	34646
7. Net income	9329	11117	9216	9405	11941	13907	14200	17387	21003	19666
8. Provisions (net)	3377	4518	3872	2374	4467	6328	6317	10313	11746	9573
9. Profit before tax	5952	6599	5344	7031	7474	7579	7883	7074	9257	10093
10. Income tax	3234	3481	2737	3839	3994	3434	3883	3821	3705	3685
11. Profit after tax	2718	3118	2607	3192	3480	4145	4000	3253	5552	6408
12. Distributed profit	1889	2329	2202	2309	2584	3041	2840	2894	4224	4584
13. Retained profit	829	789	405	883	896	1104	1160	359	1328	1824
Memoranda										
14. Staff costs	10465	12336	12985	13729	14259	15555	17477	18961	20452	20947
15. Provisions on loans	3183	4304	3697	2353	4314	5983	6157	10046	11539	9469
16. Provisions on securities (2)	..	..	..	..	..	..	..	..	..	..
BALANCE SHEET										
Assets										
17. Cash & balance with Central bank	29095	29491	30940	28116	32043	35665	37627	38792	35404	25057
18. Interbank deposits	187019	213482	230538	254751	283241	311569	314517	345687	392646	429534
19. Loans	438301	506244	537300	602864	664124	757560	865040	938289	1055138	1105296
20. Securities	100452	108981	111209	117005	132739	156499	177994	205865	296656	315399
21. Other assets	15655	21459	22180	24399	26549	25353	26308	34854	42200	38270
Liabilities										
22. Capital & reserves	32633	40298	44399	47034	55417	64922	72356	82228	91355	106070
23. Borrowing from Central bank	34776	41126	34090	50803	60371	57210	60178	56101	99026	74264
24. Interbank deposits	211301	247319	266114	293506	314931	348978	362609	415905	441897	545674
25. Non-bank deposits	377964	423698	454523	501012	551267	634532	727226	784343	885548	849713
26. Bonds	77443	81095	84686	84760	101409	115170	125832	141938	196115	236239
27. Other liabilities	36405	46121	48355	50020	55301	65834	73285	82972	108103	101596
Balance sheet total										
28. End-year total	770522	879657	932167	1027135	1138696	1286646	1421486	1563487	1822044	1913556
29. Average total	719619	818825	889239	968536	1072589	1203377	1350934	1495870	1697098	1852710
Memoranda										
30. Short-term securities	22960	18210	17037	16986	13915	23196	38346	39895	62240	48808
31. Bonds	52792	60112	61295	65546	75707	76814	79780	98773	152047	178096
32. Shares and participations	24700	30659	32877	34473	43117	56489	59868	67197	82369	88495
33. Claims on non-residents	185372	227950	246090	298773	330289	397119	405332	437475	552554	596035
34. Liabilities to non-residents	190391	195971	211822	252393	260075	306926	319405	373253	410965	480595
SUPPLEMENTARY INFORMATION										
35. Number of institutions	173	252	255	259	264	274	281	276	270	273
36. Number of branches	5449	6346	6260	6242	6252	6255	6044	6394	7331	7303
37. Number of employees (x 1000)	NA	NA	NA	NA	NA	NA	NA	NA	NA	NA

COMPTE DE RESULTATS
1. Produits financiers
2. Frais financiers
3. Produits financiers nets
4. Produits non financiers (nets)
5. Résultat brut
6. Frais d'exploitation
7. Résultat net
8. Provisions (nettes)
9. Bénéfices avant impôt
10. Impôt
11. Bénéfices après impôt
12. Bénéfices distribués
13. Bénéfices mis en réserve

Pour mémoire
14. Frais de personnel
15. Provisions sur prêts
16. Provisions sur titres (2)

BILAN

Actif
17. Caisse & solde auprès de la Banque centrale
18. Dépôts interbancaires
19. Prêts
20. Valeurs mobilières
21. Autres actifs

Passif
22. Capital et réserves
23. Emprunts auprès de la Banque centrale
24. Dépôts interbancaires
25. Dépôts non bancaires
26. Obligations
27. Autres engagements

Total du bilan
28. En fin d'exercice
29. Moyen

Pour mémoire
30. Titres à court terme
31. Obligations
32. Actions et participations
33. Créances sur des non résidents
34. Engagements envers des non résidents

RENSEIGNEMENTS COMPLEMENTAIRES
35. Nombre d'institutions
36. Nombre de succursales
37. Nombre de salariés (x 1000)

Commercial banks — Banques commerciales

Per cent — *Pourcentage*

INCOME STATEMENT ANALYSIS — ANALYSE DU COMPTE DE RESULTATS

	1985	1986	1987	1988	1989	1990	1991	1992	1993 (1)	1994		
% of average balance sheet total												**% du total moyen du bilan**
38. Interest income	7.21	6.68	6.19	6.27	7.08	7.77	8.13	8.37	7.56	6.65	38.	Produits financiers
39. Interest expenses	4.77	4.10	3.89	4.07	5.04	5.73	5.96	6.16	5.37	4.47	39.	Frais financiers
40. Net interest income	2.44	2.58	2.30	2.19	2.04	2.04	2.16	2.21	2.18	2.18	40.	Produits financiers nets
41. Non-interest income (net)	1.05	1.08	0.98	0.96	1.15	1.14	0.95	0.99	1.00	0.75	41.	Produits non financiers (nets)
42. Gross income	3.49	3.67	3.28	3.15	3.19	3.19	3.11	3.20	3.18	2.93	42.	Résultat brut
43. Operating expenses	2.20	2.31	2.25	2.18	2.07	2.03	2.06	2.04	1.95	1.87	43.	Frais d'exploitation
44. Net income	1.30	1.36	1.04	0.97	1.11	1.16	1.05	1.16	1.24	1.06	44.	Résultat net
45. Provisions (net)	0.47	0.55	0.44	0.25	0.42	0.53	0.47	0.69	0.69	0.52	45.	Provisions (nettes)
46. Profit before tax	0.83	0.81	0.60	0.73	0.70	0.63	0.58	0.47	0.55	0.54	46.	Bénéfices avant impôt
47. Income tax	0.45	0.43	0.31	0.40	0.37	0.29	0.29	0.26	0.22	0.20	47.	Impôt
48. Profit after tax	0.38	0.38	0.29	0.33	0.32	0.34	0.30	0.22	0.33	0.35	48.	Bénéfices après impôt
49. Distributed profit	0.26	0.28	0.25	0.24	0.24	0.25	0.21	0.19	0.25	0.25	49.	Bénéfices distribués
50. Retained profit	0.12	0.10	0.05	0.09	0.08	0.09	0.09	0.02	0.08	0.10	50.	Bénéfices mis en réserve
51. Staff costs	1.45	1.51	1.46	1.42	1.33	1.29	1.29	1.27	1.21	1.13	51.	Frais de personnel
52. Provisions on loans	0.44	0.53	0.42	0.24	0.40	0.50	0.46	0.67	0.68	0.51	52.	Provisions sur prêts
53. Provisions on securities (2)	:	:	:	:	:	:	:	:	:	:	53.	Provisions sur titres (2)
% of gross income												**% du total du résultat brut**
54. Net interest income	69.95	70.45	70.17	69.61	63.98	64.15	69.49	69.20	68.57	74.52	54.	Produits financiers nets
55. Non-interest income (net)	30.05	29.55	29.83	30.39	36.02	35.85	30.51	30.80	31.43	25.48	55.	Produits non financiers (nets)
56. Operating expenses	62.87	62.98	68.43	69.21	65.07	63.72	66.22	63.65	61.13	63.79	56.	Frais d'exploitation
57. Net income	37.13	37.02	31.57	30.79	34.93	36.28	33.78	36.35	38.87	36.21	57.	Résultat net
58. Provisions (net)	13.44	15.05	13.26	7.77	13.07	16.51	15.03	21.56	21.74	17.63	58.	Provisions (nettes)
59. Profit before tax	23.69	21.98	18.31	23.02	21.86	19.77	18.75	14.79	17.13	18.58	59.	Bénéfices avant impôt
60. Income tax	12.87	11.59	9.38	12.57	11.68	8.96	9.24	7.99	6.86	6.78	60.	Impôt
61. Profit after tax	10.82	10.38	8.93	10.45	10.18	10.81	9.52	6.80	10.28	11.80	61.	Bénéfices après impôt
62. Staff costs	41.65	41.08	44.48	44.95	41.71	40.58	41.58	39.64	37.85	38.57	62.	Frais de personnel
% of net income												**% du total du résultat net**
63. Provisions (net)	36.20	40.64	42.01	25.24	37.41	45.50	44.49	59.31	55.93	48.68	63.	Provisions (nettes)
64. Profit before tax	63.80	59.36	57.99	74.76	62.59	54.50	55.51	40.69	44.07	51.32	64.	Bénéfices avant impôt
65. Income tax	34.67	31.31	29.70	40.82	33.45	24.69	27.35	21.98	17.64	18.74	65.	Impôt
66. Profit after tax	29.13	28.05	28.29	33.94	29.14	29.81	28.17	18.71	26.43	32.58	66.	Bénéfices après impôt

GERMANY

Commercial banks

ALLEMAGNE

Banques commerciales

Per cent	1985	1986	1987	1988	1989	1990	1991	1992	1993 (1)	1994	Pourcentage
BALANCE SHEET ANALYSIS											**ANALYSE DU BILAN**
% of year-end balance sheet total											*% du total du bilan en fin d'exercice*
Assets											**Actif**
67. Cash & balance with Central bank	3.78	3.35	3.32	2.74	2.81	2.77	2.65	2.48	1.94	1.31	67. Caisse & solde auprès de la Banque centrale
68. Interbank deposits	24.27	24.27	24.73	24.80	24.87	24.22	22.13	22.11	21.55	22.45	68. Dépôts interbancaires
69. Loans	56.88	57.55	57.64	58.69	58.32	58.88	60.85	60.01	57.91	57.76	69. Prêts
70. Securities	13.04	12.39	11.93	11.39	11.66	12.16	12.52	13.17	16.28	16.48	70. Valeurs mobilières
71. Other assets	2.03	2.44	2.38	2.38	2.33	1.97	1.85	2.23	2.32	2.00	71. Autres actifs
Liabilities											**Passif**
72. Capital & reserves	4.24	4.58	4.76	4.58	4.87	5.05	5.09	5.26	5.01	5.54	72. Capital et réserves
73. Borrowing from Central bank	4.51	4.68	3.66	4.95	5.30	4.45	4.23	3.59	5.43	3.88	73. Emprunts auprès de la Banque centrale
74. Interbank deposits	27.42	28.12	28.55	28.58	27.66	27.12	25.51	26.60	24.25	28.52	74. Dépôts interbancaires
75. Non-bank deposits	49.05	48.17	48.76	48.78	48.41	49.32	51.16	50.17	48.60	44.40	75. Dépôts non bancaires
76. Bonds	10.05	9.22	9.08	8.25	8.91	8.95	8.85	9.08	10.76	12.35	76. Obligations
77. Other liabilities	4.72	5.24	5.19	4.87	4.86	5.12	5.16	5.31	5.93	5.31	77. Autres engagements
Memoranda											*Pour mémoire*
78. Short-term securities	2.98	2.07	1.83	1.65	1.22	1.80	2.70	2.55	3.42	2.55	78. Titres à court terme
79. Bonds	6.85	6.83	6.58	6.38	6.65	5.97	5.61	6.32	8.34	9.31	79. Obligations
80. Shares and participations	3.21	3.49	3.53	3.36	3.79	4.39	4.21	4.30	4.52	4.62	80. Actions et participations
81. Claims on non-residents	24.06	25.91	26.40	29.09	29.01	30.86	28.51	27.98	30.33	31.15	81. Créances sur des non résidents
82. Liabilities to non-residents	24.71	22.28	22.72	24.57	22.84	23.85	22.47	23.87	22.56	25.12	82. Engagements envers des non résidents

1. Break in series due to change in methodology.

2. Included under "Provisions on loans" (item 15 or item 52).

Notes

• Average balance sheet totals (item 29) are based on twelve end-month data.

Change in methodology:

• As from 1986, the so called Instalment sales financing institutions are included in the data.

• As from 1993, data include eastern German credit institutions and are in accordance with the new accounting regulations.

1. Rupture de comparabilité dans les séries dûe aux changements méthodologiques.

2. Inclus sous "Provisions sur prêts" (poste 15 ou poste 52).

Notes

• La moyenne du total des actifs/passifs (poste 29) est basée sur douze données de fin de mois.

Changement méthodologique :

• Depuis 1986, les données comprennent les Etablissements de financement des ventes à crédit.

• Depuis 1993, les données comprennent les organismes de crédit d'Allemagne orientale et sont conformes aux nouvelles règles de comptabilité.

GERMANY / ALLEMAGNE

Large commercial banks / Grandes banques commerciales

Million DM / Millions de DM

	1985	1986	1987	1988	1989	1990	1991	1992	1993 (1)	1994	
INCOME STATEMENT											**COMPTE DE RESULTATS**
1. Interest income	24185	24338	24256	28090	35221	43650	50489	55719	56093	51849	1. Produits financiers
2. Interest expenses	14769	13370	14257	17400	23823	30612	34827	38594	37872	33191	2. Frais financiers
3. Net interest income	9416	10968	9999	10690	11398	13038	15662	17125	18221	18658	3. Produits financiers nets
4. Non-interest income (net)	4261	4169	4313	4901	5773	6997	6315	8204	9625	7805	4. Produits non financiers (nets)
5. Gross income	13677	15137	14312	15591	17171	20035	21977	25329	27846	26463	5. Résultat brut
6. Operating expenses	9063	10056	10442	11105	11571	12657	14795	16027	17075	17780	6. Frais d'exploitation
7. Net income	4614	5081	3870	4486	5600	7378	7182	9302	10771	8683	7. Résultat net
8. Provisions (net)	1095	1443	1452	517	1053	2708	2395	4423	6372	3877	8. Provisions (nettes)
9. Profit before tax	3519	3638	2418	3969	4547	4670	4787	4879	4399	4806	9. Bénéfices avant impôt
10. Income tax	2017	1987	1201	2245	2493	1915	2320	1999	1706	1680	10. Impôt
11. Profit after tax	1502	1651	1217	1724	2054	2755	2467	2880	2693	3126	11. Bénéfices après impôt
12. Distributed profit	862	1114	1003	1037	1304	1962	1543	1586	1668	1976	12. Bénéfices distribués
13. Retained profit	640	537	214	687	750	793	924	1294	1025	1150	13. Bénéfices mis en réserve
Memoranda											*Pour mémoire*
14. Staff costs	*6104*	*6770*	*7012*	*7457*	*7702*	*8348*	*9671*	*10378*	*11105*	*11314*	*14. Frais de personnel*
15. Provisions on loans	*933*	*1296*	*1329*	*504*	*1035*	*2491*	*2327*	*4217*	*6259*	*3877*	*15. Provisions sur prêts*
16. Provisions on securities (2)	..	..	..	..	..	..	..	..	..	..	*16. Provisions sur titres (2)*
BALANCE SHEET											**BILAN**
Assets											**Actif**
17. Cash & balance with Central bank	15575	15771	17090	14265	17006	20034	22041	21456	20936	14594	17. Caisse & solde auprès de la Banque centrale
18. Interbank deposits	93352	101248	110062	126057	135759	155820	151688	173501	185179	220925	18. Dépôts interbancaires
19. Loans	191921	212505	227226	267545	296500	345721	405306	418642	447449	457923	19. Prêts
20. Securities	50246	55225	53877	55507	63955	74472	83023	92907	140141	146082	20. Valeurs mobilières
21. Other assets	6983	7391	7735	8133	8385	8254	8240	10760	14481	12093	21. Autres actifs
Liabilities											**Passif**
22. Capital & reserves	15839	18766	20761	22133	26944	31303	34258	38059	42120	46446	22. Capital et réserves
23. Borrowing from Central bank	15539	16388	13552	17319	23045	17203	24044	18426	20868	26561	23. Emprunts auprès de la Banque centrale
24. Interbank deposits	91277	99229	105502	123272	127905	151037	148965	175391	181824	247249	24. Dépôts interbancaires
25. Non-bank deposits	200721	217879	233581	264367	291839	343846	402067	423614	473267	431910	25. Dépôts non bancaires
26. Bonds	13948	16008	17005	17585	23021	26870	26312	28232	48934	58833	26. Obligations
27. Other liabilities	20753	23870	25589	26831	28851	34042	34652	33544	41173	40618	27. Autres engagements
Balance sheet total											**Total du bilan**
28. End-year total	358077	392140	415990	471507	521605	604301	670298	717266	808186	851617	28. En fin d'exercice
29. Average total	335269	365894	399553	446084	494426	563239	641255	694382	768766	829919	29. Moyen
Memoranda											*Pour mémoire*
30. Short-term securities	*12216*	*9151*	*7653*	*8334*	*8291*	*10071*	*14800*	*15548*	*28641*	*26708*	*30. Titres à court terme*
31. Bonds	*22016*	*24818*	*23050*	*24103*	*26290*	*25355*	*28915*	*33627*	*59251*	*66615*	*31. Obligations*
32. Shares and participations	*16014*	*21256*	*23174*	*23070*	*29374*	*39046*	*39308*	*43732*	*52249*	*52759*	*32. Actions et participations*
33. Claims on non-residents	*114577*	*138091*	*147374*	*183131*	*194585*	*233940*	*235265*	*257909*	*311555*	*351591*	*33. Créances sur des non résidents*
34. Liabilities to non-residents	*119745*	*124004*	*131661*	*163674*	*166807*	*197384*	*202878*	*232226*	*252796*	*305451*	*34. Engagements envers des non résidents*
SUPPLEMENTARY INFORMATION											**RENSEIGNEMENTS COMPLEMENTAIRES**
35. Number of institutions	6	6	6	6	6	6	4	4	3	3	35. Nombre d'institutions
36. Number of branches	3115	3118	3120	3108	3110	3105	3043	3036	3598	3621	36. Nombre de succursales
37. Number of employees (x 1000)	NA	NA	NA	NA	NA	NA	NA	NA	NA	NA	37. Nombre de salariés (x 1000)

GERMANY

Large commercial banks

ALLEMAGNE

Grandes banques commerciales

Per cent / *Pourcentage*

	1985	1986	1987	1988	1989	1990	1991	1992	1993 (1)	1994	
INCOME STATEMENT ANALYSIS											**ANALYSE DU COMPTE DE RESULTATS**
% of average balance sheet total											**% du total moyen du bilan**
38. Interest income	7.21	6.65	6.07	6.30	7.12	7.75	7.87	8.02	7.30	6.25	38. Produits financiers
39. Interest expenses	4.41	3.65	3.57	3.90	4.82	5.43	5.43	5.56	4.93	4.00	39. Frais financiers
40. Net interest income	2.81	3.00	2.50	2.40	2.31	2.31	2.44	2.47	2.37	2.25	40. Produits financiers nets
41. Non-interest income (net)	1.27	1.14	1.08	1.10	-1.17	1.24	0.98	1.18	1.25	0.94	41. Produits non financiers (nets)
42. Gross income	4.08	4.14	3.58	3.50	3.47	3.56	3.43	3.65	3.62	3.19	42. Résultat brut
43. Operating expenses	2.70	2.75	2.61	2.49	2.34	2.25	2.31	2.31	2.22	2.14	43. Frais d'exploitation
44. Net income	1.38	1.39	0.97	1.01	1.13	1.31	1.12	1.34	1.40	1.05	44. Résultat net
45. Provisions (net)	0.33	0.39	0.36	0.12	0.21	0.48	0.37	0.64	0.83	0.47	45. Provisions (nettes)
46. Profit before tax	1.05	0.99	0.61	0.89	0.92	0.83	0.75	0.70	0.57	0.58	46. Bénéfices avant impôt
47. Income tax	0.60	0.54	0.30	0.50	0.50	0.34	0.36	0.29	0.22	0.20	47. Impôt
48. Profit after tax	0.45	0.45	0.30	0.39	0.42	0.49	0.38	0.41	0.35	0.38	48. Bénéfices après impôt
49. Distributed profit	0.26	0.30	0.25	0.23	0.26	0.35	0.24	0.23	0.22	0.24	49. Bénéfices distribués
50. Retained profit	0.19	0.15	0.05	0.15	0.15	0.14	0.14	0.19	0.13	0.14	50. Bénéfices mis en réserve
51. Staff costs	1.82	1.85	1.75	1.67	1.56	1.48	1.51	1.49	1.44	1.36	51. Frais de personnel
52. Provisions on loans	0.28	0.35	0.33	0.11	0.21	0.44	0.36	0.61	0.81	0.47	52. Provisions sur prêts
53. Provisions on securities (2)	..	..	..	..	..	..	..	..	..	..	53. Provisions sur titres (2)
% of gross income											**% du total du résultat brut**
54. Net interest income	68.85	72.46	69.86	68.57	66.38	65.08	71.27	67.61	65.43	70.51	54. Produits financiers nets
55. Non-interest income (net)	31.15	27.54	30.14	31.43	33.62	34.92	28.73	32.39	34.57	29.49	55. Produits non financiers (nets)
56. Operating expenses	66.26	66.43	72.96	71.23	67.39	63.17	67.32	63.28	61.32	67.19	56. Frais d'exploitation
57. Net income	33.74	33.57	27.04	28.77	32.61	36.83	32.68	36.72	38.68	32.81	57. Résultat net
58. Provisions (net)	8.01	9.53	10.15	3.32	6.13	13.52	10.90	17.46	22.88	14.65	58. Provisions (nettes)
59. Profit before tax	25.73	24.03	16.89	25.46	26.48	23.31	21.78	19.26	15.80	18.16	59. Bénéfices avant impôt
60. Income tax	14.75	13.13	8.39	14.40	14.52	9.56	10.56	7.89	6.13	6.35	60. Impôt
61. Profit after tax	10.98	10.91	8.50	11.06	11.96	13.75	11.23	11.37	9.67	11.81	61. Bénéfices après impôt
62. Staff costs	44.63	44.72	48.99	47.83	44.85	41.67	44.01	40.97	39.88	42.75	62. Frais de personnel
% of net income											**% du total du résultat net**
63. Provisions (net)	23.73	28.40	37.52	11.52	18.80	36.70	33.35	47.55	59.16	44.65	63. Provisions (nettes)
64. Profit before tax	76.27	71.60	62.48	88.48	81.20	63.30	66.65	52.45	40.84	55.35	64. Bénéfices avant impôt
65. Income tax	43.71	39.11	31.03	50.04	44.52	25.96	32.30	21.49	15.84	19.35	65. Impôt
66. Profit after tax	32.55	32.49	31.45	38.43	36.68	37.34	34.35	30.96	25.00	36.00	66. Bénéfices après impôt

GERMANY

Large commercial banks

Grandes banques commerciales

Per cent / *Pourcentage*

BALANCE SHEET ANALYSIS / **ANALYSE DU BILAN**

% of year-end balance sheet total / **% du total du bilan en fin d'exercice**

	1985	1986	1987	1988	1989	1990	1991	1992	1993 (1)	1994		
Assets												**Actif**
67. Cash & balance with Central bank	4.35	4.02	4.11	3.03	3.26	3.32	3.29	2.99	2.59	1.71	67.	Caisse & solde auprès de la Banque centrale
68. Interbank deposits	26.07	25.82	26.46	26.73	26.03	25.79	22.63	24.19	22.91	25.94	68.	Dépôts interbancaires
69. Loans	53.60	54.19	54.62	56.74	56.84	57.21	60.47	58.37	55.36	53.77	69.	Prêts
70. Securities	14.03	14.08	12.95	11.77	12.26	12.32	12.39	12.95	17.34	17.15	70.	Valeurs mobilières
71. Other assets	1.95	1.88	1.86	1.72	1.61	1.37	1.23	1.50	1.79	1.42	71.	Autres actifs
Liabilities												**Passif**
72. Capital & reserves	4.42	4.79	4.99	4.69	5.17	5.18	5.11	5.31	5.21	5.45	72.	Capital et réserves
73. Borrowing from Central bank	4.34	4.18	3.26	3.67	4.42	2.85	3.59	2.57	2.58	3.12	73.	Emprunts auprès de la Banque centrale
74. Interbank deposits	25.49	25.30	25.36	26.14	24.52	24.99	22.22	24.45	22.50	29.03	74.	Dépôts interbancaires
75. Non-bank deposits	56.06	55.56	56.15	56.07	55.95	56.90	59.98	59.06	58.56	50.72	75.	Dépôts non bancaires
76. Bonds	3.90	4.08	4.09	3.73	4.41	4.45	3.93	3.94	6.05	6.91	76.	Obligations
77. Other liabilities	5.80	6.09	6.15	5.69	5.53	5.63	5.17	4.68	5.09	4.77	77.	Autres engagements
Memoranda												*Pour mémoire*
78. Short-term securities	*3.41*	*2.33*	*1.84*	*1.77*	*1.59*	*1.67*	*2.21*	*2.17*	*3.54*	*3.14*	*78.*	*Titres à court terme*
79. Bonds	*6.15*	*6.33*	*5.54*	*5.11*	*5.04*	*4.20*	*4.31*	*4.69*	*7.33*	*7.82*	*79.*	*Obligations*
80. Shares and participations	*4.47*	*5.42*	*5.57*	*4.89*	*5.63*	*6.46*	*5.86*	*6.10*	*6.46*	*6.20*	*80.*	*Actions et participations*
81. Claims on non-residents	*32.00*	*35.21*	*35.43*	*38.84*	*37.31*	*38.71*	*35.10*	*35.96*	*38.55*	*41.29*	*81.*	*Créances sur des non résidents*
82. Liabilities to non-residents	*33.44*	*31.62*	*31.65*	*34.71*	*31.98*	*32.66*	*30.27*	*32.38*	*31.28*	*35.87*	*82.*	*Engagements envers des non résidents*

1. Break in series due to change in methodology.
2. Included under "Provisions on loans" (item 15 or item 52).

Notes

- Large commercial banks are a sub-group of Commercial banks.

- Average balance sheet totals (item 29) are based on twelve end-month data.

Change in methodology:

- As from 1993, data include eastern German credit institutions and are in accordance with the new accounting regulations.

1. Rupture de comparabilité dans les séries due aux changements méthodologiques.
2. Inclus sous "Provisions sur prêts" (poste 15 ou poste 52).

Notes

- Les Grandes banques commerciales sont un sous-groupe des Banques commerciales.

- La moyenne du total des actifs/passifs (poste 29) est basée sur douze données de fin de mois.

Changement méthodologique :

- Depuis 1993, les données comprennent les organismes de crédit d'Allemagne orientale et sont conformes aux nouvelles règles de comptabilité.

Regional giro institutions

Organismes régionaux de compensation

Million DM	1985	1986	1987	1988	1989	1990	1991	1992	1993 (1)	1994	Millions de DM
INCOME STATEMENT											**COMPTE DE RESULTATS**
1. Interest income	38132	37898	38471	40388	46856	56817	67101	76780	82029	85756	1. Produits financiers
2. Interest expenses	33348	33068	33756	35646	42153	52078	61750	70142	74208	75737	2. Frais financiers
3. Net interest income	4784	4830	4715	4742	4703	4739	5351	6638	7821	10019	3. Produits financiers nets
4. Non-interest income (net)	1797	1389	1287	1188	1473	1349	1857	2006	2701	1388	4. Produits non financiers (nets)
5. Gross income	6581	6219	6002	5930	6176	6088	7208	8644	10522	11407	5. Résultat brut
6. Operating expenses	2576	2776	2919	3117	3308	3604	3873	5063	5524	5970	6. Frais d'exploitation
7. Net income	4005	3443	3083	2813	2868	2484	3335	3581	4998	5437	7. Résultat net
8. Provisions (net)	2788	2104	1839	1200	1122	1579	1899	1771	2399	2823	8. Provisions (nettes)
9. Profit before tax	1217	1339	1244	1613	1746	905	1436	1810	2599	2614	9. Bénéfices avant impôt
10. Income tax	796	880	747	1089	1016	433	766	889	1328	1115	10. Impôt
11. Profit after tax	421	459	497	524	730	472	670	921	1271	1499	11. Bénéfices après impôt
12. Distributed profit	283	321	350	359	374	336	327	434	503	550	12. Bénéfices distribués
13. Retained profit	138	138	147	165	356	136	343	487	768	949	13. Bénéfices mis en réserve
Memoranda											*Pour mémoire*
14. Staff costs	1738	1842	1942	2069	2171	2393	2468	3220	3401	3486	14. Frais de personnel
15. Provisions on loans	2740	2005	1787	1174	1090	1551	1825	1697	2398	2656	15. Provisions sur prêts
16. Provisions on securities (1)	..	..	..	..	..	..	..	..	..	..	16. Provisions sur titres (1)
BALANCE SHEET											**BILAN**
Assets											**Actif**
17. Cash & balance with Central bank	4543	4590	3708	4030	5325	7106	4334	5357	5550	3240	17. Caisse & solde auprès de la Banque centrale
18. Interbank deposits	154205	187446	218430	254734	286439	317729	329932	368961	433992	460760	18. Dépôts interbancaires
19. Loans	328885	333939	342577	349487	354110	382774	444196	523715	628712	672947	19. Prêts
20. Securities	59383	59305	60068	62549	69504	116932	124858	158334	201622	224794	20. Valeurs mobilières
21. Other assets	9215	9595	11052	12591	13529	14559	16378	20179	30832	33454	21. Autres actifs
Liabilities											**Passif**
22. Capital & reserves	12160	13341	13930	14624	16331	17442	20265	29846	36348	40788	22. Capital et réserves
23. Borrowing from Central bank	13920	7879	6816	21939	25183	32448	43979	31831	67281	46009	23. Emprunts auprès de la Banque centrale
24. Interbank deposits	141307	158442	171508	198227	213735	280076	305577	371072	419636	446589	24. Dépôts interbancaires
25. Non-bank deposits	112754	130238	149124	165298	178316	191566	211546	260784	309832	346858	25. Dépôts non bancaires
26. Bonds	260911	268873	279056	266228	277285	295797	312236	344492	411510	461832	26. Obligations
27. Other liabilities	15179	16102	15401	17075	18057	21771	26095	38521	56101	53119	27. Autres engagements
Balance sheet total											**Total du bilan**
28. End-year total	556231	594875	635835	683391	728907	839100	919698	1076546	1300708	1395195	28. En fin d'exercice
29. Average total	533905	573933	617561	655600	699495	774961	872439	1021846	1194272	1321304	29. Moyen
Memoranda											*Pour mémoire*
30. Short-term securities	15398	12062	10605	7331	7514	40637	44877	42029	39899	29343	30. Titres à court terme
31. Bonds	37879	40633	42226	47644	52600	63689	65843	97520	138342	167236	31. Obligations
32. Shares and participations	6106	6610	7237	7574	9390	12606	14138	18785	23381	28215	32. Actions et participations
33. Claims on non-residents	94562	118012	130839	155053	184436	272157	222613	247934	304288	284607	33. Créances sur des non résidents
34. Liabilities to non-residents	46261	43867	50691	61614	61469	104877	87723	134346	134531	175500	34. Engagements envers des non résidents
SUPPLEMENTARY INFORMATION											**RENSEIGNEMENTS COMPLEMENTAIRES**
35. Number of institutions	12	12	12	12	11	11	11	12	13	13	35. Nombre d'institutions
36. Number of branches	239	235	231	226	219	309	290	329	436	433	36. Nombre de succursales
37. Number of employees (x 1000)	NA	NA	NA	NA	NA	NA	NA	NA	NA	NA	37. Nombre de salariés (x 1000)

GERMANY

Regional giro institutions

ALLEMAGNE

Organismes régionaux de compensation

Per cent — *Pourcentage*

	1985	1986	1987	1988	1989	1990	1991	1992	1993 (1)	1994	
INCOME STATEMENT ANALYSIS											**ANALYSE DU COMPTE DE RESULTATS**
% of average balance sheet total											**% du total moyen du bilan**
38. Interest income	7.14	6.60	6.23	6.16	6.70	7.33	7.69	7.51	6.87	6.49	38. Produits financiers
39. Interest expenses	6.25	5.76	5.47	5.44	6.03	6.72	7.08	6.86	6.21	5.73	39. Frais financiers
40. Net interest income	0.90	0.84	0.76	0.72	0.67	0.61	0.61	0.65	0.65	0.76	40. Produits financiers nets
41. Non-interest income (net)	0.34	0.24	0.21	0.18	0.21	0.17	0.21	0.20	0.23	0.11	41. Produits non financiers (nets)
42. Gross income	1.23	1.08	0.97	0.90	0.88	0.79	0.83	0.85	0.88	0.86	42. Résultat brut
43. Operating expenses	0.48	0.48	0.47	0.48	0.47	0.47	0.44	0.50	0.46	0.45	43. Frais d'exploitation
44. Net income	0.75	0.60	0.50	0.43	0.41	0.32	0.38	0.35	0.42	0.41	44. Résultat net
45. Provisions (net)	0.52	0.37	0.30	0.18	0.16	0.20	0.22	0.17	0.20	0.21	45. Provisions (nettes)
46. Profit before tax	0.23	0.23	0.20	0.25	0.25	0.12	0.16	0.18	0.22	0.20	46. Bénéfices avant impôt
47. Income tax	0.15	0.15	0.12	0.17	0.15	0.06	0.09	0.09	0.11	0.08	47. Impôt
48. Profit after tax	0.08	0.08	0.08	0.08	0.10	0.06	0.08	0.09	0.11	0.11	48. Bénéfices après impôt
49. Distributed profit	0.05	0.06	0.06	0.05	0.05	0.04	0.04	0.04	0.04	0.04	49. Bénéfices distribués
50. Retained profit	0.03	0.02	0.02	0.03	0.05	0.02	0.04	0.05	0.06	0.07	50. Bénéfices mis en réserve
51. Staff costs	0.33	0.32	0.31	0.32	0.31	0.31	0.28	0.32	0.28	0.26	51. Frais de personnel
52. Provisions on loans	0.51	0.35	0.29	0.18	0.16	0.20	0.21	0.17	0.20	0.20	52. Provisions sur prêts
53. Provisions on securities (1)	:	:	:	:	:	:	:	:	:	:	53. Provisions sur titres (1)
% of gross income											**% du total du résultat brut**
54. Net interest income	72.69	77.67	78.56	79.97	76.15	77.84	74.24	76.79	74.33	87.83	54. Produits financiers nets
55. Non-interest income (net)	27.31	22.33	21.44	20.03	23.85	22.16	25.76	23.21	25.67	12.17	55. Produits non financiers (nets)
56. Operating expenses	39.14	44.64	48.63	52.56	53.56	59.20	53.73	58.57	52.50	52.34	56. Frais d'exploitation
57. Net income	60.86	55.36	51.37	47.44	46.44	40.80	46.27	41.43	47.50	47.66	57. Résultat net
58. Provisions (net)	42.36	33.83	30.64	20.24	18.17	25.94	26.35	20.49	22.80	24.75	58. Provisions (nettes)
59. Profit before tax	18.49	21.53	20.73	27.20	28.27	14.87	19.92	20.94	24.70	22.92	59. Bénéfices avant impôt
60. Income tax	12.10	14.15	12.45	18.36	16.45	7.11	10.63	10.28	12.62	9.77	60. Impôt
61. Profit after tax	6.40	7.38	8.28	8.84	11.82	7.75	9.30	10.65	12.08	13.14	61. Bénéfices après impôt
62. Staff costs	26.41	29.62	32.36	34.89	35.15	39.31	34.24	37.25	32.32	30.56	62. Frais de personnel
% of net income											**% du total du résultat net**
63. Provisions (net)	69.61	61.11	59.65	42.66	39.12	63.57	56.94	49.46	48.00	51.92	63. Provisions (nettes)
64. Profit before tax	30.39	38.89	40.35	57.34	60.88	36.43	43.06	50.54	52.00	48.08	64. Bénéfices avant impôt
65. Income tax	19.88	25.56	24.23	38.71	35.43	17.43	22.97	24.83	26.57	20.51	65. Impôt
66. Profit after tax	10.51	13.33	16.12	18.63	25.45	19.00	20.09	25.72	25.43	27.57	66. Bénéfices après impôt

GERMANY

Regional giro institutions

Per cent

BALANCE SHEET ANALYSIS

% of year-end balance sheet total

	1985	1986	1987	1988	1989	1990	1991	1992	1993 (1)	1994
Assets										
67. Cash & balance with Central bank	0.82	0.77	0.58	0.59	0.73	0.85	0.47	0.50	0.43	0.23
68. Interbank deposits	27.72	31.51	34.35	37.28	39.30	37.87	35.87	34.27	33.37	33.02
69. Loans	59.13	56.14	53.88	51.14	48.58	45.62	48.30	48.65	48.34	48.23
70. Securities	10.68	9.97	9.45	9.15	9.54	13.94	13.58	14.71	15.50	16.11
71. Other assets	1.66	1.61	1.74	1.84	1.86	1.74	1.78	1.87	2.37	2.40
Liabilities										
72. Capital & reserves	2.19	2.24	2.19	2.14	2.24	2.08	2.20	2.77	2.79	2.92
73. Borrowing from Central bank	2.50	1.32	1.07	3.21	3.45	3.87	4.78	2.96	5.17	3.30
74. Interbank deposits	25.40	26.63	26.97	29.01	29.32	33.38	33.23	34.47	32.26	32.01
75. Non-bank deposits	20.27	21.89	23.45	24.19	24.46	22.83	23.00	24.22	23.82	24.86
76. Bonds	46.91	45.20	43.89	38.96	38.04	35.25	33.95	32.00	31.64	33.10
77. Other liabilities	2.73	2.71	2.42	2.50	2.48	2.59	2.84	3.58	4.31	3.81
Memoranda										
78. Short-term securities	2.77	2.03	1.67	1.07	1.03	4.84	4.88	3.90	3.07	2.10
79. Bonds	6.81	6.83	6.64	6.97	7.22	7.59	7.16	9.06	10.64	11.99
80. Shares and participations	1.10	1.11	1.14	1.11	1.29	1.50	1.54	1.74	1.80	2.02
81. Claims on non-residents	17.00	19.84	20.58	22.69	25.30	32.43	24.21	23.03	23.39	20.40
82. Liabilities to non-residents	8.32	7.37	7.97	9.02	8.43	12.50	9.54	12.48	10.34	12.58

1. Break in series due to change in methodology.
2. Included under "Provisions on loans" (item 15 or item 52).

Notes

- Average balance sheet totals (item 29) are based on twelve end-month data.

- **Change in methodology:**

- As from 1993, data include eastern German credit institutions and are in accordance with the new accounting regulations.

ALLEMAGNE

Organismes régionaux de compensation

Pourcentage

ANALYSE DU BILAN

% du total du bilan en fin d'exercice

Actif
67. Caisse & solde auprès de la Banque centrale
68. Dépôts interbancaires
69. Prêts
70. Valeurs mobilières
71. Autres actifs

Passif
72. Capital et réserves
73. Emprunts auprès de la Banque centrale
74. Dépôts interbancaires
75. Dépôts non bancaires
76. Obligations
77. Autres engagements

Pour mémoire
78. Titres à court terme
79. Obligations
80. Actions et participations
81. Créances sur des non résidents
82. Engagements envers des non résidents

1. Rupture de comparabilité dans les séries due aux changements méthodologiques.
2. Inclus sous "Provisions sur prêts" (poste 15 ou poste 52).

Notes

- La moyenne du total des actifs/passifs (poste 29) est basée sur douze données de fin de mois.

Changement méthodologique :

- Depuis 1993, les données comprennent les organismes de crédit d'Allemagne orientale et sont conformes aux nouvelles règles de comptabilité.

GERMANY

Savings banks

Million DM

ALLEMAGNE

Caisses d'épargne

Millions de DM

	1985	1986	1987	1988	1989	1990	1991	1992	1993 (1)	1994		
INCOME STATEMENT												**COMPTE DE RESULTATS**
1. Interest income	50911	50338	50450	51762	57466	67561	78362	85138	99669	100302	1.	Produits financiers
2. Interest expenses	28055	26984	26864	27319	33152	42593	50204	55437	61591	57192	2.	Frais financiers
3. Net interest income	22856	23354	23586	24443	24314	24968	28158	29701	38078	43110	3.	Produits financiers nets
4. Non-interest income (net)	2390	2588	2728	1837	4097	5387	5633	6164	7374	6949	4.	Produits non financiers (nets)
5. Gross income	25246	25942	26314	26280	28411	30355	33791	35865	45452	50059	5.	Résultat brut
6. Operating expenses	14946	15881	16876	17680	18409	19731	21782	22991	28638	29250	6.	Frais d'exploitation
7. Net income	10300	10061	9438	8600	10002	10624	12009	12874	16814	20809	7.	Résultat net
8. Provisions (net)	3202	3160	3216	2425	5859	5681	3573	3467	5977	10987	8.	Provisions (nettes)
9. Profit before tax	7098	6901	6222	6175	4143	4943	8436	9407	10837	9822	9.	Bénéfices avant impôt
10. Income tax	4900	4762	4224	4095	2466	3133	5612	6475	7006	5762	10.	Impôt
11. Profit after tax	2198	2139	1998	2080	1677	1810	2824	2932	3831	4060	11.	Bénéfices après impôt
12. Distributed profit	1379	1377	1317	1345	1159	1240	1614	1726	2269	2457	12.	Bénéfices distribués
13. Retained profit	819	762	681	735	518	570	1210	1206	1562	1603	13.	Bénéfices mis en réserve
Memoranda												*Pour mémoire*
14. Staff costs	*9677*	*10283*	*11045*	*11542*	*11864*	*12776*	*14231*	*15040*	*17728*	*18279*	*14.*	*Frais de personnel*
15. Provisions on loans	*3181*	*3142*	*3205*	*2420*	*5850*	*5671*	*3550*	*3446*	*5878*	*10110*	*15.*	*Provisions sur prêts*
16. Provisions on securities (2)	:	:	:	:	:	:	:	:	:	:	*16.*	*Provisions sur titres (2)*
BALANCE SHEET												**BILAN**
Assets												**Actif**
17. Cash & balance with Central bank	21726	22576	25753	27440	29921	30259	29855	33908	33658	28734	17.	Caisse & solde auprès de la Banque centrale
18. Interbank deposits	59931	73203	70015	76311	95999	107769	112200	92305	135787	109603	18.	Dépôts interbancaires
19. Loans	466780	482066	501094	528417	561165	595639	652187	685475	800910	869221	19.	Prêts
20. Securities	141064	160719	186938	203826	200023	213906	220649	230666	322312	382643	20.	Valeurs mobilières
21. Other assets	27331	27950	28136	28016	28700	31408	36680	32972	38344	37917	21.	Autres actifs
Liabilities												**Passif**
22. Capital & reserves	26540	28541	30564	32526	34655	36411	38900	40977	49544	54119	22.	Capital et réserves
23. Borrowing from Central bank	19853	17492	15744	27825	38355	42747	48466	38075	42726	47242	23.	Emprunts auprès de la Banque centrale
24. Interbank deposits	68608	77549	86147	91503	94993	100577	110026	118366	158962	198913	24.	Dépôts interbancaires
25. Non-bank deposits	569248	606075	636267	660439	684637	721904	760428	775360	961866	993253	25.	Dépôts non bancaires
26. Bonds	4000	6783	11589	18246	28102	40537	52476	58781	63860	77037	26.	Obligations
27. Other liabilities	28583	30074	31625	33471	35066	36805	41275	43767	54053	57554	27.	Autres engagements
Balance sheet total												**Total du bilan**
28. End-year total	716832	766514	811936	864010	915808	978981	1051571	1075326	1331011	1428118	28.	En fin d'exercice
29. Average total	689295	733290	783133	831211	875042	934259	999930	1029488	1253312	1367636	29.	Moyen
Memoranda												*Pour mémoire*
30. Short-term securities	*13683*	*17580*	*20792*	*18534*	*16671*	*20248*	*23108*	*22241*	*29184*	*33717*	*30.*	*Titres à court terme*
31. Bonds	*122644*	*137562*	*159219*	*177850*	*174336*	*181083*	*180251*	*185685*	*260719*	*306844*	*31.*	*Obligations*
32. Shares and participations	*4737*	*5577*	*6927*	*7442*	*9016*	*12575*	*17290*	*22740*	*32409*	*42082*	*32.*	*Actions et participations*
33. Claims on non-residents	*4253*	*7521*	*8416*	*11326*	*21563*	*27051*	*24154*	*17581*	*26976*	*24001*	*33.*	*Créances sur des non résidents*
34. Liabilities to non-residents	*5097*	*5116*	*5863*	*6864*	*7637*	*12385*	*7891*	*11002*	*14234*	*14684*	*34.*	*Engagements envers des non résidents*
SUPPLEMENTARY INFORMATION												**RENSEIGNEMENTS COMPLEMENTAIRES**
35. Number of institutions	590	589	586	585	583	575	558	542	704	657	35.	Nombre d'institutions
36. Number of branches	17204	17248	17307	17355	17359	17212	17033	16923	19510	19271	36.	Nombre de succursales
37. Number of employees (x 1000)	NA	NA	NA	NA	NA	NA	NA	NA	NA	NA	37.	Nombre de salariés (x 1000)

GERMANY

Savings banks

ALLEMAGNE

Caisses d'épargne

Per cent	1985	1986	1987	1988	1989	1990	1991	1992	1993 (1)	1994		Pourcentage
INCOME STATEMENT ANALYSIS												**ANALYSE DU COMPTE DE RESULTATS**
% of average balance sheet total												**% du total moyen du bilan**
38. Interest income	7.39	6.86	6.44	6.23	6.57	7.23	7.84	8.27	7.95	7.33		38. Produits financiers
39. Interest expenses	4.07	3.68	3.43	3.29	3.79	4.56	5.02	5.38	4.91	4.18		39. Frais financiers
40. Net interest income	3.32	3.18	3.01	2.94	2.78	2.67	2.82	2.89	3.04	3.15		40. Produits financiers nets
41. Non-interest income (net)	0.35	0.35	0.35	0.22	0.47	0.58	0.56	0.60	0.59	0.51		41. Produits non financiers (nets)
42. Gross income	3.66	3.54	3.36	3.16	3.25	3.25	3.38	3.48	3.63	3.66		42. Résultat brut
43. Operating expenses	2.17	2.17	2.15	2.13	2.10	2.11	2.18	2.23	2.28	2.14		43. Frais d'exploitation
44. Net income	1.49	1.37	1.21	1.03	1.14	1.14	1.20	1.25	1.34	1.52		44. Résultat net
45. Provisions (net)	0.46	0.43	0.41	0.29	0.67	0.61	0.36	0.34	0.48	0.80		45. Provisions (nettes)
46. Profit before tax	1.03	0.94	0.79	0.74	0.47	0.53	0.84	0.91	0.86	0.72		46. Bénéfices avant impôt
47. Income tax	0.71	0.65	0.54	0.49	0.28	0.34	0.56	0.63	0.56	0.42		47. Impôt
48. Profit after tax	0.32	0.29	0.26	0.25	0.19	0.19	0.28	0.28	0.31	0.30		48. Bénéfices après impôt
49. Distributed profit	0.20	0.19	0.17	0.16	0.13	0.13	0.16	0.17	0.18	0.18		49. Bénéfices distribués
50. Retained profit	0.12	0.10	0.09	0.09	0.06	0.06	0.12	0.12	0.12	0.12		50. Bénéfices mis en réserve
51. Staff costs	1.40	1.40	1.41	1.39	1.36	1.37	1.42	1.46	1.41	1.34		51. Frais de personnel
52. Provisions on loans	0.46	0.43	0.41	0.29	0.67	0.61	0.36	0.33	0.47	0.74		52. Provisions sur prêts
53. Provisions on securities (2)	:	:	:	:	:	:	:	:	:	:		53. Provisions sur titres (2)
% of gross income												**% du total du résultat brut**
54. Net interest income	90.53	90.02	89.63	93.01	85.58	82.25	83.33	82.81	83.78	86.12		54. Produits financiers nets
55. Non-interest income (net)	9.47	9.98	10.37	6.99	14.42	17.75	16.67	17.19	16.22	13.88		55. Produits non financiers (nets)
56. Operating expenses	59.20	61.22	64.13	67.28	64.80	65.00	64.46	64.10	63.01	58.43		56. Frais d'exploitation
57. Net income	40.80	38.78	35.87	32.72	35.20	35.00	35.54	35.90	36.99	41.57		57. Résultat net
58. Provisions (net)	12.68	12.18	12.22	9.23	20.62	18.72	10.57	9.67	13.15	21.95		58. Provisions (nettes)
59. Profit before tax	28.12	26.60	23.65	23.50	14.58	16.28	24.97	26.23	23.84	19.62		59. Bénéfices avant impôt
60. Income tax	19.41	18.36	16.05	15.58	8.68	10.32	16.61	18.05	15.41	11.51		60. Impôt
61. Profit after tax	8.71	8.25	7.59	7.91	5.90	5.96	8.36	8.18	8.43	8.11		61. Bénéfices après impôt
62. Staff costs	38.33	39.64	41.97	43.92	41.76	42.09	42.11	41.94	39.00	36.51		62. Frais de personnel
% of net income												**% du total du résultat net**
63. Provisions (net)	31.09	31.41	34.08	28.20	58.58	53.47	29.75	26.93	35.55	52.80		63. Provisions (nettes)
64. Profit before tax	68.91	68.59	65.92	71.80	41.42	46.53	70.25	73.07	64.45	47.20		64. Bénéfices avant impôt
65. Income tax	47.57	47.33	44.76	47.62	24.66	29.49	46.73	50.30	41.67	27.69		65. Impôt
66. Profit after tax	21.34	21.26	21.17	24.19	16.77	17.04	23.52	22.77	22.78	19.51		66. Bénéfices après impôt

GERMANY

Savings banks

ALLEMAGNE

Caisses d'épargne

Per cent / *Pourcentage*

BALANCE SHEET ANALYSIS / **ANALYSE DU BILAN**

% of year-end balance sheet total / % du total du bilan en fin d'exercice

	1985	1986	1987	1988	1989	1990	1991	1992	1993 (1)	1994	
Assets											**Actif**
67. Cash & balance with Central bank	3.03	2.95	3.17	3.18	3.27	3.09	2.84	3.15	2.53	2.01	67. Caisse & solde auprès de la Banque centrale
68. Interbank deposits	8.36	9.55	8.62	8.83	10.48	11.01	10.67	8.58	10.20	7.67	68. Dépôts interbancaires
69. Loans	65.12	62.89	61.72	61.16	61.28	60.84	62.02	63.75	60.17	60.86	69. Prêts
70. Securities	19.68	20.97	23.02	23.59	21.84	21.85	20.98	21.45	24.22	26.79	70. Valeurs mobilières
71. Other assets	3.81	3.65	3.47	3.24	3.13	3.21	3.49	3.07	2.88	2.66	71. Autres actifs
Liabilities											**Passif**
72. Capital & reserves	3.70	3.72	3.76	3.76	3.78	3.72	3.70	3.81	3.72	3.79	72. Capital et réserves
73. Borrowing from Central bank	2.77	2.28	1.94	3.22	4.19	4.37	4.61	3.54	3.21	3.31	73. Emprunts auprès de la Banque centrale
74. Interbank deposits	9.57	10.12	10.61	10.59	10.37	10.27	10.46	11.01	11.94	13.93	74. Dépôts interbancaires
75. Non-bank deposits	79.41	79.07	78.36	76.44	74.76	73.74	72.31	72.10	72.27	69.55	75. Dépôts non bancaires
76. Bonds	0.56	0.88	1.43	2.11	3.07	4.14	4.99	5.47	4.80	5.39	76. Obligations
77. Other liabilities	3.99	3.92	3.90	3.87	3.83	3.76	3.93	4.07	4.06	4.03	77. Autres engagements
Memoranda											*Pour mémoire*
78. Short-term securities	*1.91*	*2.29*	*2.56*	*2.15*	*1.82*	*2.07*	*2.20*	*2.07*	*2.19*	*2.36*	*78. Titres à court terme*
79. Bonds	*17.11*	*17.95*	*19.61*	*20.58*	*19.04*	*18.50*	*17.14*	*17.27*	*19.59*	*21.49*	*79. Obligations*
80. Shares and participations	*0.66*	*0.73*	*0.85*	*0.86*	*0.98*	*1.28*	*1.64*	*2.11*	*2.43*	*2.95*	*80. Actions et participations*
81. Claims on non-residents	*0.59*	*0.98*	*1.04*	*1.31*	*2.35*	*2.76*	*2.30*	*1.63*	*2.03*	*1.68*	*81. Créances sur des non résidents*
82. Liabilities to non-residents	*0.71*	*0.67*	*0.72*	*0.79*	*0.83*	*1.27*	*0.75*	*1.02*	*1.07*	*1.03*	*82. Engagements envers des non résidents*

1. Break in series due to change in methodology.
2. Included under "Provisions on loans" (item 15 or item 52).

Notes

- Average balance sheet totals (item 29) are based on twelve end-month data.

Change in methodology:

- As from 1993, data include eastern German credit institutions and are in accordance with the new accounting regulations.

1. Rupture de comparabilité dans les séries due aux changements méthodologiques.
2. Inclus sous "Provisions sur prêts" (poste 15 ou poste 52).

Notes

- La moyenne du total des actifs/passifs (poste 29) est basée sur douze données de fin de mois.

Changement méthodologique :

- Depuis 1993, les données comprennent les organismes de crédit d'Allemagne orientale et sont conformes aux nouvelles règles de comptabilité.

Regional institutions of co-operative banks

Institutions régionales des banques mutualistes

Million DM	1985	1986	1987	1988	1989	1990	1991	1992	1993 (1)	1994	Millions de DM
INCOME STATEMENT											**COMPTE DE RESULTATS**
1. Interest income	9675	9036	9216	9630	11113	14172	15773	16099	15530	14851	1. Produits financiers
2. Interest expenses	8098	7329	7413	7898	9891	12999	14684	14635	13693	11867	2. Frais financiers
3. Net interest income	1577	1707	1803	1732	1222	1173	1089	1464	1837	2984	3. Produits financiers nets
4. Non-interest income (net)	1160	578	433	358	938	1307	1271	585	756	1329	4. Produits non financiers (nets)
5. Gross income	2737	2285	2236	2090	2160	2480	2360	2049	2593	4313	5. Résultat brut
6. Operating expenses	906	1032	1053	1029	1055	1175	1222	1344	1457	1527	6. Frais d'exploitation
7. Net income	1831	1253	1183	1061	1105	1305	1138	705	1136	2786	7. Résultat net
8. Provisions (net)	1206	290	245	47	623	844	728	244	700	1692	8. Provisions (nettes)
9. Profit before tax	625	963	938	1014	482	461	410	461	436	1094	9. Bénéfices avant impôt
10. Income tax	506	529	542	585	93	177	228	261	260	543	10. Impôt
11. Profit after tax	119	434	396	429	389	284	182	200	176	551	11. Bénéfices après impôt
12. Distributed profit	148	276	200	219	559	219	119	78	91	185	12. Bénéfices distribués
13. Retained profit	-29	158	196	210	-170	65	63	122	85	366	13. Bénéfices mis en réserve
Memoranda											*Pour mémoire*
14. Staff costs	*524*	*536*	*572*	*554*	*577*	*647*	*660*	*723*	*769*	*801*	*14. Frais de personnel*
15. Provisions on loans	*1198*	*283*	*234*	*34*	*623*	*725*	*670*	*189*	*698*	*1691*	*15. Provisions sur prêts*
16. Provisions on securities (2)	..	..	..	..	..	..	..	..	..	..	*16. Provisions sur titres (2)*
BALANCE SHEET											**BILAN**
Assets											**Actif**
17. Cash & balance with Central bank	3029	3319	2351	2389	2739	2247	2925	2102	1195	998	17. Caisse & solde auprès de la Banque centrale
18. Interbank deposits	78937	90268	103468	106397	102158	107746	102957	106576	117859	128297	18. Dépôts interbancaires
19. Loans	29305	28722	31166	35220	36028	38412	51773	58011	57046	58457	19. Prêts
20. Securities	32501	31844	33460	35375	38995	40883	38670	39914	49568	52943	20. Valeurs mobilières
21. Other assets	2904	2707	2596	2167	4217	4258	14284	3980	3887	4565	21. Autres actifs
Liabilities											**Passif**
22. Capital & reserves	5394	5556	6013	6218	6725	6446	7180	7890	8513	9349	22. Capital et réserves
23. Borrowing from Central bank	7069	4842	4802	10001	11529	11993	15690	10254	8228	14600	23. Emprunts auprès de la Banque centrale
24. Interbank deposits	106247	116949	129249	131965	130758	139772	145210	148468	160210	156250	24. Dépôts interbancaires
25. Non-bank deposits	12603	12734	12874	12595	12563	14712	17599	19028	21946	25462	25. Dépôts non bancaires
26. Bonds	12477	13676	16677	16654	18525	15454	18346	19042	21349	28982	26. Obligations
27. Other liabilities	2886	3103	3426	4115	4037	5169	6584	5901	9309	10617	27. Autres engagements
Balance sheet total											**Total du bilan**
28. End-year total	146676	156860	173041	181548	184137	193546	210609	210583	229555	245260	28. En fin d'exercice
29. Average total	136874	144403	159944	171195	173658	178846	194435	188434	200135	230507	29. Moyen
Memoranda											*Pour mémoire*
30. Short-term securities	*9033*	*7351*	*7352*	*3575*	*2446*	*7982*	*10499*	*11801*	*14428*	*10899*	*30. Titres à court terme*
31. Bonds	*19406*	*19908*	*20656*	*25849*	*30436*	*27049*	*21166*	*20777*	*26538*	*32886*	*31. Obligations*
32. Shares and participations	*4062*	*4585*	*5452*	*5951*	*6113*	*5852*	*7005*	*7336*	*8602*	*9158*	*32. Actions et participations*
33. Claims on non-residents	*12952*	*19246*	*25807*	*25893*	*31136*	*42780*	*34701*	*27719*	*34757*	*35554*	*33. Créances sur des non résidents*
34. Liabilities to non-residents	*3979*	*3128*	*3150*	*3530*	*3745*	*10054*	*7674*	*7998*	*8091*	*11830*	*34. Engagements envers des non résidents*
SUPPLEMENTARY INFORMATION											**RENSEIGNEMENTS COMPLEMENTAIRES**
35. Number of institutions	9	8	7	6	6	4	4	4	4	4	35. Nombre d'institutions
36. Number of branches	46	48	36	32	32	31	29	31	46	46	36. Nombre de succursales
37. Number of employees (x 1000)	NA	NA	NA	NA	NA	NA	NA	NA	NA	NA	37. Nombre de salariés (x 1000)

89

GERMANY

Regional institutions of co-operative banks

ALLEMAGNE

Institutions régionales des banques mutualistes

Per cent / *Pourcentage*

INCOME STATEMENT ANALYSIS / **ANALYSE DU COMPTE DE RESULTATS**

	1985	1986	1987	1988	1989	1990	1991	1992	1993 (1)	1994	
% of average balance sheet total											**% du total moyen du bilan**
38. Interest income	7.07	6.26	5.76	5.63	6.40	7.92	8.11	8.54	7.76	6.44	38. Produits financiers
39. Interest expenses	5.92	5.08	4.63	4.61	5.70	7.27	7.55	7.77	6.84	5.15	39. Frais financiers
40. Net interest income	1.15	1.18	1.13	1.01	0.70	0.66	0.56	0.78	0.92	1.29	40. Produits financiers nets
41. Non-interest income (net)	0.85	0.40	0.27	0.21	0.54	0.73	0.65	0.31	0.38	0.58	41. Produits non financiers (nets)
42. Gross income	2.00	1.58	1.40	1.22	1.24	1.39	1.21	1.09	1.30	1.87	42. Résultat brut
43. Operating expenses	0.66	0.71	0.66	0.60	0.61	0.66	0.63	0.71	0.73	0.66	43. Frais d'exploitation
44. Net income	1.34	0.87	0.74	0.62	0.64	0.73	0.59	0.37	0.57	1.21	44. Résultat net
45. Provisions (net)	0.88	0.20	0.15	0.03	0.36	0.47	0.37	0.13	0.35	0.73	45. Provisions (nettes)
46. Profit before tax	0.46	0.67	0.59	0.59	0.28	0.26	0.21	0.24	0.22	0.47	46. Bénéfices avant impôt
47. Income tax	0.37	0.37	0.34	0.34	0.05	0.10	0.12	0.14	0.13	0.24	47. Impôt
48. Profit after tax	0.09	0.30	0.25	0.25	0.22	0.16	0.09	0.11	0.09	0.24	48. Bénéfices après impôt
49. Distributed profit	0.11	0.19	0.13	0.13	0.32	0.12	0.06	0.04	0.05	0.08	49. Bénéfices distribués
50. Retained profit	-0.02	0.11	0.12	0.12	-0.10	0.04	0.03	0.06	0.04	0.16	50. Bénéfices mis en réserve
51. Staff costs	0.38	0.37	0.36	0.32	0.33	0.36	0.34	0.38	0.38	0.35	51. Frais de personnel
52. Provisions on loans	0.88	0.20	0.15	0.02	0.36	0.41	0.34	0.10	0.35	0.73	52. Provisions sur prêts
53. Provisions on securities (2)	:	:	:	:	:	:	:	:	:	:	53. Provisions sur titres (2)
% of gross income											**% du total du résultat brut**
54. Net interest income	57.62	74.70	80.64	82.87	56.57	47.30	46.14	71.45	70.84	69.19	54. Produits financiers nets
55. Non-interest income (net)	42.38	25.30	19.36	17.13	43.43	52.70	53.86	28.55	29.16	30.81	55. Produits non financiers (nets)
56. Operating expenses	33.10	45.16	47.09	49.23	48.84	47.38	51.78	65.59	56.19	35.40	56. Frais d'exploitation
57. Net income	66.90	54.84	52.91	50.77	51.16	52.62	48.22	34.41	43.81	64.60	57. Résultat net
58. Provisions (net)	44.06	12.69	10.96	2.25	28.84	34.03	30.85	11.91	27.00	39.23	58. Provisions (nettes)
59. Profit before tax	22.84	42.14	41.95	48.52	22.31	18.59	17.37	22.50	16.81	25.37	59. Bénéfices avant impôt
60. Income tax	18.49	23.15	24.24	27.99	4.31	7.14	9.66	12.74	10.03	12.59	60. Impôt
61. Profit after tax	4.35	18.99	17.71	20.53	18.01	11.45	7.71	9.76	6.79	12.78	61. Bénéfices après impôt
62. Staff costs	19.15	23.46	25.58	26.51	26.71	26.09	27.97	35.29	29.66	18.57	62. Frais de personnel
% of net income											**% du total du résultat net**
63. Provisions (net)	65.87	23.14	20.71	4.43	56.38	64.67	63.97	34.61	61.62	60.73	63. Provisions (nettes)
64. Profit before tax	34.13	76.86	79.29	95.57	43.62	35.33	36.03	65.39	38.38	39.27	64. Bénéfices avant impôt
65. Income tax	27.64	42.22	45.82	55.14	8.42	13.56	20.04	37.02	22.89	19.49	65. Impôt
66. Profit after tax	6.50	34.64	33.47	40.43	35.20	21.76	15.99	28.37	15.49	19.78	66. Bénéfices après impôt

GERMANY

Regional institutions of co-operative banks

ALLEMAGNE

Institutions régionales des banques mutualistes

Per cent / Pourcentage	1985	1986	1987	1988	1989	1990	1991	1992	1993 (1)	1994		
BALANCE SHEET ANALYSIS											**ANALYSE DU BILAN**	
% of year-end balance sheet total											**% du total du bilan en fin d'exercice**	
Assets											**Actif**	
67. Cash & balance with Central bank	2.07	2.12	1.36	1.32	1.49	1.16	1.39	1.00	0.52	0.41	67. Caisse & solde auprès de la Banque centrale	
68. Interbank deposits	53.82	57.55	59.79	58.61	55.48	55.67	48.89	50.61	51.34	52.31	68. Dépôts interbancaires	
69. Loans	19.98	18.31	18.01	19.40	19.57	19.85	24.58	27.55	24.85	23.83	69. Prêts	
70. Securities	22.16	20.30	19.34	19.49	21.18	21.12	18.36	18.95	21.59	21.59	70. Valeurs mobilières	
71. Other assets	1.98	1.73	1.50	1.19	2.29	2.20	6.78	1.89	1.69	1.86	71. Autres actifs	
Liabilities											**Passif**	
72. Capital & reserves	3.68	3.54	3.47	3.42	3.65	3.33	3.41	3.75	3.71	3.81	72. Capital et réserves	
73. Borrowing from Central bank	4.82	3.09	2.78	5.51	6.26	6.20	7.45	4.87	3.58	5.95	73. Emprunts auprès de la Banque centrale	
74. Interbank deposits	72.44	74.56	74.69	72.69	71.01	72.22	68.95	70.50	69.79	63.71	74. Dépôts interbancaires	
75. Non-bank deposits	8.59	8.12	7.44	6.94	6.82	7.60	8.36	9.04	9.56	10.38	75. Dépôts non bancaires	
76. Bonds	8.51	8.72	9.64	9.17	10.06	7.98	8.71	9.04	9.30	11.82	76. Obligations	
77. Other liabilities	1.97	1.98	1.98	2.27	2.19	2.67	3.13	2.80	4.06	4.33	77. Autres engagements	
Memoranda											*Pour mémoire*	
78. *Short-term securities*	*6.16*	*4.69*	*4.25*	*1.97*	*1.33*	*4.12*	*4.99*	*5.60*	*6.29*	*4.44*	78. *Titres à court terme*	
79. *Bonds*	*13.23*	*12.69*	*11.94*	*14.24*	*16.53*	*13.98*	*10.05*	*9.87*	*11.56*	*13.41*	79. *Obligations*	
80. *Shares and participations*	*2.77*	*2.92*	*3.15*	*3.28*	*3.32*	*3.02*	*3.33*	*3.48*	*3.75*	*3.73*	80. *Actions et participations*	
81. *Claims on non-residents*	*8.83*	*12.27*	*14.91*	*14.26*	*16.91*	*22.10*	*16.48*	*13.16*	*15.14*	*14.50*	81. *Créances sur des non résidents*	
82. *Liabilities to non-residents*	*2.71*	*1.99*	*1.82*	*1.94*	*2.03*	*5.19*	*3.64*	*3.80*	*3.52*	*4.82*	82. *Engagements envers des non résidents*	

1. Break in series due to change in methodology.
2. Included under "Provisions on loans" (item 15 or item 52).

Notes

• Average balance sheet totals (item 29) are based on twelve end-month data.

Change in methodology:

• As from 1993, data include eastern German credit institutions and are in accordance with the new accounting regulations.

1. Rupture de comparabilité dans les séries dûe aux changements méthodologiques.
2. Inclus sous "Provisions sur prêts" (poste 15 ou poste 52).

Notes

• La moyenne du total des actifs/passifs (poste 29) est basée sur douze données de fin de mois.

Changement méthodologique :

• Depuis 1993, les données comprennent les organismes de crédit d'Allemagne orientale et sont conformes aux nouvelles règles de comptabilité.

GERMANY

Co-operative banks

Million DM

ALLEMAGNE

Banques mutualistes

Millions de DM

	1985	1986	1987	1988	1989	1990	1991	1992	1993 (1)	1994	
INCOME STATEMENT											**COMPTE DE RESULTATS**
1. Interest income	29893	29179	28961	29323	33387	40361	46925	53748	58603	57888	1. Produits financiers
2. Interest expenses	16852	15878	15268	15278	18638	24620	29438	34507	35941	33050	2. Frais financiers
3. Net interest income	13041	13301	13693	14045	14749	15741	17487	19241	22662	24838	3. Produits financiers nets
4. Non-interest income (net)	2617	2908	2974	2776	4134	4270	4203	4760	5515	5779	4. Produits non financiers (nets)
5. Gross income	15658	16209	16667	16821	18883	20011	21690	24001	28177	30617	5. Résultat brut
6. Operating expenses	11400	11930	12352	12635	12976	14050	15068	16557	19183	20041	6. Frais d'exploitation
7. Net income	4258	4279	4315	4186	5907	5961	6622	7444	8994	10576	7. Résultat net
8. Provisions (net)	1385	1416	1305	762	3223	2375	1491	1530	2541	4885	8. Provisions (nettes)
9. Profit before tax	2873	2863	3010	3424	2684	3586	5131	5914	6453	5691	9. Bénéfices avant impôt
10. Income tax	1957	1943	2066	2357	1706	2231	3096	3820	4014	3230	10. Impôt
11. Profit after tax	916	920	944	1067	978	1355	2035	2094	2439	2461	11. Bénéfices après impôt
12. Distributed profit	718	760	775	856	830	992	1292	1390	1625	1688	12. Bénéfices distribués
13. Retained profit	198	160	169	211	148	363	743	704	814	773	13. Bénéfices mis en réserve
Memoranda											*Pour mémoire*
14. Staff costs	*6975*	*7331*	*7636*	*7876*	*8100*	*8807*	*9428*	*10357*	*11599*	*12137*	14. Frais de personnel
15. Provisions on loans	*1359*	*1408*	*1295*	*755*	*3216*	*2365*	*1478*	*1522*	*2529*	*4528*	15. Provisions sur prêts
16. Provisions on securities (2)	*..*	*..*	*..*	*..*	*..*	*..*	*..*	*..*	*..*	*..*	16. Provisions sur titres (2)
BALANCE SHEET											**BILAN**
Assets											**Actif**
17. Cash & balance with Central bank	11442	11552	12726	14152	15830	17170	18317	21756	19195	19295	17. Caisse & solde auprès de la Banque centrale
18. Interbank deposits	61694	77475	80670	80874	87254	98019	101699	99288	125575	111758	18. Dépôts interbancaires
19. Loans	262650	265473	272516	286326	308096	328660	360749	395299	447100	491988	19. Prêts
20. Securities	65318	72516	84681	92621	94108	99721	105973	119457	153590	182578	20. Valeurs mobilières
21. Other assets	17957	18299	17776	17669	17907	19449	20833	21221	22424	23918	21. Autres actifs
Liabilities											**Passif**
22. Capital & reserves	16096	17279	18353	19353	20352	21223	23008	26460	31894	36177	22. Capital et réserves
23. Borrowing from Central bank	11515	10549	10111	14595	18523	19645	17945	16430	14095	16325	23. Emprunts auprès de la Banque centrale
24. Interbank deposits	40537	40505	41513	42971	43988	45417	45706	49800	65179	81515	24. Dépôts interbancaires
25. Non-bank deposits	335914	360226	379948	394167	416252	447499	485201	521466	604672	635073	25. Dépôts non bancaires
26. Bonds	3386	4380	5635	7036	9476	13078	17288	22229	27348	34560	26. Obligations
27. Other liabilities	11613	12376	12809	13520	14604	16157	18423	20636	24696	25887	27. Autres engagements
Balance sheet total											**Total du bilan**
28. End-year total	419061	445315	468369	491642	523195	563019	607571	657021	767884	829537	28. En fin d'exercice
29. Average total	402107	424901	451136	474491	497789	534273	575708	624292	716971	788684	29. Moyen
Memoranda											*Pour mémoire*
30. Short-term securities	*8565*	*9088*	*11294*	*11750*	*11313*	*12885*	*15821*	*18236*	*25528*	*25458*	30. Titres à court terme
31. Bonds	*54691*	*60724*	*70037*	*77256*	*79170*	*82820*	*85535*	*95354*	*118926*	*146152*	31. Obligations
32. Shares and participations	*2062*	*2704*	*3350*	*3615*	*3625*	*4016*	*4617*	*5867*	*9136*	*10968*	32. Actions et participations
33. Claims on non-residents	*1506*	*1970*	*2619*	*3393*	*5401*	*6795*	*8269*	*7585*	*15519*	*15268*	33. Créances sur des non résidents
34. Liabilities to non-residents	*3857*	*3840*	*3998*	*4217*	*4491*	*5836*	*4973*	*6989*	*9146*	*10878*	34. Engagements envers des non résidents
SUPPLEMENTARY INFORMATION											**RENSEIGNEMENTS COMPLEMENTAIRES**
35. Number of institutions	3655	3604	3480	3361	3225	3049	2862	2683	2778	2666	35. Nombre d'institutions
36. Number of branches	15929	15935	15910	15824	15789	15769	15815	15618	17599	17383	36. Nombre de succursales
37. Number of employees (x 1000)	NA	NA	NA	NA	NA	NA	NA	NA	NA	NA	37. Nombre de salariés (x 1000)

Per cent / *Pourcentage*

	1985	1986	1987	1988	1989	1990	1991	1992	1993 (1)	1994		
INCOME STATEMENT ANALYSIS												**ANALYSE DU COMPTE DE RESULTATS**
% of average balance sheet total												**% du total moyen du bilan**
38. Interest income	7.43	6.87	6.42	6.18	6.71	7.55	8.15	8.61	8.17	7.34	38.	Produits financiers
39. Interest expenses	4.19	3.74	3.38	3.22	3.74	4.61	5.11	5.53	5.01	4.19	39.	Frais financiers
40. Net interest income	3.24	3.13	3.04	2.96	2.96	2.95	3.04	3.08	3.16	3.15	40.	Produits financiers nets
41. Non-interest income (net)	0.65	0.68	0.66	0.59	0.83	0.80	0.73	0.76	0.77	0.73	41.	Produits non financiers (nets)
42. Gross income	3.89	3.81	3.69	3.55	3.79	3.75	3.77	3.84	3.93	3.88	42.	Résultat brut
43. Operating expenses	2.84	2.81	2.74	2.66	2.61	2.63	2.62	2.65	2.68	2.54	43.	Frais d'exploitation
44. Net income	1.06	1.01	0.96	0.88	1.19	1.12	1.15	1.19	1.25	1.34	44.	Résultat net
45. Provisions (net)	0.34	0.33	0.29	0.16	0.65	0.44	0.26	0.25	0.35	0.62	45.	Provisions (nettes)
46. Profit before tax	0.71	0.67	0.67	0.72	0.54	0.67	0.89	0.95	0.90	0.72	46.	Bénéfices avant impôt
47. Income tax	0.49	0.46	0.46	0.50	0.34	0.42	0.54	0.61	0.56	0.41	47.	Impôt
48. Profit after tax	0.23	0.22	0.21	0.22	0.20	0.25	0.35	0.34	0.34	0.31	48.	Bénéfices après impôt
49. Distributed profit	0.18	0.18	0.17	0.18	0.17	0.19	0.22	0.22	0.23	0.21	49.	Bénéfices distribués
50. Retained profit	0.05	0.04	0.04	0.04	0.03	0.07	0.13	0.11	0.11	0.10	50.	Bénéfices mis en réserve
51. Staff costs	1.73	1.73	1.69	1.66	1.63	1.65	1.64	1.66	1.62	1.54	51.	Frais de personnel
52. Provisions on loans	0.34	0.33	0.29	0.16	0.65	0.44	0.26	0.24	0.35	0.57	52.	Provisions sur prêts
53. Provisions on securities (2)	:	:	:	:	:	:	:	:	:	:	53.	Provisions sur titres (2)
% of gross income												**% du total du résultat brut**
54. Net interest income	83.29	82.06	82.16	83.50	78.11	78.66	80.62	80.17	80.43	81.12	54.	Produits financiers nets
55. Non-interest income (net)	16.71	17.94	17.84	16.50	21.89	21.34	19.38	19.83	19.57	18.88	55.	Produits non financiers (nets)
56. Operating expenses	72.81	73.60	74.11	75.11	68.72	70.21	69.47	68.98	68.08	65.46	56.	Frais d'exploitation
57. Net income	27.19	26.40	25.89	24.89	31.28	29.79	30.53	31.02	31.92	34.54	57.	Résultat net
58. Provisions (net)	8.85	8.74	7.83	4.53	17.07	11.87	6.87	6.37	9.02	15.96	58.	Provisions (nettes)
59. Profit before tax	18.35	17.66	18.06	20.36	14.21	17.92	23.66	24.64	22.90	18.59	59.	Bénéfices avant impôt
60. Income tax	12.50	11.99	12.40	14.01	9.03	11.15	14.27	15.92	14.25	10.55	60.	Impôt
61. Profit after tax	5.85	5.68	5.66	6.34	5.18	6.77	9.38	8.72	8.66	8.04	61.	Bénéfices après impôt
62. Staff costs	44.55	45.23	45.82	46.82	42.90	44.01	43.47	43.15	41.16	39.64	62.	Frais de personnel
% of net income												**% du total du résultat net**
63. Provisions (net)	32.53	33.09	30.24	18.20	54.56	39.84	22.52	20.55	28.25	46.19	63.	Provisions (nettes)
64. Profit before tax	67.47	66.91	69.76	81.80	45.44	60.16	77.48	79.45	71.75	53.81	64.	Bénéfices avant impôt
65. Income tax	45.96	45.41	47.88	56.31	28.88	37.43	46.75	51.32	44.63	30.54	65.	Impôt
66. Profit after tax	21.51	21.50	21.88	25.49	16.56	22.73	30.73	28.13	27.12	23.27	66.	Bénéfices après impôt

Co-operative banks — Banques mutualistes

Per cent — *Pourcentage*

BALANCE SHEET ANALYSIS — **ANALYSE DU BILAN**

% of year-end balance sheet total — % du total du bilan en fin d'exercice

	1985	1986	1987	1988	1989	1990	1991	1992	1993 (1)	1994	
Assets											**Actif**
67. Cash & balance with Central bank	2.73	2.59	2.72	2.88	3.03	3.05	3.01	3.31	2.50	2.33	67. Caisse & solde auprès de la Banque centrale
68. Interbank deposits	14.72	17.40	17.22	16.45	16.68	17.41	16.74	15.11	16.35	13.47	68. Dépôts interbancaires
69. Loans	62.68	59.61	58.18	58.24	58.89	58.37	59.38	60.17	58.22	59.31	69. Prêts
70. Securities	15.59	16.28	18.08	18.84	17.99	17.71	17.44	18.18	20.00	22.01	70. Valeurs mobilières
71. Other assets	4.29	4.11	3.80	3.59	3.42	3.45	3.43	3.23	2.92	2.88	71. Autres actifs
Liabilities											**Passif**
72. Capital & reserves	3.84	3.88	3.92	3.94	3.89	3.77	3.79	4.03	4.15	4.36	72. Capital et réserves
73. Borrowing from Central bank	2.75	2.37	2.16	2.97	3.54	3.49	2.95	2.50	1.84	1.97	73. Emprunts auprès de la Banque centrale
74. Interbank deposits	9.67	9.10	8.86	8.74	8.41	8.07	7.52	7.58	8.49	9.83	74. Dépôts interbancaires
75. Non-bank deposits	80.16	80.89	81.12	80.17	79.56	79.48	79.86	79.37	78.75	76.56	75. Dépôts non bancaires
76. Bonds	0.81	0.98	1.20	1.43	1.81	2.32	2.85	3.38	3.56	4.17	76. Obligations
77. Other liabilities	2.77	2.78	2.73	2.75	2.79	2.87	3.03	3.14	3.22	3.12	77. Autres engagements
Memoranda											*Pour mémoire*
78. Short-term securities	2.04	2.04	2.41	2.39	2.16	2.29	2.60	2.78	3.32	3.07	78. Titres à court terme
79. Bonds	13.05	13.64	14.95	15.71	15.13	14.71	14.08	14.51	15.49	17.62	79. Obligations
80. Shares and participations	0.49	0.61	0.72	0.74	0.69	0.71	0.76	0.89	1.19	1.32	80. Actions et participations
81. Claims on non-residents	0.36	0.44	0.56	0.69	1.03	1.21	1.36	1.15	2.02	1.84	81. Créances sur des non résidents
82. Liabilities to non-residents	0.92	0.86	0.85	0.86	0.86	1.04	0.82	1.06	1.19	1.31	82. Engagements envers des non résidents

1. Break in series due to change in methodology.
2. Included under "Provisions on loans" (item 15 or item 52).

Notes

- Average balance sheet totals (item 29) are based on twelve end-month data.

Change in methodology:

- As from 1985, all credit co-operatives are included in the data.

- As from 1993, data include eastern German credit institutions and are in accordance with the new accounting regulations.

1. Rupture de comparabilité dans les séries due aux changements méthodologiques.
2. Inclus sous "Provisions sur prêts" (poste 15 ou poste 52).

Notes

- La moyenne du total des actifs/passifs (poste 29) est basée sur douze données de fin de mois.

Changement méthodologique :

- Depuis 1985, les données comprennent l'ensemble des banques mutualistes.

- Depuis 1993, les données comprennent les organismes de crédit d'Allemagne orientale et sont conformes aux nouvelles règles de comptabilité.

GREECE

Commercial banks

GRECE

Banques commerciales

Million drachmas / *Millions de drachmes*

			1989	1990	1991	1992	1993	1994
INCOME STATEMENT		**COMPTE DE RESULTATS**						
1.	Interest income	Produits financiers	810801	1036099	1262406	1433138	1589503	1821510
2.	Interest expenses	Frais financiers	726260	906804	1058188	1254678	1383660	1621449
3.	Net interest income	Produits financiers nets	84541	129295	204218	178460	205843	200061
4.	Non-interest income (net)	Produits non financiers (nets)	124699	162721	233967	244891	286193	420906
5.	Gross income	Résultat brut	209240	292016	438185	423351	492036	620967
6.	Operating expenses	Frais d'exploitation	156387	187198	224921	258439	308571	369367
7.	Net income	Résultat net	52853	104818	213264	164912	183465	251600
8.	Provisions (net)	Provisions (nettes)	22034	35758	63983	35905	44700	57981
9.	Profit before tax	Bénéfices avant impôt	30819	69060	149281	129007	138765	193619
10.	Income tax	Impôt	3847	14306	24108	42032	46105	54599
11.	Profit after tax	Bénéfices après impôt	26972	54754	125173	86975	92660	139020
12.	Distributed profit	Bénéfices distribués	15572	32859	59333	42248	54204	73996
13.	Retained profit	Bénéfices mis en réserve	11400	21895	65840	44727	38456	65024
	Memoranda	***Pour mémoire***						
14.	*Staff costs*	*Frais de personnel*	*119771*	*143740*	*170408*	*184861*	*214426*	*259686*
15.	*Provisions on loans*	*Provisions sur prêts*	*18589*	*32052*	*60506*	*32988*	*44261*	*194520*
16.	*Provisions on securities*	*Provisions sur titres*	..	..	..	..	..	..
BALANCE SHEET (1)		**BILAN (1)**						
	Assets	**Actif**						
17.	Cash & balance with Central bank	Caisse & solde auprès de la Banque centrale	1320877	1491539	1767795	2155478	2490771	2837652
18.	Interbank deposits	Dépôts interbancaires	398722	449363	571899	796507	1101032	1706498
19.	Loans	Prêts	2297698	2424713	2610509	2939091	3358861	3858319
20.	Securities	Valeurs mobilières	2694366	3287455	3869357	4441205	5156437	5489608
21.	Other assets	Autres actifs	632496	847931	1280489	1782388	2018707	1438616
	Liabilities	**Passif**						
22.	Capital & reserves	Capital et réserves	230484	331782	473424	558540	642884	746500
23.	Borrowing from Central bank	Emprunts auprès de la Banque centrale	29734	37482	30198	25045	26399	22354
24.	Interbank deposits	Dépôts interbancaires	138630	114612	210746	265597	395454	940169
25.	Non-bank deposits	Dépôts non bancaires	6035693	6884165	7993838	9432922	11093788	11519309
26.	Bonds	Obligations			119125	119125	120122	120096
27.	Other liabilities	Autres engagements	909618	1132960	1272718	1713440	1847161	1982265
	Balance sheet total	**Total du bilan**						
28.	End-year total	En fin d'exercice	7344159	8501001	10100049	12114669	14125808	15330693
29.	Average total	Moyen	6734317	7922580	9300525	11107359	13120238	14728251
	Memoranda	***Pour mémoire***						
30.	*Short-term securities*	*Titres à court terme*	*2287331*	*2609230*	*1331164*	*766113*	*234529*	*339189*
31.	*Bonds*	*Obligations*	*156967*	*380370*	*2166431*	*3194076*	*4356727*	*4380005*
32.	*Shares and participations*	*Actions et participations*	*250068*	*297855*	*371762*	*481016*	*565221*	*770414*
33.	*Claims on non-residents*	*Créances sur des non résidents*	..	..	..	..	..	..
34.	*Liabilities to non-residents*	*Engagements envers des non résidents*	..	..	..	..	..	..
SUPPLEMENTARY INFORMATION		**RENSEIGNEMENTS COMPLEMENTAIRES**						
35.	Number of institutions	Nombre d'institutions	15	15	19	19	20	19
36.	Number of branches	Nombre de succursales	1065	1079	1117	1154	1200	1244
37.	Number of employees (x 1000)	Nombre de salariés (x 1000)	37.22	36.4	37.17	37.1	37.54	39.57

95

GREECE

Commercial banks

GREECE

Banques commerciales

Per cent

Pourcentage

	1989	1990	1991	1992	1993	1994		
INCOME STATEMENT ANALYSIS								**ANALYSE DU COMPTE DE RESULTATS**
% of average balance sheet total								**% du total moyen du bilan**
38. Interest income	12.04	13.08	13.57	12.90	12.11	12.37	38.	Produits financiers
39. Interest expenses	10.78	11.45	11.38	11.30	10.55	11.01	39.	Frais financiers
40. Net interest income	1.26	1.63	2.20	1.61	1.57	1.36	40.	Produits financiers nets
41. Non-interest income (net)	1.85	2.05	2.52	2.20	2.18	2.86	41.	Produits non financiers (nets)
42. Gross income	3.11	3.69	4.71	3.81	3.75	4.22	42.	Résultat brut
43. Operating expenses	2.32	2.36	2.42	2.33	2.35	2.51	43.	Frais d'exploitation
44. Net income	0.78	1.32	2.29	1.48	1.40	1.71	44.	Résultat net
45. Provisions (net)	0.33	0.45	0.69	0.32	0.34	0.39	45.	Provisions (nettes)
46. Profit before tax	0.46	0.87	1.61	1.16	1.06	1.31	46.	Bénéfices avant impôt
47. Income tax	0.06	0.18	0.26	0.38	0.35	0.37	47.	Impôt
48. Profit after tax	0.40	0.69	1.35	0.78	0.71	0.94	48.	Bénéfices après impôt
49. Distributed profit	0.23	0.41	0.64	0.38	0.41	0.50	49.	Bénéfices distribués
50. Retained profit	0.17	0.28	0.71	0.40	0.29	0.44	50.	Bénéfices mis en réserve
51. Staff costs	1.78	1.81	1.83	1.66	1.63	1.76	51.	Frais de personnel
52. Provisions on loans	0.28	0.40	0.65	0.30	0.34	1.32	52.	Provisions sur prêts
53. Provisions on securities	:	:	:	:	:	:	53.	Provisions sur titres
% of gross income								**% du total du résultat brut**
54. Net interest income	40.40	44.28	46.61	42.15	41.83	32.22	54.	Produits financiers nets
55. Non-interest income (net)	59.60	55.72	53.39	57.85	58.17	67.78	55.	Produits non financiers (nets)
56. Operating expenses	74.74	64.11	51.33	61.05	62.71	59.48	56.	Frais d'exploitation
57. Net income	25.26	35.89	48.67	38.95	37.29	40.52	57.	Résultat net
58. Provisions (net)	10.53	12.25	14.60	8.48	9.08	9.34	58.	Provisions (nettes)
59. Profit before tax	14.73	23.65	34.07	30.47	28.20	31.18	59.	Bénéfices avant impôt
60. Income tax	1.84	4.90	5.50	9.93	9.37	8.79	60.	Impôt
61. Profit after tax	12.89	18.75	28.57	20.54	18.83	22.39	61.	Bénéfices après impôt
62. Staff costs	57.24	49.22	38.89	43.67	43.58	41.82	62.	Frais de personnel
% of net income								**% du total du résultat net**
63. Provisions (net)	41.69	34.11	30.00	21.77	24.36	23.04	63.	Provisions (nettes)
64. Profit before tax	58.31	65.89	70.00	78.23	75.64	76.96	64.	Bénéfices avant impôt
65. Income tax	7.28	13.65	11.30	25.49	25.13	21.70	65.	Impôt
66. Profit after tax	51.03	52.24	58.69	52.74	50.51	55.25	66.	Bénéfices après impôt

GREECE

Commercial banks

Per cent

BALANCE SHEET ANALYSIS (1)

	1989	1990	1991	1992	1993	1994
% of year-end balance sheet total						
Assets						
67. Cash & balance with Central bank	17.99	17.55	17.50	17.79	17.63	18.51
68. Interbank deposits	5.43	5.29	5.66	6.57	7.79	11.13
69. Loans	31.29	28.52	25.85	24.26	23.78	25.17
70. Securities	36.69	38.67	38.31	36.66	36.50	35.81
71. Other assets	8.61	9.97	12.68	14.71	14.29	9.38
Liabilities						
72. Capital & reserves	3.14	3.90	4.69	4.61	4.55	4.87
73. Borrowing from Central bank	0.40	0.44	0.30	0.21	0.19	0.15
74. Interbank deposits	1.89	1.35	2.09	2.19	2.80	6.13
75. Non-bank deposits	82.18	80.98	79.15	77.86	78.54	75.14
76. Bonds	-	-	1.18	0.98	0.85	0.78
77. Other liabilities	12.39	13.33	12.60	14.14	13.08	12.93
Memoranda						
78. Short-term securities	*31.14*	*30.69*	*13.18*	*6.32*	*1.66*	*2.21*
79. Bonds	*2.14*	*4.47*	*21.45*	*26.37*	*30.84*	*28.57*
80. Shares and participations	*3.40*	*3.50*	*3.68*	*3.97*	*4.00*	*5.03*
81. Claims on non-residents	..	..	..	..	..	..
82. Liabilities to non-residents	..	..	..	..	..	..

1. Due to changes in the reporting system, balance-sheet data have been revised to include off-shore activities of bank branches

GRECE

Banques commerciales

Pourcentage

ANALYSE DU BILAN (1)

% du total du bilan en fin d'exercice

Actif
67. Caisse & solde auprès de la Banque centrale
68. Dépôts interbancaires
69. Prêts
70. Valeurs mobilières
71. Autres actifs

Passif
72. Capital et réserves
73. Emprunts auprès de la Banque centrale
74. Dépôts interbancaires
75. Dépôts non bancaires
76. Obligations
77. Autres engagements

Pour mémoire
78. Titres à court terme
79. Obligations
80. Actions et participations
81. Créances sur des non résidents
82. Engagements envers des non résidents

1. Suite aux changements dans le règlement en vigueur, les données du bilan ont été révisées afin d'inclure les activités des succursales à l'étranger.

GREECE

Large commercial banks

Million drachmas

GREECE

Grandes banques commerciales

Millions de drachmes

		1985	1986	1987	1988	1989	1990	1991	1992	1993	1994	
INCOME STATEMENT												**COMPTE DE RESULTATS**
1.	Interest income	362938	421524	470044	575166	708956	890880	1068795	1214742	1308178	1440979	Produits financiers
2.	Interest expenses	327762	380934	444522	538274	644999	798348	912049	1085177	1159732	1321417	Frais financiers
3.	Net interest income	35176	40590	25522	36892	63957	92532	156746	129565	148846	119562	Produits financiers nets
4.	Non-interest income (net)	46042	56926	80966	96544	103671	135770	196760	185477	215507	349770	Produits non financiers (nets)
5.	Gross income	81218	97516	106488	133436	167628	228302	353506	315042	363953	469332	Résultat brut
6.	Operating expenses	63849	73121	83179	108286	128358	151969	178455	198993	233028	275646	Frais d'exploitation
7.	Net income	17369	24395	23309	25150	39270	76333	175051	116049	130925	193686	Résultat net
8.	Provisions (net)	8598	10344	9491	10760	19350	31240	59044	24506	30252	44356	Provisions (nettes)
9.	Profit before tax	8771	14051	13818	14390	19920	45093	116007	91543	100673	149330	Bénéfices avant impôt
10.	Income tax	990	1243	2288	2244	2714	9498	17547	26789	30387	38534	Impôt
11.	Profit after tax	7781	12808	11530	12146	17206	35595	98460	64754	70286	110796	Bénéfices après impôt
12.	Distributed profit	3765	6810	8572	9763	8768	19583	41679	29745	39918	56433	Bénéfices distribués
13.	Retained profit	4016	5998	2958	2383	8438	16012	56781	35009	30368	54363	Bénéfices mis en réserve
	Memoranda											*Pour mémoire*
14.	*Staff costs*	*51695*	*58343*	*63957*	*83952*	*100241*	*118929*	*138279*	*147857*	*168130*	*202185*	*Frais de personnel*
15.	*Provisions on loans*	*..*	*..*	*9491*	*9920*	*16178*	*29200*	*56171*	*24112*	*29882*	*148941*	*Provisions sur prêts*
16.	*Provisions on securities*	*..*	*..*	*..*	*..*	*..*	*..*	*..*	*..*	*..*	*..*	*Provisions sur titres*
BALANCE SHEET (1)												**BILAN (1)**
Assets												**Actif**
17.	Cash & balance with Central bank	509022	512909	737241	1165163	1153461	1373922	1604560	1913734	2207539	2378388	Caisse & solde auprès de la Banque centrale
18.	Interbank deposits	202194	155764	159245	281820	296536	320288	388178	582607	807989	1058011	Dépôts interbancaires
19.	Loans	1074734	1295144	1410280	1647158	1948042	1996282	2120142	2293430	2590358	2917673	Prêts
20.	Securities	969482	1210724	1509263	1949543	2527840	2968372	3453143	3823378	4575126	4922240	Valeurs mobilières
21.	Other assets	173612	294366	216138	338723	513998	721156	1082620	1612072	1622812	1239852	Autres actifs
Liabilities												**Passif**
22.	Capital & reserves	71217	77377	81929	149671	167870	247835	351624	408236	477322	586903	Capital et réserves
23.	Borrowing from Central bank	194405	186261	136750	41278	5523	12086	5896	1385	1370	666	Emprunts auprès de la Banque centrale
24.	Interbank deposits	44946	34488	37923	66746	74608	78980	154198	179240	289281	805002	Dépôts interbancaires
25.	Non-bank deposits	2507426	2998305	3675497	4453687	5395410	6035308	6843311	8017463	9322416	9432971	Dépôts non bancaires
26.	Bonds							119125	119125	119125	119125	Obligations
27.	Other liabilities	111050	172476	100068	671025	796466	1005811	1169489	1499772	1594310	1571497	Autres engagements
Balance sheet total												**Total du bilan**
28.	End-year total	2929044	3468907	4032167	5382407	6439877	7380020	8648643	10225221	11803824	12516164	En fin d'exercice
29.	Average total	2606795	3198976	3750537	4919463	5911142	6909949	8014322	9436932	11014523	12159994	Moyen
	Memoranda											*Pour mémoire*
30.	*Short-term securities*	*893488*	*1073423*	*1235980*	*1607086*	*2133756*	*2317709*	*969054*	*506022*	*160917*	*282618*	*Titres à court terme*
31.	*Bonds*	*21494*	*31206*	*73101*	*115355*	*149571*	*366025*	*2135623*	*2916980*	*3884467*	*3924375*	*Obligations*
32.	*Shares and participations*	*54500*	*106095*	*200182*	*227102*	*244513*	*284638*	*348466*	*400376*	*529742*	*715247*	*Actions et participations*
33.	*Claims on non-residents*	*..*	*..*	*..*	*..*	*..*	*..*	*..*	*..*	*..*	*..*	*Créances sur des non résidents*
34.	*Liabilities to non-residents*	*..*	*..*	*..*	*..*	*..*	*..*	*..*	*..*	*..*	*..*	*Engagements envers des non résidents*
SUPPLEMENTARY INFORMATION												**RENSEIGNEMENTS COMPLEMENTAIRES**
35.	Number of institutions	4	4	4	4	4	4	4	4	4	4	Nombre d'institutions
36.	Number of branches	782	795	794	797	799	802	812	824	843	856	Nombre de succursales
37.	Number of employees (x 1000)	27.4	28.4	29.0	29.4	29.7	28.7	28.7	28.3	28.2	29.4	Nombre de salariés (x 1000)

GREECE

Large commercial banks

GRECE

Grandes banques commerciales

Per cent	1985	1986	1987	1988	1989	1990	1991	1992	1993	1994	Pourcentage	
INCOME STATEMENT ANALYSIS											**ANALYSE DU COMPTE DE RESULTATS**	
% of average balance sheet total											**% du total moyen du bilan**	
38. Interest income	13.92	13.18	12.53	11.69	11.99	12.89	13.34	12.87	11.88	11.85	38. Produits financiers	
39. Interest expenses	12.57	11.91	11.85	10.94	10.91	11.55	11.38	11.50	10.53	10.87	39. Frais financiers	
40. Net interest income	1.35	1.27	0.68	0.75	1.08	1.34	1.96	1.37	1.35	0.98	40. Produits financiers nets	
41. Non-interest income (net)	1.77	1.78	2.16	1.96	1.75	1.96	2.46	1.97	1.96	2.88	41. Produits non financiers (nets)	
42. Gross income	3.12	3.05	2.84	2.71	2.84	3.30	4.41	3.34	3.30	3.86	42. Résultat brut	
43. Operating expenses	2.45	2.29	2.22	2.20	2.17	2.20	2.23	2.11	2.12	2.27	43. Frais d'exploitation	
44. Net income	0.67	0.76	0.62	0.51	0.66	1.10	2.18	1.23	1.19	1.59	44. Résultat net	
45. Provisions (net)	0.33	0.32	0.25	0.22	0.33	0.45	0.74	0.26	0.27	0.36	45. Provisions (nettes)	
46. Profit before tax	0.34	0.44	0.37	0.29	0.34	0.65	1.45	0.97	0.91	1.23	46. Bénéfices avant impôt	
47. Income tax	0.04	0.04	0.06	0.05	0.05	0.14	0.22	0.28	0.28	0.32	47. Impôt	
48. Profit after tax	0.30	0.40	0.31	0.25	0.29	0.52	1.23	0.69	0.64	0.91	48. Bénéfices après impôt	
49. Distributed profit	0.14	0.21	0.23	0.20	0.15	0.28	0.52	0.32	0.36	0.46	49. Bénéfices distribués	
50. Retained profit	0.15	0.19	0.08	0.05	0.14	0.23	0.71	0.37	0.28	0.45	50. Bénéfices mis en réserve	
51. Staff costs	1.98	1.82	1.71	1.71	1.70	1.72	1.73	1.57	1.53	1.66	51. Frais de personnel	
52. Provisions on loans	:	:	0.25	0.20	0.27	0.42	0.70	0.26	0.27	1.22	52. Provisions sur prêts	
53. Provisions on securities	:	:	:	:	:	:	:	:	:	:	53. Provisions sur titres	
% of gross income											**% du total du résultat brut**	
54. Net interest income	43.31	41.62	23.97	27.65	38.15	40.53	44.34	41.13	40.79	25.47	54. Produits financiers nets	
55. Non-interest income (net)	56.69	58.38	76.03	72.35	61.85	59.47	55.66	58.87	59.21	74.53	55. Produits non financiers (nets)	
56. Operating expenses	78.61	74.98	78.11	81.15	76.57	66.56	50.48	63.16	64.03	58.73	56. Frais d'exploitation	
57. Net income	21.39	25.02	21.89	18.85	23.43	33.44	49.52	36.84	35.97	41.27	57. Résultat net	
58. Provisions (net)	10.59	10.61	8.91	8.06	11.54	13.68	16.70	7.78	8.31	9.45	58. Provisions (nettes)	
59. Profit before tax	10.80	14.41	12.98	10.78	11.88	19.75	32.82	29.06	27.66	31.82	59. Bénéfices avant impôt	
60. Income tax	1.22	1.27	2.15	1.68	1.62	4.16	4.96	8.50	8.35	8.21	60. Impôt	
61. Profit after tax	9.58	13.13	10.83	9.10	10.26	15.59	27.85	20.55	19.31	23.61	61. Bénéfices après impôt	
62. Staff costs	63.65	59.83	60.06	62.92	59.80	52.09	39.12	46.93	46.20	43.08	62. Frais de personnel	
% of net income											**% du total du résultat net**	
63. Provisions (net)	49.50	42.40	40.72	42.78	49.27	40.93	33.73	21.12	23.11	22.90	63. Provisions (nettes)	
64. Profit before tax	50.50	57.60	59.28	57.22	50.73	59.07	66.27	78.88	76.89	77.10	64. Bénéfices avant impôt	
65. Income tax	5.70	5.10	9.82	8.92	6.91	12.44	10.02	23.08	23.21	19.90	65. Impôt	
66. Profit after tax	44.80	52.50	49.47	48.29	43.81	46.63	56.25	55.80	53.68	57.20	66. Bénéfices après impôt	

Large commercial banks

Per cent

BALANCE SHEET ANALYSIS (1)

% of year-end balance sheet total

	1985	1986	1987	1988	1989	1990	1991	1992	1993	1994
Assets										
67. Cash & balance with Central bank	17.38	14.79	18.28	21.65	17.91	18.62	18.55	18.72	18.70	19.00
68. Interbank deposits	6.90	4.49	3.95	5.24	4.60	4.34	4.49	5.70	6.85	8.45
69. Loans	36.69	37.34	34.98	30.60	30.25	27.05	24.51	22.43	21.95	23.31
70. Securities	33.10	34.90	37.43	36.22	39.25	40.22	39.93	37.39	38.76	39.33
71. Other assets	5.93	8.49	5.36	6.29	7.98	9.77	12.52	15.77	13.75	9.91
Liabilities										
72. Capital & reserves	2.43	2.23	2.03	2.78	2.61	3.36	4.07	3.99	4.04	4.69
73. Borrowing from Central bank	6.64	5.37	3.39	0.77	0.09	0.16	0.07	0.01	0.01	0.01
74. Interbank deposits	1.53	0.99	0.94	1.24	1.16	1.07	1.78	1.75	2.45	6.43
75. Non-bank deposits	85.61	86.43	91.15	82.75	83.78	81.78	79.18	78.41	78.98	75.37
76. Bonds	-						1.38	1.17	1.01	0.95
77. Other liabilities	3.79	4.97	2.48	12.47	12.37	13.63	13.52	14.67	13.51	12.56
Memoranda										
78. Short-term securities	*30.50*	*30.94*	*30.65*	*29.86*	*33.13*	*31.41*	*11.20*	*4.95*	*1.36*	*2.26*
79. Bonds	*0.73*	*0.90*	*1.81*	*2.14*	*2.32*	*4.96*	*24.69*	*28.53*	*32.91*	*31.35*
80. Shares and participations	*1.86*	*3.06*	*4.96*	*4.22*	*3.80*	*3.86*	*4.03*	*3.92*	*4.49*	*5.71*
81. Claims on non-residents	*..*	*..*	*..*	*..*	*..*	*..*	*..*	*..*		
82. Liabilities to non-residents	*..*	*..*	*..*	*..*	*..*	*..*	*..*			

1. Break in series. Due to changes in the reporting system, beginning 1988, balance-sheet data have been revised to include off-shore activities of bank branches.

Notes

• Large commercial banks are a sub-group of Commercial banks.

Grandes banques commerciales

Pourcentage

ANALYSE DU BILAN (1)

% du total du bilan en fin d'exercice

Actif
67. Caisse & solde auprès de la Banque centrale
68. Dépôts interbancaires
69. Prêts
70. Valeurs mobilières
71. Autres actifs

Passif
72. Capital et réserves
73. Emprunts auprès de la Banque centrale
74. Dépôts interbancaires
75. Dépôts non bancaires
76. Obligations
77. Autres engagements

Pour mémoire
78. Titres à court terme
79. Obligations
80. Actions et participations
81. Créances sur des non résidents
82. Engagements envers des non résidents

1. Rupture dans les séries. Suite aux changements dans le règlement en vigueur, à partir de 1988, les données du bilan ont été révisées afin d'inclure les activités des succursales à l'étranger.

Notes

• La catégorie Grandes banques commerciales est un sous-groupe des Banques commerciales.

Commercial banks and savings banks (1)
Banques commerciales et caisses d'épargne (1)

Million Icelandic krónur — *Millions de couronnes islandaises*

		1985	1986	1987	1988	1989	1990	1991	1992	1993	1994	
INCOME STATEMENT												**COMPTE DE RESULTATS**
1.	Interest income	14161	12215	20664	31450	37854	29516	33827	26546	27916	22455	1. Produits financiers
2.	Interest expenses	10843	8277	14351	22647	28694	18830	22429	14572	15366	10490	2. Frais financiers
3.	Net interest income	3318	3938	6313	8803	9160	10686	11398	11974	12550	11965	3. Produits financiers nets
4.	Non-interest income (net)	920	1156	1886	2665	4300	4273	4475	4583	5334	6147	4. Produits non financiers (nets)
5.	Gross income	4238	5094	8199	11468	13460	14959	15873	16557	17884	18112	5. Résultat brut
6.	Operating expenses	3320	4625	6528	8963	9937	11080	12440	12425	11584	12169	6. Frais d'exploitation
7.	Net income	918	469	1671	2505	3523	3879	3433	4132	6300	5943	7. Résultat net
8.	Provisions (net)	652	295	699	976	1530	2585	2530	6802	6047	4715	8. Provisions (nettes)
9.	Profit before tax	266	174	972	1529	1993	1294	903	-2670	253	1228	9. Bénéfices avant impôt
10.	Income tax	230	77	485	597	744	297	395	97	421	480	10. Impôt
11.	Profit after tax	36	97	487	932	1249	997	508	-2767	-168	748	11. Bénéfices après impôt
12.	Distributed profit	-	26	31	109	169	50	288	189	97	159	12. Bénéfices distribués
13.	Retained profit	36	71	456	823	1080	947	220	-2956	-265	589	13. Bénéfices mis en réserve
Memoranda												*Pour mémoire*
14.	*Staff costs*	1888	2612	3770	4936	5433	5472	5994	6021	5727	5907	14. *Frais de personnel*
15.	*Provisions on loans*	652	295	699	976	1530	2585	2530	6802	6047	4715	15. *Provisions sur prêts*
16.	*Provisions on securities*	-	-	-	-	-	-	-	-	-	-	16. *Provisions sur titres*
BALANCE SHEET												**BILAN**
Assets												**Actif**
17.	Cash & balance with Central bank	9215	12290	13182	14453	19633	15188	16873	14642	11901	11740	17. Caisse & solde auprès de la Banque centrale
18.	Interbank deposits	1475	2143	3816	5199	6058	6339	6898	6211	10799	11511	18. Dépôts interbancaires
19.	Loans	53009	62004	87125	123547	152548	158736	178640	185216	191021	194164	19. Prêts
20.	Securities	646	636	1598	3467	8035	20496	20232	23861	27655	19318	20. Valeurs mobilières
21.	Other assets	5276	7455	10299	8670	11236	12609	14858	15135	15485	14658	21. Autres actifs
Liabilities												**Passif**
22.	Capital & reserves	4710	6125	9238	11943	15975	16163	19536	16718	19025	19885	22. Capital et réserves
23.	Borrowing from Central bank	5634	6034	5076	4587	4737	3625	3378	2520	1599	3107	23. Emprunts auprès de la Banque centrale
24.	Interbank deposits	1062	639	1288	2332	2582	2192	2475	2404	1812	2147	24. Dépôts interbancaires
25.	Non-bank deposits	37337	50464	68452	84774	108543	124645	142809	147998	157888	160736	25. Dépôts non bancaires
26.	Bonds	-	-	853	8817	13792	17453	19181	20666	22549	22273	26. Obligations
27.	Other liabilities	20878	21266	31113	42883	51881	49290	50122	54759	53988	43243	27. Autres engagements
Balance sheet total												**Total du bilan**
28.	End-year total	69621	84528	116020	155336	197510	213368	237501	245065	256861	251391	28. En fin d'exercice
29.	Average total	61127	77075	100273	135678	176423	205439	225435	241283	250963	254126	29. Moyen
Memoranda												*Pour mémoire*
30.	*Short-term securities*	646	-	395	168	2833	5870	5226	8361	7202	2191	30. *Titres à court terme*
31.	*Bonds*	176	636	1203	3299	5202	14626	15006	15500	20453	17127	31. *Obligations*
32.	*Shares and participations*	176	300	514	748	1479	2026	3678	4000	4023	4138	32. *Actions et participations*
33.	*Claims on non-residents*	1968	1762	2279	2942	3766	4488	4645	4524	6812	8105	33. *Créances sur des non résidents*
34.	*Liabilities to non-residents*	17752	16887	22603	35109	42728	39071	39900	43769	43126	31843	34. *Engagements envers des non résidents*
SUPPLEMENTARY INFORMATION												**RENSEIGNEMENTS COMPLEMENTAIRES**
35.	Number of institutions	45	45	44	41	41	35	36	36	34	33	35. Nombre d'institutions
36.	Number of branches	173	180	184	183	183	176	177	178	174	176	36. Nombre de succursales
37.	Number of employees (x 1000)	2.75	2.89	3.01	3.07	2.93	2.81	2.82	2.71	2.55	2.53	37. Nombre de salariés (x 1000)

ICELAND

Commercial banks and savings banks (1)

ISLANDE

Banques commerciales et caisses d'épargne (1)

Per cent / *Pourcentage*

INCOME STATEMENT ANALYSIS / ANALYSE DU COMPTE DE RESULTATS

	1985	1986	1987	1988	1989	1990	1991	1992	1993	1994	
% of average balance sheet total											**% du total moyen du bilan**
38. Interest income	23.17	15.85	20.61	23.18	21.46	14.37	15.01	11.00	11.12	8.84	38. Produits financiers
39. Interest expenses	17.74	10.74	14.31	16.69	16.26	9.17	9.95	6.04	6.12	4.13	39. Frais financiers
40. Net interest income	5.43	5.11	6.30	6.49	5.19	5.20	5.06	4.96	5.00	4.71	40. Produits financiers nets
41. Non-interest income (net)	1.51	1.50	1.88	1.96	2.44	2.08	1.99	1.90	2.13	2.42	41. Produits non financiers (nets)
42. Gross income	6.93	6.61	8.18	8.45	7.63	7.28	7.04	6.86	7.13	7.13	42. Résultat brut
43. Operating expenses	5.43	6.00	6.51	6.61	5.63	5.39	5.52	5.15	4.62	4.79	43. Frais d'exploitation
44. Net income	1.50	0.61	1.67	1.85	2.00	1.89	1.52	1.71	2.51	2.34	44. Résultat net
45. Provisions (net)	1.07	0.38	0.70	0.72	0.87	1.26	1.12	2.82	2.41	1.86	45. Provisions (nettes)
46. Profit before tax	0.44	0.23	0.97	1.13	1.13	0.63	0.40	-1.11	0.10	0.48	46. Bénéfices avant impôt
47. Income tax	0.38	0.10	0.48	0.44	0.42	0.14	0.18	0.04	0.17	0.19	47. Impôt
48. Profit after tax	0.06	0.13	0.49	0.69	0.71	0.49	0.23	-1.15	-0.07	0.29	48. Bénéfices après impôt
49. Distributed profit		0.03	0.03	0.08	0.10	0.02	0.13	0.08	0.04	0.06	49. Bénéfices distribués
50. Retained profit	0.06	0.09	0.45	0.61	0.61	0.46	0.10	-1.23	-0.11	0.23	50. Bénéfices mis en réserve
51. Staff costs	3.09	3.39	3.76	3.64	3.08	2.66	2.66	2.50	2.28	2.32	51. Frais de personnel
52. Provisions on loans	1.07	0.38	0.70	0.72	0.87	1.26	1.12	2.82	2.41	1.86	52. Provisions sur prêts
53. Provisions on securities											53. Provisions sur titres
% of gross income											**% du total du résultat brut**
54. Net interest income	78.29	77.31	77.00	76.76	68.05	71.44	71.81	72.32	70.17	66.06	54. Produits financiers nets
55. Non-interest income (net)	21.71	22.69	23.00	23.24	31.95	28.56	28.19	27.68	29.83	33.94	55. Produits non financiers (nets)
56. Operating expenses	78.34	90.79	79.62	78.16	73.83	74.07	78.37	75.04	64.77	67.19	56. Frais d'exploitation
57. Net income	21.66	9.21	20.38	21.84	26.17	25.93	21.63	24.96	35.23	32.81	57. Résultat net
58. Provisions (net)	15.38	5.79	8.53	8.51	11.37	17.28	15.94	41.08	33.81	26.03	58. Provisions (nettes)
59. Profit before tax	6.28	3.42	11.86	13.33	14.81	8.65	5.69	-16.13	1.41	6.78	59. Bénéfices avant impôt
60. Income tax	5.43	1.51	5.92	5.21	5.53	1.99	2.49	0.59	2.35	2.65	60. Impôt
61. Profit after tax	0.85	1.90	5.94	8.13	9.28	6.66	3.20	-16.71	-0.94	4.13	61. Bénéfices après impôt
62. Staff costs	44.55	51.28	45.98	43.04	40.36	36.58	37.76	36.37	32.02	32.61	62. Frais de personnel
% of net income											**% du total du résultat net**
63. Provisions (net)	71.02	62.90	41.83	38.96	43.43	66.64	73.70	164.62	95.98	79.34	63. Provisions (nettes)
64. Profit before tax	28.98	37.10	58.17	61.04	56.57	33.36	26.30	-64.62	4.02	20.66	64. Bénéfices avant impôt
65. Income tax	25.05	16.42	29.02	23.83	21.12	7.66	11.51	2.35	6.68	8.08	65. Impôt
66. Profit after tax	3.92	20.68	29.14	37.21	35.45	25.70	14.80	-66.97	-2.67	12.59	66. Bénéfices après impôt

ICELAND

Commercial banks and savings banks (1)

ISLANDE

Banques commerciales et caisses d'épargne (1)

Per cent / *Pourcentage*

BALANCE SHEET ANALYSIS / **ANALYSE DU BILAN**

% of year-end balance sheet total / % du total du bilan en fin d'exercice

	1985	1986	1987	1988	1989	1990	1991	1992	1993	1994		
Assets												**Actif**
67. Cash & balance with Central bank	13.24	14.54	11.36	9.30	9.94	7.12	7.10	5.97	4.63	4.67	67.	Caisse & solde auprès de la Banque centrale
68. Interbank deposits	2.12	2.54	3.29	3.35	3.07	2.97	2.90	2.53	4.20	4.58	68.	Dépôts interbancaires
69. Loans	76.14	73.35	75.09	79.54	77.24	74.40	75.22	75.58	74.37	77.24	69.	Prêts
70. Securities	0.93	0.75	1.38	2.23	4.07	9.61	8.52	9.74	10.77	7.68	70.	Valeurs mobilières
71. Other assets	7.58	8.82	8.88	5.58	5.69	5.91	6.26	6.18	6.03	5.83	71.	Autres actifs
Liabilities												**Passif**
72. Capital & reserves	6.77	7.25	7.96	7.69	8.09	7.58	8.23	6.82	7.41	7.91	72.	Capital et réserves
73. Borrowing from Central bank	8.09	7.14	4.38	2.95	2.40	1.70	1.42	1.03	0.62	1.24	73.	Emprunts auprès de la Banque centrale
74. Interbank deposits	1.53	0.76	1.11	1.50	1.31	1.03	1.04	0.98	0.71	0.85	74.	Dépôts interbancaires
75. Non-bank deposits	53.63	59.70	59.00	54.57	54.96	58.42	60.13	60.39	61.47	63.94	75.	Dépôts non bancaires
76. Bonds		-	0.74	5.68	6.98	8.18	8.08	8.43	8.78	8.86	76.	Obligations
77. Other liabilities	29.99	25.16	26.82	27.61	26.27	23.10	21.10	22.34	21.02	17.20	77.	Autres engagements
Memoranda												*Pour mémoire*
78. Short-term securities	-		0.34	0.11	1.43	2.75	2.20	3.41	2.80	0.87	78.	Titres à court terme
79. Bonds	0.93	0.75	1.04	2.12	2.63	6.85	6.32	6.32	7.96	6.81	79.	Obligations
80. Shares and participations	0.25	0.35	0.44	0.48	0.75	0.95	1.55	1.63	1.57	1.65	80.	Actions et participations
81. Claims on non-residents	2.83	2.08	1.96	1.89	1.91	2.10	1.96	1.85	2.65	3.22	81.	Créances sur des non résidents
82. Liabilities to non-residents	25.50	19.98	19.48	22.60	21.63	18.31	16.80	17.86	16.79	12.67	82.	Engagements envers des non résidents

1. Includes all commercial banks and savings banks operating in Iceland.

1. Comprend toutes les banques commerciales et les caisses d'épargne en activité en Islande.

ITALY

All banks (1)

ITALIE

Ensemble des banques (1)

Billion lire / *Milliards de lires*

	English	Français	1989	1990	1991	1992	1993	1994
	INCOME STATEMENT (2)	**COMPTE DE RESULTATS (2)**						
1.	Interest income	Produits financiers	132026	148748	160288	187721	190857	166971
2.	Interest expenses	Frais financiers	86264	97251	104852	123408	125766	104656
3.	Net interest income	Produits financiers nets	45762	51497	55436	64313	65091	62315
4.	Non-interest income (net)	Produits non financiers (nets)	13097	15314	16895	14381	26105	19310
5.	Gross income	Résultat brut	58859	66811	72331	78694	91196	81625
6.	Operating expenses	Frais d'exploitation	36316	40920	45806	50200	54117	53017
7.	Net income	Résultat net	22543	25891	26525	28494	37079	28608
8.	Provisions (net)	Provisions (nettes)	6271	7933	6746	9919	15220	18916
9.	Profit before tax	Bénéfices avant impôt	16272	17958	19779	18575	21859	9692
10.	Income tax	Impôt	9057	9898	11224	11982	18310	8857
11.	Profit after tax	Bénéfices après impôt	7215	8060	8555	6593	3549	835
12.	Distributed profit	Bénéfices distribués	2236	2690	2943	3448	3265	2613
13.	Retained profit	Bénéfices mis en réserve	4979	5370	5612	3145	284	-1778
	Memoranda	*Pour mémoire*						
14.	*Staff costs*	*Frais de personnel*	*24415*	*27207*	*30369*	*33269*	*34496*	*36231*
15.	*Provisions on loans*	*Provisions sur prêts*	*7171*	*8447*	*8656*	*9877*	*12349*	*8366*
16.	*Provisions on securities*	*Provisions sur titres*	*1755*	*1185*	*1398*	*3944*	*1450*	*8009*
	BALANCE SHEET	**BILAN**						
	Assets	**Actif**						
17.	Cash & balance with Central bank	Caisse & solde auprès de la Banque centrale	116895	128921	133038	132054	108626	92888
18.	Interbank deposits	Dépôts interbancaires	116797	95018	97374	157728	171104	165436
19.	Loans	Prêts	667177	775334	885151	988280	1028446	1039792
20.	Securities	Valeurs mobilières	224628	221493	274021	327281	349770	385969
21.	Other assets	Autres actifs	448725	476290	546332	644825	756859	782439
	Liabilities	**Passif**						
22.	Capital & reserves	Capital et réserves	115834	126562	162279	189760	206017	219387
23.	Borrowing from Central bank	Emprunts auprès de la Banque centrale	6334	7600	8858	8936	2722	2834
24.	Interbank deposits	Dépôts interbancaires	133963	105370	103176	159186	179086	166671
25.	Non-bank deposits	Dépôts non bancaires	678142	751263	819277	851220	919115	923371
26.	Bonds	Obligations	129641	135872	153174	166407	194113	217028
27.	Other liabilities	Autres engagements	510309	570390	689152	874659	913752	937233
	Balance sheet total	**Total du bilan**						
28.	End-year total	En fin d'exercice	1574223	1697056	1935916	2250169	2414806	2466524
29.	Average total	Moyen	1395675	1545903	1703201	2030379	2250183	2365999
	Memoranda	*Pour mémoire*						
30.	*Short-term securities*	*Titres à court terme*	*24706*	*29388*	*31635*	*31209*	*74863*	*68456*
31.	*Bonds*	*Obligations*	*199922*	*192104*	*242386*	*296072*	*274908*	*317513*
32.	*Shares and participations*	*Actions et participations*	*24029*	*26348*	*37551*	*41763*	*43427*	*50067*
33.	*Claims on non-residents*	*Créances sur des non résidents*	*110370*	*116102*	*124897*	*165178*	*229057*	*201953*
34.	*Liabilities to non-residents*	*Engagements envers des non résidents*	*205534*	*232106*	*279740*	*367477*	*369979*	*375663*
	SUPPLEMENTARY INFORMATION	**RENSEIGNEMENTS COMPLEMENTAIRES**						
35.	Number of institutions	Nombre d'institutions	384	377	367	340	333	281
36.	Number of branches	Nombre de succursales	13697	14734	16372	17653	18960	19984
37.	Number of employees (x 1000)	Nombre de salariés (x 1000)	325.1	330.9	336.6	338.2	340.9	339.1

All banks (1)

Ensemble des banques (1)

Per cent	1989	1990	1991	1992	1993	1994		Pourcentage
INCOME STATEMENT ANALYSIS (2)								**ANALYSE DU COMPTE DE RESULTATS (2)**
% of average balance sheet total								**% du total moyen du bilan**
38. Interest income	9.46	9.62	9.41	9.25	8.48	7.06	38.	Produits financiers
39. Interest expenses	6.18	6.29	6.16	6.08	5.59	4.42	39.	Frais financiers
40. Net interest income	3.28	3.33	3.25	3.17	2.89	2.63	40.	Produits financiers nets
41. Non-interest income (net)	0.94	0.99	0.99	0.71	1.16	0.82	41.	Produits non financiers (nets)
42. Gross income	4.22	4.32	4.25	3.88	4.05	3.45	42.	Résultat brut
43. Operating expenses	2.60	2.65	2.69	2.47	2.41	2.24	43.	Frais d'exploitation
44. Net income	1.62	1.67	1.56	1.40	1.65	1.21	44.	Résultat net
45. Provisions (net)	0.45	0.51	0.40	0.49	0.68	0.80	45.	Provisions (nettes)
46. Profit before tax	1.17	1.16	1.16	0.91	0.97	0.41	46.	Bénéfices avant impôt
47. Income tax	0.65	0.64	0.66	0.59	0.81	0.37	47.	Impôt
48. Profit after tax	0.52	0.52	0.50	0.32	0.16	0.04	48.	Bénéfices après impôt
49. Distributed profit	0.16	0.17	0.17	0.17	0.15	0.11	49.	Bénéfices distribués
50. Retained profit	0.36	0.35	0.33	0.15	0.01	-0.08	50.	Bénéfices mis en réserve
51. Staff costs	1.75	1.76	1.78	1.64	1.53	1.53	51.	Frais de personnel
52. Provisions on loans	0.51	0.55	0.51	0.49	0.55	0.35	52.	Provisions sur prêts
53. Provisions on securities	0.13	0.08	0.08	0.19	0.06	0.34	53.	Provisions sur titres
% of gross income								**% du total du résultat brut**
54. Net interest income	77.75	77.08	76.64	81.73	71.37	76.34	54.	Produits financiers nets
55. Non-interest income (net)	22.25	22.92	23.36	18.27	28.63	23.66	55.	Produits non financiers (nets)
56. Operating expenses	61.70	61.25	63.33	63.79	59.34	64.95	56.	Frais d'exploitation
57. Net income	38.30	38.75	36.67	36.21	40.66	35.05	57.	Résultat net
58. Provisions (net)	10.65	11.87	9.33	12.60	16.69	23.17	58.	Provisions (nettes)
59. Profit before tax	27.65	26.88	27.35	23.60	23.97	11.87	59.	Bénéfices avant impôt
60. Income tax	15.39	14.81	15.52	15.23	20.08	10.85	60.	Impôt
61. Profit after tax	12.26	12.06	11.83	8.38	3.89	1.02	61.	Bénéfices après impôt
62. Staff costs	41.48	40.72	41.99	42.28	37.83	44.39	62.	Frais de personnel
% of net income								**% du total du résultat net**
63. Provisions (net)	27.82	30.64	25.43	34.81	41.05	66.12	63.	Provisions (nettes)
64. Profit before tax	72.18	69.36	74.57	65.19	58.95	33.88	64.	Bénéfices avant impôt
65. Income tax	40.18	38.23	42.31	42.05	49.38	30.96	65.	Impôt
66. Profit after tax	32.01	31.13	32.25	23.14	9.57	2.92	66.	Bénéfices après impôt

ITALY

All banks (1)

Per cent

BALANCE SHEET ANALYSIS

% of year-end balance sheet total

	1989	1990	1991	1992	1993	1994
Assets						
67. Cash & balance with Central bank	7.43	7.60	6.87	5.87	4.50	3.77
68. Interbank deposits	7.42	5.60	5.03	7.01	7.09	6.71
69. Loans	42.38	45.69	45.72	43.92	42.59	42.16
70. Securities	14.27	13.05	14.15	14.54	14.48	15.65
71. Other assets	28.50	28.07	28.22	28.66	31.34	31.72
Liabilities						
72. Capital & reserves	7.36	7.46	8.38	8.43	8.53	8.89
73. Borrowing from Central bank	0.40	0.45	0.46	0.40	0.11	0.11
74. Interbank deposits	8.51	6.21	5.33	7.07	7.42	6.76
75. Non-bank deposits	43.08	44.27	42.32	37.83	38.06	37.44
76. Bonds	8.24	8.01	7.91	7.40	8.04	8.80
77. Other liabilities	32.42	33.61	35.60	38.87	37.84	38.00
Memoranda						
78. Short-term securities	*1.57*	*1.73*	*1.63*	*1.39*	*3.10*	*2.78*
79. Bonds	*12.70*	*11.32*	*12.52*	*13.16*	*11.38*	*12.87*
80. Shares and participations	*1.53*	*1.55*	*1.94*	*1.86*	*1.80*	*2.03*
81. Claims on non-residents	*7.01*	*6.84*	*6.45*	*7.34*	*9.49*	*8.19*
82. Liabilities to non-residents	*13.06*	*13.68*	*14.45*	*16.33*	*15.32*	*15.23*

1. New series: "All banks". Further to the new banking statutes of 1993, the distinction between banks and special credit institutions was abolished. "All banks" comprises the following categories of banks:
   - Limited company banks
   - Co-operative banks
   - Main mutual banks
   - Central credit institutions
   - Branches of foreign banks

2. Break in series. As from 1992, income statement excludes one bank from the survey. However, this bank is included in the balance sheet data.

Notes

• Average balance sheet totals (item 29) are based on twelve end-month data.

ITALIE

Ensemble des banques (1)

Pourcentage

ANALYSE DU BILAN

% du total du bilan en fin d'exercice

Actif
67. Caisse & solde auprès de la Banque centrale
68. Dépôts interbancaires
69. Prêts
70. Valeurs mobilières
71. Autres actifs

Passif
72. Capital et réserves
73. Emprunts auprès de la Banque centrale
74. Dépôts interbancaires
75. Dépôts non bancaires
76. Obligations
77. Autres engagements

Pour mémoire
78. Titres à court terme
79. Obligations
80. Actions et participations
81. Créances sur des non résidents
82. Engagements envers des non résidents

1. Nouvelle série: "Ensemble des banques". Suite au nouveau code de 1993 concernant le secteur bancaire, la distinction entre banques et institutions spécialisées de crédit a été supprimée. "L'Ensemble des banques" regroupe les catégories suivantes:
   - Banques société anonyme
   - Banques mutualistes
   - Mutuelles principales
   - Institutions centrales de crédit
   - Succursales de banques étrangères

2. Rupture dans la série. Depuis 1992, le compte de résultat exclue une banque de l'enquête. Cependant cette banque est comptabilisée dans les données du bilan.

Notes

• La moyenne du total des actifs/passifs (poste 29) est basée sur douze données de fin de mois.

106

JAPAN

Commercial banks

100 million Japanese yen

JAPON

Banques commerciales

100 millions de yen japonais

	1985	1986	1987	1988	1989	1990	1991	1992	1993	1994	COMPTE DE RESULTATS
INCOME STATEMENT											
1. Interest income	212785	205504	225242	281848	388258	481476	462453	360912	301478	281579	1. Produits financiers
2. Interest expenses	166626	152514	168596	211888	318008	413323	379443	269818	214466	189919	2. Frais financiers
3. Net interest income	46159	52990	56646	69960	70250	68153	83010	91094	87012	91660	3. Produits financiers nets
4. Non-interest income (net)	12311	12988	18998	24369	21992	21663	10197	3489	2702	-2945	4. Produits non financiers (nets)
5. Gross income	58470	65978	75644	94329	92242	89816	93207	94583	89714	88715	5. Résultat brut
6. Operating expenses	40353	42516	45629	52811	56619	60639	64193	66294	67111	67730	6. Frais d'exploitation
7. Net income	18117	23462	30015	41518	35623	29177	29014	28289	22603	20985	7. Résultat net
8. Provisions (net)	723	1596	1631	3147	3101	2125	5335	9612	9739	13054	8. Provisions (nettes)
9. Profit before tax	17394	21866	28384	38371	32522	27052	23679	18677	12864	7931	9. Bénéfices avant impôt
10. Income tax	9209	11770	15625	20235	15521	12743	12628	11084	6137	5849	10. Impôt
11. Profit after tax	8185	10096	12759	18136	17001	14309	11051	7593	6727	2082	11. Bénéfices après impôt
12. Distributed profit	2089	2274	2337	1493	1638	1694	1697	1706	1685	1756	12. Bénéfices distribués
13. Retained profit	6096	7822	10422	16643	15363	12615	9354	5887	5042	326	13. Bénéfices mis en réserve
Memoranda											*Pour mémoire*
14. Staff costs	23032	23600	23774	29558	30796	32255	33713	34624	35312	35507	14. Frais de personnel
15. Provisions on loans	494	1085	1320	2851	2937	2009	5480	9329	9550	13019	15. Provisions sur prêts
16. Provisions on securities	229	511	311	296	164	116	-145	283	189	35	16. Provisions sur titres
BALANCE SHEET											**BILAN**
Assets											*Actif*
17. Cash & balance with Central bank(1)	594525	724358	820228	994636	1232259	1010134	845110	710380	737768	679009	17. Caisse & solde auprès de la Banque centrale(1)
18. Interbank deposits	..	..	..	..	..	..	..	..	..	..	18. Dépôts interbancaires
19. Loans	2175910	2456586	2783332	3537651	4098926	4330109	4484647	4538361	4520965	4520184	19. Prêts
20. Securities	474340	581051	648140	835621	1014487	1022177	978035	960568	952841	983659	20. Valeurs mobilières
21. Other assets	657274	674373	758522	1037496	1287869	1170455	1138940	786390	711979	705356	21. Autres actifs
Liabilities											*Passif*
22. Capital & reserves	91335	101614	124197	175958	226715	239712	249044	253907	258587	258042	22. Capital et réserves
23. Borrowing from Central bank	26192	40878	47166	46336	33141	35555	30535	39738	39515	28183	23. Emprunts auprès de la Banque centrale
24. Interbank deposits (2)	..	..	..	..	..	..	..	..	..	..	24. Dépôts interbancaires (2)
25. Non-bank deposits	2959597	3361047	3797408	4906164	5808225	5736884	5554169	5357468	5363045	5394567	25. Dépôts non bancaires
26. Bonds	30934	33266	44854	57657	58214	55069	56237	56566	54374	58466	26. Obligations
27. Other liabilities	793991	899563	996597	1219289	1507246	1465655	1556746	1288020	1208032	1148950	27. Autres engagements
Balance sheet total											**Total du bilan**
28. End-year total	3902049	4436368	5010222	6405404	7633541	7532875	7446732	6995699	6923553	6888208	28. En fin d'exercice
29. Average total	3794356	4169208	4723295	5971836	7019472	7583208	7489804	7221216	6959626	6905881	29. Moyen
Memoranda											*Pour mémoire*
30. Short-term securities	84597	94218	122050	173678	219140	247808	258658	258058	271948	300249	30. Titres à court terme
31. Bonds	..	..	..	..	..	..	..	..	..	..	31. Obligations
32. Shares and participations	..	..	..	..	..	..	..	..	..	..	32. Actions et participations
33. Claims on non-residents	..	..	..	..	..	..	..	..	..	..	33. Créances sur des non résidents
34. Liabilities to non-residents	..	..	..	..	..	..	..	..	..	..	34. Engagements envers des non résidents
SUPPLEMENTARY INFORMATION											**RENSEIGNEMENTS COMPLEMENTAIRES**
35. Number of institutions	77	77	77	145	145	144	143	141	140	140	35. Nombre d'institutions
36. Number of branches	9037	9251	9355	13727	14045	14325	14632	14782	14804	14823	36. Nombre de succursales
37. Number of employees (x 1000)	325	320	314	397	397	399	406	412	417	414	37. Nombre de salariés (x 1000)

JAPAN

Commercial banks

Per cent

INCOME STATEMENT ANALYSIS

JAPON

Banques commerciales

Pourcentage

ANALYSE DU COMPTE DE RESULTATS

	1985	1986	1987	1988	1989	1990	1991	1992	1993	1994	
% of average balance sheet total											**% du total moyen du bilan**
38. Interest income	5.61	4.93	4.77	4.72	5.53	6.35	6.17	5.00	4.33	4.08	38. Produits financiers
39. Interest expenses	4.39	3.66	3.57	3.55	4.53	5.45	5.07	3.74	3.08	2.75	39. Frais financiers
40. Net interest income	1.22	1.27	1.20	1.17	1.00	0.90	1.11	1.26	1.25	1.33	40. Produits financiers nets
41. Non-interest income (net)	0.32	0.31	0.40	0.41	0.31	0.29	0.14	0.05	0.04	-0.04	41. Produits non financiers (nets)
42. Gross income	1.54	1.58	1.60	1.58	1.31	1.18	1.24	1.31	1.29	1.28	42. Résultat brut
43. Operating expenses	1.06	1.02	0.97	0.88	0.81	0.80	0.86	0.92	0.96	0.98	43. Frais d'exploitation
44. Net income	0.48	0.56	0.64	0.70	0.51	0.38	0.39	0.39	0.32	0.30	44. Résultat net
45. Provisions (net)	0.02	0.04	0.03	0.05	0.04	0.03	0.07	0.13	0.14	0.19	45. Provisions (nettes)
46. Profit before tax	0.46	0.52	0.60	0.64	0.46	0.36	0.32	0.26	0.18	0.11	46. Bénéfices avant impôt
47. Income tax	0.24	0.28	0.33	0.34	0.22	0.17	0.17	0.15	0.09	0.08	47. Impôt
48. Profit after tax	0.22	0.24	0.27	0.30	0.24	0.19	0.15	0.11	0.10	0.03	48. Bénéfices après impôt
49. Distributed profit	0.06	0.05	0.05	0.03	0.02	0.02	0.02	0.02	0.02	0.03	49. Bénéfices distribués
50. Retained profit	0.16	0.19	0.22	0.28	0.22	0.17	0.12	0.08	0.07	0.00	50. Bénéfices mis en réserve
51. Staff costs	0.61	0.57	0.50	0.49	0.44	0.43	0.45	0.48	0.51	0.51	51. Frais de personnel
52. Provisions on loans	0.01	0.03	0.03	0.05	0.04	0.03	0.07	0.13	0.14	0.19	52. Provisions sur prêts
53. Provisions on securities	0.01	0.01	0.01	0.00	0.00	0.00	0.00	0.00	0.00	0.00	53. Provisions sur titres
% of gross income											**% du total du résultat brut**
54. Net interest income	78.94	80.31	74.88	74.17	76.16	75.88	89.06	96.31	96.99	103.32	54. Produits financiers nets
55. Non-interest income (net)	21.06	19.69	25.12	25.83	23.84	24.12	10.94	3.69	3.01	-3.32	55. Produits non financiers (nets)
56. Operating expenses	69.01	64.44	60.32	55.99	61.38	67.51	68.87	70.09	74.81	76.35	56. Frais d'exploitation
57. Net income	30.99	35.56	39.68	44.01	38.62	32.49	31.13	29.91	25.19	23.65	57. Résultat net
58. Provisions (net)	1.24	2.42	2.16	3.34	3.36	2.37	5.72	10.16	10.86	14.71	58. Provisions (nettes)
59. Profit before tax	29.75	33.14	37.52	40.68	35.26	30.12	25.40	19.75	14.34	8.94	59. Bénéfices avant impôt
60. Income tax	15.75	17.84	20.66	21.45	16.83	14.19	13.55	11.72	6.84	6.59	60. Impôt
61. Profit after tax	14.00	15.30	16.87	19.23	18.43	15.93	11.86	8.03	7.50	2.35	61. Bénéfices après impôt
62. Staff costs	39.39	35.77	31.43	31.34	33.39	35.91	36.17	36.61	39.36	40.02	62. Frais de personnel
% of net income											**% du total du résultat net**
63. Provisions (net)	3.99	6.80	5.43	7.58	8.71	7.28	18.39	33.98	43.09	62.21	63. Provisions (nettes)
64. Profit before tax	96.01	93.20	94.57	92.42	91.29	92.72	81.61	66.02	56.91	37.79	64. Bénéfices avant impôt
65. Income tax	50.83	50.17	52.06	48.74	43.57	43.67	43.52	39.18	27.15	27.87	65. Impôt
66. Profit after tax	45.18	43.03	42.51	43.68	47.72	49.04	38.09	26.84	29.76	9.92	66. Bénéfices après impôt

JAPAN

Commercial banks

Per cent

BALANCE SHEET ANALYSIS

% of year-end balance sheet total

	1985	1986	1987	1988	1989	1990	1991	1992	1993	1994
Assets										
67. Cash & balance with Central bank (1)	..	..	..	..	..	..	..	..	..	..
68. Interbank deposits	15.24	16.33	16.37	15.53	16.14	13.41	11.35	10.15	10.66	9.86
69. Loans	55.76	55.37	55.55	55.23	53.70	57.48	60.22	64.87	65.30	65.62
70. Securities	12.16	13.10	12.94	13.05	13.29	13.57	13.13	13.73	13.76	14.28
71. Other assets	16.84	15.20	15.14	16.20	16.87	15.54	15.29	11.24	10.28	10.24
Liabilities										
72. Capital & reserves	2.34	2.29	2.48	2.75	2.97	3.18	3.34	3.63	3.73	3.75
73. Borrowing from Central bank	0.67	0.92	0.94	0.72	0.43	0.47	0.41	0.57	0.57	0.41
74. Interbank deposits (2)	..	..	..	..	..	..	..	..	..	..
75. Non-bank deposits	75.85	75.76	75.79	76.59	76.09	76.16	74.59	76.58	77.46	78.32
76. Bonds	0.79	0.75	0.90	0.90	0.76	0.73	0.76	0.81	0.79	0.85
77. Other liabilities	20.35	20.28	19.89	19.04	19.75	19.46	20.91	18.41	17.45	16.68
Memoranda										
78. Short-term securities	..	..	..	..	..	..	..	..	..	..
79. Bonds	..	..	..	..	..	..	..	..	..	..
80. Shares and participations	2.17	2.12	2.44	2.71	2.87	3.29	3.47	3.69	3.93	4.36
81. Claims on non-residents	..	..	..	..	..	..	..	..	..	..
82. Liabilities to non-residents	..	..	..	..	..	..	..	..	..	..

Notes

1. Included under "Interbank deposits" (item 18 or item 68).
2. Included under "Non-bank deposits" (item 25 or item 75).

Notes

- Data relate to fiscal years ending 31st March.

Change in methodology

- As from 1988, data also include Sogo banks (banks for medium- and small-size industries).

JAPON

Banques commerciales

Pourcentage

ANALYSE DU BILAN

% du total du bilan en fin d'exercice

Actif
67. Caisse & solde auprès de la Banque centrale(1)
68. Dépôts interbancaires
69. Prêts
70. Valeurs mobilières
71. Autres actifs

Passif
72. Capital et réserves
73. Emprunts auprès de la Banque centrale
74. Dépôts interbancaires (2)
75. Dépôts non bancaires
76. Obligations
77. Autres engagements

Pour mémoire
78. Titres à court terme
79. Obligations
80. Actions et participations
81. Créances sur des non résidents
82. Engagements envers des non résidents

1. Inclus sous "Dépôts interbancaires" (poste 18 ou poste 68).
2. Inclus sous "Dépôts non bancaires" (poste 25 ou poste 75).

Notes

- Les données portent sur l'exercice financier, qui se termine le 31 mars.

Changement méthodologique

- Depuis 1988, sont aussi reprises dans les données des Sogo Banks (les banques pour les petites et moyennes entreprises).

JAPAN

Large commercial banks

100 million Japanese yen

JAPON

Grandes banques commerciales

100 millions de yen japonais

No.	Item (EN)	Item (FR)	1985	1986	1987	1988	1989	1990	1991	1992	1993	1994
	INCOME STATEMENT	**COMPTE DE RESULTATS**										
1.	Interest income	Produits financiers	150656	144688	163562	204088	270559	323647	298368	226675	188626	177263
2.	Interest expenses	Frais financiers	125425	114577	130371	167313	238474	293346	257605	180932	145110	135250
3.	Net interest income	Produits financiers nets	25231	30111	33191	36775	32085	30301	40763	45743	43516	42013
4.	Non-interest income (net)	Produits non financiers (nets)	9140	9787	15787	24566	19003	17000	9026	2807	548	-241
5.	Gross income	Résultat brut	34371	39898	48978	61341	51088	47301	49789	48550	44064	41772
6.	Operating expenses	Frais d'exploitation	22554	24074	26620	28559	27233	29367	31018	31779	32023	32239
7.	Net income	Résultat net	11817	15824	22358	32782	23855	17934	18771	16771	12041	9533
8.	Provisions (net)	Provisions (nettes)	368	928	1091	6361	2354	1503	4330	7368	6438	8884
9.	Profit before tax	Bénéfices avant impôt	11449	14896	21267	26421	21501	16431	14441	9403	5603	649
10.	Income tax	Impôt	5868	7836	12066	13940	10470	7577	7965	5727	2418	1342
11.	Profit after tax	Bénéfices après impôt	5581	7060	9201	12481	11031	8854	6476	3676	3185	-693
12.	Distributed profit	Bénéfices distribués	1417	1581	1624	1838	1069	1115	1113	1113	1105	1130
13.	Retained profit	Bénéfices mis en réserve	4164	5479	7577	10643	9962	7739	5363	2563	2080	-1823
	Memoranda	*Pour mémoire*										
14.	*Staff costs*	*Frais de personnel*	*12070*	*12511*	*12498*	*12772*	*13378*	*14079*	*14658*	*14970*	*15140*	*15135*
15.	*Provisions on loans*	*Provisions sur prêts*	*214*	*576*	*925*	*2080*	*2224*	*1425*	*4354*	*7114*	*6816*	*8809*
16.	*Provisions on securities*	*Provisions sur titres*	*154*	*352*	*166*	*4281*	*130*	*78*	*-24*	*254*	*122*	*75*
	BALANCE SHEET	**BILAN**										
	Assets	*Actif*										
17.	Cash & balance with Central bank(1)	Caisse & solde auprès de la Banque centrale(1)	..	..	..	..	..	..	..	..	..	..
18.	Interbank deposits	Dépôts interbancaires	527488	648761	723304	883583	1046119	858603	694322	556503	568884	517242
19.	Loans	Prêts	1453591	1672764	1909408	2159315	2520336	2660295	2736541	2743890	2703186	2670535
20.	Securities	Valeurs mobilières	289760	344058	391775	449216	560295	538856	513847	513673	504841	531647
21.	Other assets	Autres actifs	485490	518040	583935	720189	956143	858749	804944	546982	481154	473919
	Liabilities	*Passif*										
22.	Capital & reserves	Capital et réserves	53621	60837	78740	104939	137039	144097	148493	149928	152224	149560
23.	Borrowing from Central bank	Emprunts auprès de la Banque centrale	24265	38492	44685	43204	27135	28024	26353	34859	34790	23605
24.	Interbank deposits (2)	Dépôts interbancaires (2)	..	..	..	..	..	..	..	..	..	..
25.	Non-bank deposits	Dépôts non bancaires	1991385	2303880	2622945	3045140	3644553	3535869	3292328	3087810	3060102	3034603
26.	Bonds	Obligations	30934	32908	41384	52623	53948	51568	53546	54181	52944	57213
27.	Other liabilities	Autres engagements	656124	747506	820668	966397	1220218	1156945	1228934	1034270	958005	928363
	Balance sheet total	*Total du bilan*										
28.	End-year total	En fin d'exercice	2756329	3183623	3608422	4212303	5082893	4916503	4749654	4361048	4258065	4193343
29.	Average total	Moyen	2691715	2969976	3396022	3910362	4647598	4999698	4833079	4555351	4309557	4225704
	Memoranda	*Pour mémoire*										
30.	*Short-term securities*	*Titres à court terme*	*..*	*..*	*..*	*..*	*..*	*..*	*..*	*..*	*..*	*..*
31.	*Bonds*	*Obligations*	*..*	*..*	*..*	*..*	*..*	*..*	*..*	*..*	*..*	*..*
32.	*Shares and participations*	*Actions et participations*	*67468*	*74847*	*97885*	*132497*	*169114*	*192011*	*201849*	*200637*	*211988*	*238626*
33.	*Claims on non-residents*	*Créances sur des non résidents*	*..*	*..*	*..*	*..*	*..*	*..*	*..*	*..*	*..*	*..*
34.	*Liabilities to non-residents*	*Engagements envers des non résidents*	*..*	*..*	*..*	*..*	*..*	*..*	*..*	*..*	*..*	*..*
	SUPPLEMENTARY INFORMATION	**RENSEIGNEMENTS COMPLEMENTAIRES**										
35.	Number of institutions	Nombre d'institutions	13	13	13	13	13	12	11	11	11	11
36.	Number of branches	Nombre de succursales	2904	3032	3050	3099	3182	3249	3280	3293	3238	3224
37.	Number of employees (x 1000)	Nombre de salariés (x 1000)	160	157	154	152	152	152	154	157	158	155

JAPAN

Large commercial banks

Per cent	1985	1986	1987	1988	1989	1990	1991	1992	1993	1994		*Pourcentage*
INCOME STATEMENT ANALYSIS												**ANALYSE DU COMPTE DE RESULTATS**
% of average balance sheet total												**% du total moyen du bilan**
38. Interest income	5.60	4.87	4.82	5.22	5.82	6.47	6.17	4.98	4.38	4.19	38.	Produits financiers
39. Interest expenses	4.66	3.86	3.84	4.28	5.13	5.87	5.33	3.97	3.37	3.20	39.	Frais financiers
40. Net interest income	0.94	1.01	0.98	0.94	0.69	0.61	0.84	1.00	1.01	0.99	40.	Produits financiers nets
41. Non-interest income (net)	0.34	0.33	0.46	0.63	0.41	0.34	0.19	0.06	0.01	-0.01	41.	Produits non financiers (nets)
42. Gross income	1.28	1.34	1.44	1.57	1.10	0.95	1.03	1.07	1.02	0.99	42.	Résultat brut
43. Operating expenses	0.84	0.81	0.78	0.73	0.59	0.59	0.64	0.70	0.74	0.76	43.	Frais d'exploitation
44. Net income	0.44	0.53	0.66	0.84	0.51	0.36	0.39	0.37	0.28	0.23	44.	Résultat net
45. Provisions (net)	0.01	0.03	0.03	0.16	0.05	0.03	0.09	0.16	0.15	0.21	45.	Provisions (nettes)
46. Profit before tax	0.43	0.50	0.63	0.68	0.46	0.33	0.30	0.21	0.13	0.02	46.	Bénéfices avant impôt
47. Income tax	0.22	0.26	0.36	0.36	0.23	0.15	0.16	0.13	0.06	0.03	47.	Impôt
48. Profit after tax	0.21	0.24	0.27	0.32	0.24	0.18	0.13	0.08	0.07	-0.02	48.	Bénéfices après impôt
49. Distributed profit	0.05	0.05	0.05	0.05	0.02	0.02	0.02	0.02	0.03	0.03	49.	Bénéfices distribués
50. Retained profit	0.15	0.18	0.22	0.27	0.21	0.15	0.11	0.06	0.05	-0.04	50.	Bénéfices mis en réserve
51. Staff costs	0.45	0.42	0.37	0.33	0.29	0.28	0.30	0.33	0.35	0.36	51.	Frais de personnel
52. Provisions on loans	0.01	0.02	0.03	0.05	0.05	0.03	0.09	0.16	0.16	0.21	52.	Provisions sur prêts
53. Provisions on securities	0.01	0.01	-	0.11	-	-	-	0.01	-	-	53.	Provisions sur titres
% of gross income												**% du total du résultat brut**
54. Net interest income	73.41	75.47	67.77	59.95	62.80	64.06	81.87	94.22	98.76	100.58	54.	Produits financiers nets
55. Non-interest income (net)	26.59	24.53	32.23	40.05	37.20	35.94	18.13	5.78	1.24	-0.58	55.	Produits non financiers (nets)
56. Operating expenses	65.62	60.34	54.35	46.56	53.31	62.09	62.30	65.46	72.67	77.18	56.	Frais d'exploitation
57. Net income	34.38	39.66	45.65	53.44	46.69	37.91	37.70	34.54	27.33	22.82	57.	Résultat net
58. Provisions (net)	1.07	2.33	2.23	10.37	4.61	3.18	8.70	15.18	14.61	21.27	58.	Provisions (nettes)
59. Profit before tax	33.31	37.34	43.42	43.07	42.09	34.74	29.00	19.37	12.72	1.55	59.	Bénéfices avant impôt
60. Income tax	17.07	19.64	24.64	22.73	20.49	16.02	16.00	11.80	5.49	3.21	60.	Impôt
61. Profit after tax	16.24	17.70	18.79	20.35	21.59	18.72	13.01	7.57	7.23	-1.66	61.	Bénéfices après impôt
62. Staff costs	35.12	31.36	25.52	20.82	26.19	29.76	29.44	30.83	34.36	36.23	62.	Frais de personnel
% of net income												**% du total du résultat net**
63. Provisions (net)	3.11	5.86	4.88	19.40	9.87	8.38	23.07	43.93	53.47	93.19	63.	Provisions (nettes)
64. Profit before tax	96.89	94.14	95.12	80.60	90.13	91.62	76.93	56.07	46.53	6.81	64.	Bénéfices avant impôt
65. Income tax	49.66	49.52	53.97	42.52	43.89	42.25	42.43	34.15	20.08	14.08	65.	Impôt
66. Profit after tax	47.23	44.62	41.15	38.07	46.24	49.37	34.50	21.92	26.45	-7.27	66.	Bénéfices après impôt

JAPAN

Large commercial banks

Per cent

BALANCE SHEET ANALYSIS

% of year-end balance sheet total

	1985	1986	1987	1988	1989	1990	1991	1992	1993	1994
Assets										
67. Cash & balance with Central bank (1)	..	..	..	..	..	..	..	..	..	..
68. Interbank deposits	19.14	20.38	20.04	20.98	20.58	17.46	14.62	12.76	13.36	12.33
69. Loans	52.74	52.54	52.92	51.26	49.58	54.11	57.62	62.92	63.48	63.69
70. Securities	10.51	10.81	10.86	10.66	11.02	10.96	10.82	11.78	11.86	12.68
71. Other assets	17.61	16.27	16.18	17.10	18.81	17.47	16.95	12.54	11.30	11.30
Liabilities										
72. Capital & reserves	1.95	1.91	2.18	2.49	2.70	2.93	3.13	3.44	3.57	3.57
73. Borrowing from Central bank	0.88	1.21	1.24	1.03	0.53	0.57	0.55	0.80	0.82	0.56
74. Interbank deposits (2)	..	..	..	..	..	..	..	..	..	..
75. Non-bank deposits	72.25	72.37	72.69	72.29	71.70	71.92	69.32	70.80	71.87	72.37
76. Bonds	1.12	1.03	1.15	1.25	1.06	1.05	1.13	1.24	1.24	1.36
77. Other liabilities	23.80	23.48	22.74	22.94	24.01	23.53	25.87	23.72	22.50	22.14
Memoranda										
78. Short-term securities	..	..	..	..	..	..	..	..	..	..
79. Bonds	..	..	..	..	..	..	..	..	..	..
80. Shares and participations	*2.45*	*2.35*	*2.71*	*3.15*	*3.33*	*3.91*	*4.25*	*4.60*	*4.98*	*5.69*
81. Claims on non-residents	..	..	..	..	..	..	..	..	..	..
82. Liabilities to non-residents	..	..	..	..	..	..	..	..	..	..

1. Included under "Interbank deposits" (item 18 or item 68).
2. Included under "Non-bank deposits" (item 25 or item 75).

Notes

- Data are based on the annual publication of the Federation of Bankers Associations of Japan "Analysis of Financial Statements of All Banks". The term Large commercial banks corresponds to the term City banks used in Japanese publications.
- Data relate to fiscal years ending 31st March.

JAPON

Grandes banques commerciales

Pourcentage

ANALYSE DU BILAN

% du total du bilan en fin d'exercice

Actif

67. Caisse & solde auprès de la Banque centrale(1)
68. Dépôts interbancaires
69. Prêts
70. Valeurs mobilières
71. Autres actifs

Passif

72. Capital et réserves
73. Emprunts auprès de la Banque centrale
74. Dépôts interbancaires (2)
75. Dépôts non bancaires
76. Obligations
77. Autres engagements

Pour mémoire

78. Titres à court terme
79. Obligations
80. Actions et participations
81. Créances sur des non résidents
82. Engagements envers des non résidents

1. Inclus sous "Dépôts interbancaires" (poste 18 ou poste 68).
2. Inclus sous "Dépôts non bancaires" (poste 25 ou poste 75).

Notes

- Les données sont extraites d'une publication annuelle de la Fédération des associations de banquiers du Japon "Analysis of Financial Statements of All Banks". Le terme, Grandes banques commerciales correspond au terme City banks utilisé dans les publications japonaises.
- Les données portent sur l'exercice financier, qui se termine le 31 mars.

LUXEMBOURG

Commercial banks / Banques commerciales

Million Luxembourg francs / Millions de francs luxembourgeois

	1985	1986	1987	1988	1989	1990	1991	1992	1993	1994
INCOME STATEMENT / COMPTE DE RESULTATS										
1. Interest income / Produits financiers	659869	593525	605706	702452	1001719	1185123	1251957	1375962	1306736	1165813
2. Interest expenses / Frais financiers	571174	506503	519999	612743	910018	1090911	1143722	1259077	1188477	1041088
3. Net interest income / Produits financiers nets	88695	87022	85707	89709	91701	94212	108235	116885	118259	124725
4. Non-interest income (net) / Produits non financiers (nets)	21712	23657	21418	28762	36062	50738	39044	48172	77335	61299
5. Gross income / Résultat brut	110407	110679	107125	118471	127763	144950	147279	165057	195594	186024
6. Operating expenses / Frais d'exploitation	30777	34110	37767	45361	52259	54089	59720	65000	74261	83278
7. Net income / Résultat net	79630	76569	69358	73110	75504	90861	87559	100057	121333	102746
8. Provisions (net) / Provisions (nettes)	54515	50973	42488	35000	41357	63860	54302	55180	41160	14093
9. Profit before tax / Bénéfices avant impôt	25115	25596	26870	38110	34147	27001	33257	44877	80173	88653
10. Income tax / Impôt	11817	11426	11246	14579	10912	7919	9539	16498	25635	26012
11. Profit after tax / Bénéfices après impôt	13298	14170	15624	23531	23235	19082	23718	28379	54538	62641
12. Distributed profit / Bénéfices distribués	5437	5753	7861	8716	NA	NA	NA	NA	NA	NA
13. Retained profit / Bénéfices mis en réserve	7861	8417	7763	14815	NA	NA	NA	NA	NA	NA
Memoranda / Pour mémoire										
14. Staff costs / Frais de personnel	16751	18717	20810	24038	27326	28291	31205	33820	38155	44102
15. Provisions on loans / Provisions sur prêts	..	..	..	..	..	..	..	..	..	..
16. Provisions on securities / Provisions sur titres	..	..	..	..	..	..	..	..	..	..
BALANCE SHEET / BILAN										
Assets / Actif										
17. Cash & balance with Central bank / Caisse & solde auprès de la Banque centrale	15896	17822	14954	22731	22550	21999	23912	25247	138581	59853
18. Interbank deposits / Dépôts interbancaires	4153414	4493575	5091042	5895411	6827903	7542436	7595436	8514637	9359103	10610714
19. Loans / Prêts	2444418	2291377	2239670	2488137	2705253	2991164	3111790	3560101	3570761	3257258
20. Securities / Valeurs mobilières	519801	626933	644846	747022	825196	947786	1030649	1366487	2379016	3078582
21. Other assets / Autres actifs	494278	577407	695968	784481	955869	976829	989324	957609	573503	662785
Liabilities / Passif										
22. Capital & reserves / Capital et réserves	264572	278847	292956	326944	362536	400727	437490	509944	402292	424215
23. Borrowing from Central bank / Emprunts auprès de la Banque centrale										
24. Interbank deposits / Dépôts interbancaires	5087914	5021751	5213590	5456033	5664861	5862019	5781106	6308312	7029508	7992635
25. Non-bank deposits / Dépôts non bancaires	1756196	2165763	2567373	3338309	4362287	5018640	5233632	6122701	7074785	7486709
26. Bonds / Obligations	110723	108212	133500	291661	361339	557124	643922	683190	684930	864671
27. Other liabilities / Autres engagements	408402	432541	479061	524835	585748	641704	654961	799934	829449	900962
Balance sheet total / Total du bilan										
28. End-year total / En fin d'exercice	7627807	8007114	8686480	9937782	11336771	12480214	12751111	14424081	16020964	17669192
29. Average total / Moyen	7509547	7669959	8275464	9467853	11126632	12212272	13003686	13841317	15450298	16710459
Memoranda / Pour mémoire										
30. Short-term securities / Titres à court terme	..	..	..	..	..	..	..	..	..	..
31. Bonds / Obligations	292268	310070	308259	333652	324005	380893	480731	700081	767318	1046597
32. Shares and participations / Actions et participations	31087	33769	35795	49897	86293	121414	86639	89378	79085	97430
33. Claims on non-residents / Créances sur des non résidents	6598617	6941873	7525666	8663424	10020284	11050104	11263515	12563961	..	..
34. Liabilities to non-residents / Engagements envers des non résidents	6373914	6645544	7068412	8015812	9226691	10258514	10468546	11558901	..	..
SUPPLEMENTARY INFORMATION / RENSEIGNEMENTS COMPLEMENTAIRES										
35. Number of institutions / Nombre d'institutions	118	122	127	143	166	177	187	213	218	222
36. Number of branches / Nombre de succursales	243	250	258	258	295	297	308	303	306	367
37. Number of employees (x1000) / Nombre de salariés (x1000)	10.2	11.4	12.7	13.7	15.2	16.3	17.1	17.6	18.5	19.7

113

LUXEMBOURG

Commercial banks

Per cent

Banques commerciales

Pourcentage

INCOME STATEMENT ANALYSIS	1985	1986	1987	1988	1989	1990	1991	1992	1993	1994	ANALYSE DU COMPTE DE RESULTATS	
% of average balance sheet total											**% du total moyen du bilan**	
38. Interest income	8.79	7.74	7.32	7.42	9.00	9.70	9.63	9.94	8.46	6.98	Produits financiers	38.
39. Interest expenses	7.61	6.60	6.28	6.47	8.18	8.93	8.80	9.10	7.69	6.23	Frais financiers	39.
40. Net interest income	1.18	1.13	1.04	0.95	0.82	0.77	0.83	0.84	0.77	0.75	Produits financiers nets	40.
41. Non-interest income (net)	0.29	0.31	0.26	0.30	0.32	0.42	0.30	0.35	0.50	0.37	Produits non financiers (nets)	41.
42. Gross income	1.47	1.44	1.29	1.25	1.15	1.19	1.13	1.19	1.27	1.11	Résultat brut	42.
43. Operating expenses	0.41	0.44	0.46	0.48	0.47	0.44	0.46	0.47	0.48	0.50	Frais d'exploitation	43.
44. Net income	1.06	1.00	0.84	0.77	0.68	0.74	0.67	0.72	0.79	0.61	Résultat net	44.
45. Provisions (net)	0.73	0.66	0.51	0.37	0.37	0.52	0.42	0.40	0.27	0.08	Provisions (nettes)	45.
46. Profit before tax	0.33	0.33	0.32	0.40	0.31	0.22	0.26	0.32	0.52	0.53	Bénéfices avant impôt	46.
47. Income tax	0.16	0.15	0.14	0.15	0.10	0.06	0.07	0.12	0.17	0.16	Impôt	47.
48. Profit after tax	0.18	0.18	0.19	0.25	0.21	0.16	0.18	0.21	0.35	0.37	Bénéfices après impôt	48.
49. Distributed profit	0.07	0.08	0.09	0.09	NA	NA	NA	NA	NA	NA	Bénéfices distribués	49.
50. Retained profit	0.10	0.11	0.09	0.16	NA	NA	NA	NA	NA	NA	Bénéfices mis en réserve	50.
51. Staff costs	0.22	0.24	0.25	0.25	0.25	0.23	0.24	0.24	0.25	0.26	Frais de personnel	51.
52. Provisions on loans	..	..	..	..	..	..	..	..	..	..	Provisions sur prêts	52.
53. Provisions on securities	..	..	..	..	..	..	..	..	..	..	Provisions sur titres	53.
% of gross income											**% du total du résultat brut**	
54. Net interest income	80.33	78.63	80.01	75.72	71.77	65.00	73.49	70.81	60.46	67.05	Produits financiers nets	54.
55. Non-interest income (net)	19.67	21.37	19.99	24.28	28.23	35.00	26.51	29.19	39.54	32.95	Produits non financiers (nets)	55.
56. Operating expenses	27.88	30.82	35.26	38.29	40.90	37.32	40.55	39.38	37.97	44.77	Frais d'exploitation	56.
57. Net income	72.12	69.18	64.74	61.71	59.10	62.68	59.45	60.62	62.03	55.23	Résultat net	57.
58. Provisions (net)	49.38	46.05	39.66	29.54	32.37	44.06	36.87	33.43	21.04	7.58	Provisions (nettes)	58.
59. Profit before tax	22.75	23.13	25.08	32.17	26.73	18.63	22.58	27.19	40.99	47.66	Bénéfices avant impôt	59.
60. Income tax	10.70	10.32	10.50	12.31	8.54	5.46	6.48	10.00	13.11	13.98	Impôt	60.
61. Profit after tax	12.04	12.80	14.58	19.86	18.19	13.16	16.10	17.19	27.88	33.67	Bénéfices après impôt	61.
62. Staff costs	15.17	16.91	19.43	20.29	21.39	19.52	21.19	20.49	19.51	23.71	Frais de personnel	62.
% of net income											**% du total du résultat net**	
63. Provisions (net)	68.46	66.57	61.26	47.87	54.77	70.28	62.02	55.15	33.92	13.72	Provisions (nettes)	63.
64. Profit before tax	31.54	33.43	38.74	52.13	45.23	29.72	37.98	44.85	66.08	86.28	Bénéfices avant impôt	64.
65. Income tax	14.84	14.92	16.21	19.94	14.45	8.72	10.89	16.49	21.13	25.32	Impôt	65.
66. Profit after tax	16.70	18.51	22.53	32.19	30.77	21.00	27.09	28.36	44.95	60.97	Bénéfices après impôt	66.

LUXEMBOURG

Commercial banks

Per cent

BALANCE SHEET ANALYSIS

% of year-end balance sheet total

	1985	1986	1987	1988	1989	1990	1991	1992	1993	1994
Assets										
67. Cash & balance with Central bank	0.21	0.22	0.17	0.23	0.20	0.18	0.19	0.18	0.86	0.34
68. Interbank deposits	54.45	56.12	58.61	59.32	60.23	60.44	59.57	59.03	58.42	60.05
69. Loans	32.05	28.62	25.78	25.04	23.86	23.97	24.40	24.68	22.29	18.43
70. Securities	6.81	7.83	7.42	7.52	7.28	7.59	8.08	9.47	14.85	17.42
71. Other assets	6.48	7.21	8.01	7.89	8.43	7.83	7.76	6.64	3.58	3.75
Liabilities										
72. Capital & reserves	3.47	3.48	3.37	3.29	3.20	3.21	3.43	3.54	2.51	2.40
73. Borrowing from Central bank	-	-	-	-	-	-	-	-	-	-
74. Interbank deposits	66.70	62.72	60.02	54.90	49.97	46.97	45.34	43.73	43.88	45.23
75. Non-bank deposits	23.02	27.05	29.56	33.59	38.48	40.21	41.04	42.45	44.16	42.37
76. Bonds	1.45	1.35	1.54	2.93	3.19	4.46	5.05	4.74	4.28	4.89
77. Other liabilities	5.35	5.40	5.52	5.28	5.17	5.14	5.14	5.55	5.18	5.10
Memoranda										
78. Short-term securities	..	..	..	..	..	..	..	..	..	..
79. Bonds	3.83	3.87	3.55	3.36	2.86	3.05	3.77	4.85	4.79	5.92
80. Shares and participations	0.41	0.42	0.41	0.50	0.76	0.97	0.68	0.62	0.49	0.55
81. Claims on non-residents	86.51	86.70	86.64	87.18	88.39	88.54	88.33	87.10	..	..
82. Liabilities to non-residents	83.56	83.00	81.37	80.66	81.39	82.20	82.10	80.14	..	..

Notes

- Average balance sheet totals (item 29) are based on thirteen end-month data.

LUXEMBOURG

Banques commerciales

Pourcentage

ANALYSE DU BILAN

% du total du bilan en fin d'exercice

Actif
67. Caisse & solde auprès de la Banque centrale
68. Dépôts interbancaires
69. Prêts
70. Valeurs mobilières
71. Autres actifs

Passif
72. Capital et réserves
73. Emprunts auprès de la Banque centrale
74. Dépôts interbancaires
75. Dépôts non bancaires
76. Obligations
77. Autres engagements

Pour mémoire
78. Titres à court terme
79. Obligations
80. Actions et participations
81. Créances sur des non résidents
82. Engagements envers des non résidents

Notes

- La moyenne du total des actifs/passifs (poste 29) est basée sur treize données de fin de mois.

115

MEXICO

Commercial banks (1)

Million pesos

MEXIQUE

Banques commerciales (1)

Millions de pesos

No.	Item / Poste	1985	1986	1987	1988	1989	1990	1991	1992	1993	1994
	INCOME STATEMENT / COMPTE DE RESULTATS										
1.	Interest income / Produits financiers	4162.1	9663.1	24860.4	33390.7	31152.0	52738.0	61862.4	73980.4	92987.0	104324.9
2.	Interest expenses / Frais financiers	3727.0	8766.1	22845.4	28966.8	24883.8	41965.8	46168.9	50531.6	63501.4	72930.9
3.	Net interest income / Produits financiers nets	435.1	897.0	2015.0	4423.9	6268.2	10772.2	15693.5	23448.8	29485.6	31394.0
4.	Non-interest income (net) / Produits non financiers (nets)	243.0	472.4	1461.2	2754.6	2298.5	3360.5	5587.2	7030.7	9501.8	8672.9
5.	Gross income / Résultat brut	678.1	1369.4	3476.2	7178.5	8566.7	14132.7	21280.7	30479.5	38987.4	40066.9
6.	Operating expenses / Frais d'exploitation	574.3	1085.9	2581.6	5469.2	5946.8	9752.9	14295.0	18044.9	21534.0	25720.0
7.	Net income / Résultat net	103.8	283.5	894.6	1709.3	2619.9	4379.8	6985.7	12434.6	17453.4	14346.9
8.	Provisions (net) / Provisions (nettes)	-	-	-	-	278.9	278.9	1266.4	3501.7	6884.6	9618.8
9.	Profit before tax / Bénéfices avant impôt	103.8	283.5	894.6	1709.3	2619.9	4100.9	5719.3	8932.9	10568.8	4728.1
10.	Income tax / Impôt	NA	NA	NA	NA	589.8	1099.9	1642.6	2414.0	2160.1	1047.7
11.	Profit after tax / Bénéfices après impôt	NA	NA	NA	NA	2030.1	3001.0	4076.7	6518.9	8408.7	3680.4
12.	Distributed profit / Bénéfices distribués	NA	NA	NA	NA	231.5	401.6	565.1	690.7	624.0	253.5
13.	Retained profit / Bénéfices mis en réserve	NA	NA	NA	NA	1798.6	2599.4	3511.6	5828.2	7784.7	3426.9
	Memoranda / Pour mémoire										
14.	Staff costs / Frais de personnel	..	..	..	..	2663.1	4223.7	6002.4	8626.4	10661.1	12301.1
15.	Provisions on loans / Provisions sur prêts	-	-	-	-	-	278.9	1266.4	3501.7	6884.6	9618.8
16.	Provisions on securities / Provisions sur titres	..	..	..	..	..	..	..	..	..	..
	BALANCE SHEET / BILAN										
	Assets / Actif										
17.	Cash & balance with Central bank / Caisse & solde auprès de la Banque centrale	1334.0	3258.0	6294.0	7558.0	8665.0	6204.1	7269.8	6945.1	5849.8	9528.8
18.	Interbank deposits (2) (3) / Dépôts interbancaires (2) (3)	..	..	..	..	..	4111.5	5687.5	4055.6	5283.8	7646.3
19.	Loans / Prêts	8033.0	17086.0	43775.0	51050.0	80628.0	126251.0	187832.8	263653.5	321495.2	444599.8
20.	Securities / Valeurs mobilières	3446.0	6267.0	12326.0	23774.0	28853.0	49881.8	103665.3	75690.6	93242.9	153306.3
21.	Other assets / Autres actifs	895.0	2385.0	6166.0	13171.0	23387.0	43475.0	50021.5	64786.7	84933.4	112333.9
	Liabilities / Passif										
22.	Capital & reserves / Capital et réserves	428.2	990.1	3183.3	6760.5	9180.0	14339.9	19304.8	26028.1	33711.6	40034.6
23.	Borrowing from Central bank / Emprunts auprès de la Banque centrale	-	-	-	-	1172.0	1907.9	3059.0	4575.6	5293.6	6836.8
24.	Interbank deposits (4) / Dépôts interbancaires (4)	-	-	-	-	17363.0	25460.9	29146.1	33203.9	43843.4	104164.7
25.	Non-bank deposits / Dépôts non bancaires	8430.0	17125.0	43107.0	58622.0	87398.0	165845.2	268747.5	314100.4	386315.0	479618.3
26.	Bonds (5) / Obligations (5)	..	..	..	..	..	..	..	..	..	..
27.	Other liabilities / Autres engagements	4849.0	10881.0	22271.0	30171.0	26419.0	22369.6	34218.6	37223.6	41641.5	96760.7
	Balance sheet total / Total du bilan										
28.	End-year total / En fin d'exercice	13708.0	28996.0	68561.0	95553.0	141533.0	229923.5	354476.9	415131.7	510805.1	727415.4
29.	Average total / Moyen	NA	21352.0	48778.5	82057.0	118543.0	185728.3	292200.2	384804.3	462968.4	619110.3
	Memoranda / Pour mémoire										
30.	Short-term securities / Titres à court terme	..	..	..	..	..	..	..	..	..	..
31.	Bonds / Obligations	..	..	..	..	..	..	..	..	..	..
32.	Shares and participations / Actions et participations	..	..	..	..	..	1929.5	4358.3	4163.9	5762.3	12815.1
33.	Claims on non-residents / Créances sur des non résidents	..	..	..	..	..	..	..	..	..	..
34.	Liabilities to non-residents / Engagements envers des non résidents	..	..	..	..	..	..	..	..	..	..
	SUPPLEMENTARY INFORMATION / RENSEIGNEMENTS COMPLEMENTAIRES										
35.	Number of institutions / Nombre d'institutions	13	13	13	13	13	13	13	13	14	26
36.	Number of branches / Nombre de succursales	3573	3564	3613	3636	3647	3624	3621	3535	3763	4338
37.	Number of employees (x 1000) / Nombre de salariés (x 1000)	124584	125187	130024	130072	131596	137294	137511	138860	131235	126852

MEXICO / MEXIQUE

Commercial banks (1) / Banques commerciales (1)

Per cent / Pourcentage

INCOME STATEMENT ANALYSIS / ANALYSE DU COMPTE DE RESULTATS

No.	Item	1985	1986	1987	1988	1989	1990	1991	1992	1993	1994	Item (FR)
	% of average balance sheet total											**% du total moyen du bilan**
38.	Interest income	NA	45.26	50.97	40.69	26.28	28.40	21.17	19.23	20.08	16.85	Produits financiers
39.	Interest expenses	NA	41.06	46.83	35.30	20.99	22.60	15.80	13.13	13.72	11.78	Frais financiers
40.	Net interest income	NA	4.20	4.13	5.39	5.29	5.80	5.37	6.09	6.37	5.07	Produits financiers nets
41.	Non-interest income (net)	NA	2.21	3.00	3.36	1.94	1.81	1.91	1.83	2.05	1.40	Produits non financiers (nets)
42.	Gross income	NA	6.41	7.13	8.75	7.23	7.61	7.28	7.92	8.42	6.47	Résultat brut
43.	Operating expenses	NA	5.09	5.29	6.67	5.02	5.25	4.89	4.69	4.65	4.15	Frais d'exploitation
44.	Net income	NA	1.33	1.83	2.08	2.21	2.36	2.39	3.23	3.77	2.32	Résultat net
45.	Provisions (net)	-	-	-	-	-	0.15	0.43	0.91	1.49	1.55	Provisions (nettes)
46.	Profit before tax	NA	1.33	1.83	2.08	2.21	2.21	1.96	2.32	2.28	0.76	Bénéfices avant impôt
47.	Income tax	NA	NA	NA	NA	0.50	0.59	0.56	0.63	0.47	0.17	Impôt
48.	Profit after tax	NA	NA	NA	NA	1.71	1.62	1.40	1.69	1.82	0.59	Bénéfices après impôt
49.	Distributed profit	NA	NA	NA	NA	0.20	0.22	0.19	0.18	0.13	0.04	Bénéfices distribués
50.	Retained profit	NA	NA	NA	NA	1.52	1.40	1.20	1.51	1.68	0.55	Bénéfices mis en réserve
51.	Staff costs	:	:	:	:	2.25	2.27	2.05	2.24	2.30	1.99	Frais de personnel
52.	Provisions on loans	:	-	:	:	-	0.15	0.43	0.91	1.49	1.55	Provisions sur prêts
53.	Provisions on securities	:	:	:	:	:	:	:	:	:	:	Provisions sur titres
	% of gross income											**% du total du résultat brut**
54.	Net interest income	64.16	65.50	57.97	61.63	73.17	76.22	73.75	76.93	75.63	78.35	Produits financiers nets
55.	Non-interest income (net)	35.84	34.50	42.03	38.37	26.83	23.78	26.25	23.07	24.37	21.65	Produits non financiers (nets)
56.	Operating expenses	84.69	79.30	74.27	76.19	69.42	69.01	67.17	59.20	55.23	64.19	Frais d'exploitation
57.	Net income	15.31	20.70	25.73	23.81	30.58	30.99	32.83	40.80	44.77	35.81	Résultat net
58.	Provisions (net)	-	-	-	-	-	1.97	5.95	11.49	17.66	24.01	Provisions (nettes)
59.	Profit before tax	15.31	20.70	25.73	23.81	30.58	29.02	26.88	29.31	27.11	11.80	Bénéfices avant impôt
60.	Income tax	NA	NA	NA	NA	6.88	7.78	7.72	7.92	5.54	2.61	Impôt
61.	Profit after tax	NA	NA	NA	NA	23.70	21.23	19.16	21.39	21.57	9.19	Bénéfices après impôt
62.	Staff costs	:	:	:	:	31.09	29.89	28.21	28.30	27.34	30.70	Frais de personnel
	% of net income											**% du total du résultat net**
63.	Provisions (net)	-	-	-	-	-	6.37	18.13	28.16	39.45	67.04	Provisions (nettes)
64.	Profit before tax	100.00	100.00	100.00	100.00	100.00	93.63	81.87	71.84	60.55	32.96	Bénéfices avant impôt
65.	Income tax	NA	NA	NA	NA	22.51	25.11	23.51	19.41	12.38	7.30	Impôt
66.	Profit after tax	NA	NA	NA	NA	77.49	68.52	58.36	52.43	48.18	25.65	Bénéfices après impôt

117

MEXICO

Commercial banks (1)

Per cent

BALANCE SHEET ANALYSIS

% of year-end balance sheet total

	1985	1986	1987	1988	1989	1990	1991	1992	1993	1994
Assets										
67. Cash & balance with Central bank	9.73	11.24	9.18	7.91	6.12	2.70	2.05	1.67	1.15	1.31
68. Interbank deposits (2) (3)	..	..	..	-	-	1.79	1.60	0.98	1.03	1.05
69. Loans	58.60	58.93	63.85	53.43	56.97	54.91	52.99	63.51	62.94	61.12
70. Securities	25.14	21.61	17.98	24.88	20.39	21.69	29.24	18.23	18.25	21.08
71. Other assets	6.53	8.23	8.99	13.78	16.52	18.91	14.11	15.61	16.63	15.44
Liabilities										
72. Capital & reserves	3.12	3.41	4.64	7.08	6.49	6.24	5.45	6.27	6.60	5.50
73. Borrowing from Central bank	-	-	-	-	0.83	0.83	0.86	1.10	1.04	0.94
74. Interbank deposits (4)	-	-	-	-	12.27	11.07	8.22	8.00	8.58	14.32
75. Non-bank deposits	61.50	59.06	62.87	61.35	61.75	72.13	75.82	75.66	75.63	65.93
76. Bonds (5)	..	..	..	..	..	..	..	..	..	..
77. Other liabilities	35.37	37.53	32.48	31.58	18.67	9.73	9.65	8.97	8.15	13.30
Memoranda										
78. Short-term securities	:	:	:	:	:	:	:	:	:	:
79. Bonds	:	:	:	:	:	:	:	:	:	:
80. Shares and participations	:	:	:	:	:	0.84	1.23	1.00	1.13	1.76
81. Claims on non-residents	:	:	:	:	:	:	:	:	:	:
82. Liabilities to non-residents	:	:	:	:	:	:	:	:	:	:

1. The following banks are excluded from the coverage because of their special situation: Inverlat, Union, Cremi, Centro, Banpais, Oriente, Obrero, and Interestatal.
2. Until 1990, included under "Cash and balance with Central bank" (item 17 or item 67).
3. Includes deposits in domestic and foreign banks.
4. Includes deposits and loans in domestic and foreign banks.
5. Included under "Capital and reserves" (item 22 or item 72).

MEXIQUE

Banques commerciales (1)

Pourcentage

ANALYSE DU BILAN

% du total du bilan en fin d'exercice

Actif
67. Caisse & solde auprès de la Banque centrale
68. Dépôts interbancaires (2) (3)
69. Prêts
70. Valeurs mobilières
71. Autres actifs

Passif
72. Capital et réserves
73. Emprunts auprès de la Banque centrale
74. Dépôts interbancaires (4)
75. Dépôts non bancaires
76. Obligations (5)
77. Autres engagements

Pour mémoire
78. Titres à court terme
79. Obligations
80. Actions et participations
81. Créances sur des non résidents
82. Engagements envers des non résidents

1. En raison de leur situation spéciale, les banques suivantes ne sont pas prises en compte: Inverlat, Union, Cremi, Centro, Banpais, Oriente, Obrero et Interestatal.
2. Jusqu'en 1990, inclus sous la rubrique "Caisse et solde auprès de la Banque centrale" (item 17 ou item 67).
3. Sont compris les dépôts dans les banques domestiques et étrangères.
4. Y compris les dépôts et les prêts dans les banques domestiques et étrangères.
5. Inclus sous "Capital et réserves" (poste 22 ou poste 72).

NETHERLANDS

All banks

Million guilders

PAYS-BAS

Ensemble des banques

Millions de florins

	1985	1986	1987	1988	1989 (1)	1990 (1)	1991	1992	1993 (2)	1994	
INCOME STATEMENT											**COMPTE DE RESULTATS**
1. Interest income	..	..	..	..	..	..	..	..	99664	94750	1. Produits financiers
2. Interest expenses	..	..	..	..	..	..	..	..	75842	68617	2. Frais financiers
3. Net interest income	11182	13478	14036	15038	16987	18309	20331	22215	23822	26133	3. Produits financiers nets
4. Non-interest income (net)	3858	4237	4918	5632	7062	7336	8360	8912	11959	10690	4. Produits non financiers (nets)
5. Gross income	15040	17715	18954	20670	24049	25645	28691	31127	35781	36823	5. Résultat brut
6. Operating expenses	9436	11682	13053	13986	15862	17612	19510	21074	23930	24576	6. Frais d'exploitation
7. Net income	5604	6033	5901	6684	8187	8033	9181	10053	11851	12247	7. Résultat net
8. Provisions (net)	1843	1892	1161	2741	2931	3006	3293	3609	3966	3850	8. Provisions (nettes)
9. Profit before tax	3761	4141	4740	3943	5256	5027	5888	6444	7885	8397	9. Bénéfices avant impôt
10. Income tax	..	..	1374	1102	1254	1273	1683	1933	2425	2413	10. Impôt
11. Profit after tax	..	..	3366	2841	4002	3754	4205	4511	5460	5984	11. Bénéfices après impôt
12. Distributed profit	..	..	..	..	..	..	..	..	..	..	12. Bénéfices distribués
13. Retained profit	..	..	..	..	..	..	..	..	..	..	13. Bénéfices mis en réserve
Memoranda											*Pour mémoire*
14. Staff costs	*6150*	*7085*	*7925*	*8371*	*9162*	*10183*	*11242*	*12245*	*13274*	*13585*	*14. Frais de personnel*
15. Provisions on loans	*..*	*..*	*..*	*..*	*..*	*..*	*..*	*..*	*..*	*..*	*15. Provisions sur prêts*
16. Provisions on securities	*..*	*..*	*..*	*..*	*..*	*..*	*..*	*..*	*..*	*..*	*16. Provisions sur titres*
BALANCE SHEET											**BILAN**
Assets											**Actif**
17. Cash & bal. with Central bank	4679	6077	8377	7622	22879	26110	22511	29446	36154	37349	17. Caisse & solde auprès de la Banque centrale
18. Interbank deposits	153339	151908	161571	186233	223004	261984	259165	265622	280384	262497	18. Dépôts interbancaires
19. Loans	280217	332268	338626	374264	501308	685356	731174	789757	856348	883475	19. Prêts
20. Securities	47132	69246	66150	73059	77642	118789	122342	139692	158231	183931	20. Valeurs mobilières
21. Other assets	31122	37466	42822	48856	62595	30251	32468	31019	32790	34742	21. Autres actifs
Liabilities											**Passif**
22. Capital & reserves	19296	23717	26532	29058	38756	45047	47634	50459	56031	59681	22. Capital et réserves
23. Borrowing from Central bank	5610	10701	7351	6093	4891	9328	3045	6647	4056	7921	23. Emprunts auprès de la Banque centrale
24. Interbank deposits	150742	154974	164676	179108	197499	265314	285345	296965	329205	324057	24. Dépôts interbancaires
25. Non-bank deposits	253320	307565	311773	342967	422644	510650	535246	580987	618785	623038	25. Dépôts non bancaires
26. Bonds	42909	49600	54773	67145	138017	167192	167845	168702	185287	217687	26. Obligations
27. Other liabilities	44612	50408	52441	65663	85621	124959	128545	151776	170543	169610	27. Autres engagements
Balance sheet total											**Total du bilan**
28. End-year total	516489	596965	617546	690034	887428	1122490	1167660	1255536	1363907	1401994	28. En fin d'exercice
29. Average total	507819	556727	607256	653790	817041	1004959	1145075	1211598	1309722	1382951	29. Moyen
Memoranda											*Pour mémoire*
30. Short-term securities (3)	*45863*	*66459*	*63459*	*69532*	*74111*	*27525*	*23333*	*24900*	*25350*	*34092*	*30. Titres à court terme (3)*
31. Bonds	*1269*	*2787*	*2691*	*3527*	*3531*	*86122*	*93604*	*110535*	*126878*	*143462*	*31. Obligations*
32. Shares and participations						*6281*	*6708*	*6898*	*6890*	*7117*	*32. Actions et participations*
33. Claims on non-residents	*199717*	*199689*	*203974*	*238791*	*280183*	*314206*	*321725*	*343747*	*379936*	*347670*	*33. Créances sur des non résidents*
34. Liabilities to non-residents	*181741*	*182778*	*192450*	*220035*	*232405*	*259304*	*267940*	*298789*	*328408*	*323608*	*34. Engagements envers des non résidents*
SUPPLEMENTARY INFORMATION											**RENSEIGNEMENTS COMPLEMENTAIRES**
35. Number of institutions	84	83	85	86	170	180	173	177	175	173	35. Nombre d'institutions
36. Number of branches	4786	7388	7352	7233	8006	7992	7827	7518	7167	7269	36. Nombre de succursales
37. Number of employees(x 1000)	92.4	104.1	106.0	106.4	117.4	122.9	119.9	119.9	115.4	109.0	37. Nombre de salariés (x 1000)

NETHERLANDS

All banks

Per cent

INCOME STATEMENT ANALYSIS

PAYS-BAS

Ensemble des banques

Pourcentage

ANALYSE DU COMPTE DE RESULTATS

	1985	1986	1987	1988	1989 (1)	1990 (1)	1991	1992	1993 (2)	1994		
% of average balance sheet total												**% du total moyen du bilan**
38. Interest income	..	..	..	..	..	..	..	..	7.61	6.85	38.	Produits financiers
39. Interest expenses	..	..	..	..	..	..	..	..	5.79	4.96	39.	Frais financiers
40. Net interest income	2.20	2.42	2.31	2.30	2.08	1.82	1.78	1.83	1.82	1.89	40.	Produits financiers nets
41. Non-interest income (net)	0.76	0.76	0.81	0.86	0.86	0.73	0.73	0.74	0.91	0.77	41.	Produits non financiers (nets)
42. Gross income	2.96	3.18	3.12	3.16	2.94	2.55	2.51	2.57	2.73	2.66	42.	Résultat brut
43. Operating expenses	1.86	2.10	2.15	2.14	1.94	1.75	1.70	1.74	1.83	1.78	43.	Frais d'exploitation
44. Net income	1.10	1.08	0.97	1.02	1.00	0.80	0.80	0.83	0.90	0.89	44.	Résultat net
45. Provisions (net)	0.36	0.34	0.19	0.42	0.36	0.30	0.29	0.30	0.30	0.28	45.	Provisions (nettes)
46. Profit before tax	0.74	0.74	0.78	0.60	0.64	0.50	0.51	0.53	0.60	0.61	46.	Bénéfices avant impôt
47. Income tax	..	..	0.23	0.17	0.15	0.13	0.15	0.16	0.19	0.17	47.	Impôt
48. Profit after tax	..	..	0.55	0.43	0.49	0.37	0.37	0.37	0.42	0.43	48.	Bénéfices après impôt
49. Distributed profit	..	..	..	..	..	..	..	..	..	..	49.	Bénéfices distribués
50. Retained profit	..	..	..	..	..	..	..	..	..	..	50.	Bénéfices mis en réserve
51. Staff costs	1.21	1.27	1.31	1.28	1.12	1.01	0.98	1.01	1.01	0.98	51.	Frais de personnel
52. Provisions on loans	..	..	..	..	..	..	..	..	..	..	52.	Provisions sur prêts
53. Provisions on securities	..	..	..	..	..	..	..	..	..	..	53.	Provisions sur titres
% of gross income												**% du total du résultat brut**
54. Net interest income	74.35	76.08	74.05	72.75	70.63	71.39	70.86	71.37	66.58	70.97	54.	Produits financiers nets
55. Non-interest income (net)	25.65	23.92	25.95	27.25	29.37	28.61	29.14	28.63	33.42	29.03	55.	Produits non financiers (nets)
56. Operating expenses	62.74	65.94	68.87	67.66	65.96	68.68	68.00	67.70	66.88	66.74	56.	Frais d'exploitation
57. Net income	37.26	34.06	31.13	32.34	34.04	31.32	32.00	32.30	33.12	33.26	57.	Résultat net
58. Provisions (net)	12.25	10.68	6.13	13.26	12.19	11.72	11.48	11.59	11.08	10.46	58.	Provisions (nettes)
59. Profit before tax	25.01	23.38	25.01	19.08	21.86	19.60	20.52	20.70	22.04	22.80	59.	Bénéfices avant impôt
60. Income tax	..	..	7.25	5.33	5.21	4.96	5.87	6.21	6.78	6.55	60.	Impôt
61. Profit after tax	..	..	17.76	13.74	16.64	14.64	14.66	14.49	15.26	16.25	61.	Bénéfices après impôt
62. Staff costs	40.89	39.99	41.81	40.50	38.10	39.71	39.18	39.34	37.10	36.89	62.	Frais de personnel
% of net income												**% du total du résultat net**
63. Provisions (net)	32.89	31.36	19.67	41.01	35.80	37.42	35.87	35.90	33.47	31.44	63.	Provisions (nettes)
64. Profit before tax	67.11	68.64	80.33	58.99	64.20	62.58	64.13	64.10	66.53	68.56	64.	Bénéfices avant impôt
65. Income tax	..	..	23.28	16.49	15.32	15.85	18.33	19.23	20.46	19.70	65.	Impôt
66. Profit after tax	..	..	57.04	42.50	48.88	46.73	45.80	44.87	46.07	48.86	66.	Bénéfices après impôt

NETHERLANDS

All banks

PAYS-BAS

Ensemble des banques

Per cent / *Pourcentage*

BALANCE SHEET ANALYSIS / **ANALYSE DU BILAN**

% of year-end balance sheet total / % du total du bilan en fin d'exercice

	1985	1986	1987	1988	1989 (1)	1990 (1)	1991	1992	1993 (2)	1994	
Assets											**Actif**
67. Cash & bal. with Central bank	0.91	1.02	1.36	1.10	2.58	2.33	1.93	2.35	2.65	2.66	67. Caisse & solde auprès de la Banque centrale
68. Interbank deposits	29.69	25.45	26.16	26.99	25.13	23.34	22.20	21.16	20.56	18.72	68. Dépôts interbancaires
69. Loans	54.25	55.66	54.83	54.24	56.49	61.06	62.62	62.90	62.79	63.02	69. Prêts
70. Securities	9.13	11.60	10.71	10.59	8.75	10.58	10.48	11.13	11.60	13.12	70. Valeurs mobilières
71. Other assets	6.03	6.28	6.93	7.08	7.05	2.69	2.78	2.47	2.40	2.48	71. Autres actifs
Liabilities											**Passif**
72. Capital & reserves	3.74	3.97	4.30	4.21	4.37	4.01	4.08	4.02	4.11	4.26	72. Capital et réserves
73. Borrowing from Central bank	1.09	1.79	1.19	0.88	0.55	0.83	0.26	0.53	0.30	0.56	73. Emprunts auprès de la Banque centrale
74. Interbank deposits	29.19	25.96	26.67	25.96	22.26	23.64	24.44	23.65	24.14	23.11	74. Dépôts interbancaires
75. Non-bank deposits	49.05	51.52	50.49	49.70	47.63	45.49	45.84	46.27	45.37	44.44	75. Dépôts non bancaires
76. Bonds	8.31	8.31	8.87	9.73	15.55	14.89	14.37	13.44	13.59	15.53	76. Obligations
77. Other liabilities	8.64	8.44	8.49	9.52	9.65	11.13	11.01	12.09	12.50	12.10	77. Autres engagements
Memoranda											*Pour mémoire*
78. Short-term securities (3)	*..*	*..*	*..*	*..*	*..*	*2.45*	*2.00*	*1.98*	*1.86*	*2.43*	*78. Titres à court terme (3)*
79. Bonds	*8.88*	*11.13*	*10.28*	*10.08*	*8.35*	*7.67*	*8.02*	*8.80*	*9.30*	*10.23*	*79. Obligations*
80. Shares and participations	*0.25*	*0.47*	*0.44*	*0.51*	*0.40*	*0.56*	*0.57*	*0.55*	*0.51*	*0.51*	*80. Actions et participations*
81. Claims on non-residents	*38.67*	*33.45*	*33.03*	*34.61*	*31.57*	*27.99*	*27.55*	*27.38*	*27.86*	*24.80*	*81. Créances sur des non résidents*
82. Liabilities to non-residents	*35.19*	*30.62*	*31.16*	*31.89*	*26.19*	*23.10*	*22.95*	*23.80*	*24.08*	*23.08*	*82. Engagements envers des non résidents*

1. New series. See change in methodology.
2. Break in series in 1993 due to changes in methodology.
3. Up to 1990 (old series), included under "Bonds" (item 31 or item 79).

Change in methodology:

• As from 1986, the data include the Postbank.

• As from 1988, Provisions (net) (item 8) consists of "transfers to the provision for general business risks". The addition to the lending/country risk provision out of this "provision for general business risks" in 1990 (new series), 1991 and 1992 amounts to Gld 2 410 million, Gld 3 328 million and Gld 3 283 respectively. In 1993, the item "transfers to the provision for general banking risks" was replaced by "value adjustments to receivables". The latter includes a transfer to an undisclosed reserve called "4% under valuation". In 1993 and 1994 this transfer amounted to Gld 592 million and Gld 1190 million.

• As from 1989, balance sheet data, in addition to universal banks and banks organised on a co-operative basis (old series), also include savings banks, mortgage banks, capital market institutions and security credit institutions. The income statement data, for the same series (1989 and 1990 old series), include universal banks, banks organised on a credit co-operative basis and savings banks. The old series for 1989 and 1990 appeared in Bank Profitability (OECD, Paris), 1992 and 1993 editions.

• The new series for 1990 cover, both for income statement and balance sheet data, universal banks, banks organised on a co-operative basis, savings banks, mortgage banks, capital market institutions and security credit institutions.

• As from 1993, the reporting system underlying the income statement has been adapted to legal changes.

1. Nouvelle série. Voir changement méthodologique.
2. En 1993, rupture dans les séries consécutive aux changements méthodologiques.
3. Jusqu'à 1990 (ancienne série) inclus sous "Obligations" (poste 31 ou poste 79).

Changement méthodologique :

• A compter de 1986, les données incluent la Banque postale.

• Depuis 1988, les Provisions (nettes) (poste 8), concernent les "dotations aux provisions pour risques généraux". La partie correspondant à la "provision pour risques" dans cette provision générale s'est élevée en 1990 (nouvelle série), 1991 et 1992 à fl 2 410 millions, fl 3 328 millions et fl 3 283 millions respectivement. En 1993, les "dotations aux provisions pour risques généraux" ont été remplacées par les "ajustements de valeur aux comptes recevables". Ce dernier comprend un transfert vers une réserve non divulguée, nommée "4 % de sous valuation". En 1993 et 1994 le montant de ce transfert était de fl 592 millions et fl 1190 millions.

• A partir de 1989, les données de bilan, en plus des banques universelles et des banques organisées en mutuelles (anciennes séries), incluent également les caisses d'épargne, les banques hypothécaires, les institutions du marché financier et les institutions des titres de crédit. Les données du compte de résultat, pour les mêmes séries (1989 et 1990 ancienne série), incluent les banques universelles, les banques organisées en mutuelles et les caisses d'épargne. Les anciennes séries pour 1989 et 1990 ont été publiées dans Rentabilité des banques (OCDE, Paris), éditions 1992 et 1993.

• La nouvelle série pour 1990 concerne, aussi bien pour les données du compte de résultat que pour celles du bilan, les banques universelles, les banques organisées en mutuelles, les caisses d'épargne, les banques hypothécaires, les institutions du marché financier et les institutions du marché financier et les institutions du titres de crédit.

• Depuis 1993, le règlement en vigueur sur lequel repose le compte de résultats a été adapté en fonction des modifications legislatives.

All banks

Million Norwegian kroner

	1985	1986	1987	1988	1989	1990	1991	1992	1993	1994	
INCOME STATEMENT											**COMPTE DE RESULTATS**
1. Interest income	40872	55270	73541	80265	76422	75021	70070	67670	58660	46728	1. Produits financiers
2. Interest expenses	28976	40490	55847	61632	55286	54808	50888	46937	35813	25764	2. Frais financiers
3. Net interest income	11896	14780	17694	18633	21136	20213	19182	20733	22847	20964	3. Produits financiers nets
4. Non-interest income (net)	4557	5805	3740	6320	7455	5155	3604	5555	8777	4582	4. Produits non financiers (nets)
5. Gross income	16453	20585	21434	24953	28591	25368	22786	26288	31624	25546	5. Résultat brut
6. Operating expenses (1)	11720	13926	16322	17438	17250	17933	20051	15859	15942	16196	6. Frais d'exploitation (1)
7. Net income	4733	6659	5112	7515	11341	7435	2735	10429	15682	9350	7. Résultat net
8. Provisions (net) (1)	2745	4049	4444	8882	9891	11655	21632	11670	8822	1265	8. Provisions (nettes) (1)
9. Profit before tax	1988	2610	668	-1367	1450	-4220	-18897	-1241	6860	8085	9. Bénéfices avant impôt
10. Income tax	403	468	384	279	570	272	201	404	917	943	10. Impôt
11. Profit after tax	1585	2142	284	-1646	880	-4492	-19098	-1645	5943	7142	11. Bénéfices après impôt
12. Distributed profit	651	501	239	167	775	35	25	122	619	2161	12. Bénéfices distribués
13. Retained profit	934	1641	45	-1813	105	-4527	-19123	-1767	5324	4981	13. Bénéfices mis en réserve
Memoranda											*Pour mémoire*
14. Staff costs	*5787*	*6868*	*7670*	*8436*	*8262*	*8557*	*8416*	*7868*	*7762*	*7821*	14. Frais de personnel
15. Provisions on loans	*1432*	*1720*	*4432*	*8769*	*10481*	*10919*	*21370*	*11691*	*7336*	*700*	15. Provisions sur prêts
16. Provisions on securities	..	..	..	..	..	..	..	..	..	..	16. Provisions sur titres
BALANCE SHEET											**BILAN**
Assets											**Actif**
17. Cash & balance with Central bank	2529	2893	3881	3136	3083	3136	3634	4890	3151	4333	17. Caisse & solde auprès de la Banque centrale
18. Interbank deposits	21717	40840	35734	23367	17799	20753	28470	41658	24143	26759	18. Dépôts interbancaires
19. Loans	263201	350155	405581	427506	459632	474753	451560	468575	461767	480055	19. Prêts
20. Securities	86863	83299	117509	96853	91045	84430	65803	67493	69792	63135	20. Valeurs mobilières
21. Other assets	8051	13107	27968	32167	33147	31573	28612	28094	27578	28577	21. Autres actifs
Liabilities											**Passif**
22. Capital & reserves	19450	23168	23461	22831	26204	23768	16785	21512	33910	41871	22. Capital et réserves
23. Borrowing from Central bank	2982	67676	73727	76254	58562	55880	44492	39112	16973	5207	23. Emprunts auprès de la Banque centrale
24. Interbank deposits	58975	69789	97704	80146	77217	76437	68072	50734	40048	40723	24. Dépôts interbancaires
25. Non-bank deposits	262064	268106	312465	326167	354185	370880	374350	407414	400569	418620	25. Dépôts non bancaires
26. Bonds	10147	32310	34569	43738	48038	50602	43858	64784	64576	61382	26. Obligations
27. Other liabilities	28743	29245	48746	33899	40499	37077	30523	27155	30356	35055	27. Autres engagements
Balance sheet total											**Total du bilan**
28. End-year total	382361	490294	590672	583033	604707	614645	578080	610710	586431	602859	28. En fin d'exercice
29. Average total	364215	458355	541430	613904	612183	639192	621560	591255	611885	608831	29. Moyen
Memoranda											*Pour mémoire*
30. Short-term securities	*28935*	*20470*	*33266*	*10354*	*9813*	*13128*	*8549*	*5420*	*10216*	*16150*	30. Titres à court terme
31. Bonds	*49769*	*51655*	*73705*	*75859*	*69770*	*58263*	*47245*	*52360*	*48807*	*34551*	31. Obligations
32. Shares and participations	*8158*	*11174*	*10539*	*10640*	*11462*	*13037*	*10008*	*9713*	*10770*	*12434*	32. Actions et participations
33. Claims on non-residents	*27843*	*49049*	*31792*	*26135*	*31201*	*34083*	*30838*	*43157*	*32321*	*27868*	33. Créances sur des non résidents
34. Liabilities to non-residents	*70471*	*98120*	*132070*	*131271*	*134193*	*129315*	*96144*	*75435*	*70414*	*59906*	34. Engagements envers des non résidents
SUPPLEMENTARY INFORMATION											**RENSEIGNEMENTS COMPLEMENTAIRES**
35. Number of institutions	225	221	201	187	179	164	156	155	153	150	35. Nombre d'institutions
36. Number of branches	2001	1930	2166	2032	1796	1796	1661	1593	1561	1552	36. Nombre de succursales
37. Number of employees (x 1000)	29.9	32.7	34.6	34.4	32.0	31.2	27.8	26.7	25.9	25.2	37. Nombre de salariés (x 1000)

NORWAY

All banks

NORVEGE

Ensemble des banques

Per cent	1985	1986	1987	1988	1989	1990	1991	1992	1993	1994	Pourcentage
INCOME STATEMENT ANALYSIS											**ANALYSE DU COMPTE DE RESULTATS**
% of average balance sheet total											**% du total moyen du bilan**
38. Interest income	11.22	12.06	13.58	13.07	12.48	11.74	11.27	11.45	9.59	7.68	38. Produits financiers
39. Interest expenses	7.96	8.83	10.31	10.04	9.03	8.57	8.19	7.94	5.85	4.23	39. Frais financiers
40. Net interest income	3.27	3.22	3.27	3.04	3.45	3.16	3.09	3.51	3.73	3.44	40. Produits financiers nets
41. Non-interest income (net)	1.25	1.27	0.69	1.03	1.22	0.81	0.58	0.94	1.43	0.75	41. Produits non financiers (nets)
42. Gross income	4.52	4.49	3.96	4.06	4.67	3.97	3.67	4.45	5.17	4.20	42. Résultat brut
43. Operating expenses (1)	3.22	3.04	3.01	2.84	2.82	2.81	3.23	2.68	2.61	2.66	43. Frais d'exploitation (1)
44. Net income	1.30	1.45	0.94	1.22	1.85	1.16	0.44	1.76	2.56	1.54	44. Résultat net
45. Provisions (net) (1)	0.75	0.88	0.82	1.45	1.62	1.82	3.48	1.97	1.44	0.21	45. Provisions (nettes) (1)
46. Profit before tax	0.55	0.57	0.12	-0.22	0.24	-0.66	-3.04	-0.21	1.12	1.33	46. Bénéfices avant impôt
47. Income tax	0.11	0.10	0.07	0.05	0.09	0.04	0.03	0.07	0.15	0.15	47. Impôt
48. Profit after tax	0.44	0.47	0.05	-0.27	0.14	-0.70	-3.07	-0.28	0.97	1.17	48. Bénéfices après impôt
49. Distributed profit	0.18	0.11	0.04	0.03	0.13	0.01	0.00	0.02	0.10	0.35	49. Bénéfices distribués
50. Retained profit	0.26	0.36	0.01	-0.30	0.02	-0.71	-3.08	-0.30	0.87	0.82	50. Bénéfices mis en réserve
51. Staff costs	1.59	1.50	1.42	1.37	1.35	1.34	1.35	1.33	1.27	1.28	51. Frais de personnel
52. Provisions on loans	0.39	0.38	0.82	1.43	1.71	1.71	3.44	1.98	1.20	0.11	52. Provisions sur prêts
53. Provisions on securities	..	..	..	..	..	..	..	..	..	..	53. Provisions sur titres
% of gross income											**% du total du résultat brut**
54. Net interest income	72.30	71.80	82.55	74.67	73.93	79.68	84.18	78.87	72.25	82.06	54. Produits financiers nets
55. Non-interest income (net)	27.70	28.20	17.45	25.33	26.07	20.32	15.82	21.13	27.75	17.94	55. Produits non financiers (nets)
56. Operating expenses (1)	71.23	67.65	76.15	69.88	60.33	70.69	88.00	60.33	50.41	63.40	56. Frais d'exploitation (1)
57. Net income	28.77	32.35	23.85	30.12	39.67	29.31	12.00	39.67	49.59	36.60	57. Résultat net
58. Provisions (net) (1)	16.68	19.67	20.73	35.59	34.59	45.94	94.94	44.39	27.90	4.95	58. Provisions (nettes) (1)
59. Profit before tax	12.08	12.68	3.12	-5.48	5.07	-16.64	-82.93	-4.72	21.69	31.65	59. Bénéfices avant impôt
60. Income tax	2.45	2.27	1.79	1.12	1.99	1.07	0.88	1.54	2.90	3.69	60. Impôt
61. Profit after tax	9.63	10.41	1.32	-6.60	3.08	-17.71	-83.81	-6.26	18.79	27.96	61. Bénéfices après impôt
62. Staff costs	35.17	33.36	35.78	33.81	28.90	33.73	36.93	29.93	24.54	30.62	62. Frais de personnel
% of net income											**% du total du résultat net**
63. Provisions (net)	58.00	60.80	86.93	118.19	87.21	156.76	..	111.90	56.26	13.53	63. Provisions (nettes)
64. Profit before tax	42.00	39.20	13.07	-18.19	12.79	-56.76	..	-11.90	43.74	86.47	64. Bénéfices avant impôt
65. Income tax	8.51	7.03	7.51	3.71	5.03	3.66	..	3.87	5.85	10.09	65. Impôt
66. Profit after tax	33.49	32.17	5.56	-21.90	7.76	-60.42	..	-15.77	37.90	76.39	66. Bénéfices après impôt

NORWAY

All banks

Per cent

BALANCE SHEET ANALYSIS

% of year-end balance sheet total

NORVEGE

Ensemble des banques

Pourcentage

ANALYSE DU BILAN

% du total du bilan en fin d'exercice

	1985	1986	1987	1988	1989	1990	1991	1992	1993	1994	
Assets											**Actif**
67. Cash & balance with Central bank	0.66	0.59	0.66	0.54	0.51	0.51	0.63	0.80	0.54	0.72	67. Caisse & solde auprès de la Banque centrale
68. Interbank deposits	5.68	8.33	6.05	4.01	2.94	3.38	4.92	6.82	4.12	4.44	68. Dépôts interbancaires
69. Loans	68.84	71.42	68.66	73.32	76.01	77.24	78.11	76.73	78.74	79.63	69. Prêts
70. Securities	22.72	16.99	19.89	16.61	15.06	13.74	11.38	11.05	11.90	10.47	70. Valeurs mobilières
71. Other assets	2.11	2.67	4.73	5.52	5.48	5.14	4.95	4.60	4.70	4.74	71. Autres actifs
Liabilities											**Passif**
72. Capital & reserves	5.09	4.73	3.97	3.92	4.33	3.87	2.90	3.52	5.78	6.95	72. Capital et réserves
73. Borrowing from Central bank	0.78	13.80	12.48	13.08	9.68	9.09	7.70	6.40	2.89	0.86	73. Emprunts auprès de la Banque centrale
74. Interbank deposits	15.42	14.23	16.54	13.75	12.77	12.44	11.78	8.31	6.83	6.75	74. Dépôts interbancaires
75. Non-bank deposits	68.54	54.68	52.90	55.94	58.57	60.34	64.76	66.71	68.31	69.44	75. Dépôts non bancaires
76. Bonds	2.65	6.59	5.85	7.50	7.94	8.23	7.59	10.61	11.01	10.18	76. Obligations
77. Other liabilities	7.52	5.96	8.25	5.81	6.70	6.03	5.28	4.45	5.18	5.81	77. Autres engagements
Memoranda											*Pour mémoire*
78. Short-term securities	*7.57*	*4.18*	*5.63*	*1.78*	*1.62*	*2.14*	*1.48*	*0.89*	*1.74*	*2.68*	*78. Titres à court terme*
79. Bonds	*13.02*	*10.54*	*12.48*	*13.01*	*11.54*	*9.48*	*8.17*	*8.57*	*8.32*	*5.73*	*79. Obligations*
80. Shares and participations	*2.13*	*2.28*	*1.78*	*1.82*	*1.90*	*2.12*	*1.73*	*1.59*	*1.84*	*2.06*	*80. Actions et participations*
81. Claims on non-residents	*7.28*	*10.00*	*5.38*	*4.48*	*5.16*	*5.55*	*5.33*	*7.07*	*5.51*	*4.62*	*81. Créances sur des non résidents*
82. Liabilities to non-residents	*18.43*	*20.01*	*22.36*	*22.52*	*22.19*	*21.04*	*16.63*	*12.35*	*12.01*	*9.94*	*82. Engagements envers des non résidents*

1. Change in methodology.

1. Changement méthodologique.

Notes

- Average balance sheet totals (item 29) are based on thirteen end-month data.
- All banks include Commercial banks and Savings banks.

Change in methodology:

- Due to methodological changes, in 1991, value adjustments (NKr 1.1 billion in 1990) are included under "Operating expenses" (item 6 or item 43 or item 56) and no longer under "Provisions (net)" (item 8 or item 45 or item 58).

Notes

- La moyenne du total des actifs/passifs (poste 29) est basée sur treize données de fin de mois.
- L'Ensemble des banques comprend les Banques commerciales et les Caisses d'épargne.

Changement méthodologique :

- Dû aux changements méthodologiques, pour l'année 1991, les ajustements en valeur (1,1 milliard de KrN en 1990) sont inclus sous la rubrique "Frais d'exploitation" (poste 6 ou poste 43 ou poste 56) et non plus sous la rubrique "Provisions (nettes)" (poste 8 ou poste 45 ou poste 58).

NORWAY

Commercial banks

Million Norwegian kroner

	1985	1986	1987	1988	1989	1990	1991	1992	1993	1994
INCOME STATEMENT										
1. Interest income	23179	30974	42243	45572	43709	43631	40234	38821	32757	25966
2. Interest expenses	16945	23289	33352	36088	33093	33431	30930	28587	21644	15833
3. Net interest income	6234	7685	8891	9484	10616	10200	9304	10234	11113	10133
4. Non-interest income (net)	3551	4400	2443	4739	5229	3570	2188	3850	5433	3437
5. Gross income	9785	12085	11334	14223	15845	13770	11492	14084	16546	13570
6. Operating expenses (1)	6676	7857	9358	9681	9522	10151	11742	8659	8602	8606
7. Net income	3109	4228	1976	4542	6323	3619	-250	5425	7944	4964
8. Provisions (net) (1)	1684	2500	2734	5712	5710	7593	16780	9842	6082	468
9. Profit before tax	1425	1728	-758	-1170	613	-3974	-17030	-4417	1862	4496
10. Income tax	298	328	151	78	287	61	8	77	262	162
11. Profit after tax	1127	1400	-909	-1248	326	-4035	-17038	-4494	1600	4334
12. Distributed profit	651	501	239	157	699	15	13	105	199	1511
13. Retained profit	476	899	-1148	-1405	-373	-4050	-17051	-4599	1401	2823
Memoranda										
14. Staff costs	3250	3925	4441	4833	4723	4928	4751	4348	4392	4256
15. Provisions on loans	736	794	2688	5673	5308	7051	16663	7800	4836	-183
16. Provisions on securities	..	..	..	..	..	..	..	..	..	..
BALANCE SHEET										
Assets										
17. Cash & balance with Central bank	1001	1136	1756	1512	1404	1283	1797	2535	1079	1879
18. Interbank deposits	14832	27382	23939	17293	13416	17261	23493	36086	20082	20915
19. Loans	152128	203608	237502	245541	272208	281433	258981	273155	256624	260848
20. Securities	50296	52925	76414	54137	50082	48439	33969	40519	39824	34547
21. Other assets	5832	10226	20062	22231	23933	22850	19944	19628	19644	19911
Liabilities										
22. Capital & reserves	11271	14046	13906	13493	15202	13153	7122	8167	15163	21147
23. Borrowing from Central bank	793	41936	41261	39518	27636	32814	29881	28544	8261	2437
24. Interbank deposits	44224	52510	72292	58967	60811	62804	51388	39492	33450	31434
25. Non-bank deposits	137290	135619	165776	169189	186288	193183	190008	218413	204360	213341
26. Bonds	7910	27949	31955	38615	43067	44105	38446	56546	54837	47471
27. Other liabilities	22601	23217	34483	20932	28038	25207	21339	20761	21183	22271
Balance sheet total										
28. End-year total	224089	295277	359673	340713	361042	371266	338184	371923	337255	338101
29. Average total	220953	270976	320318	361442	361350	387647	373090	349682	360924	347261
Memoranda										
30. Short-term securities	17382	14086	26421	5546	6941	10318	5327	3807	6933	10834
31. Bonds	26420	30045	42132	40352	34291	28024	21172	29839	26335	15885
32. Shares and participations	6493	8794	7861	8238	8850	10095	7470	6872	6556	7829
33. Claims on non-residents	22673	41215	25853	20660	26830	30023	27120	39798	28978	23911
34. Liabilities to non-residents	58367	85603	110579	106520	114870	112266	82903	66734	60748	50090
SUPPLEMENTARY INFORMATION										
35. Number of institutions	27	29	28	29	28	22	21	21	20	18
36. Number of branches	673	702	740	713	602	602	540	488	451	462
37. Number of employees (x 1000)	17.1	17.9	19.0	18.7	17.0	16.6	14.5	13.3	13.1	12.5

NORVEGE

Banques commerciales

Millions de couronnes norvégiennes

COMPTE DE RESULTATS
1. Produits financiers
2. Frais financiers
3. Produits financiers nets
4. Produits non financiers (nets)
5. Résultat brut
6. Frais d'exploitation (1)
7. Résultat net
8. Provisions (nettes) (1)
9. Bénéfices avant impôt
10. Impôt
11. Bénéfices après impôt
12. Bénéfices distribués
13. Bénéfices mis en réserve

Pour mémoire
14. Frais de personnel
15. Provisions sur prêts
16. Provisions sur titres

BILAN

Actif
17. Caisse & solde auprès de la Banque centrale
18. Dépôts interbancaires
19. Prêts
20. Valeurs mobilières
21. Autres actifs

Passif
22. Capital et réserves
23. Emprunts auprès de la Banque centrale
24. Dépôts interbancaires
25. Dépôts non bancaires
26. Obligations
27. Autres engagements

Total du bilan
28. En fin d'exercice
29. Moyen

Pour mémoire
30. Titres à court terme
31. Obligations
32. Actions et participations
33. Créances sur des non résidents
34. Engagements envers des non résidents

RENSEIGNEMENTS COMPLEMENTAIRES
35. Nombre d'institutions
36. Nombre de succursales
37. Nombre de salariés (x 1000)

NORWAY

Commercial banks

Per cent	1985	1986	1987	1988	1989	1990	1991	1992	1993	1994
INCOME STATEMENT ANALYSIS										
% of average balance sheet total										
38. Interest income	10.49	11.43	13.19	12.61	12.10	11.26	10.78	11.10	9.08	7.48
39. Interest expenses	7.67	8.59	10.41	9.98	9.16	8.62	8.29	8.18	6.00	4.56
40. Net interest income	2.82	2.84	2.78	2.62	2.94	2.63	2.49	2.93	3.08	2.92
41. Non-interest income (net)	1.61	1.62	0.76	1.31	1.45	0.92	0.59	1.10	1.51	0.99
42. Gross income	4.43	4.46	3.54	3.94	4.38	3.55	3.08	4.03	4.58	3.91
43. Operating expenses (1)	3.02	2.90	2.92	2.68	2.64	2.62	3.15	2.48	2.38	2.48
44. Net income	1.41	1.56	0.62	1.26	1.75	0.93	-0.07	1.55	2.20	1.43
45. Provisions (net) (1)	0.76	0.92	0.85	1.58	1.58	1.96	4.50	2.81	1.69	0.13
46. Profit before tax	0.64	0.64	-0.24	-0.32	0.17	-1.03	-4.56	-1.26	0.52	1.29
47. Income tax	0.13	0.12	0.05	0.02	0.08	0.02	0.00	0.02	0.07	0.05
48. Profit after tax	0.51	0.52	-0.28	-0.35	0.09	-1.04	-4.57	-1.29	0.44	1.25
49. Distributed profit	0.29	0.18	0.07	0.04	0.19	0.00	0.00	0.03	0.06	0.44
50. Retained profit	0.22	0.33	-0.36	-0.39	-0.10	-1.04	-4.57	-1.32	0.39	0.81
51. Staff costs	1.47	1.45	1.39	1.34	1.31	1.27	1.27	1.24	1.22	1.23
52. Provisions on loans	0.33	0.29	0.84	1.57	1.47	1.82	4.47	2.23	1.34	-0.05
53. Provisions on securities	:	:	:	:	:	:	:	:	:	:
% of gross income										
54. Net interest income	63.71	63.59	78.45	66.68	67.00	74.07	80.96	72.66	67.16	74.67
55. Non-interest income (net)	36.29	36.41	21.55	33.32	33.00	25.93	19.04	27.34	32.84	25.33
56. Operating expenses (1)	68.23	65.01	82.57	68.07	60.09	73.72	102.18	61.48	51.99	63.42
57. Net income	31.77	34.99	17.43	31.93	39.91	26.28	-2.18	38.52	48.01	36.58
58. Provisions (net) (1)	17.21	20.69	24.12	40.16	36.04	55.14	146.01	69.88	36.76	3.45
59. Profit before tax	14.56	14.30	-6.69	-8.23	3.87	-28.86	-148.19	-31.36	11.25	33.13
60. Income tax	3.05	2.71	1.33	0.55	1.81	0.44	0.07	0.55	1.58	1.19
61. Profit after tax	11.52	11.58	-8.02	-8.77	2.06	-29.30	-148.26	-31.91	9.67	31.94
62. Staff costs	33.21	32.48	39.18	33.98	29.81	35.79	41.34	30.87	26.54	31.36
% of net income										
63. Provisions (net)	54.17	59.13	138.36	125.76	90.31	209.81	:	181.42	76.56	9.43
64. Profit before tax	45.83	40.87	-38.36	-25.76	9.69	-109.81	:	-81.42	23.44	90.57
65. Income tax	9.59	7.76	7.64	1.72	4.54	1.69	:	1.42	3.30	3.26
66. Profit after tax	36.25	33.11	-46.00	-27.48	5.16	-111.49	:	-82.84	20.14	87.31

NORVEGE

Banques commerciales

Pourcentage

ANALYSE DU COMPTE DE RESULTATS

% du total moyen du bilan
38. Produits financiers
39. Frais financiers
40. Produits financiers nets
41. Produits non financiers (nets)
42. Résultat brut
43. Frais d'exploitation (1)
44. Résultat net
45. Provisions (nettes) (1)
46. Bénéfices avant impôt
47. Impôt
48. Bénéfices après impôt
49. Bénéfices distribués
50. Bénéfices mis en réserve

51. Frais de personnel
52. Provisions sur prêts
53. Provisions sur titres

% du total du résultat brut
54. Produits financiers nets
55. Produits non financiers (nets)
56. Frais d'exploitation (1)
57. Résultat net
58. Provisions (nettes) (1)
59. Bénéfices avant impôt
60. Impôt
61. Bénéfices après impôt
62. Frais de personnel

% du total du résultat net
63. Provisions (nettes)
64. Bénéfices avant impôt
65. Impôt
66. Bénéfices après impôt

126

Commercial banks

Per cent

BALANCE SHEET ANALYSIS

% of year-end balance sheet total

	1985	1986	1987	1988	1989	1990	1991	1992	1993	1994
Assets										
67. Cash & balance with Central bank	0.45	0.38	0.49	0.44	0.39	0.35	0.53	0.68	0.32	0.56
68. Interbank deposits	6.62	9.27	6.66	5.08	3.72	4.65	6.95	9.70	5.95	6.19
69. Loans	67.89	68.95	66.03	72.07	75.40	75.80	76.58	73.44	76.09	77.15
70. Securities	22.44	17.92	21.25	15.89	13.87	13.05	10.04	10.89	11.81	10.22
71. Other assets	2.60	3.46	5.58	6.52	6.63	6.15	5.90	5.28	5.82	5.89
Liabilities										
72. Capital & reserves	5.03	4.76	3.87	3.96	4.21	3.54	2.11	2.20	4.50	6.25
73. Borrowing from Central bank	0.35	14.20	11.47	11.60	7.65	8.84	8.84	7.67	2.45	0.72
74. Interbank deposits	19.74	17.78	20.10	17.31	16.84	16.92	15.20	10.62	9.92	9.30
75. Non-bank deposits	61.27	45.93	46.09	49.66	51.60	52.03	56.18	58.73	60.60	63.10
76. Bonds	3.53	9.47	8.88	11.33	11.93	11.88	11.37	15.20	16.26	14.04
77. Other liabilities	10.09	7.86	9.59	6.14	7.77	6.79	6.31	5.58	6.28	6.59
Memoranda										
78. Short-term securities	*7.76*	*4.77*	*7.35*	*1.63*	*1.92*	*2.78*	*1.58*	*1.02*	*2.06*	*3.20*
79. Bonds	*11.79*	*10.18*	*11.71*	*11.84*	*9.50*	*7.55*	*6.26*	*8.02*	*7.81*	*4.70*
80. Shares and participations	*2.90*	*2.98*	*2.19*	*2.42*	*2.45*	*2.72*	*2.21*	*1.85*	*1.94*	*2.32*
81. Claims on non-residents	*10.12*	*13.96*	*7.19*	*6.06*	*7.43*	*8.09*	*8.02*	*10.70*	*8.59*	*7.07*
82. Liabilities to non-residents	*26.05*	*28.99*	*30.74*	*31.26*	*31.82*	*30.24*	*24.51*	*17.94*	*18.01*	*14.82*

1. Change in methodology.

Notes

• Average balance sheet totals (item 29) are based on thirteen end-month data.

Change in methodology:

• Due to methodological changes, in 1991, value adjustments are included under "Operating expenses" (item 6 or item 43 or item 56) and no longer under "Provisions (net)" (item 8 or item 45 or item 58).

NORVEGE

Banques commerciales

Pourcentage

ANALYSE DU BILAN

% du total du bilan en fin d'exercice

Actif
67. Caisse & solde auprès de la Banque centrale
68. Dépôts interbancaires
69. Prêts
70. Valeurs mobilières
71. Autres actifs

Passif
72. Capital et réserves
73. Emprunts auprès de la Banque centrale
74. Dépôts interbancaires
75. Dépôts non bancaires
76. Obligations
77. Autres engagements

Pour mémoire
78. Titres à court terme
79. Obligations
80. Actions et participations
81. Créances sur des non résidents
82. Engagements envers des non résidents

1. Changement méthodologique.

Notes

• La moyenne du total des actifs/passifs (poste 29) est basée sur treize données de fin de mois.

Changement méthodologique :

• Dû aux changements méthodologiques, pour l'année 1991, les ajustements en valeur sont inclus sous la rubrique "Frais d'exploitation" (poste 6 ou poste 43 ou poste 56) et non plus sous la rubrique "Provisions (nettes)" (poste 8 ou poste 45 ou poste 58).

NORWAY

Savings banks

NORVEGE

Caisses d'épargne

Million Norwegian kroner / *Millions de couronnes norvégiennes*

	1985	1986	1987	1988	1989	1990	1991	1992	1993	1994	
INCOME STATEMENT											**COMPTE DE RESULTATS**
1. Interest income	17693	24296	31298	34693	32713	31391	29836	28849	25903	20762	1. Produits financiers
2. Interest expenses	12031	17201	22495	25544	22193	21376	19958	18350	14169	9932	2. Frais financiers
3. Net interest income	5662	7095	8803	9149	10520	10015	9878	10499	11734	10830	3. Produits financiers nets
4. Non-interest income (net)	1006	1405	1297	1581	2226	1585	1416	1705	3343	1146	4. Produits non financiers (nets)
5. Gross income	6668	8500	10100	10730	12746	11600	11294	12204	15077	11976	5. Résultat brut
6. Operating expenses (1)	5044	6069	6964	7757	7728	7782	8309	7200	7340	7591	6. Frais d'exploitation (1)
7. Net income	1624	2431	3136	2973	5018	3818	2985	5004	7737	4385	7. Résultat net
8. Provisions (net) (1)	1061	1549	1710	3170	4181	4062	4852	1828	2740	797	8. Provisions (nettes) (1)
9. Profit before tax	563	882	1426	-197	837	-244	-1867	3176	4997	3588	9. Bénéfices avant impôt
10. Income tax	105	140	233	201	283	212	192	327	655	781	10. Impôt
11. Profit after tax	458	742	1193	-398	554	-456	-2059	2849	4342	2807	11. Bénéfices après impôt
12. Distributed profit	-	-	-	10	76	21	11	17	420	650	12. Bénéfices distribués
13. Retained profit	458	742	1193	-408	478	-477	-2070	2832	3922	2157	13. Bénéfices mis en réserve
Memoranda											*Pour mémoire*
14. Staff costs	*2537*	*2943*	*3229*	*3603*	*3539*	*3629*	*3665*	*3520*	*3370*	*3564*	14. Frais de personnel
15. Provisions on loans	*696*	*926*	*1744*	*3095*	*5173*	*3868*	*4708*	*3891*	*2500*	*883*	15. Provisions sur prêts
16. Provisions on securities	*:*	*:*	*:*	*:*	*:*	*:*	*:*	*:*	*:*	*:*	16. Provisions sur titres
BALANCE SHEET											**BILAN**
Assets											**Actif**
17. Cash & balance with Central bank	1528	1757	2124	1624	1679	1853	1837	2355	2072	2454	17. Caisse & solde auprès de la Banque cen
18. Interbank deposits	6885	13458	11794	6074	4383	3492	4977	5572	4060	5844	18. Dépôts interbancaires
19. Loans	111073	146547	168079	181965	187424	193320	192579	195420	205142	219207	19. Prêts
20. Securities	36567	30374	41095	42716	40963	35991	31834	26974	29968	28588	20. Valeurs mobilières
21. Other assets	2219	2881	7906	9936	9214	8723	8669	8466	7934	8666	21. Autres actifs
Liabilities											**Passif**
22. Capital & reserves	8179	9122	9555	9338	11002	10615	9663	13345	18746	20723	22. Capital et réserves
23. Borrowing from Central bank	2189	25740	32466	36736	30926	23066	14611	10567	8712	2770	23. Emprunts auprès de la Banque centrale
24. Interbank deposits	14751	17279	25412	21179	16406	13633	16684	11242	6598	9289	24. Dépôts interbancaires
25. Non-bank deposits	124774	132487	146689	156978	167897	177698	184342	189000	196209	205280	25. Dépôts non bancaires
26. Bonds	2237	4361	2614	5123	4971	6496	5413	8238	9738	13911	26. Obligations
27. Other liabilities	6142	6028	14263	12967	12461	11870	9183	6394	9173	12784	27. Autres engagements
Balance sheet total											**Total du bilan**
28. End-year total	158272	195017	230999	242320	243665	243379	239896	238787	249176	264758	28. En fin d'exercice
29. Average total	143262	187379	221112	252462	250833	251542	248570	241573	250961	261571	29. Moyen
Memoranda											*Pour mémoire*
30. Short-term securities	*11553*	*6384*	*6845*	*4808*	*2872*	*2810*	*3222*	*1613*	*3283*	*5316*	30. Titres à court terme
31. Bonds	*23349*	*21610*	*31573*	*35507*	*35479*	*30238*	*26073*	*22521*	*22471*	*18666*	31. Obligations
32. Shares and participations	*1665*	*2380*	*2678*	*2402*	*2612*	*2942*	*2539*	*2841*	*4214*	*4605*	32. Actions et participations
33. Claims on non-residents	*5170*	*7834*	*5939*	*5475*	*4371*	*4060*	*3718*	*3358*	*3343*	*3957*	33. Créances sur des non résidents
34. Liabilities to non-residents	*12104*	*12517*	*21491*	*24751*	*19323*	*17049*	*13240*	*8701*	*9666*	*9816*	34. Engagements envers des non résidents
SUPPLEMENTARY INFORMATION											**RENSEIGNEMENTS COMPLEMENTAIRES**
35. Number of institutions	198	192	173	158	151	142	135	134	133	132	35. Nombre d'institutions
36. Number of branches	1328	1228	1426	1319	1194	1194	1121	1105	1110	1090	36. Nombre de succursales
37. Number of employees (x 1000)	12.8	14.7	15.6	15.7	14.9	14.6	13.3	13.4	12.8	12.7	37. Nombre de salariés (x 1000)

NORWAY

Savings banks

NORVEGE

Caisses d'épargne

Per cent / *Pourcentage*

INCOME STATEMENT ANALYSIS / ANALYSE DU COMPTE DE RESULTATS

	1985	1986	1987	1988	1989	1990	1991	1992	1993	1994	
% of average balance sheet total											**% du total moyen du bilan**
38. Interest income	12.35	12.97	14.15	13.74	13.04	12.48	12.00	11.94	10.32	7.94	38. Produits financiers
39. Interest expenses	8.40	9.18	10.17	10.12	8.85	8.50	8.03	7.60	5.65	3.80	39. Frais financiers
40. Net interest income	3.95	3.79	3.98	3.62	4.19	3.98	3.97	4.35	4.68	4.14	40. Produits financiers nets
41. Non-interest income (net)	0.70	0.75	0.59	0.63	0.89	0.63	0.57	0.71	1.33	0.44	41. Produits non financiers (nets)
42. Gross income	4.65	4.54	4.57	4.25	5.08	4.61	4.54	5.05	6.01	4.58	42. Résultat brut
43. Operating expenses (1)	3.52	3.24	3.15	3.07	3.08	3.09	3.34	2.98	2.92	2.90	43. Frais d'exploitation (1)
44. Net income	1.13	1.30	1.42	1.18	2.00	1.52	1.20	2.07	3.08	1.68	44. Résultat net
45. Provisions (net) (1)	0.74	0.83	0.77	1.26	1.67	1.61	1.95	0.76	1.09	0.30	45. Provisions (nettes) (1)
46. Profit before tax	0.39	0.47	0.64	-0.08	0.33	-0.10	-0.75	1.31	1.99	1.37	46. Bénéfices avant impôt
47. Income tax	0.07	0.07	0.11	0.08	0.11	0.08	0.08	0.14	0.26	0.30	47. Impôt
48. Profit after tax	0.32	0.40	0.54	-0.16	0.22	-0.18	-0.83	1.18	1.73	1.07	48. Bénéfices après impôt
49. Distributed profit			-	0.00	0.03	0.01	0.00	0.01	0.17	0.25	49. Bénéfices distribués
50. Retained profit	0.32	0.40	0.54	-0.16	0.19	-0.19	-0.83	1.17	1.56	0.82	50. Bénéfices mis en réserve
51. Staff costs	1.77	1.57	1.46	1.43	1.41	1.44	1.47	1.46	1.34	1.36	51. Frais de personnel
52. Provisions on loans	0.49	0.49	0.79	1.23	2.06	1.54	1.89	1.61	1.00	0.34	52. Provisions sur prêts
53. Provisions on securities	:	:	:	:	:	:	:	:	:	:	53. Provisions sur titres
% of gross income											**% du total du résultat brut**
54. Net interest income	84.91	83.47	87.16	85.27	82.54	86.34	87.46	86.03	77.83	90.43	54. Produits financiers nets
55. Non-interest income (net)	15.09	16.53	12.84	14.73	17.46	13.66	12.54	13.97	22.17	9.57	55. Produits non financiers (nets)
56. Operating expenses (1)	75.64	71.40	68.95	72.29	60.63	67.09	73.57	59.00	48.68	63.39	56. Frais d'exploitation (1)
57. Net income	24.36	28.60	31.05	27.71	39.37	32.91	26.43	41.00	51.32	36.61	57. Résultat net
58. Provisions (net) (1)	15.91	18.22	16.93	29.54	32.80	35.02	42.96	14.98	18.17	6.65	58. Provisions (nettes) (1)
59. Profit before tax	8.44	10.38	14.12	-1.84	6.57	-2.10	-16.53	26.02	33.14	29.96	59. Bénéfices avant impôt
60. Income tax	1.57	1.65	2.31	1.87	2.22	1.83	1.70	2.68	4.34	6.52	60. Impôt
61. Profit after tax	6.87	8.73	11.81	-3.71	4.35	-3.93	-18.23	23.34	28.80	23.44	61. Bénéfices après impôt
62. Staff costs	38.05	34.62	31.97	33.58	27.77	31.28	32.45	28.84	22.35	29.76	62. Frais de personnel
% of net income											**% du total du résultat net**
63. Provisions (net)	65.33	63.72	54.53	106.63	83.32	106.39	162.55	36.53	35.41	18.18	63. Provisions (nettes)
64. Profit before tax	34.67	36.28	45.47	-6.63	16.68	-6.39	-62.55	63.47	64.59	81.82	64. Bénéfices avant impôt
65. Income tax	6.47	5.76	7.43	6.76	5.64	5.55	6.43	6.53	8.47	17.81	65. Impôt
66. Profit after tax	28.20	30.52	38.04	-13.39	11.04	-11.94	-68.98	56.93	56.12	64.01	66. Bénéfices après impôt

NORWAY

Savings banks

NORVEGE

Caisses d'épargne

Per cent / *Pourcentage*

BALANCE SHEET ANALYSIS / **ANALYSE DU BILAN**

% of year-end balance sheet total / % du total du bilan en fin d'exercice

	1985	1986	1987	1988	1989	1990	1991	1992	1993	1994	
Assets											**Actif**
67. Cash & balance with Central bank	0.97	0.90	0.92	0.67	0.69	0.76	0.77	0.99	0.83	0.93	67. Caisse & solde auprès de la Banque centrale
68. Interbank deposits	4.35	6.90	5.11	2.51	1.80	1.43	2.07	2.33	1.63	2.21	68. Dépôts interbancaires
69. Loans	70.18	75.15	72.76	75.09	76.92	79.43	80.28	81.84	82.33	82.80	69. Prêts
70. Securities	23.10	15.58	17.79	17.63	16.81	14.79	13.27	11.30	12.03	10.80	70. Valeurs mobilières
71. Other assets	1.40	1.48	3.42	4.10	3.78	3.58	3.61	3.55	3.18	3.27	71. Autres actifs
Liabilities											**Passif**
72. Capital & reserves	5.17	4.68	4.14	3.85	4.52	4.36	4.03	5.59	7.52	7.83	72. Capital et réserves
73. Borrowing from Central bank	1.38	13.20	14.05	15.16	12.69	9.48	6.09	4.43	3.50	1.05	73. Emprunts auprès de la Banque centrale
74. Interbank deposits	9.32	8.86	11.00	8.74	6.73	5.60	6.95	4.71	2.65	3.51	74. Dépôts interbancaires
75. Non-bank deposits	78.84	67.94	63.50	64.78	68.90	73.01	76.84	79.15	78.74	77.53	75. Dépôts non bancaires
76. Bonds	1.41	2.24	1.13	2.11	2.04	2.67	2.26	3.45	3.91	5.25	76. Obligations
77. Other liabilities	3.88	3.09	6.17	5.35	5.11	4.88	3.83	2.68	3.68	4.83	77. Autres engagements
Memoranda											*Pour mémoire*
78. Short-term securities	*7.30*	*3.27*	*2.96*	*1.98*	*1.18*	*1.15*	*1.34*	*0.68*	*1.32*	*2.01*	*78. Titres à court terme*
79. Bonds	*14.75*	*11.08*	*13.67*	*14.65*	*14.56*	*12.42*	*10.87*	*9.43*	*9.02*	*7.05*	*79. Obligations*
80. Shares and participations	*1.05*	*1.22*	*1.16*	*0.99*	*1.07*	*1.21*	*1.06*	*1.19*	*1.69*	*1.74*	*80. Actions et participations*
81. Claims on non-residents	*3.27*	*4.02*	*2.57*	*2.26*	*1.79*	*1.67*	*1.55*	*1.41*	*1.34*	*1.49*	*81. Créances sur des non résidents*
82. Liabilities to non-residents	*7.65*	*6.42*	*9.30*	*10.21*	*7.93*	*7.01*	*5.52*	*3.64*	*3.88*	*3.71*	*82. Engagements envers des non résidents*

1. Change in methodology.

1. Changement méthodologique.

Notes

• Average balance sheet totals (item 29) are based on thirteen end-month data.

Change in methodology:

• Due to methodological changes, in 1991, value adjustments are included under "Operating expenses" (item 6 or item 43 or item 56) and no longer under "Provisions (net)" (item 8 or item 45 or item 58).

Notes

• La moyenne du total des actifs/passifs (poste 29) est basée sur treize données de fin de mois.

Changement méthodologique :

• Dû aux changements méthodologiques, pour l'année 1991, les ajustements en valeur sont inclus sous la rubrique "Frais d'exploitation" (poste 6 ou poste 43 ou poste 56) et non plus sous la rubrique "Provisions (nettes)" (poste 8 ou poste 45 ou poste 58).

PORTUGAL

All banks

Million escudos

PORTUGAL

Ensemble des banques

Millions d'escudos

	1985	1986	1987	1988	1989	1990 (1)	1991	1992	1993	1994	
INCOME STATEMENT											**COMPTE DE RESULTATS**
1. Interest income	939400	880775	848092	944041	1171919	1543263	1910743	2266576	2283156	2189039	1. Produits financiers
2. Interest expenses	821707	718557	614871	649072	780109	995986	1246944	1592212	1605301	1524868	2. Frais financiers
3. Net interest income	117693	162218	233221	294969	391810	547277	663799	674364	677855	664171	3. Produits financiers nets
4. Non-interest income (net)	37271	36132	52303	64212	76182	127345	154924	222693	266462	249085	4. Produits non financiers (nets)
5. Gross income	154964	198350	285524	359181	467992	674622	818723	897057	944317	913256	5. Résultat brut
6. Operating expenses	107744	132113	154510	183213	219080	280913	367679	461264	505583	531773	6. Frais d'exploitation
7. Net income	47220	66237	131014	175968	248912	393709	451044	435793	438734	381483	7. Résultat net
8. Provisions (net)	30831	49399	92362	115176	151446	231939	236953	255558	235295	224782	8. Provisions (nettes)
9. Profit before tax	16389	16838	38652	60792	97466	161770	214091	180235	203439	156701	9. Bénéfices avant impôt
10. Income tax	1622	1668	1846	4053	23304	38814	55937	39516	44625	38421	10. Impôt
11. Profit after tax	14767	15170	36806	56739	74162	122956	158154	140719	158814	118280	11. Bénéfices après impôt
12. Distributed profit	..	..	..	..	..	..	..	..	..	..	12. Bénéfices distribués
13. Retained profit	..	..	..	..	..	..	..	..	..	..	13. Bénéfices mis en réserve
Memoranda											*Pour mémoire*
14. Staff costs	76547	92062	106888	121684	141475	172842	216208	262331	282884	295363	14. Frais de personnel
15. Provisions on loans	..	..	..	..	..	220648	218120	225991	251133	233688	15. Provisions sur prêts
16. Provisions on securities	..	..	..	..	..	11493	19225	57115	24712	29040	16. Provisions sur titres
BALANCE SHEET											**BILAN**
Assets											*Actif*
17. Cash & balance with Central bank	311083	284202	396356	465639	1319298	1424899	1807694	2006298	2172598	428084	17. Caisse & solde auprès de la Banque centrale
18. Interbank deposits	798040	1072002	1192065	1263484	1242249	2334765	2102738	3480830	5172973	8062323	18. Dépôts interbancaires
19. Loans	2923807	3257965	3384853	3631461	3851876	4765890	5952732	7074854	7732441	8283476	19. Prêts
20. Securities	432504	573087	972915	1407330	1545134	2221676	4089252	4421027	4724133	5833440	20. Valeurs mobilières
21. Other assets	987459	1132528	1432713	1971423	2342169	1017021	1000235	1227762	2270184	3135461	21. Autres actifs
Liabilities											*Passif*
22. Capital & reserves	305897	421556	609487	836160	1063216	1289880	1732169	2120942	2370745	2582171	22. Capital et réserves
23. Borrowing from Central bank	57127	77083	60445	21686	30932	45412	196482	28497	244250	542114	23. Emprunts auprès de la Banque centrale
24. Interbank deposits	86839	106330	245149	333275	505209	1240662	1795270	2557152	3662537	4891034	24. Dépôts interbancaires
25. Non-bank deposits	4203635	4952503	5586231	6465273	7539688	8047619	9763854	11961252	13299301	14454570	25. Dépôts non bancaires
26. Bonds	43152	42025	69277	91676	92159	134255	184859	234356	361361	322904	26. Obligations
27. Other liabilities	756243	720287	808313	991267	1069522	1006423	1280017	1308572	2134135	2949991	27. Autres engagements
Balance sheet total											**Total du bilan**
28. End-year total	5452893	6319784	7378902	8739337	10300726	11764251	14952651	18210771	22072329	25742784	28. En fin d'exercice
29. Average total	4956980	5886339	6849343	8059120	9520032	NA	13358451	16581711	20141550	23907557	29. Moyen
Memoranda											*Pour mémoire*
30. Short-term securities	45711	156355	293109	302597	522655	708908	1375478	1022246	905737	1266904	30. Titres à court terme
31. Bonds	345710	371191	572003	845926	816299	1164697	2141720	2135984	2953901	3304043	31. Obligations
32. Shares and participations	43628	46503	109391	131635	184629	280616	428802	752903	717082	801546	32. Actions et participations
33. Claims on non-residents	357334	339334	403409	611988	698218	810947	1168368	2012590	3504158	4506949	33. Créances sur des non résidents
34. Liabilities to non-residents	257699	221513	229801	301338	466196	772540	1305575	1800705	2453201	3423794	34. Engagements envers des non résidents
SUPPLEMENTARY INFORMATION											**RENSEIGNEMENTS COMPLÉMENTAIRES**
35. Number of institutions	24	27	27	27	29	33	35	35	42	44	35. Nombre d'institutions
36. Number of branches	1494	1510	1531	1607	1741	1999	2520	2874	3169	3401	36. Nombre de succursales
37. Number of employees (x 1000)	59.1	59.2	59.0	58.4	58.1	59.2	61.1	60.8	59.7	61.6	37. Nombre de salariés (x 1000)

PORTUGAL

All banks

Per cent

INCOME STATEMENT ANALYSIS

	1985	1986	1987	1988	1989	1990 (1)	1991	1992	1993	1994
% of average balance sheet total										
38. Interest income	18.95	14.96	12.38	11.71	12.31	NA	14.30	13.67	11.34	9.16
39. Interest expenses	16.58	12.21	8.98	8.05	8.19	NA	9.33	9.60	7.97	6.38
40. Net interest income	2.37	2.76	3.41	3.66	4.12	NA	4.97	4.07	3.37	2.78
41. Non-interest income (net)	0.75	0.61	0.76	0.80	0.80	NA	1.16	1.34	1.32	1.04
42. Gross income	3.13	3.37	4.17	4.46	4.92	NA	6.13	5.41	4.69	3.82
43. Operating expenses	2.17	2.24	2.26	2.27	2.30	NA	2.75	2.78	2.51	2.22
44. Net income	0.95	1.13	1.91	2.18	2.61	NA	3.38	2.63	2.18	1.60
45. Provisions (net)	0.62	0.84	1.35	1.43	1.59	NA	1.77	1.54	1.17	0.94
46. Profit before tax	0.33	0.29	0.56	0.75	1.02	NA	1.60	1.09	1.01	0.66
47. Income tax	0.03	0.03	0.03	0.05	0.24	NA	0.42	0.24	0.22	0.16
48. Profit after tax	0.30	0.26	0.54	0.70	0.78	NA	1.18	0.85	0.79	0.49
49. Distributed profit	..	..	..	..	..	..	..	..	..	..
50. Retained profit	..	..	..	..	..	..	..	..	..	..
51. Staff costs	1.54	1.56	1.56	1.51	1.49	NA	1.62	1.58	1.40	1.24
52. Provisions on loans	..	..	..	..	..	NA	1.63	1.36	1.25	0.98
53. Provisions on securities	..	..	..	..	..	NA	0.14	0.34	0.12	0.12
% of gross income										
54. Net interest income	75.95	81.78	81.68	82.12	83.72	81.12	81.08	75.18	71.78	72.73
55. Non-interest income (net)	24.05	18.22	18.32	17.88	16.28	18.88	18.92	24.82	28.22	27.27
56. Operating expenses	69.53	66.61	54.11	51.01	46.81	41.64	44.91	51.42	53.54	58.23
57. Net income	30.47	33.39	45.89	48.99	53.19	58.36	55.09	48.58	46.46	41.77
58. Provisions (net)	19.90	24.90	32.35	32.07	32.36	34.38	28.94	28.49	24.92	24.61
59. Profit before tax	10.58	8.49	13.54	16.93	20.83	23.98	26.15	20.09	21.54	17.16
60. Income tax	1.05	0.84	0.65	1.13	4.98	5.75	6.83	4.41	4.73	4.21
61. Profit after tax	9.53	7.65	12.89	15.80	15.85	18.23	19.32	15.69	16.82	12.95
62. Staff costs	49.40	46.41	37.44	33.88	30.23	25.62	26.41	29.24	29.96	32.34
% of net income										
63. Provisions (net)	65.29	74.58	70.50	65.45	60.84	58.91	52.53	58.64	53.63	58.92
64. Profit before tax	34.71	25.42	29.50	34.55	39.16	41.09	47.47	41.36	46.37	41.08
65. Income tax	3.43	2.52	1.41	2.30	9.36	9.86	12.40	9.07	10.17	10.07
66. Profit after tax	31.27	22.90	28.09	32.24	29.79	31.23	35.06	32.29	36.20	31.01

PORTUGAL

Ensemble des banques

Pourcentage

ANALYSE DU COMPTE DE RESULTATS

% du total moyen du bilan
38. Produits financiers
39. Frais financiers
40. Produits financiers nets
41. Produits non financiers (nets)
42. Résultat brut
43. Frais d'exploitation
44. Résultat net
45. Provisions (nettes)
46. Bénéfices avant impôt
47. Impôt
48. Bénéfices après impôt
49. Bénéfices distribués
50. Bénéfices mis en réserve
51. Frais de personnel
52. Provisions sur prêts
53. Provisions sur titres

% du total du résultat brut
54. Produits financiers nets
55. Produits non financiers (nets)
56. Frais d'exploitation
57. Résultat net
58. Provisions (nettes)
59. Bénéfices avant impôt
60. Impôt
61. Bénéfices après impôt
62. Frais de personnel

% du total du résultat net
63. Provisions (nettes)
64. Bénéfices avant impôt
65. Impôt
66. Bénéfices après impôt

132

All banks

Ensemble des banques

BALANCE SHEET ANALYSIS

Per cent — *Pourcentage*

ANALYSE DU BILAN

% of year-end balance sheet total — % du total du bilan en fin d'exercice

	1985	1986	1987	1988	1989	1990 (1)	1991	1992	1993	1994	
Assets											**Actif**
67. Cash & balance with Central bank	5.70	4.50	5.37	5.33	12.81	12.11	12.09	11.02	9.84	1.66	67. Caisse & solde auprès de la Banque centrale
68. Interbank deposits	14.64	16.96	16.16	14.46	12.06	19.85	14.06	19.11	23.44	31.32	68. Dépôts interbancaires
69. Loans	53.62	51.55	45.87	41.55	37.39	40.51	39.81	38.85	35.03	32.18	69. Prêts
70. Securities	7.93	9.07	13.19	16.10	15.00	18.88	27.35	24.28	21.40	22.66	70. Valeurs mobilières
71. Other assets	18.11	17.92	19.42	22.56	22.74	8.65	6.69	6.74	10.29	12.18	71. Autres actifs
Liabilities											**Passif**
72. Capital & reserves	5.61	6.67	8.26	9.57	10.32	10.96	11.58	11.65	10.74	10.03	72. Capital et réserves
73. Borrowing from Central bank	1.05	1.22	0.82	0.25	0.30	0.39	1.31	0.16	1.11	2.11	73. Emprunts auprès de la Banque centrale
74. Interbank deposits	1.59	1.68	3.32	3.81	4.90	10.55	12.01	14.04	16.59	19.00	74. Dépôts interbancaires
75. Non-bank deposits	77.09	78.37	75.71	73.98	73.20	68.41	65.30	65.68	60.25	56.15	75. Dépôts non bancaires
76. Bonds	0.79	0.66	0.94	1.05	0.89	1.14	1.24	1.29	1.64	1.25	76. Obligations
77. Other liabilities	13.87	11.40	10.95	11.34	10.38	8.55	8.56	7.19	9.67	11.46	77. Autres engagements
Memoranda											*Pour mémoire*
78. Short-term securities	*0.84*	*2.47*	*3.97*	*3.46*	*5.07*	*6.03*	*9.20*	*5.61*	*4.10*	*4.92*	*78. Titres à court terme*
79. Bonds	*6.34*	*5.87*	*7.75*	*9.68*	*7.92*	*9.90*	*14.32*	*11.73*	*13.38*	*12.83*	*79. Obligations*
80. Shares and participations	*0.80*	*0.74*	*1.48*	*1.51*	*1.79*	*2.39*	*2.87*	*4.13*	*3.25*	*3.11*	*80. Actions et participations*
81. Claims on non-residents	*6.55*	*5.37*	*5.47*	*7.00*	*6.78*	*6.89*	*7.81*	*11.05*	*15.88*	*17.51*	*81. Créances sur des non résidents*
82. Liabilities to non-residents	*4.73*	*3.51*	*3.11*	*3.45*	*4.53*	*6.57*	*8.73*	*9.89*	*11.11*	*13.30*	*82. Engagements envers des non résidents*

1. Break in series due to changes in methodology.

Change in methodology:

- Until 1989, time deposits with the Central bank are included under "Interbank deposits" (item 18).

- As from 1990, data are based on the new accounting framework for the Portugese banking sector, introduced in January 1990. Also from 1990, data were revised taking into account the European Directives regarding capital funds and reserves. In addition, branches in off-shore centres of Madeira and Santa Maria Islands are also included.

1. Rupture dans les séries consécutive aux changements méthodologiques.

Changement méthodologique :

- Jusqu'en 1989, les dépôts à terme auprès de la Banque centrale sont inclus sous "Dépôts interbancaires" (poste 18).

- A partir de 1990, les données sont établies à l'aide du nouveau cadre comptable pour le secteur bancaire portugais introduit en janvier 1990. Egalement à partir de 1990, les données ont été révisées en prenant en compte les directives européennes concernant les capitaux et réserves. De plus, les succursales des centres extraterritoriaux des îles de Madère et Santa Maria sont également inclues.

SPAIN

All banks

Billion pesetas

ESPAGNE

Ensemble des banques

Milliards de pesetas

	1985	1986	1987	1988	1989	1990	1991	1992	1993 (1)	1994 (2)	
INCOME STATEMENT											**COMPTE DE RESULTATS**
1. Interest income	4033	4225	4854	5237	6373	7676	8558	8972	10230	9251	1. Produits financiers
2. Interest expenses	2535	2520	2907	3054	3961	5039	5624	5961	7099	5977	2. Frais financiers
3. Net interest income	1498	1705	1947	2183	2412	2637	2934	3011	3131	3274	3. Produits financiers nets
4. Non-interest income (net)	277	317	419	525	515	588	689	766	1090	902	4. Produits non financiers (nets)
5. Gross income	1775	2022	2366	2708	2927	3225	3623	3777	4221	4176	5. Résultat brut
6. Operating expenses	1145	1366	1461	1740	1784	1970	2118	2280	2518	2493	6. Frais d'exploitation
7. Net income	630	656	905	968	1143	1255	1505	1497	1703	1683	7. Résultat net
8. Provisions (net)	311	292	390	363	312	380	477	599	1359	845	8. Provisions (nettes)
9. Profit before tax	319	364	515	605	831	875	1028	898	344	838	9. Bénéfices avant impôt
10. Income tax	69	85	120	158	231	239	249	219	228	197	10. Impôt
11. Profit after tax	250	279	395	447	600	636	779	679	116	641	11. Bénéfices après impôt
12. Distributed profit	94	102	135	188	243	262	317	315	317	346	12. Bénéfices distribués
13. Retained profit	156	177	260	259	357	374	462	364	-201	295	13. Bénéfices mis en réserve
Memoranda											*Pour mémoire*
14. *Staff costs*	*756*	*945*	*983*	*1200*	*1164*	*1229*	*1284*	*1385*	*1560*	*1517*	14. *Frais de personnel*
15. *Provisions on loans*	*186*	*137*	*183*	*208*	*157*	*195*	*378*	*523*	*1040*	*557*	15. *Provisions sur prêts*
16. *Provisions on securities*	*27*	*9*	*39*	*26*	*21*	*79*	*46*	*92*	*195*	*273*	16. *Provisions sur titres*
BALANCE SHEET											**BILAN**
Assets											**Actif**
17. Cash & balance with Central bank	3668	3787	5033	5141	5930	5034	5788	4984	4306	4300	17. Caisse & solde auprès de la Banque centrale
18. Interbank deposits	5146	5406	5750	6773	8301	9721	11744	14307	19416	17501	18. Dépôts interbancaires
19. Loans	16828	18251	20650	23800	28055	31457	37341	40786	43125	48589	19. Prêts
20. Securities	8671	10907	11735	13042	14159	15469	14277	15116	17552	21542	20. Valeurs mobilières
21. Other assets	5891	5679	5920	6197	7049	8456	9720	11716	18948	18760	21. Autres actifs
Liabilities											**Passif**
22. Capital & reserves	3164	3497	4132	4907	5572	6451	8231	8428	9160	10219	22. Capital et réserves
23. Borrowing from Central bank	980	1426	1384	957	2112	1590	1572	4282	6525	6063	23. Emprunts auprès de la Banque centrale
24. Interbank deposits	5496	5584	5562	6250	6804	7563	9863	11574	16930	17971	24. Dépôts interbancaires
25. Non-bank deposits	24851	27102	30873	35170	40280	44500	48383	51277	56329	60805	25. Dépôts non bancaires
26. Bonds	1314	1717	1480	1379	1107	1007	1210	1276	1758	3071	26. Obligations
27. Other liabilities	4398	4704	5658	6290	7618	9026	9611	10073	12646	12563	27. Autres engagements
Balance sheet total											**Total du bilan**
28. End-year total	40203	44029	49089	54953	63493	70137	78868	86910	103347	110692	28. En fin d'exercice
29. Average total	38154	42116	46559	52021	59223	66815	74503	82889	95128	109096	29. Moyen
Memoranda											*Pour mémoire*
30. *Short-term securities*	*3831*	*4484*	*5412*	*6204*	*7237*	*8142*	*6064*	*6456*	*5839*	*6370*	30. *Titres à court terme*
31. *Bonds*	*4056*	*5531*	*5308*	*5382*	*5194*	*5378*	*5480*	*5745*	*8299*	*11492*	31. *Obligations*
32. *Shares and participations*	*784*	*893*	*1015*	*1456*	*1728*	*1949*	*2732*	*2915*	*3415*	*3680*	32. *Actions et participations*
33. *Claims on non-residents*	*3089*	*3152*	*2804*	*2800*	*3019*	*3792*	*4511*	*7857*	*16518*	*14583*	33. *Créances sur des non résidents*
34. *Liabilities to non-residents*	*3228*	*3372*	*3629*	*4246*	*4876*	*6447*	*7373*	*9342*	*12308*	*13261*	34. *Engagements envers des non résidents*
SUPPLEMENTARY INFORMATION											**RENSEIGNEMENTS COMPLEMENTAIRES**
35. Number of institutions	364	355	346	334	333	327	323	319	316	316	35. Nombre d'institutions
36. Number of branches	32503	32731	33282	33757	34511	35234	34873	35476	35240	35591	36. Nombre de succursales
37. Number of employees (x 1000)	243.5	240.7	240.0	242.4	248.3	251.6	256.0	253.2	246.8	246.1	37. Nombre de salariés (x 1000)

SPAIN

All banks

Per cent

ESPAGNE

Ensemble des banques

Pourcentage

	1985	1986	1987	1988	1989	1990	1991	1992	1993 (1)	1994 (2)		
INCOME STATEMENT ANALYSIS												**ANALYSE DU COMPTE DE RESULTATS**
% of average balance sheet total												**% du total moyen du bilan**
38. Interest income	10.57	10.03	10.43	10.07	10.76	11.49	11.49	10.82	10.75	8.48	38.	Produits financiers
39. Interest expenses	6.64	5.98	6.24	5.87	6.69	7.54	7.55	7.19	7.46	5.48	39.	Frais financiers
40. Net interest income	3.93	4.05	4.18	4.20	4.07	3.95	3.94	3.63	3.29	3.00	40.	Produits financiers nets
41. Non-interest income (net)	0.73	0.75	0.90	1.01	0.87	0.88	0.92	0.92	1.15	0.83	41.	Produits non financiers (nets)
42. Gross income	4.65	4.80	5.08	5.21	4.94	4.83	4.86	4.56	4.44	3.83	42.	Résultat brut
43. Operating expenses	3.00	3.24	3.14	3.34	3.01	2.95	2.84	2.75	2.65	2.29	43.	Frais d'exploitation
44. Net income	1.65	1.56	1.94	1.86	1.93	1.88	2.02	1.81	1.79	1.54	44.	Résultat net
45. Provisions (net)	0.82	0.69	0.84	0.70	0.53	0.57	0.64	0.72	1.43	0.77	45.	Provisions (nettes)
46. Profit before tax	0.84	0.86	1.11	1.16	1.40	1.31	1.38	1.08	0.36	0.77	46.	Bénéfices avant impôt
47. Income tax	0.18	0.20	0.26	0.30	0.39	0.36	0.33	0.26	0.24	0.18	47.	Impôt
48. Profit after tax	0.66	0.66	0.85	0.86	1.01	0.95	1.05	0.82	0.12	0.59	48.	Bénéfices après impôt
49. Distributed profit	0.25	0.24	0.29	0.36	0.41	0.39	0.43	0.38	0.33	0.32	49.	Bénéfices distribués
50. Retained profit	0.41	0.42	0.56	0.50	0.60	0.56	0.62	0.44	-0.21	0.27	50.	Bénéfices mis en réserve
51. Staff costs	1.98	2.24	2.11	2.31	1.97	1.84	1.72	1.67	1.64	1.39	51.	Frais de personnel
52. Provisions on loans	0.49	0.33	0.39	0.40	0.27	0.29	0.51	0.63	1.09	0.51	52.	Provisions sur prêts
53. Provisions on securities	0.07	0.02	0.08	0.05	0.04	0.12	0.06	0.11	0.20	0.25	53.	Provisions sur titres
% of gross income												**% du total du résultat brut**
54. Net interest income	84.39	84.32	82.29	80.61	82.41	81.77	80.98	79.72	74.18	78.40	54.	Produits financiers nets
55. Non-interest income (net)	15.61	15.68	17.71	19.39	17.59	18.23	19.02	20.28	25.82	21.60	55.	Produits non financiers (nets)
56. Operating expenses	64.51	67.56	61.75	64.25	60.95	61.09	58.46	60.37	59.65	59.70	56.	Frais d'exploitation
57. Net income	35.49	32.44	38.25	35.75	39.05	38.91	41.54	39.63	40.35	40.30	57.	Résultat net
58. Provisions (net)	17.52	14.44	16.48	13.40	10.66	11.78	13.17	15.86	32.20	20.23	58.	Provisions (nettes)
59. Profit before tax	17.97	18.00	21.77	22.34	28.39	27.13	28.37	23.78	8.15	20.07	59.	Bénéfices avant impôt
60. Income tax	3.89	4.20	5.07	5.83	7.89	7.41	6.87	5.80	5.40	4.72	60.	Impôt
61. Profit after tax	14.08	13.80	16.69	16.51	20.50	19.72	21.50	17.98	2.75	15.35	61.	Bénéfices après impôt
62. Staff costs	42.59	46.74	41.55	44.31	39.77	38.11	35.44	36.67	36.96	36.33	62.	Frais de personnel
% of net income												**% du total du résultat net**
63. Provisions (net)	49.37	44.51	43.09	37.50	27.30	30.28	31.69	40.01	79.80	50.21	63.	Provisions (nettes)
64. Profit before tax	50.63	55.49	56.91	62.50	72.70	69.72	68.31	59.99	20.20	49.79	64.	Bénéfices avant impôt
65. Income tax	10.95	12.96	13.26	16.32	20.21	19.04	16.54	14.63	13.39	11.71	65.	Impôt
66. Profit after tax	39.68	42.53	43.65	46.18	52.49	50.68	51.76	45.36	6.81	38.09	66.	Bénéfices après impôt

SPAIN

All banks

Per cent

BALANCE SHEET ANALYSIS

% of year-end balance sheet total

ESPAGNE

Ensemble des banques

Pourcentage

ANALYSE DU BILAN

% du total du bilan en fin d'exercice

	1985	1986	1987	1988	1989	1990	1991	1992	1993 (1)	1994 (2)	
Assets											**Actif**
67. Cash & balance with Central bank	9.12	8.60	10.25	9.36	9.34	7.18	7.34	5.73	4.17	3.88	67. Caisse & solde auprès de la Banque centrale
68. Interbank deposits	12.80	12.28	11.71	12.33	13.07	13.86	14.89	16.46	18.79	15.81	68. Dépôts interbancaires
69. Loans	41.86	41.45	42.07	43.31	44.19	44.85	47.35	46.93	41.73	43.90	69. Prêts
70. Securities	21.57	24.77	23.91	23.73	22.30	22.06	18.10	17.39	16.98	19.46	70. Valeurs mobilières
71. Other assets	14.65	12.90	12.06	11.28	11.10	12.06	12.32	13.48	18.33	16.95	71. Autres actifs
Liabilities											**Passif**
72. Capital & reserves	7.87	7.94	8.42	8.93	8.78	9.20	10.44	9.70	8.86	9.23	72. Capital et réserves
73. Borrowing from Central bank	2.44	3.24	2.82	1.74	3.33	2.27	1.99	4.93	6.31	5.48	73. Emprunts auprès de la Banque centrale
74. Interbank deposits	13.67	12.68	11.33	11.37	10.72	10.78	12.51	13.32	16.38	16.24	74. Dépôts interbancaires
75. Non-bank deposits	61.81	61.55	62.89	64.00	63.44	63.45	61.35	59.00	54.50	54.93	75. Dépôts non bancaires
76. Bonds	3.27	3.90	3.01	2.51	1.74	1.44	1.53	1.47	1.70	2.77	76. Obligations
77. Other liabilities	10.94	10.68	11.53	11.45	12.00	12.87	12.19	11.59	12.24	11.35	77. Autres engagements
Memoranda											*Pour mémoire*
78. Short-term securities	*9.53*	*10.18*	*11.02*	*11.29*	*11.40*	*11.61*	*7.69*	*7.43*	*5.65*	*5.75*	*78. Titres à court terme*
79. Bonds	*10.09*	*12.56*	*10.81*	*9.79*	*8.18*	*7.67*	*6.95*	*6.61*	*8.03*	*10.38*	*79. Obligations*
80. Shares and participations	*1.95*	*2.03*	*2.07*	*2.65*	*2.72*	*2.78*	*3.46*	*3.35*	*3.30*	*3.32*	*80. Actions et participations*
81. Claims on non-residents	*7.68*	*7.16*	*5.71*	*5.10*	*4.75*	*5.41*	*5.72*	*9.04*	*15.98*	*13.17*	*81. Créances sur des non résidents*
82. Liabilities to non-residents	*8.03*	*7.66*	*7.39*	*7.73*	*7.68*	*9.19*	*9.35*	*10.75*	*11.91*	*11.98*	*82. Engagements envers des non résidents*

1. Break in series in 1993 due to restructuring of a major bank.

2. Break in series in 1994. Three official credit banks were classified as Commercial banks and no longer as Official credit institutions

: Notes

• All banks include Commercial banks, Savings banks and Co-operative banks.

Change in methodology:

• Liabilities to non-resident credit institutions, included under "Non-bank deposits" in earlier editions of this publication, were revised to incorporate them in "Other liabilities".

• As from 1992, "Income tax" (item 10) includes tax on domestic activities of resident entities rather than total tax.

1. Rupture dans les séries en 1993 suite à la restructuration de l'une des principales banques.

2. Rupture dans les séries en 1994. Trois banques publiques de crédit ont été classées dans les Banques commerciales et non plus dans les Institutions publiques de crédit.

Notes

• L'Ensemble des banques comprend les Banques commerciales, les Caisses d'épargne et les Banques mutualistes.

Changement méthodologique :

• Le passif des institutions de crédit non-résidentes, inclus dans "Dépôts non bancaires" dans les éditions précédentes de cette publication, a été révisé de manière à être incorporé dans "Autres engagements".

• A partir de 1992, la rubrique "Impôt" (poste 10) inclut l'impôt sur les activités domestiques des entités résidentes plutôt que l'impôt total.

SPAIN

Commercial banks

Billion pesetas

ESPAGNE

Banques commerciales

Milliards de pesetas

	1985	1986	1987	1988	1989	1990	1991	1992	1993 (1)	1994 (2)	
INCOME STATEMENT											**COMPTE DE RESULTATS**
1. Interest income	2710	2752	3157	3308	4036	4819	5520	5664	6445	5876	1. Produits financiers
2. Interest expenses	1787	1717	2004	1977	2566	3224	3693	3886	4668	4016	2. Frais financiers
3. Net interest income	923	1035	1153	1331	1470	1595	1827	1778	1777	1860	3. Produits financiers nets
4. Non-interest income (net)	207	226	314	373	362	433	535	547	820	626	4. Produits non financiers (nets)
5. Gross income	1130	1261	1467	1704	1832	2028	2362	2325	2597	2486	5. Résultat brut
6. Operating expenses	727	830	906	1005	1049	1182	1322	1408	1546	1470	6. Frais d'exploitation
7. Net income	403	431	561	699	783	846	1040	917	1051	1016	7. Résultat net
8. Provisions (net)	217	205	262	252	208	223	318	342	1046	538	8. Provisions (nettes)
9. Profit before tax	186	226	299	447	575	623	722	575	5	478	9. Bénéfices avant impôt
10. Income tax	48	61	83	134	179	189	185	145	146	119	10. Impôt
11. Profit after tax	138	165	216	313	396	434	537	430	-141	359	11. Bénéfices après impôt
12. Distributed profit	61	68	91	141	186	207	262	255	245	276	12. Bénéfices distribués
13. Retained profit	77	97	125	172	210	227	275	175	-386	83	13. Bénéfices mis en réserve
Memoranda											*Pour mémoire*
14. Staff costs	*486*	*577*	*627*	*688*	*689*	*750*	*810*	*867*	*977*	*893*	14. Frais de personnel
15. Provisions on loans	*152*	*152*	*176*	*219*	*138*	*127*	*258*	*335*	*736*	*329*	15. Provisions sur prêts
16. Provisions on securities	*22*	*4*	*26*	*24*	*17*	*47*	*41*	*46*	*211*	*215*	16. Provisions sur titres
BALANCE SHEET											**BILAN**
Assets											**Actif**
17. Cash & balance with Central bank	1938	1811	2791	2751	2979	2516	3105	2513	2181	2151	17. Caisse & solde auprès de la Banque centrale
18. Interbank deposits	3418	3481	4000	4585	5504	6384	7636	8678	12521	11795	18. Dépôts interbancaires
19. Loans	11943	12566	13722	15359	17773	19723	23922	25006	25993	29254	19. Prêts
20. Securities	5094	6623	6809	7020	7697	8508	8385	8873	11568	13282	20. Valeurs mobilières
21. Other assets	4538	4166	4220	4343	4791	5508	6640	8466	14451	13916	21. Autres actifs
Liabilities											**Passif**
22. Capital & reserves	2142	2342	2732	3318	3728	4231	5719	5639	6002	6641	22. Capital et réserves
23. Borrowing from Central bank	919	1303	1257	919	1553	1296	1243	2593	5417	4793	23. Emprunts auprès de la Banque centrale
24. Interbank deposits	4791	4941	4986	5512	5978	6241	8554	9881	14860	15425	24. Dépôts interbancaires
25. Non-bank deposits	14722	15468	17390	18975	21334	23800	26142	26649	28842	30472	25. Dépôts non bancaires
26. Bonds	712	896	753	689	591	586	720	707	1026	2308	26. Obligations
27. Other liabilities	3646	3698	4424	4646	5558	6487	7311	8066	10566	10760	27. Autres engagements
Balance sheet total											**Total du bilan**
28. End-year total	26930	28648	31542	34059	38743	42639	49688	53535	66713	70399	28. En fin d'exercice
29. Average total	25873	27789	30095	32800	36401	40691	46164	51612	60124	70633	29. Moyen
Memoranda											*Pour mémoire*
30. Short-term securities	*2330*	*3184*	*3486*	*3733*	*4016*	*4445*	*3221*	*3396*	*3337*	*3483*	30. Titres à court terme
31. Bonds	*2115*	*2743*	*2542*	*2175*	*2395*	*2628*	*2979*	*3214*	*5599*	*6984*	31. Obligations
32. Shares and participations	*650*	*696*	*782*	*1112*	*1285*	*1436*	*2185*	*2263*	*2633*	*2815*	32. Actions et participations
33. Claims on non-residents	*3020*	*3030*	*2676*	*2665*	*2821*	*3375*	*3983*	*6777*	*14204*	*12267*	33. Créances sur des non résidents
34. Liabilities to non-residents	*2976*	*3099*	*3312*	*3841*	*4420*	*5739*	*6603*	*8523*	*11327*	*12202*	34. Engagements envers des non résidents
SUPPLEMENTARY INFORMATION											**RENSEIGNEMENTS COMPLÉMENTAIRES**
35. Number of institutions	139	138	138	138	145	154	160	164	164	165	35. Nombre d'institutions
36. Number of branches	16606	16518	16498	16691	16677	16917	17824	18058	17636	17557	36. Nombre de succursales
37. Number of employees (x 1000)	161.6	157.8	155.3	154.7	155.7	157.0	162.0	159.3	152.8	151.2	37. Nombre de salariés (x 1000)

SPAIN

Commercial banks

Per cent	1985	1986	1987	1988	1989	1990	1991	1992	1993 (1)	1994 (2)		Pourcentage
INCOME STATEMENT ANALYSIS												**ANALYSE DU COMPTE DE RESULTATS**
% of average balance sheet total												**% du total moyen du bilan**
38. Interest income	10.47	9.90	10.49	10.09	11.09	11.84	11.96	10.97	10.72	8.32	38.	Produits financiers
39. Interest expenses	6.91	6.18	6.66	6.03	7.05	7.92	8.00	7.53	7.76	5.69	39.	Frais financiers
40. Net interest income	3.57	3.72	3.83	4.06	4.04	3.92	3.96	3.44	2.96	2.63	40.	Produits financiers nets
41. Non-interest income (net)	0.80	0.81	1.04	1.14	0.99	1.06	1.16	1.06	1.36	0.89	41.	Produits non financiers (nets)
42. Gross income	4.37	4.54	4.87	5.20	5.03	4.98	5.12	4.50	4.32	3.52	42.	Résultat brut
43. Operating expenses	2.81	2.99	3.01	3.06	2.88	2.90	2.86	2.73	2.57	2.08	43.	Frais d'exploitation
44. Net income	1.56	1.55	1.86	2.13	2.15	2.08	2.25	1.78	1.75	1.44	44.	Résultat net
45. Provisions (net)	0.84	0.74	0.87	0.77	0.57	0.55	0.69	0.66	1.74	0.76	45.	Provisions (nettes)
46. Profit before tax	0.72	0.81	0.99	1.36	1.58	1.53	1.56	1.11	0.01	0.68	46.	Bénéfices avant impôt
47. Income tax	0.19	0.22	0.28	0.41	0.49	0.46	0.40	0.28	0.24	0.17	47.	Impôt
48. Profit after tax	0.53	0.59	0.72	0.95	1.09	1.07	1.16	0.83	-0.23	0.51	48.	Bénéfices après impôt
49. Distributed profit	0.24	0.24	0.30	0.43	0.51	0.51	0.57	0.49	0.41	0.39	49.	Bénéfices distribués
50. Retained profit	0.30	0.35	0.42	0.52	0.58	0.56	0.60	0.34	-0.64	0.12	50.	Bénéfices mis en réserve
51. Staff costs	1.88	2.08	2.08	2.10	1.89	1.84	1.75	1.68	1.62	1.26	51.	Frais de personnel
52. Provisions on loans	0.59	0.55	0.58	0.67	0.38	0.31	0.56	0.65	1.22	0.47	52.	Provisions sur prêts
53. Provisions on securities	0.09	0.01	0.09	0.07	0.05	0.12	0.09	0.09	0.35	0.30	53.	Provisions sur titres
% of gross income												**% du total du résultat brut**
54. Net interest income	81.68	82.08	78.60	78.11	80.24	78.65	77.35	76.47	68.43	74.82	54.	Produits financiers nets
55. Non-interest income (net)	18.32	17.92	21.40	21.89	19.76	21.35	22.65	23.53	31.57	25.18	55.	Produits non financiers (nets)
56. Operating expenses	64.34	65.82	61.76	58.98	57.26	58.28	55.97	60.56	59.53	59.13	56.	Frais d'exploitation
57. Net income	35.66	34.18	38.24	41.02	42.74	41.72	44.03	39.44	40.47	40.87	57.	Résultat net
58. Provisions (net)	19.20	16.26	17.86	14.79	11.35	11.00	13.46	14.71	40.28	21.64	58.	Provisions (nettes)
59. Profit before tax	16.46	17.92	20.38	26.23	31.39	30.72	30.57	24.73	0.19	19.23	59.	Bénéfices avant impôt
60. Income tax	4.25	4.84	5.66	7.86	9.77	9.32	7.83	6.24	5.62	4.79	60.	Impôt
61. Profit after tax	12.21	13.08	14.72	18.37	21.62	21.40	22.73	18.49	-5.43	14.44	61.	Bénéfices après impôt
62. Staff costs	43.01	45.76	42.74	40.38	37.61	36.98	34.29	37.29	37.62	35.92	62.	Frais de personnel
% of net income												**% du total du résultat net**
63. Provisions (net)	53.85	47.56	46.70	36.05	26.56	26.36	30.58	37.30	99.52	52.35	63.	Provisions (nettes)
64. Profit before tax	46.15	52.44	53.30	63.95	73.44	73.64	69.42	62.70	0.48	47.05	64.	Bénéfices avant impôt
65. Income tax	11.91	14.15	14.80	19.17	22.86	22.34	17.79	15.81	13.89	11.71	65.	Impôt
66. Profit after tax	34.24	38.28	38.50	44.78	50.57	51.30	51.63	46.89	-13.42	35.33	66.	Bénéfices après impôt

SPAIN

Commercial banks

ESPAGNE

Banques commerciales

Per cent — *Pourcentage*

BALANCE SHEET ANALYSIS — ANALYSE DU BILAN

	1985	1986	1987	1988	1989	1990	1991	1992	1993 (1)	1994 (2)	
% of year-end balance sheet total											**% du total du bilan en fin d'exercice**
Assets											**Actif**
67. Cash & balance with Central bank	7.20	6.32	8.85	8.08	7.69	5.90	6.25	4.69	3.27	3.06	67. Caisse & solde auprès de la Banque centrale
68. Interbank deposits	12.69	12.15	12.68	13.46	14.21	14.97	15.37	16.21	18.77	16.75	68. Dépôts interbancaires
69. Loans	44.35	43.86	43.50	45.10	45.87	46.26	48.14	46.71	38.96	41.55	69. Prêts
70. Securities	18.92	23.12	21.59	20.61	19.87	19.95	16.88	16.57	17.34	18.87	70. Valeurs mobilières
71. Other assets	16.85	14.54	13.38	12.75	12.37	12.92	13.36	15.81	21.66	19.77	71. Autres actifs
Liabilities											**Passif**
72. Capital & reserves	7.95	8.18	8.66	9.74	9.62	9.92	11.51	10.53	9.00	9.43	72. Capital et réserves
73. Borrowing from Central bank	3.41	4.55	3.99	2.70	4.01	3.04	2.50	4.84	8.12	6.81	73. Emprunts auprès de la Banque centrale
74. Interbank deposits	17.79	17.25	15.81	16.18	15.43	14.64	17.22	18.46	22.27	21.91	74. Dépôts interbancaires
75. Non-bank deposits	54.67	53.99	55.13	55.71	55.07	55.82	52.61	49.78	43.23	43.28	75. Dépôts non bancaires
76. Bonds	2.64	3.13	2.39	2.02	1.53	1.37	1.45	1.32	1.54	3.28	76. Obligations
77. Other liabilities	13.54	12.91	14.03	13.64	14.35	15.21	14.71	15.07	15.84	15.28	77. Autres engagements
Memoranda											*Pour mémoire*
78. Short-term securities	8.65	11.11	11.05	10.96	10.37	10.42	6.48	6.34	5.00	4.95	78. Titres à court terme
79. Bonds	7.85	9.57	8.06	6.39	6.18	6.16	6.00	6.00	8.39	9.92	79. Obligations
80. Shares and participations	2.41	2.43	2.48	3.26	3.32	3.37	4.40	4.23	3.95	4.00	80. Actions et participations
81. Claims on non-residents	11.21	10.58	8.48	7.82	7.28	7.92	8.02	12.66	21.29	17.42	81. Créances sur des non résidents
82. Liabilities to non-residents	11.05	10.82	10.50	11.28	11.41	13.46	13.29	15.92	16.98	17.33	82. Engagements envers des non résidents

1. Break in series in 1993 due to restructuring of a major bank.

2. Break in series in 1994. Three official credit banks were classified as Commercial banks and no longer as Official credit institutions

Change in methodology:

- Liabilities to non-resident credit institutions, included under "Non-bank deposits" in earlier editions of this publication, were revised to incorporate them in "Other liabilities".

- As from 1992, "Income tax" (item 10) includes tax on domestic activities of resident entities rather than total tax.

1. Rupture dans les séries en 1993 suite à la restructuration de l'une des principales banques.

2. Rupture dans les séries en 1994. Trois banques publiques de crédit ont été classées dans les Banques commerciales et non plus dans les Institutions publiques de crédit.

Changement méthodologique :

- Le passif des institutions de crédit non-résidentes, inclus dans "Dépôts non bancaires" dans les éditions précédentes de cette publication, a été révisé de manière à être incorporé dans "Autres engagements".

- A partir de 1992, la rubrique "Impôt" (poste 10) inclut l'impôt sur les activités domestiques des entités résidentes plutôt que l'impôt total.

SPAIN

Savings banks

Billion pesetas

ESPAGNE

Caisses d'épargne

Milliards de pesetas

	1985	1986	1987	1988	1989	1990	1991	1992	1993	1994	
INCOME STATEMENT											**COMPTE DE RESULTATS**
1. Interest income	1192	1331	1533	1761	2151	2637	2782	3027	3461	3079	1. Produits financiers
2. Interest expenses	674	729	821	989	1298	1693	1788	1920	2248	1811	2. Frais financiers
3. Net interest income	518	602	712	772	853	944	994	1107	1213	1268	3. Produits financiers nets
4. Non-interest income (net)	61	87	101	147	148	150	148	212	258	264	4. Produits non financiers (nets)
5. Gross income	579	689	813	919	1001	1094	1142	1319	1471	1532	5. Résultat brut
6. Operating expenses	378	494	508	683	678	723	722	790	881	927	6. Frais d'exploitation
7. Net income	201	195	305	236	323	371	420	529	590	605	7. Résultat net
8. Provisions (net)	84	79	116	102	97	147	148	244	286	288	8. Provisions (nettes)
9. Profit before tax	117	116	189	134	226	224	272	285	304	317	9. Bénéfices avant impôt
10. Income tax	20	23	35	22	49	47	59	68	76	72	10. Impôt
11. Profit after tax	97	93	154	112	177	177	213	217	228	245	11. Bénéfices après impôt
12. Distributed profit	27	28	38	43	50	47	47	50	62	60	12. Bénéfices distribués
13. Retained profit	70	65	116	69	127	130	166	167	166	185	13. Bénéfices mis en réserve
Memoranda											*Pour mémoire*
14. Staff costs	*245*	*341*	*326*	*480*	*440*	*440*	*430*	*470*	*531*	*567*	14. Frais de personnel
15. Provisions on loans	*54*	*28*	*57*	*59*	*37*	*58*	*122*	*175*	*282*	*207*	15. Provisions sur prêts
16. Provisions on securities	*5*	*5*	*12*	*2*	*3*	*29*	*4*	*46*	*-17*	*54*	16. Provisions sur titres
BALANCE SHEET											**BILAN**
Assets											**Actif**
17. Cash & balance with Central bank	1595	1825	2043	2183	2698	2249	2418	2253	1928	1956	17. Caisse & solde auprès de la Banque centrale
18. Interbank deposits	1402	1592	1428	1800	2412	2827	3494	4923	5885	4822	18. Dépôts interbancaires
19. Loans	4347	5094	6247	7735	9482	10824	12319	14484	15724	17687	19. Prêts
20. Securities	3446	4081	4683	5762	6216	6736	5667	6039	5792	7850	20. Valeurs mobilières
21. Other assets	1234	1391	1576	1738	2139	2812	2927	3090	4321	4625	21. Autres actifs
Liabilities											**Passif**
22. Capital & reserves	916	1026	1239	1408	1640	1987	2244	2493	2816	3188	22. Capital et réserves
23. Borrowing from Central bank	62	123	127	39	559	294	329	1688	1077	1200	23. Emprunts auprès de la Banque centrale
24. Interbank deposits	627	552	471	640	739	1210	1205	1567	1950	2421	24. Dépôts interbancaires
25. Non-bank deposits	9126	10557	12277	14886	17515	19086	20352	22531	25073	27631	25. Dépôts non bancaires
26. Bonds	594	802	710	681	514	421	490	569	731	763	26. Obligations
27. Other liabilities	698	922	1151	1565	1980	2449	2207	1940	2003	1737	27. Autres engagements
Balance sheet total											**Total du bilan**
28. End-year total	12023	13982	15976	19218	22947	25448	26825	30788	33650	36940	28. En fin d'exercice
29. Average total	11136	13003	14979	17597	21083	24198	26137	28807	32219	35295	29. Moyen
Memoranda											*Pour mémoire*
30. Short-term securities	*1479*	*1246*	*1813*	*2335*	*3081*	*3556*	*2703*	*2959*	*2414*	*2769*	30. Titres à court terme
31. Bonds	*1838*	*2647*	*2643*	*3091*	*2700*	*2679*	*2432*	*2446*	*2619*	*4246*	31. Obligations
32. Shares and participations	*129*	*188*	*226*	*336*	*435*	*501*	*532*	*633*	*760*	*835*	32. Actions et participations
33. Claims on non-residents	*68*	*122*	*128*	*134*	*196*	*415*	*527*	*1065*	*2288*	*2286*	33. Créances sur des non résidents
34. Liabilities to non-residents	*245*	*266*	*309*	*399*	*450*	*699*	*758*	*804*	*961*	*1036*	34. Engagements envers des non résidents
SUPPLEMENTARY INFORMATION											**RENSEIGNEMENTS COMPLEMENTAIRES**
35. Number of institutions	79	79	79	79	78	66	57	54	52	52	35. Nombre d'institutions
36. Number of branches	10797	11061	11754	12252	13168	13642	14031	14291	14485	14880	36. Nombre de succursales
37. Number of employees (x 1000)	71.0	72.7	74.5	78.0	83.0	84.6	83.4	82.9	82.7	83.8	37. Nombre de salariés (x 1000)

140

Savings banks   **Caisses d'épargne**

Per cent   *Pourcentage*

INCOME STATEMENT ANALYSIS   **ANALYSE DU COMPTE DE RESULTATS**

	1985	1986	1987	1988	1989	1990	1991	1992	1993	1994	
% of average balance sheet total											**% du total moyen du bilan**
38. Interest income	10.70	10.24	10.23	10.01	10.20	10.90	10.64	10.51	10.74	8.72	38. Produits financiers
39. Interest expenses	6.05	5.61	5.48	5.62	6.16	7.00	6.84	6.67	6.98	5.13	39. Frais financiers
40. Net interest income	4.65	4.63	4.75	4.39	4.05	3.90	3.80	3.84	3.76	3.59	40. Produits financiers nets
41. Non-interest income (net)	0.55	0.67	0.67	0.84	0.70	0.62	0.57	0.74	0.80	0.75	41. Produits non financiers (nets)
42. Gross income	5.20	5.30	5.43	5.22	4.75	4.52	4.37	4.58	4.57	4.34	42. Résultat brut
43. Operating expenses	3.39	3.80	3.39	3.88	3.22	2.99	2.76	2.74	2.73	2.63	43. Frais d'exploitation
44. Net income	1.80	1.50	2.04	1.34	1.53	1.53	1.61	1.84	1.83	1.71	44. Résultat net
45. Provisions (net)	0.75	0.61	0.77	0.58	0.46	0.61	0.57	0.85	0.89	0.82	45. Provisions (nettes)
46. Profit before tax	1.05	0.89	1.26	0.76	1.07	0.93	1.04	0.99	0.94	0.90	46. Bénéfices avant impôt
47. Income tax	0.18	0.18	0.23	0.13	0.23	0.19	0.23	0.24	0.24	0.20	47. Impôt
48. Profit after tax	0.87	0.72	1.03	0.64	0.84	0.73	0.81	0.75	0.71	0.69	48. Bénéfices après impôt
49. Distributed profit	0.24	0.22	0.25	0.24	0.24	0.19	0.18	0.17	0.19	0.17	49. Bénéfices distribués
50. Retained profit	0.63	0.50	0.77	0.39	0.60	0.54	0.64	0.58	0.52	0.52	50. Bénéfices mis en réserve
51. Staff costs	0.48	0.22	0.38	0.34	0.18	0.24	0.47	0.61	0.88	1.61	51. Frais de personnel
52. Provisions on loans	0.04	0.04	0.08	0.01	0.01	0.12	0.02	0.16	-0.05	0.59	52. Provisions sur prêts
53. Provisions on securities	0.04	0.04	0.08	0.01	0.01	0.12	0.02	0.16	-0.05	0.15	53. Provisions sur titres
% of gross income											**% du total du résultat brut**
54. Net interest income	89.46	87.37	87.58	84.00	85.21	86.29	87.04	83.93	82.46	82.77	54. Produits financiers nets
55. Non-interest income (net)	10.54	12.63	12.42	16.00	14.79	13.71	12.96	16.07	17.54	17.23	55. Produits non financiers (nets)
56. Operating expenses	65.28	71.70	62.48	74.32	67.73	66.09	63.22	59.89	59.89	60.51	56. Frais d'exploitation
57. Net income	34.72	28.30	37.52	25.68	32.27	33.91	36.78	40.11	40.11	39.49	57. Résultat net
58. Provisions (net)	14.51	11.47	14.27	11.10	9.69	13.44	12.96	18.50	19.44	18.80	58. Provisions (nettes)
59. Profit before tax	20.21	16.84	23.25	14.58	22.58	20.48	23.82	21.61	20.67	20.69	59. Bénéfices avant impôt
60. Income tax	3.45	3.34	4.31	2.39	4.90	4.30	5.17	5.16	5.17	4.70	60. Impôt
61. Profit after tax	16.75	13.50	18.94	12.19	17.68	16.18	18.65	16.45	15.50	15.99	61. Bénéfices après impôt
62. Staff costs	9.33	4.06	7.01	6.42	3.70	5.30	10.68	13.27	19.17	37.01	62. Frais de personnel
% of net income											**% du total du résultat net**
63. Provisions (net)	41.79	40.51	38.03	43.22	30.03	39.62	35.24	46.12	48.47	47.60	63. Provisions (nettes)
64. Profit before tax	58.21	59.49	61.97	56.78	69.97	60.38	64.76	53.88	51.53	52.40	64. Bénéfices avant impôt
65. Income tax	9.95	11.79	11.48	9.32	15.17	12.67	14.05	12.85	12.88	11.90	65. Impôt
66. Profit after tax	48.26	47.69	50.49	47.46	54.80	47.71	50.71	41.02	38.64	40.50	66. Bénéfices après impôt

SPAIN

Savings banks

ESPAGNE

Caisses d'épargne

Per cent — *Pourcentage*

BALANCE SHEET ANALYSIS — **ANALYSE DU BILAN**

% of year-end balance sheet total — **% du total du bilan en fin d'exercice**

	1985	1986	1987	1988	1989	1990	1991	1992	1993	1994		
Assets												**Actif**
67. Cash & balance with Central bank	13.27	13.05	12.79	11.36	11.76	8.84	9.01	7.32	5.73	5.30	67.	Caisse & solde auprès de la Banque centrale
68. Interbank deposits	11.66	11.39	8.94	9.37	10.51	11.11	13.03	15.99	17.49	13.05	68.	Dépôts interbancaires
69. Loans	36.16	36.43	39.10	40.25	41.32	42.53	45.92	47.04	46.73	47.88	69.	Prêts
70. Securities	28.66	29.19	29.31	29.98	27.09	26.47	21.13	19.61	17.21	21.25	70.	Valeurs mobilières
71. Other assets	10.26	9.95	9.86	9.04	9.32	11.05	10.91	10.04	12.84	12.52	71.	Autres actifs
Liabilities												**Passif**
72. Capital & reserves	7.62	7.34	7.76	7.33	7.15	7.81	8.37	8.10	8.37	8.63	72.	Capital et réserves
73. Borrowing from Central bank	0.52	0.88	0.79	0.20	2.44	1.16	1.23	5.48	3.20	3.25	73.	Emprunts auprès de la Banque centrale
74. Interbank deposits	5.22	3.95	2.95	3.33	3.22	4.75	4.49	5.09	5.79	6.55	74.	Dépôts interbancaires
75. Non-bank deposits	75.90	75.50	76.85	77.46	76.33	75.00	75.87	73.18	74.51	74.80	75.	Dépôts non bancaires
76. Bonds	4.94	5.74	4.44	3.54	2.24	1.65	1.83	1.85	2.17	2.07	76.	Obligations
77. Other liabilities	5.81	6.59	7.20	8.14	8.63	9.62	8.23	6.30	5.95	4.70	77.	Autres engagements
Memoranda												*Pour mémoire*
78. Short-term securities	*12.30*	*8.91*	*11.35*	*12.15*	*13.43*	*13.97*	*10.08*	*9.61*	*7.17*	*7.50*	*78.*	*Titres à court terme*
79. Bonds	*15.29*	*18.93*	*16.54*	*16.08*	*11.77*	*10.53*	*9.07*	*7.94*	*7.78*	*11.49*	*79.*	*Obligations*
80. Shares and participations	*1.07*	*1.34*	*1.41*	*1.75*	*1.90*	*1.97*	*1.98*	*2.06*	*2.26*	*2.26*	*80.*	*Actions et participations*
81. Claims on non-residents	*0.57*	*0.87*	*0.80*	*0.70*	*0.85*	*1.63*	*1.96*	*3.46*	*6.80*	*6.19*	*81.*	*Créances sur des non résidents*
82. Liabilities to non-residents	*2.04*	*1.90*	*1.93*	*2.08*	*1.96*	*2.75*	*2.83*	*2.61*	*2.86*	*2.80*	*82.*	*Engagements envers des non résidents*

Change in methodology:

- Liabilities to non-resident credit institutions, included under "Non-bank deposits" in earlier editions of this publication, were revised to incorporate them in "Other liabilities".
- As from 1992, "Income tax" (item 10) includes tax on domestic activities of resident entities rather than total tax.

Changement méthodologique :

- Le passif des institutions de crédit non-résidentes, inclus dans "Dépôts non bancaires" dans les éditions précédentes de cette publication, a été révisé de manière à être incorporé dans "Autres engagements".
- A partir de 1992, la rubrique "Impôt" (poste 10) inclut l'impôt sur les activités domestiques des entités résidentes plutôt que l'impôt total.

SPAIN ESPAGNE

Co-operative banks Banques mutualistes

Billion pesetas / *Milliards de pesetas*

	1985	1986	1987	1988	1989	1990	1991	1992	1993	1994	
INCOME STATEMENT											**COMPTE DE RESULTATS**
1. Interest income	130	142	164	167	186	221	256	281	324	296	1. Produits financiers
2. Interest expenses	74	75	82	88	97	122	143	156	182	151	2. Frais financiers
3. Net interest income	56	67	82	79	89	99	113	125	142	145	3. Produits financiers nets
4. Non-interest income (net)	9	5	4	4	5	6	7	7	11	12	4. Produits non financiers (nets)
5. Gross income	65	72	86	83	94	105	120	132	153	157	5. Résultat brut
6. Operating expenses	40	42	48	51	57	65	74	82	91	96	6. Frais d'exploitation
7. Net income	25	30	38	32	37	40	46	50	62	61	7. Résultat net
8. Provisions (net)	10	9	12	9	7	10	11	13	27	20	8. Provisions (nettes)
9. Profit before tax	15	21	26	23	30	30	35	37	35	41	9. Bénéfices avant impôt
10. Income tax	1	2	2	2	3	3	5	6	6	6	10. Impôt
11. Profit after tax	14	19	24	21	27	27	30	31	29	35	11. Bénéfices après impôt
12. Distributed profit	5	6	6	5	7	8	9	10	10	11	12. Bénéfices distribués
13. Retained profit	9	13	18	16	20	19	21	21	19	24	13. Bénéfices mis en réserve
Memoranda											*Pour mémoire*
14. Staff costs	26	27	30	33	35	39	44	48	52	56	14. Frais de personnel
15. Provisions on loans	10	9	12	8	6	7	9	14	29	17	15. Provisions sur prêts
16. Provisions on securities	-	-	-	-	1	2	1	1	-	5	16. Provisions sur titres
BALANCE SHEET											**BILAN**
Assets											**Actif**
17. Cash & balance with Central bank	136	151	199	207	253	269	265	219	197	193	17. Caisse & solde auprès de la Banque centrale
18. Interbank deposits	326	332	323	388	385	511	613	707	1011	883	18. Dépôts interbancaires
19. Loans	538	591	681	706	800	910	1100	1296	1408	1649	19. Prêts
20. Securities	130	203	243	260	247	225	225	205	192	410	20. Valeurs mobilières
21. Other assets	119	122	124	115	119	136	152	160	176	218	21. Autres actifs
Liabilities											**Passif**
22. Capital & reserves	107	128	160	181	204	234	269	296	342	390	22. Capital et réserves
23. Borrowing from Central bank	-	-	-	-	-	-	-	-	32	70	23. Emprunts auprès de la Banque centrale
24. Interbank deposits	78	91	105	98	87	112	104	127	119	125	24. Dépôts interbancaires
25. Non-bank deposits	1003	1076	1205	1310	1431	1615	1889	2097	2415	2702	25. Dépôts non bancaires
26. Bonds	8	19	17	9	1	1	-	-	-	-	26. Obligations
27. Other liabilities	54	84	83	78	80	89	93	67	76	66	27. Autres engagements
Balance sheet total											**Total du bilan**
28. End-year total	1250	1399	1571	1676	1804	2050	2355	2587	2985	3353	28. En fin d'exercice
29. Average total	1145	1324	1485	1623	1740	1927	2203	2471	2786	3169	29. Moyen
Memoranda											*Pour mémoire*
30. Short-term securities	22	54	113	135	140	141	141	101	88	118	30. Titres à court terme
31. Bonds	104	141	123	117	99	71	70	86	81	262	31. Obligations
32. Shares and participations	5	8	7	8	8	13	15	18	22	30	32. Actions et participations
33. Claims on non-residents	1	-	-	1	1	1	2	15	26	31	33. Créances sur des non résidents
34. Liabilities to non-residents	7	7	8	5	6	9	12	15	20	23	34. Engagements envers des non résidents
SUPPLEMENTARY INFORMATION											**RENSEIGNEMENTS COMPLEMENTAIRES**
35. Number of institutions	146	138	129	117	110	107	106	101	100	99	35. Nombre d'institutions
36. Number of branches	3350	3382	3248	3029	2890	2919	3018	3127	3119	3154	36. Nombre de succursales
37. Number of employees (x 1000)	10.8	10.2	10.2	9.7	9.6	10.0	10.6	11.0	11.2	11.2	37. Nombre de salariés (x 1000)

SPAIN

Co-operative banks

ESPAGNE

Banques mutualistes

Per cent	1985	1986	1987	1988	1989	1990	1991	1992	1993	1994	*Pourcentage*
INCOME STATEMENT ANALYSIS											**ANALYSE DU COMPTE DE RESULTATS**
% of average balance sheet total											**% du total moyen du bilan**
38. Interest income	11.35	10.73	11.04	10.29	10.69	11.47	11.62	11.37	11.63	9.34	38. Produits financiers
39. Interest expenses	6.46	5.66	5.52	5.42	5.57	6.33	6.49	6.31	6.53	4.76	39. Frais financiers
40. Net interest income	4.89	5.06	5.52	4.87	5.11	5.14	5.13	5.06	5.10	4.58	40. Produits financiers nets
41. Non-interest income (net)	0.79	0.38	0.27	0.25	0.29	0.31	0.32	0.28	0.39	0.38	41. Produits non financiers (nets)
42. Gross income	5.68	5.44	5.79	5.11	5.40	5.45	5.45	5.34	5.49	4.95	42. Résultat brut
43. Operating expenses	3.49	3.17	3.23	3.14	3.28	3.37	3.36	3.32	3.27	3.03	43. Frais d'exploitation
44. Net income	2.18	2.27	2.56	1.97	2.13	2.08	2.09	2.02	2.23	1.92	44. Résultat net
45. Provisions (net)	0.87	0.68	0.81	0.55	0.40	0.52	0.50	0.53	0.97	0.63	45. Provisions (nettes)
46. Profit before tax	1.31	1.59	1.75	1.42	1.72	1.56	1.59	1.50	1.26	1.29	46. Bénéfices avant impôt
47. Income tax	0.09	0.15	0.13	0.12	0.17	0.16	0.23	0.24	0.22	0.19	47. Impôt
48. Profit after tax	1.22	1.44	1.62	1.29	1.55	1.40	1.36	1.25	1.04	1.10	48. Bénéfices après impôt
49. Distributed profit	0.44	0.45	0.40	0.31	0.40	0.42	0.41	0.40	0.36	0.35	49. Bénéfices distribués
50. Retained profit	0.79	0.98	1.21	0.99	1.15	0.99	0.95	0.85	0.68	0.76	50. Bénéfices mis en réserve
51. Staff costs	2.27	2.04	2.02	2.03	2.01	2.02	2.00	1.94	1.87	1.77	51. Frais de personnel
52. Provisions on loans	0.87	0.68	0.81	0.49	0.34	0.36	0.41	0.57	1.04	0.54	52. Provisions sur prêts
53. Provisions on securities	.	.	.	.	0.06	0.10	0.05	0.04	.	0.16	53. Provisions sur titres
% of gross income											**% du total du résultat brut**
54. Net interest income	86.15	93.06	95.35	95.18	94.68	94.29	94.17	94.70	92.81	92.36	54. Produits financiers nets
55. Non-interest income (net)	13.85	6.94	4.65	4.82	5.32	5.71	5.83	5.30	7.19	7.64	55. Produits non financiers (nets)
56. Operating expenses	61.54	58.33	55.81	61.45	60.64	61.90	61.67	62.12	59.48	61.15	56. Frais d'exploitation
57. Net income	38.46	41.67	44.19	38.55	39.36	38.10	38.33	37.88	40.52	38.85	57. Résultat net
58. Provisions (net)	15.38	12.50	13.95	10.84	7.45	9.52	9.17	9.85	17.65	12.74	58. Provisions (nettes)
59. Profit before tax	23.08	29.17	30.23	27.71	31.91	28.57	29.17	28.03	22.88	26.11	59. Bénéfices avant impôt
60. Income tax	1.54	2.78	2.33	2.41	3.19	2.86	4.17	4.55	3.92	3.82	60. Impôt
61. Profit after tax	21.54	26.39	27.91	25.30	28.72	25.71	25.00	23.48	18.95	22.29	61. Bénéfices après impôt
62. Staff costs	40.00	37.50	34.88	39.76	37.23	37.14	36.67	36.36	33.99	35.67	62. Frais de personnel
% of net income											**% du total du résultat net**
63. Provisions (net)	40.00	30.00	31.58	28.13	18.92	25.00	23.91	26.00	43.55	32.79	63. Provisions (nettes)
64. Profit before tax	60.00	70.00	68.42	71.88	81.08	75.00	76.09	74.00	56.45	67.21	64. Bénéfices avant impôt
65. Income tax	4.00	6.67	5.26	6.25	8.11	7.50	10.87	12.00	9.68	9.84	65. Impôt
66. Profit after tax	56.00	63.33	63.16	65.63	72.97	67.50	65.22	62.00	46.77	57.38	66. Bénéfices après impôt

SPAIN

Co-operative banks

ESPAGNE

Banques mutualistes

Per cent	1985	1986	1987	1988	1989	1990	1991	1992	1993	1994		Pourcentage
BALANCE SHEET ANALYSIS												**ANALYSE DU BILAN**
% of year-end balance sheet total												**% du total du bilan en fin d'exercice**
Assets												**Actif**
67. Cash & balance with Central bank	10.88	10.79	12.67	12.35	14.02	13.12	11.25	8.47	6.60	5.76		67. Caisse & solde auprès de la Banque centrale
68. Interbank deposits	26.08	23.73	20.56	23.15	21.34	24.93	26.03	27.33	33.87	26.33		68. Dépôts interbancaires
69. Loans	43.04	42.24	43.35	42.12	44.35	44.39	46.71	50.10	47.17	49.18		69. Prêts
70. Securities	10.40	14.51	15.47	15.51	13.69	10.98	9.55	7.92	6.43	12.23		70. Valeurs mobilières
71. Other assets	9.52	8.72	7.89	6.86	6.60	6.63	6.45	6.18	5.90	6.50		71. Autres actifs
Liabilities												**Passif**
72. Capital & reserves	8.56	9.15	10.18	10.80	11.31	11.41	11.42	11.44	11.46	11.63		72. Capital et réserves
73. Borrowing from Central bank	-	-	-	-	-	-	-	-	1.07	2.09		73. Emprunts auprès de la Banque centrale
74. Interbank deposits	6.24	6.50	6.68	5.85	4.82	5.46	4.42	4.91	3.99	3.73		74. Dépôts interbancaires
75. Non-bank deposits	80.24	76.91	76.70	78.16	79.32	78.78	80.21	81.06	80.90	80.58		75. Dépôts non bancaires
76. Bonds	0.64	1.36	1.08	0.54	0.06	0.05	-	-	-	-		76. Obligations
77. Other liabilities	4.32	6.00	5.28	4.65	4.43	4.34	3.95	2.59	2.55	1.97		77. Autres engagements
Memoranda												*Pour mémoire*
78. Short-term securities	*1.76*	*3.86*	*7.19*	*8.05*	*7.76*	*6.88*	*5.99*	*3.90*	*2.95*	*3.52*		*78. Titres à court terme*
79. Bonds	*8.32*	*10.08*	*7.83*	*6.98*	*5.49*	*3.46*	*2.97*	*3.32*	*2.71*	*7.81*		*79. Obligations*
80. Shares and participations	*0.40*	*0.57*	*0.45*	*0.48*	*0.44*	*0.63*	*0.64*	*0.70*	*0.74*	*0.89*		*80. Actions et participations*
81. Claims on non-residents	*0.08*	-	-	*0.06*	*0.06*	*0.05*	*0.08*	*0.58*	*0.87*	*0.92*		*81. Créances sur des non résidents*
82. Liabilities to non-residents	*0.56*	*0.50*	*0.51*	*0.30*	*0.33*	*0.44*	*0.51*	*0.58*	*0.67*	*0.69*		*82. Engagements envers des non résidents*

Change in methodology:

- As from 1992, "Income tax" (item 10) includes tax on domestic activities of resident entities rather than total tax.

Changement méthodologique :

- A partir de 1992, la rubrique "Impôt" (poste 10) inclut l'impôt sur les activités domestiques des entités résidentes plutôt que l'impôt total.

SWEDEN

Commercial banks

Million Swedish kroner

SUEDE

Banques commerciales

Millions de couronnes suédoises

		1985	1986	1987	1988	1989	1990	1991	1992	1993	1994	
INCOME STATEMENT												**COMPTE DE RESULTATS**
1.	Interest income	58761	53282	58230	70837	97962	130929	131201	122619	123005	101973	1. Produits financiers
2.	Interest expenses	47811	38170	41768	51467	76559	105873	104914	96190	85426	66498	2. Frais financiers
3.	Net interest income	10950	15112	16462	19370	21403	25056	26287	26429	37579	35475	3. Produits financiers nets
4.	Non-interest income (net)	5883	8233	6482	7825	8565	8899	8848	17704	43796	20540	4. Produits non financiers (nets)
5.	Gross income	16833	23345	22944	27195	29968	33955	35135	44133	81375	56015	5. Résultat brut
6.	Operating expenses	10413	12673	12760	15112	16736	26568	42353	64668	89359	45428	6. Frais d'exploitation
7.	Net income	6420	10672	10184	12083	13232	7387	-7218	-20535	-7984	10587	7. Résultat net
8.	Provisions (net)	4526	4888	5380	7397	8582	4786	-42895	-23564	-10050	-2948	8. Provisions (nettes)
9.	Profit before tax	1894	5784	4804	4686	4650	2601	35677	3029	2066	13535	9. Bénéfices avant impôt
10.	Income tax	636	3797	1638	2507	833	647	10576	510	1482	2120	10. Impôt
11.	Profit after tax	1258	1987	3166	2179	3817	1954	25101	2519	584	11415	11. Bénéfices après impôt
12.	Distributed profit	1080	1296	1567	1873	2082	2014	2014	1727	23	1076	12. Bénéfices distribués
13.	Retained profit	178	691	1599	306	1735	-60	23087	792	561	10339	13. Bénéfices mis en réserve
Memoranda												*Pour mémoire*
14.	*Staff costs*	*4307*	*4869*	*5718*	*6254*	*7016*	*8308*	*9242*	*10442*	*13327*	*14117*	14. *Frais de personnel*
15.	*Provisions on loans (1)*	*1566*	*4989*	*5368*	*7602*	*3319*	*5680*	*47814*	*..*	*..*	*..*	15. *Provisions sur prêts (1)*
16.	*Provisions on securities (1)*	*3017*	*99*	*42*	*-*	*5482*	*1154*	*9236*	*..*	*..*	*..*	16. *Provisions sur titres (1)*
BALANCE SHEET												**BILAN**
Assets												**Actif**
17.	Cash & balance with Central bank	16407	20156	19514	21016	20754	29467	13756	20577	21982	7566	17. Caisse & solde auprès de la Banque centrale
18.	Interbank deposits	67617	100242	134207	179948	189095	237934	194122	112209	127046	133139	18. Dépôts interbancaires
19.	Loans	261746	300322	338922	450616	579838	676529	625661	670191	690861	644503	19. Prêts
20.	Securities	136173	114419	108167	106185	125842	147546	316226	272689	431645	486676	20. Valeurs mobilières
21.	Other assets	58367	59566	65384	77240	104792	173158	57982	77890	82295	72731	21. Autres actifs
Liabilities												**Passif**
22.	Capital & reserves	33606	38772	47169	56944	65273	71307	65386	52898	73313	72486	22. Capital et réserves
23.	Borrowing from Central bank	6891	4233	3455	19033	19946	14517	31415	60279	644	8	23. Emprunts auprès de la Banque centrale
24.	Interbank deposits	158724	173803	235065	314540	399495	526730	408906	300599	298288	294934	24. Dépôts interbancaires
25.	Non-bank deposits	261975	294776	292546	325616	372914	440738	503993	535982	717766	731913	25. Dépôts non bancaires
26.	Bonds	24734	22546	23905	39335	56383	85724	76723	89829	112966	107374	26. Obligations
27.	Other liabilities	54380	60578	64054	79535	106310	125616	121325	113968	150854	137900	27. Autres engagements
Balance sheet total												**Total du bilan**
28.	End-year total	540311	594707	666193	835005	1020321	1264632	1207745	1153554	1353830	1344615	28. En fin d'exercice
29.	Average total	552021	578578	660427	794416	994864	1202580	1254792	1209533	1383064	1383358	29. Moyen
Memoranda												*Pour mémoire*
30.	*Short-term securities*	*8931*	*6312*	*2122*	*2566*	*3705*	*9720*	*21402*	*136911*	*145151*	*153025*	30. *Titres à court terme*
31.	*Bonds*	*129920*	*105119*	*98359*	*92876*	*108179*	*112899*	*86868*	*77073*	*156453*	*203784*	31. *Obligations*
32.	*Shares and participations*	*5113*	*6276*	*8888*	*8386*	*13624*	*25071*	*35877*	*27575*	*39675*	*36584*	32. *Actions et participations*
33.	*Claims on non-residents*	*14560*	*14395*	*17019*	*35366*	*65010*	*104230*	*303815*	*360649*	*380901*	*341671*	33. *Créances sur des non résidents*
34.	*Liabilities to non-residents*	*17340*	*24233*	*33592*	*50483*	*68976*	*103509*	*646684*	*563031*	*616819*	*568206*	34. *Engagements envers des non résidents*
SUPPLEMENTARY INFORMATION												**RENSEIGNEMENTS COMPLEMENTAIRES**
35.	Number of institutions	15	14	14	14	14	12	9	8	9	10	35. Nombre d'institutions
36.	Number of branches	1436	1424	1403	1394	1376	1345	1288	1872	2474	2327	36. Nombre de succursales
37.	Number of employees (x 1000)	22.7	23.5	25.0	25.4	25.4	25.0	25.1	28.4	37.2	39.1	37. Nombre de salariés (x 1000)

Commercial banks

Banques commerciales

Per cent	1985	1986	1987	1988	1989	1990	1991	1992	1993	1994	Pourcentage
INCOME STATEMENT ANALYSIS											**ANALYSE DU COMPTE DE RESULTATS**
% of average balance sheet total											**% du total moyen du bilan**
38. Interest income	10.64	9.21	8.82	8.92	9.85	10.89	10.46	10.14	8.89	7.37	38. Produits financiers
39. Interest expenses	8.66	6.60	6.32	6.48	7.70	8.80	8.36	7.95	6.18	4.81	39. Frais financiers
40. Net interest income	1.98	2.61	2.49	2.44	2.15	2.08	2.09	2.19	2.72	2.56	40. Produits financiers nets
41. Non-interest income (net)	1.07	1.42	0.98	0.99	0.86	0.74	0.71	1.46	3.17	1.48	41. Produits non financiers (nets)
42. Gross income	3.05	4.03	3.47	3.42	3.01	2.82	2.80	3.65	5.88	4.05	42. Résultat brut
43. Operating expenses	1.89	2.19	1.93	1.90	1.68	2.21	3.38	5.35	6.46	3.28	43. Frais d'exploitation
44. Net income	1.16	1.84	1.54	1.52	1.33	0.61	-0.58	-1.70	-0.58	0.77	44. Résultat net
45. Provisions (net)	0.82	0.84	0.81	0.93	0.86	0.40	-3.42	-1.95	-0.73	-0.21	45. Provisions (nettes)
46. Profit before tax	0.34	1.00	0.73	0.59	0.47	0.22	2.84	0.25	0.15	0.98	46. Bénéfices avant impôt
47. Income tax	0.12	0.66	0.25	0.32	0.08	0.05	0.84	0.04	0.11	0.15	47. Impôt
48. Profit after tax	0.23	0.34	0.48	0.27	0.38	0.16	2.00	0.21	0.04	0.83	48. Bénéfices après impôt
49. Distributed profit	0.20	0.22	0.24	0.24	0.21	0.17	0.16	0.14	0.00	0.08	49. Bénéfices distribués
50. Retained profit	0.03	0.12	0.24	0.04	0.17	0.00	1.84	0.07	0.04	0.75	50. Bénéfices mis en réserve
51. Staff costs	0.78	0.84	0.87	0.79	0.71	0.69	0.74	0.86	0.96	1.02	51. Frais de personnel
52. Provisions on loans (1)	0.28	0.86	0.81	0.96	0.33	0.47	3.81	..	..	..	52. Provisions sur prêts (1)
53. Provisions on securities (1)	0.55	0.02	0.01	-	0.55	0.10	0.74	..	..	..	53. Provisions sur titres (1)
% of gross income											**% du total du résultat brut**
54. Net interest income	65.05	64.73	71.75	71.23	71.42	73.79	74.82	59.88	46.18	63.33	54. Produits financiers nets
55. Non-interest income (net)	34.95	35.27	28.25	28.77	28.58	26.21	25.18	40.12	53.82	36.67	55. Produits non financiers (nets)
56. Operating expenses	61.86	54.29	55.61	55.57	55.85	78.24	120.54	146.53	109.81	81.10	56. Frais d'exploitation
57. Net income	38.14	45.71	44.39	44.43	44.15	21.76	-20.54	-46.53	-9.81	18.90	57. Résultat net
58. Provisions (net)	26.89	20.94	23.45	27.20	28.64	14.10	-122.09	-53.39	-12.35	-5.26	58. Provisions (nettes)
59. Profit before tax	11.25	24.78	20.94	17.23	15.52	7.66	101.54	6.86	2.54	24.16	59. Bénéfices avant impôt
60. Income tax	3.78	16.26	7.14	9.22	2.78	1.91	30.10	1.16	1.82	3.78	60. Impôt
61. Profit after tax	7.47	8.51	13.80	8.01	12.74	5.75	71.44	5.71	0.72	20.38	61. Bénéfices après impôt
62. Staff costs	25.59	20.86	24.92	23.00	23.41	24.47	26.30	23.66	16.38	25.20	62. Frais de personnel
% of net income											**% du total du résultat net**
63. Provisions (net)	70.50	45.80	52.83	61.22	64.86	64.79	..	..	..	..	63. Provisions (nettes)
64. Profit before tax	29.50	54.20	47.17	38.78	35.14	35.21	..	..	..	..	64. Bénéfices avant impôt
65. Income tax	9.91	35.58	16.08	20.75	6.30	8.76	..	..	..	..	65. Impôt
66. Profit after tax	19.60	18.62	31.09	18.03	28.85	26.45	..	..	..	..	66. Bénéfices après impôt

SWEDEN

Commercial banks

SUEDE

Banques commerciales

Per cent / *Pourcentage*

BALANCE SHEET ANALYSIS / **ANALYSE DU BILAN**

% of year-end balance sheet total / **% du total du bilan en fin d'exercice**

	1985	1986	1987	1988	1989	1990	1991	1992	1993	1994	
Assets											**Actif**
67. Cash & balance with Central bank	3.04	3.39	2.93	2.52	2.03	2.33	1.14	1.78	1.62	0.56	67. Caisse & solde auprès de la Banque centrale
68. Interbank deposits	12.51	16.86	20.15	21.55	18.53	18.81	16.07	9.73	9.38	9.90	68. Dépôts interbancaires
69. Loans	48.44	50.50	50.87	53.97	56.83	53.50	51.80	58.10	51.03	47.93	69. Prêts
70. Securities	25.20	19.24	16.24	12.72	12.33	11.67	26.18	23.64	31.88	36.19	70. Valeurs mobilières
71. Other assets	10.80	10.02	9.81	9.25	10.27	13.69	4.80	6.75	6.08	5.41	71. Autres actifs
Liabilities											**Passif**
72. Capital & reserves	6.22	6.52	7.08	6.82	6.40	5.64	5.41	4.59	5.42	5.39	72. Capital et réserves
73. Borrowing from Central bank	1.28	0.71	0.52	2.28	1.95	1.15	2.60	5.23	0.05	0.00	73. Emprunts auprès de la Banque centrale
74. Interbank deposits	29.38	29.22	35.28	37.67	39.15	41.65	33.86	26.06	22.03	21.93	74. Dépôts interbancaires
75. Non-bank deposits	48.49	49.57	43.91	39.00	36.55	34.85	41.73	46.46	53.02	54.43	75. Dépôts non bancaires
76. Bonds	4.58	3.79	3.59	4.71	5.53	6.78	6.35	7.79	8.34	7.99	76. Obligations
77. Other liabilities	10.06	10.19	9.61	9.53	10.42	9.93	10.05	9.88	11.14	10.26	77. Autres engagements
Memoranda											*Pour mémoire*
78. *Short-term securities*	*1.65*	*1.06*	*0.32*	*0.31*	*0.36*	*0.77*	*1.77*	*11.87*	*10.72*	*11.38*	*78. Titres à court terme*
79. *Bonds*	*24.05*	*17.68*	*14.76*	*11.12*	*10.60*	*8.93*	*7.19*	*6.68*	*11.56*	*15.16*	*79. Obligations*
80. *Shares and participations*	*0.95*	*1.06*	*1.33*	*1.00*	*1.34*	*1.98*	*2.97*	*2.39*	*2.93*	*2.72*	*80. Actions et participations*
81. *Claims on non-residents*	*2.69*	*2.42*	*2.55*	*4.24*	*6.37*	*8.24*	*25.16*	*31.26*	*28.14*	*25.41*	*81. Créances sur des non résidents*
82. *Liabilities to non-residents*	*3.21*	*4.07*	*5.04*	*6.05*	*6.76*	*8.18*	*53.54*	*48.81*	*45.56*	*42.26*	*82. Engagements envers des non résidents*

1. As from 1992, change in methodology.

Notes

• Average balance sheet totals (item 29) are based on thirteen end-month data.

Change in methodology:

• For the year 1991, the Föreningsbankernas Bank is exceptionally included under Co-operative banks and not under Commercial banks.

• Beginning 1992, "Provisions on loans" (item 15 or item 52) and "Provisions on securities" (item 16 or item 53) are no longer available due to new accounting methods.

• As from 1992, Co-operative banks, which merged into one single commercial bank, are included under Commercial banks.

• As from 1993, Commercial banks include what was formerly the largest savings bank.

1. A partir de 1992, changement méthodologique.

Notes

• La moyenne du total des actifs/passifs (poste 29) est basée sur treize données de fin de mois.

Changement méthodologique :

• Pour l'année 1991, la Föreningsbankernas Bank est comprise exceptionnellement dans les Banques mutualistes et non pas dans les Banques commerciales.

• A partir de 1992, "Provisions sur prêts" (poste 15 ou poste 52) et "Provisions sur titres" (poste 16 ou poste 53) ne sont plus disponibles du fait de nouvelles techniques comptables.

• Depuis 1992, les Banques mutualistes, ayant fusionnées en une seule banque commerciale, sont classées dans les données concernant les Banques commerciales.

• Depuis 1993, les Banques commerciales incluent ce qui était précédemment la caisse d'épargne la plus grande.

Foreign commercial banks

Million Swedish kroner — *Millions de couronnes suédoises*

	1986	1987	1988	1989	1990	1991	1992	1993	1994	
INCOME STATEMENT										**COMPTE DE RESULTATS**
1. Interest income	417	1592	1591	2708	2959	2440	2541	2296	1680	1. Produits financiers
2. Interest expenses	322	1463	1462	2562	2722	2273	2454	1978	1390	2. Frais financiers
3. Net interest income	95	129	129	146	237	167	87	318	290	3. Produits financiers nets
4. Non-interest income (net)	103	80	80	96	121	231	451	1394	127	4. Produits non financiers (nets)
5. Gross income	198	209	209	242	358	398	538	1712	417	5. Résultat brut
6. Operating expenses	213	232	231	319	464	867	1369	538	316	6. Frais d'exploitation
7. Net income	-15	-23	-22	-77	-106	-469	-831	1174	101	7. Résultat net
8. Provisions (net)	28	-2	4	5	-38	-5	157	143	3	8. Provisions (nettes)
9. Profit before tax	-43	-21	-26	-82	-68	-464	-988	1031	98	9. Bénéfices avant impôt
10. Income tax	-	1	1	-	-	1	42	35	19	10. Impôt
11. Profit after tax	-43	-22	-27	-82	-68	-465	-1030	996	79	11. Bénéfices après impôt
12. Distributed profit	-	-	4	-	-	5	8	95	135	12. Bénéfices distribués
13. Retained profit	-43	-22	-31	-82	-68	-470	-1038	901	-56	13. Bénéfices mis en réserve
Memoranda										*Pour mémoire*
14. Staff costs	*78*	*137*	*136*	*130*	*148*	*161*	*171*	*172*	*152*	*14. Frais de personnel*
15. Provisions on loans (1)	*4*	*7*	*8*	*3*	*6171*	*13*	*..*	*..*	*..*	*15. Provisions sur prêts (1)*
16. Provisions on securities (1)	*23*	*3*	*4*	*10*	*600*	*23*	*..*	*..*	*..*	*16. Provisions sur titres (1)*
BALANCE SHEET (2)										**BILAN (2)**
Assets										**Actif**
17. Cash & balance with Central bank	210	64	57	116	209	50	2794	147	1023	17. Caisse & solde auprès de la Banque centrale
18. Interbank deposits	8341	11850	8175	8963	6380	3959	6362	9651	10463	18. Dépôts interbancaires
19. Loans	5741	9426	15337	18091	15564	13108	15732	11967	13416	19. Prêts
20. Securities	3011	2180	1086	1744	580	3033	5111	6136	9271	20. Valeurs mobilières
21. Other assets	784	1973	2834	3633	2252	640	1991	1101	3490	21. Autres actifs
Liabilities										**Passif**
22. Capital & reserves	914	887	942	890	835	528	664	1647	1401	22. Capital et réserves
23. Borrowing from Central bank	1129	113	326	603	377	169	5	-	7	23. Emprunts auprès de la Banque centrale
24. Interbank deposits	14138	21389	23726	28240	20687	16778	26951	22573	29637	24. Dépôts interbancaires
25. Non-bank deposits	364	731	1383	1145	1517	2024	2916	3223	3996	25. Dépôts non bancaires
26. Bonds	599	565	361	582	599	443	493	252	184	26. Obligations
27. Other liabilities	943	1808	753	1086	970	850	960	1305	2438	27. Autres engagements
Balance sheet total										**Total du bilan**
28. End-year total	18087	25493	27491	32547	24986	20793	31989	29000	37662	28. En fin d'exercice
29. Average total	NA	22242	28052	28568	25507	23931	25834	31936	30835	29. Moyen
Memoranda										*Pour mémoire*
30. Short-term securities	*902*	*198*	*230*	*141*	*202*	*1961*	*10260*	*7393*	*10323*	*30. Titres à court terme*
31. Bonds	*2362*	*1602*	*873*	*1515*	*140*	*90*	*100*	*606*	*1069*	*31. Obligations*
32. Shares and participations	*3*	*4*	*17*	*132*	*117*	*12*	*4*	*5*	*4*	*32. Actions et participations*
33. Claims on non-residents	*130*	*991*	*1612*	*3582*	*2907*	*5769*	*6736*	*11612*	*8145*	*33. Créances sur des non résidents*
34. Liabilities to non-residents	*72*	*108*	*486*	*396*	*524*	*17898*	*27839*	*23285*	*26114*	*34. Engagements envers des non résidents*
SUPPLEMENTARY INFORMATION										**RENSEIGNEMENTS COMPLEMENTAIRES**
35. Number of institutions	12	11	10	9	9	8	8	8	12	35. Nombre d'institutions
36. Number of branches	-	-	1	-	-	-	10	10	11	36. Nombre de succursales
37. Number of employees (x 1000)	0.3	0.3	0.4	0.3	0.3	0.3	0.3	0.3	0.3	37. Nombre de salariés (x 1000)

SWEDEN

Foreign commercial banks

Per cent

SUEDE

Banques commerciales étrangères

Pourcentage

	1986	1987	1988	1989	1990	1991	1992	1993	1994	
INCOME STATEMENT ANALYSIS										**ANALYSE DU COMPTE DE RESULTATS**
% of average balance sheet total										**% du total moyen du bilan**
38. Interest income	NA	7.16	5.67	9.48	11.60	10.20	9.84	7.19	5.45	38. Produits financiers
39. Interest expenses	NA	6.58	5.21	8.97	10.67	9.50	9.50	6.19	4.51	39. Frais financiers
40. Net interest income	NA	0.58	0.46	0.51	0.93	0.70	0.34	1.00	0.94	40. Produits financiers nets
41. Non-interest income (net)	NA	0.36	0.29	0.34	0.47	0.97	1.75	4.36	0.41	41. Produits non financiers (nets)
42. Gross income	NA	0.94	0.75	0.85	1.40	1.66	2.08	5.36	1.35	42. Résultat brut
43. Operating expenses	NA	1.04	0.82	1.12	1.82	3.62	5.30	1.68	1.02	43. Frais d'exploitation
44. Net income	NA	-0.10	-0.08	-0.27	-0.42	-1.96	-3.22	3.68	0.33	44. Résultat net
45. Provisions (net)	NA	-0.01	0.01	0.02	-0.15	-0.02	0.61	0.45	0.01	45. Provisions (nettes)
46. Profit before tax	NA	-0.09	-0.09	-0.29	-0.27	-1.94	-3.82	3.23	0.32	46. Bénéfices avant impôt
47. Income tax	-	0.00	0.00		-	0.00	0.16	0.11	0.06	47. Impôt
48. Profit after tax	NA	-0.10	-0.10	-0.29	-0.27	-1.94	-3.99	3.12	0.26	48. Bénéfices après impôt
49. Distributed profit	-		0.01		-	0.02	0.03	0.30	0.44	49. Bénéfices distribués
50. Retained profit	NA	-0.10	-0.11	-0.29	-0.27	-1.96	-4.02	2.82	-0.18	50. Bénéfices mis en réserve
51. Staff costs	NA	0.62	0.48	0.46	0.58	0.67	0.66	0.54	0.49	51. Frais de personnel
52. Provisions on loans (1)	NA	0.03	0.03	0.01	24.19	0.05	..	..	..	52. Provisions sur prêts (1)
53. Provisions on securities (1)	NA	0.01	0.01	0.04	2.35	0.10	..	..	..	53. Provisions sur titres (1)
% of gross income										**% du total du résultat brut**
54. Net interest income	47.98	61.72	61.72	60.33	66.20	41.96	16.17	18.57	69.54	54. Produits financiers nets
55. Non-interest income (net)	52.02	38.28	38.28	39.67	33.80	58.04	83.83	81.43	30.46	55. Produits non financiers (nets)
56. Operating expenses	107.58	111.00	110.53	131.82	129.61	217.84	254.46	31.43	75.78	56. Frais d'exploitation
57. Net income	-7.58	-11.00	-10.53	-31.82	-29.61	-117.84	-154.46	68.57	24.22	57. Résultat net
58. Provisions (net)	14.14	-0.96	1.91	2.07	-10.61	-1.26	29.18	8.35	0.72	58. Provisions (nettes)
59. Profit before tax	-21.72	-10.05	-12.44	-33.88	-18.99	-116.58	-183.64	60.22	23.50	59. Bénéfices avant impôt
60. Income tax	-	0.48	0.48		-	0.25	7.81	2.04	4.56	60. Impôt
61. Profit after tax	-21.72	-10.53	-12.92	-33.88	-18.99	-116.83	-191.45	58.18	18.94	61. Bénéfices après impôt
62. Staff costs	39.39	65.55	65.07	53.72	41.34	40.45	31.78	10.05	36.45	62. Frais de personnel
% of net income										**% du total du résultat net**
63. Provisions (net)	..	..	..	..	..	..	..	12.18	2.97	63. Provisions (nettes)
64. Profit before tax	..	..	..	..	..	..	..	87.82	97.03	64. Bénéfices avant impôt
65. Income tax	..	..	..	..	..	..	..	2.98	18.81	65. Impôt
66. Profit after tax	..	..	..	..	..	..	..	84.84	78.22	66. Bénéfices après impôt

SWEDEN

Foreign commercial banks

Per cent

BALANCE SHEET ANALYSIS

% of year-end balance sheet total

	1986	1987	1988	1989	1990	1991	1992	1993	1994
Assets									
67. Cash & balance with Central bank	1.16	0.25	0.21	0.36	0.84	0.24	8.73	0.51	2.72
68. Interbank deposits	46.12	46.48	29.74	27.54	25.53	19.04	19.89	33.28	27.78
69. Loans	31.74	36.97	55.79	55.58	62.29	63.04	49.18	41.27	35.62
70. Securities	16.65	8.55	3.95	5.36	2.32	14.59	15.98	21.16	24.62
71. Other assets	4.33	7.74	10.31	11.16	9.01	3.08	6.22	3.80	9.27
Liabilities									
72. Capital & reserves	5.05	3.48	3.43	2.73	3.34	2.54	2.08	5.68	3.72
73. Borrowing from Central bank	6.24	0.44	1.19	1.85	1.51	0.81	0.02	-	0.02
74. Interbank deposits	78.17	83.90	86.30	86.77	82.79	80.69	84.25	77.84	78.69
75. Non-bank deposits	2.01	2.87	5.03	3.52	6.07	9.73	9.12	11.11	10.61
76. Bonds	3.31	2.22	1.31	1.79	2.40	2.13	1.54	0.87	0.49
77. Other liabilities	5.21	7.09	2.74	3.34	3.88	4.09	3.00	4.50	6.47
Memoranda									
78. Short-term securities	*4.99*	*0.78*	*0.84*	*0.43*	*0.81*	*9.43*	*32.07*	*25.49*	*27.41*
79. Bonds	*13.06*	*6.28*	*3.18*	*4.65*	*0.56*	*0.43*	*0.31*	*2.09*	*2.84*
80. Shares and participations	*0.02*	*0.02*	*0.06*	*0.41*	*0.47*	*0.06*	*0.01*	*0.02*	*0.01*
81. Claims on non-residents	*0.72*	*3.89*	*5.86*	*11.01*	*11.63*	*27.74*	*21.06*	*40.04*	*21.63*
82. Liabilities to non-residents	*0.40*	*0.42*	*1.77*	*1.22*	*2.10*	*86.08*	*87.03*	*80.29*	*69.34*

1. As from 1992, change in methodology.
2. As from 1987, change in methodology.

Notes

- Average balance sheet totals (item 29) are based on thirteen end-month data.

Change in methodology:

- Beginning 1992, "Provisions on loans" (item 15 or item 52) and "Provisions on securities" (item 16 or item 53) are no longer available due to new accounting methods.
- As from 1987, balance sheet data are based on banks' annual balance figures. "Capital & reserves" (item 22 or item 72) also include reserves.

SUEDE

Banques commerciales étrangères

Pourcentage

ANALYSE DU BILAN

% du total du bilan en fin d'exercice

Actif
67. Caisse & solde auprès de la Banque centrale
68. Dépôts interbancaires
69. Prêts
70. Valeurs mobilières
71. Autres actifs

Passif
72. Capital et réserves
73. Emprunts auprès de la Banque centrale
74. Dépôts interbancaires
75. Dépôts non bancaires
76. Obligations
77. Autres engagements

Pour mémoire
78. Titres à court terme
79. Obligations
80. Actions et participations
81. Créances sur des non résidents
82. Engagements envers des non résidents

1. A partir de 1992, changement méthodologique.
2. A partir de 1987, changement méthodologique.

Notes

- La moyenne du total des actifs/passifs (poste 29) est basée sur treize données de fin de mois.

Changement méthodologique :

- A partir de 1992, "Provisions sur prêts" (poste 15 ou poste 52) et "Provisions sur titres" (poste 16 où poste 53) ne sont plus disponibles du fait de nouvelles techniques comptables.
- Les données du bilan de 1987 ont été recalculées à partir des soldes annuels des banques. Les "Capital et réserves" (poste 22 ou poste 72) incluent aussi les réserves.

SWEDEN

Savings banks

Million Swedish kroner

SUEDE

Caisses d'épargne

Millions de couronnes suédoises

#	Item	Libellé	1985	1986	1987	1988	1989	1990	1991	1992	1993 (2)	1994
	INCOME STATEMENT	**COMPTE DE RESULTATS**										
1.	Interest income	Produits financiers	17868	17053	18109	20328	24461	32005	31956	49806	7551	6716
2.	Interest expenses	Frais financiers	12508	10765	11356	12593	15744	20871	19994	37020	3585	3123
3.	Net interest income	Produits financiers nets	5360	6288	6753	7735	8717	11134	11962	12786	3966	3593
4.	Non-interest income (net)	Produits non financiers (nets)	1352	2137	1828	2189	2371	2695	6210	19752	860	1184
5.	Gross income	Résultat brut	6712	8425	8581	9924	11088	13829	18172	32538	4826	4777
6.	Operating expenses	Frais d'exploitation	5027	5965	6705	7406	8531	11231	19919	28310	3741	3241
7.	Net income	Résultat net	1685	2460	1876	2518	2557	2598	-1747	4228	1085	1536
8.	Provisions (net)	Provisions (nettes)	1457	1334	985	1731	2118	2448	-13356	-6458	-532	-583
9.	Profit before tax	Bénéfices avant impôt	228	1126	891	787	439	150	11609	10686	1617	2119
10.	Income tax	Impôt	121	727	487	544	130	161	3587	549	485	510
11.	Profit after tax	Bénéfices après impôt	107	399	404	243	309	-11	8022	10137	1132	1609
12.	Distributed profit	Bénéfices distribués	1	-								-
13.	Retained profit	Bénéfices mis en réserve	106	399	404	243	309	-11	8022	10137	1132	1609
	Memoranda	*Pour mémoire*										
14.	*Staff costs*	*Frais de personnel*	*2270*	*2440*	*2770*	*2088*	*3651*	*4237*	*4549*	*5203*	*1138*	*1154*
15.	*Provisions on loans (1)*	*Provisions sur prêts(1)*	*544*	*989*	*980*	*1748*	*1078*	*2035*	*14692*	*..*	*..*	*..*
16.	*Provisions on securities(1)*	*Provisions sur titres (1)*	*807*	*103*	*8*	*5*	*1073*	*644*	*2197*	*..*	*..*	*..*
	BALANCE SHEET	**BILAN**										
	Assets	**Actif**										
17.	Cash & balance with Central bank	Caisse & solde auprès de la Banque centrale	1764	2291	2766	2822	3225	4230	4592	16375	1168	998
18.	Interbank deposits	Dépôts interbancaires	13287	13839	15098	19708	20368	26163	17460	22127	9173	5471
19.	Loans	Prêts	83765	99869	111560	140385	170524	203904	189497	214186	43009	44419
20.	Securities	Valeurs mobilières	34717	38488	38437	31320	31368	33334	52710	61489	16042	20844
21.	Other assets	Autres actifs	5024	5575	5916	6742	8727	9851	9640	18925	2421	2698
	Liabilities	**Passif**										
22.	Capital & reserves	Capital et réserves	10777	12575	13938	16179	17547	19242	16241	21519	7885	8464
23.	Borrowing from Central bank	Emprunts auprès de la Banque centrale							88	8623		
24.	Interbank deposits	Dépôts interbancaires	6663	13847	18771	30976	51737	73242	48353	48931	2458	2493
25.	Non-bank deposits	Dépôts non bancaires	116956	127979	135113	145601	155530	170544	180318	197526	58016	59836
26.	Bonds	Obligations	895	1190	1735	2946	3826	3544	1139	21055	543	709
27.	Other liabilities	Autres engagements	3269	4471	4218	5274	5572	10909	27761	35448	2909	2930
	Balance sheet total	**Total du bilan**										
28.	End-year total	En fin d'exercice	138558	160063	173776	200976	234212	277482	273898	333101	71813	74431
29.	Average total	Moyen	136049	149311	166920	187376	217594	255847	275690	303500	NA	73280
	Memoranda	*Pour mémoire*										
30.	*Short-term securities*	*Titres à court terme*	*1742*	*889*	*1369*	*666*	*1426*	*4340*	*6846*	*38517*	*9783*	*10088*
31.	*Bonds*	*Obligations*	*33771*	*37412*	*37005*	*29388*	*31027*	*31037*	*24321*	*24190*	*6088*	*9165*
32.	*Shares and participations*	*Actions et participations*	*1648*	*1924*	*1686*	*1869*	*1823*	*1890*	*1519*	*10920*	*1314*	*2640*
33.	*Claims on non-residents*	*Créances sur des non résidents*	*75*	*293*	*467*	*1026*	*3405*	*8186*	*9340*	*35000*	*347*	*480*
34.	*Liabilities to non-residents*	*Engagements envers des non résidents*	*46*	*85*	*52*	*850*	*70*	*442*	*11407*	*74580*	*10*	*10*
	SUPPLEMENTARY INFORMATION	**RENSEIGNEMENTS COMPLEMENTAIRES**										
35.	Number of institutions	Nombre d'institutions	139	119	116	110	109	104	101	91	90	90
36.	Number of branches	Nombre de succursales	1179	1249	1249	1190	1273	1124	1129	1028	351	352
37.	Number of employees (x 1000)	Nombre de salariés (x 1000)	13.5	14.6	14.6	15.6	15.8	14.9	15.3	15.4	3.8	3.8

SWEDEN

Savings banks

SUEDE

Caisses d'épargne

Per cent	1985	1986	1987	1988	1989	1990	1991	1992	1993 (2)	1994	Pourcentage
INCOME STATEMENT ANALYSIS											**ANALYSE DU COMPTE DE RESULTATS**
% of average balance sheet total											**% du total moyen du bilan**
38. Interest income	13.13	11.42	10.85	10.85	11.24	12.51	11.59	16.41	NA	9.16	38. Produits financiers
39. Interest expenses	9.19	7.21	6.80	6.72	7.24	8.16	7.25	12.20	NA	4.26	39. Frais financiers
40. Net interest income	3.94	4.21	4.05	4.13	4.01	4.35	4.34	4.21	NA	4.90	40. Produits financiers nets
41. Non-interest income (net)	0.99	1.43	1.10	1.17	1.09	1.05	2.25	6.51	NA	1.62	41. Produits non financiers (nets)
42. Gross income	4.93	5.64	5.14	5.30	5.10	5.41	6.59	10.72	NA	6.52	42. Résultat brut
43. Operating expenses	3.70	4.00	4.02	3.95	3.92	4.39	7.23	9.33	NA	4.42	43. Frais d'exploitation
44. Net income	1.24	1.65	1.12	1.34	1.18	1.02	-0.63	1.39	NA	2.10	44. Résultat net
45. Provisions (net)	1.07	0.89	0.59	0.92	0.97	0.96	-4.84	-2.13	NA	-0.80	45. Provisions (nettes)
46. Profit before tax	0.17	0.75	0.53	0.42	0.20	0.06	4.21	3.52	NA	2.89	46. Bénéfices avant impôt
47. Income tax	0.09	0.49	0.29	0.29	0.06	0.06	1.30	0.18	NA	0.70	47. Impôt
48. Profit after tax	0.08	0.27	0.24	0.13	0.14	0.00	2.91	3.34	NA	2.20	48. Bénéfices après impôt
49. Distributed profit	0.00										49. Bénéfices distribués
50. Retained profit	0.08	0.27	0.24	0.13	0.14	0.00	2.91	3.34	NA	2.20	50. Bénéfices mis en réserve
51. Staff costs	1.67	1.63	1.66	1.11	1.68	1.66	1.65	1.71	NA	1.57	51. Frais de personnel
52. Provisions on loans (1)	0.40	0.66	0.59	0.93	0.50	0.80	5.33	:	:	:	52. Provisions sur prêts (1)
53. Provisions on securities (1)	0.59	0.07	0.00	0.00	0.49	0.25	0.80	:	:	:	53. Provisions sur titres (1)
% of gross income											**% du total du résultat brut**
54. Net interest income	79.86	74.64	78.70	77.94	78.62	80.51	65.83	39.30	82.18	75.21	54. Produits financiers nets
55. Non-interest income (net)	20.14	25.36	21.30	22.06	21.38	19.49	34.17	60.70	17.82	24.79	55. Produits non financiers (nets)
56. Operating expenses	74.90	70.80	78.14	74.63	76.94	81.21	109.61	87.01	77.52	67.85	56. Frais d'exploitation
57. Net income	25.10	29.20	21.86	25.37	23.06	18.79	-9.61	12.99	22.48	32.15	57. Résultat net
58. Provisions (net)	21.71	15.83	11.48	17.44	19.10	17.70	-73.50	-19.85	-11.02	-12.20	58. Provisions (nettes)
59. Profit before tax	3.40	13.36	10.38	7.93	3.96	1.08	63.88	32.84	33.51	44.36	59. Bénéfices avant impôt
60. Income tax	1.80	8.63	5.68	5.48	1.17	1.16	19.74	1.69	10.05	10.68	60. Impôt
61. Profit after tax	1.59	4.74	4.71	2.45	2.79	-0.08	44.14	31.15	23.46	33.68	61. Bénéfices après impôt
62. Staff costs	33.82	28.96	32.28	21.04	32.93	30.64	25.03	15.99	23.58	24.16	62. Frais de personnel
% of net income											**% du total du résultat net**
63. Provisions (net)	86.47	54.23	52.51	68.75	82.83	94.23	:	-152.74	-49.03	-37.96	63. Provisions (nettes)
64. Profit before tax	13.53	45.77	47.49	31.25	17.17	5.77	:	252.74	149.03	137.96	64. Bénéfices avant impôt
65. Income tax	7.18	29.55	25.96	21.60	5.08	6.20	:	12.98	44.70	33.20	65. Impôt
66. Profit after tax	6.35	16.22	21.54	9.65	12.08	-0.42	:	239.76	104.33	104.75	66. Bénéfices après impôt

SWEDEN

Savings banks

Per cent

BALANCE SHEET ANALYSIS

% of year-end balance sheet total

	1985	1986	1987	1988	1989	1990	1991	1992	1993 (2)	1994
Assets										
67. Cash & balance with Central bank	1.27	1.43	1.59	1.40	1.38	1.52	1.68	4.92	1.63	1.34
68. Interbank deposits	9.59	8.65	8.69	9.81	8.70	9.43	6.37	6.64	12.77	7.35
69. Loans	60.45	62.39	64.20	69.85	72.81	73.48	69.19	64.30	59.89	59.68
70. Securities	25.06	24.05	22.12	15.58	13.39	12.01	19.24	18.46	22.34	28.00
71. Other assets	3.63	3.48	3.40	3.35	3.73	3.55	3.52	5.68	3.37	3.62
Liabilities										
72. Capital & reserves	7.78	7.86	8.02	8.05	7.49	6.93	5.93	6.46	10.98	11.37
73. Borrowing from Central bank	-	-					0.03	2.59	-	-
74. Interbank deposits	4.81	8.65	10.80	15.41	22.09	26.40	17.65	14.69	3.42	3.35
75. Non-bank deposits	84.41	79.96	77.75	72.45	66.41	61.46	65.83	59.30	80.79	80.39
76. Bonds	0.65	0.74	1.00	1.47	1.63	1.28	0.42	6.32	0.76	0.95
77. Other liabilities	2.36	2.79	2.43	2.62	2.38	3.93	10.14	10.64	4.05	3.94
Memoranda										
78. Short-term securities	1.26	0.56	0.79	0.33	0.61	1.56	2.50	11.56	13.62	13.55
79. Bonds	24.37	23.37	21.29	14.62	13.25	11.19	8.88	7.26	8.48	12.31
80. Shares and participations	1.19	1.20	0.97	0.93	0.78	0.68	0.55	3.28	1.83	3.55
81. Claims on non-residents	0.05	0.18	0.27	0.51	1.45	2.95	3.41	10.51	0.48	0.64
82. Liabilities to non-residents	0.03	0.05	0.03	0.42	0.03	0.16	4.16	22.39	0.01	0.01

1. As from 1992, change in methodology.

2. Change in methodology.

Change in methodology:

- Beginning 1992, "Provisions on loans" (item 15 or item 52) and "Provisions on securities" (item 16 or item 53) are no longer available due to new accounting methods.

- As from 1993, what was formerly the largest savings bank is included in the category of Commercial banks.

SUEDE

Caisses d'épargne

Pourcentage

ANALYSE DU BILAN

% du total du bilan en fin d'exercice

Actif
67. Caisse & solde auprès de la Banque centrale
68. Dépôts interbancaires
69. Prêts
70. Valeurs mobilières
71. Autres actifs

Passif
72. Capital et réserves
73. Emprunts auprès de la Banque centrale
74. Dépôts interbancaires
75. Dépôts non bancaires
76. Obligations
77. Autres engagements

Pour mémoire
78. Titres à court terme
79. Obligations
80. Actions et participations
81. Créances sur des non résidents
82. Engagements envers des non résidents

1. A partir de 1992, changement méthodologique.

2. Changement méthodologique.

Changement méthodologique :

- A partir de 1992, "Provisions sur prêts" (poste 15 ou poste 52) et "Provisions sur titres" (poste 16 ou poste 53) ne sont plus disponibles du fait de nouvelles techniques comptables.

- A partir de 1993, ce qui était précédément la plus grande caisse d'épargne est incluse dans la catégorie Banques commerciales.

SWEDEN

Co-operative banks

Million Swedish kroner

SUEDE

Banques mutualistes

Millions de couronnes suédoises

	1985	1986	1987	1988	1989	1990	1991	
INCOME STATEMENT								**COMPTE DE RESULTATS**
1. Interest income	4433	4314	4556	5323	6340	8249	12157	1. Produits financiers
2. Interest expenses	3086	2687	2751	3200	3857	4942	8427	2. Frais financiers
3. Net interest income	1347	1627	1805	2123	2483	3307	3730	3. Produits financiers nets
4. Non-interest income (net)	287	328	332	391	472	602	1144	4. Produits non financiers (nets)
5. Gross income	1634	1955	2137	2514	2955	3909	4874	5. Résultat brut
6. Operating expenses	1208	1390	1625	1838	2159	2981	5717	6. Frais d'exploitation
7. Net income	426	565	512	676	796	928	-843	7. Résultat net
8. Provisions (net)	328	443	360	497	616	711	-2856	8. Provisions (nettes)
9. Profit before tax	98	122	152	179	180	217	2013	9. Bénéfices avant impôt
10. Income tax	42	54	79	101	59	67	552	10. Impôt
11. Profit after tax	56	68	73	78	121	150	1461	11. Bénéfices après impôt
12. Distributed profit	-	-	-	-	-	-	-	12. Bénéfices distribués
13. Retained profit	56	68	73	78	121	150	1461	13. Bénéfices mis en réserve
Memoranda								*Pour mémoire*
14. Staff costs	*582*	*664*	*776*	*799*	*888*	*1092*	*1377*	*14. Frais de personnel*
15. Provisions on loans	*140*	*177*	*268*	*-*	*366*	*523*	*3130*	*15. Provisions sur prêts*
16. Provisions on securities	*146*	*200*	*3*	*388*	*91*	*47*	*818*	*16. Provisions sur titres*
BALANCE SHEET (1)								**BILAN (1)**
Assets								**Actif**
17. Cash & balance with Central bank	223	269	327	368	443	593	1453	17. Caisse & solde auprès de la Banque centrale
18. Interbank deposits	4296	5654	1950	2572	1067	1515	5548	18. Dépôts interbancaires
19. Loans	19773	20825	26397	32805	40411	47201	60019	19. Prêts
20. Securities	7851	9484	10772	10009	10874	10828	23689	20. Valeurs mobilières
21. Other assets	1594	1688	1918	1499	1960	2352	3093	21. Autres actifs
Liabilities								**Passif**
22. Capital & reserves	2064	2380	4778	3407	4174	5035	4627	22. Capital et réserves
23. Borrowing from Central bank	1	1	-	-	-	-	982	23. Emprunts auprès de la Banque centrale
24. Interbank deposits			151	1533	3487	2540	20381	24. Dépôts interbancaires
25. Non-bank deposits	30262	33897	36480	41028	45690	52980	58682	25. Dépôts non bancaires
26. Bonds	104	152	264	273	332	365	2396	26. Obligations
27. Other liabilities	1306	1490	-309	1012	1073	1568	6733	27. Autres engagements
Balance sheet total								**Total du bilan**
28. End-year total	33737	37920	41364	47253	54756	62488	93803	28. En fin d'exercice
29. Average total	33152	36266	40232	45259	51406	57278	67395	29. Moyen
Memoranda								*Pour mémoire*
30. Short-term securities	*8069*	*-*	*-*	*381*	*480*	*615*	*2217*	*30. Titres à court terme*
31. Bonds	*-*	*9886*	*10064*	*10062*	*10948*	*10479*	*9047*	*31. Obligations*
32. Shares and participations	*107*	*108*	*122*	*122*	*122*	*436*	*1458*	*32. Actions et participations*
33. Claims on non-residents	*-*	*-*	*-*	*-*	*-*	*-*	*1964*	*33. Créances sur des non résidents*
34. Liabilities to non-residents	*-*	*-*	*-*	*-*	*-*	*6*	*9316*	*34. Engagements envers des non résidents*
SUPPLEMENTARY INFORMATION								**RENSEIGNEMENTS COMPLEMENTAIRES**
35. Number of institutions	12	12	12	12	12	12	12	35. Nombre d'institutions
36. Number of branches	377	389	388	391	383	373	332	36. Nombre de succursales
37. Number of employees (x 1000)	3.5	3.4	3.7	3.9	4.0	4.3	4.7	37. Nombre de salariés (x 1000)

SWEDEN

Co-operative banks

Per cent

INCOME STATEMENT ANALYSIS

SUEDE

Banques mutualistes

Pourcentage

ANALYSE DU COMPTE DE RESULTATS

	1985	1986	1987	1988	1989	1990	1991		
% of average balance sheet total									**% du total moyen du bilan**
38. Interest income	13.37	11.90	11.32	11.76	12.33	14.40	18.04	38.	Produits financiers
39. Interest expenses	9.31	7.41	6.84	7.07	7.50	8.63	12.50	39.	Frais financiers
40. Net interest income	4.06	4.49	4.49	4.69	4.83	5.77	5.53	40.	Produits financiers nets
41. Non-interest income (net)	0.87	0.90	0.83	0.86	0.92	1.05	1.70	41.	Produits non financiers (nets)
42. Gross income	4.93	5.39	5.31	5.55	5.75	6.82	7.23	42.	Résultat brut
43. Operating expenses	3.64	3.83	4.04	4.06	4.20	5.20	8.48	43.	Frais d'exploitation
44. Net income	1.28	1.56	1.27	1.49	1.55	1.62	-1.25	44.	Résultat net
45. Provisions (net)	0.99	1.22	0.89	1.10	1.20	1.24	-4.24	45.	Provisions (nettes)
46. Profit before tax	0.30	0.34	0.38	0.40	0.35	0.38	2.99	46.	Bénéfices avant impôt
47. Income tax	0.13	0.15	0.20	0.22	0.11	0.12	0.82	47.	Impôt
48. Profit after tax	0.17	0.19	0.18	0.17	0.24	0.26	2.17	48.	Bénéfices après impôt
49. Distributed profit								49.	Bénéfices distribués
50. Retained profit	0.17	0.19	0.18	0.17	0.24	0.26	2.17	50.	Bénéfices mis en réserve
51. Staff costs	1.76	1.83	1.93	1.77	1.73	1.91	2.04	51.	Frais de personnel
52. Provisions on loans	0.42	0.49	0.67		0.71	0.91	4.64	52.	Provisions sur prêts
53. Provisions on securities	0.44	0.55	0.01	0.86	0.18	0.08	1.21	53.	Provisions sur titres
% of gross income									**% du total du résultat brut**
54. Net interest income	82.44	83.22	84.46	84.45	84.03	84.60	76.53	54.	Produits financiers nets
55. Non-interest income (net)	17.56	16.78	15.54	15.55	15.97	15.40	23.47	55.	Produits non financiers (nets)
56. Operating expenses	73.93	71.10	76.04	73.11	73.06	76.26	117.30	56.	Frais d'exploitation
57. Net income	26.07	28.90	23.96	26.89	26.94	23.74	-17.30	57.	Résultat net
58. Provisions (net)	20.07	22.66	16.85	19.77	20.85	18.19	-58.60	58.	Provisions (nettes)
59. Profit before tax	6.00	6.24	7.11	7.12	6.09	5.55	41.30	59.	Bénéfices avant impôt
60. Income tax	2.57	2.76	3.70	4.02	2.00	1.71	11.33	60.	Impôt
61. Profit after tax	3.43	3.48	3.42	3.10	4.09	3.84	29.98	61.	Bénéfices après impôt
62. Staff costs	35.62	33.96	36.31	31.78	30.05	27.94	28.25	62.	Frais de personnel
% of net income									**% du total du résultat net**
63. Provisions (net)	77.00	78.41	70.31	73.52	77.39	76.62	..	63.	Provisions (nettes)
64. Profit before tax	23.00	21.59	29.69	26.48	22.61	23.38	..	64.	Bénéfices avant impôt
65. Income tax	9.86	9.56	15.43	14.94	7.41	7.22	..	65.	Impôt
66. Profit after tax	13.15	12.04	14.26	11.54	15.20	16.16	..	66.	Bénéfices après impôt

SWEDEN

Co-operative banks

Per cent	1985	1986	1987	1988	1989	1990	1991
BALANCE SHEET ANALYSIS							
% of year-end balance sheet total							
Assets							
67. Cash & balance with Central bank	0.66	0.71	0.79	0.78	0.81	0.95	1.55
68. Interbank deposits	12.73	14.91	4.71	5.44	1.95	2.42	5.91
69. Loans	58.61	54.92	63.82	69.42	73.80	75.54	63.98
70. Securities	23.27	25.01	26.04	21.18	19.86	17.33	25.25
71. Other assets	4.72	4.45	4.64	3.17	3.58	3.76	3.30
Liabilities							
72. Capital & reserves	6.12	6.28	11.55	7.21	7.62	8.06	4.93
73. Borrowing from Central bank	-	-	-	-	-	-	1.05
74. Interbank deposits	0.00	0.00	0.37	3.24	6.37	4.06	21.73
75. Non-bank deposits	89.70	89.39	88.19	86.83	83.44	84.78	62.56
76. Bonds	0.31	0.40	0.64	0.58	0.61	0.58	2.55
77. Other liabilities	3.87	3.93	-0.75	2.14	1.96	2.51	7.18
Memoranda							
78. Short-term securities	-	-	-	*0.81*	*0.88*	*0.98*	*2.36*
79. Bonds	*23.92*	*26.07*	*24.33*	*21.29*	*19.99*	*16.77*	*9.64*
80. Shares and participations	*0.32*	*0.28*	*0.29*	*0.26*	*0.22*	*0.70*	*1.55*
81. Claims on non-residents	-	-	-	-	-	-	*2.09*
82. Liabilities to non-residents	-	-	-	-	-	*0.01*	*9.93*

1. Change in methodology.

Notes

• Average balance sheet totals (item 29) are based on thirteen end-month data.

Change in methodology:

• For the year 1991, the Föreningsbankernas Bank is exceptionally included under Co-operative banks and not under Commercial banks.

• As from 1992, Co-operative banks, which merged into one single commercial bank, are included under Commercial banks.

SUEDE

Banques mutualistes

Pourcentage

ANALYSE DU BILAN

% du total du bilan en fin d'exercice

Actif

67. Caisse & solde auprès de la Banque centrale
68. Dépôts interbancaires
69. Prêts
70. Valeurs mobilières
71. Autres actifs

Passif

72. Capital et réserves
73. Emprunts auprès de la Banque centrale
74. Dépôts interbancaires
75. Dépôts non bancaires
76. Obligations
77. Autres engagements

Pour mémoire

78. Titres à court terme
79. Obligations
80. Actions et participations
81. Créances sur des non-résidents
82. Engagements envers des non résidents

1. Changement méthodologique.

Notes

• La moyenne du total des actifs/passifs (poste 29) est basée sur treize données de fin de mois.

Changement méthodologique :

• Pour l'année 1991, la Föreningsbankernas Bank est comprise exceptionnellement dans les Banques mutualistes et non pas dans les Banques commerciales.

• Depuis 1992, les Banques mutualistes, ayant fusionnées en une seule banque commerciale, sont classées dans les données concernant les Banques commerciales.

SWITZERLAND

All banks

Million Swiss francs

SUISSE

Ensemble des banques

Millions de francs suisses

		1985	1986	1987	1988	1989	1990	1991	1992	1993	1994	
INCOME STATEMENT												**COMPTE DE RESULTATS**
1.	Interest income	40021	39293	41233	45836	59594	70944	75442	74255	68499	59284	1. Produits financiers
2.	Interest expenses	30025	28705	30474	33563	46326	57257	58970	56246	47246	42638	2. Frais financiers
3.	Net interest income	9996	10588	10759	12273	13268	13687	16472	18009	21253	16646	3. Produits financiers nets
4.	Non-interest income (net)	9000	10318	11462	10929	13737	13174	16992	17961	20380	20083	4. Produits non financiers (nets)
5.	Gross income	18996	20906	22221	23202	27005	26861	33464	35970	41633	36729	5. Résultat brut
6.	Operating expenses	10084	11302	12370	13386	14934	15939	17349	18408	20183	20124	6. Frais d'exploitation
7.	Net income	8912	9604	9851	9816	12071	10922	16115	17562	21450	16605	7. Résultat net
8.	Provisions (net)	3732	3972	4236	4134	5104	5561	10127	11386	13270	10046	8. Provisions (nettes)
9.	Profit before tax	5180	5632	5615	5682	6967	5361	5988	6176	8180	6559	9. Bénéfices avant impôt
10.	Income tax	1474	1528	1531	1476	1535	1313	1382	1403	1752	1260	10. Impôt
11.	Profit after tax	3706	4104	4084	4206	5432	4048	4606	4773	6428	5299	11. Bénéfices après impôt
12.	Distributed profit	2141	2370	2488	2523	3460	2715	2805	2829	3579	3396	12. Bénéfices distribués
13.	Retained profit	1565	1734	1596	1683	1972	1333	1801	1944	2849	1903	13. Bénéfices mis en réserve
Memoranda												*Pour mémoire*
14.	*Staff costs*	*6738*	*7481*	*8189*	*8868*	*9828*	*10451*	*11419*	*11947*	*13184*	*12861*	*14. Frais de personnel*
15.	*Provisions on loans*	..	..	..	..	..	..	..	..	..	..	*15. Provisions sur prêts*
16.	*Provisions on securities*	..	..	..	..	..	..	..	..	..	..	*16. Provisions sur titres*
BALANCE SHEET												**BILAN**
Assets												**Actif**
17.	Cash & balance with Central bank	23832	25140	26375	12360	12332	11876	11715	11818	11828	10996	17. Caisse & solde auprès de la Banque centrale
18.	Interbank deposits	180879	207814	213523	226068	197365	196615	187439	196341	205946	196210	18. Dépôts interbancaires
19.	Loans	402795	431989	473369	540796	621374	670261	711407	726741	738605	744490	19. Prêts
20.	Securities	82079	91261	93583	88245	97684	105054	110906	121896	159059	164578	20. Valeurs mobilières
21.	Other assets	48555	48878	49634	48342	49591	48973	51855	55417	62368	66507	21. Autres actifs
Liabilities												**Passif**
22.	Capital & reserves	45107	50349	54177	57993	63371	66743	68676	71439	76951	79435	22. Capital et réserves
23.	Borrowing from Central bank	7008	10093	7605	4220	1585	1805	1239	1433	1670	1978	23. Emprunts auprès de la Banque centrale
24.	Interbank deposits	136182	160227	171115	179214	194091	208519	205741	209940	239523	229261	24. Dépôts interbancaires
25.	Non-bank deposits	387477	406571	432697	467158	494038	510663	534720	557064	588258	613777	25. Dépôts non bancaires
26.	Bonds	117260	130347	140314	151053	164228	181508	191779	194451	183602	174309	26. Obligations
27.	Other liabilities	45106	47495	50576	56175	61036	63546	71168	77887	87802	84022	27. Autres engagements
Balance sheet total												**Total du bilan**
28.	End-year total	738140	805082	856484	915812	978346	1032779	1073321	1112213	1177805	1182782	28. En fin d'exercice
29.	Average total	713623	771611	830783	886148	947079	1005563	1053050	1092767	1145009	1180294	29. Moyen
Memoranda												*Pour mémoire*
30.	*Short-term securities*	*31093*	*30730*	*29463*	*21328*	*25776*	*33898*	*29411*	*34438*	*34822*	*38926*	*30. Titres à court terme*
31.	*Bonds*	*42389*	*49316*	*52547*	*53313*	*55961*	*56826*	*64916*	*68459*	*92633*	*86619*	*31. Obligations*
32.	*Shares and participations*	*8597*	*11215*	*11573*	*13604*	*15947*	*14331*	*16579*	*18999*	*31605*	*39034*	*32. Actions et participations*
33.	*Claims on non-residents*	*279251*	*305547*	*317222*	*337446*	*339306*	*354848*	*372834*	*392649*	*428143*	*415068*	*33. Créances sur des non résidents*
34.	*Liabilities to non-residents*	*215294*	*234092*	*233768*	*255951*	*270950*	*293525*	*314501*	*325954*	*351526*	*349274*	*34. Engagements envers des non résidents*
SUPPLEMENTARY INFORMATION												**RENSEIGNEMENTS COMPLEMENTAIRES**
35.	Number of institutions	441	448	452	454	455	457	445	435	419	393	35. Nombre d'institutions
36.	Number of branches	5293	3948	4005	4082	4130	4191	4190	4111	3991	3807	36. Nombre de succursales
37.	Number of employees (x 1000)	98.1	105.4	112.5	115.1	119.3	121.4	120.9	118.5	117.1	116.5	37. Nombre de salariés (x 1000)

SWITZERLAND

All banks

Per cent / *Pourcentage*

INCOME STATEMENT ANALYSIS / **ANALYSE DU COMPTE DE RESULTATS**

	1985	1986	1987	1988	1989	1990	1991	1992	1993	1994	
% of average balance sheet total											**% du total moyen du bilan**
38. Interest income	5.61	5.09	4.96	5.17	6.29	7.06	7.16	6.80	5.98	5.02	38. Produits financiers
39. Interest expenses	4.21	3.72	3.67	3.79	4.89	5.69	5.60	5.15	4.13	3.61	39. Frais financiers
40. Net interest income	1.40	1.37	1.30	1.38	1.40	1.36	1.56	1.65	1.86	1.41	40. Produits financiers nets
41. Non-interest income (net)	1.26	1.34	1.38	1.23	1.45	1.31	1.61	1.64	1.78	1.70	41. Produits non financiers (nets)
42. Gross income	2.66	2.71	2.67	2.62	2.85	2.67	3.18	3.29	3.64	3.11	42. Résultat brut
43. Operating expenses	1.41	1.46	1.49	1.51	1.58	1.59	1.65	1.68	1.76	1.70	43. Frais d'exploitation
44. Net income	1.25	1.24	1.19	1.11	1.27	1.09	1.53	1.61	1.87	1.41	44. Résultat net
45. Provisions (net)	0.52	0.51	0.51	0.47	0.54	0.55	0.96	1.04	1.16	0.85	45. Provisions (nettes)
46. Profit before tax	0.73	0.73	0.68	0.64	0.74	0.53	0.57	0.57	0.71	0.56	46. Bénéfices avant impôt
47. Income tax	0.21	0.20	0.18	0.17	0.16	0.13	0.13	0.13	0.15	0.11	47. Impôt
48. Profit after tax	0.52	0.53	0.49	0.47	0.57	0.40	0.44	0.44	0.56	0.45	48. Bénéfices après impôt
49. Distributed profit	0.30	0.31	0.30	0.28	0.37	0.27	0.27	0.26	0.31	0.29	49. Bénéfices distribués
50. Retained profit	0.22	0.22	0.19	0.19	0.21	0.13	0.17	0.18	0.25	0.16	50. Bénéfices mis en réserve
51. Staff costs	0.94	0.97	0.99	1.00	1.04	1.04	1.08	1.09	1.15	1.09	51. Frais de personnel
52. Provisions on loans	:	:	:	:	:	:	:	:	:	:	52. Provisions sur prêts
53. Provisions on securities	:	:	:	:	:	:	:	:	:	:	53. Provisions sur titres
% of gross income											**% du total du résultat brut**
54. Net interest income	52.62	50.65	48.42	52.90	49.13	50.95	49.22	50.07	51.05	45.32	54. Produits financiers nets
55. Non-interest income (net)	47.38	49.35	51.58	47.10	50.87	49.05	50.78	49.93	48.95	54.68	55. Produits non financiers (nets)
56. Operating expenses	53.08	54.06	55.67	57.69	55.30	59.34	51.84	51.18	48.48	54.79	56. Frais d'exploitation
57. Net income	46.92	45.94	44.33	42.31	44.70	40.66	48.16	48.82	51.52	45.21	57. Résultat net
58. Provisions (net)	19.65	19.00	19.06	17.82	18.90	20.70	30.26	31.87	31.87	27.35	58. Provisions (nettes)
59. Profit before tax	27.27	26.94	25.27	24.49	25.80	19.96	17.89	17.17	19.65	17.86	59. Bénéfices avant impôt
60. Income tax	7.76	7.31	6.89	6.36	5.68	4.89	4.13	3.90	4.21	3.43	60. Impôt
61. Profit after tax	19.51	19.63	18.38	18.13	20.11	15.07	13.76	13.27	15.44	14.43	61. Bénéfices après impôt
62. Staff costs	35.47	35.78	36.85	38.22	36.39	38.91	34.12	33.21	31.67	35.02	62. Frais de personnel
% of net income											**% du total du résultat net**
63. Provisions (net)	41.88	41.36	43.00	42.11	42.28	50.92	62.84	64.83	61.86	60.50	63. Provisions (nettes)
64. Profit before tax	58.12	58.64	57.00	57.89	57.72	49.08	37.16	35.17	38.14	39.50	64. Bénéfices avant impôt
65. Income tax	16.54	15.91	15.54	15.04	12.72	12.02	8.58	7.99	8.17	7.59	65. Impôt
66. Profit after tax	41.58	42.73	41.46	42.85	45.00	37.06	28.58	27.18	29.97	31.91	66. Bénéfices après impôt

SWITZERLAND

All banks

SUISSE

Ensemble des banques

	1985	1986	1987	1988	1989	1990	1991	1992	1993	1994		
Per cent												*Pourcentage*
BALANCE SHEET ANALYSIS												**ANALYSE DU BILAN**
% of year-end balance sheet total												**% du total du bilan en fin d'exercice**
Assets												**Actif**
67. Cash & balance with Central bank	3.23	3.12	3.08	1.35	1.26	1.15	1.09	1.06	1.00	0.93		67. Caisse & solde auprès de la Banque centrale
68. Interbank deposits	24.50	25.81	24.93	24.68	20.17	19.04	17.46	17.65	17.49	16.59		68. Dépôts interbancaires
69. Loans	54.57	53.66	55.27	59.05	63.51	64.90	66.28	65.34	62.71	62.94		69. Prêts
70. Securities	11.12	11.34	10.93	9.64	9.98	10.17	10.33	10.96	13.50	13.91		70. Valeurs mobilières
71. Other assets	6.58	6.07	5.80	5.28	5.07	4.74	4.83	4.98	5.30	5.62		71. Autres actifs
Liabilities												**Passif**
72. Capital & reserves	6.11	6.25	6.33	6.33	6.48	6.46	6.40	6.42	6.53	6.72		72. Capital et réserves
73. Borrowing from Central bank	0.95	1.25	0.89	0.46	0.16	0.17	0.12	0.13	0.14	0.17		73. Emprunts auprès de la Banque centrale
74. Interbank deposits	18.45	19.90	19.98	19.57	19.84	20.19	19.17	18.88	20.34	19.38		74. Dépôts interbancaires
75. Non-bank deposits	52.49	50.50	50.52	51.01	50.50	49.45	49.82	50.09	49.95	51.89		75. Dépôts non bancaires
76. Bonds	15.89	16.19	16.38	16.49	16.79	17.57	17.87	17.48	15.59	14.74		76. Obligations
77. Other liabilities	6.11	5.90	5.91	6.13	6.24	6.15	6.63	7.00	7.45	7.10		77. Autres engagements
Memoranda												*Pour mémoire*
78. Short-term securities	4.21	3.82	3.44	2.33	2.63	3.28	2.74	3.10	2.96	3.29		78. Titres à court terme
79. Bonds	5.74	6.13	6.14	5.82	5.72	5.50	6.05	6.16	7.86	7.32		79. Obligations
80. Shares and participations	1.16	1.39	1.35	1.49	1.63	1.39	1.54	1.71	2.68	3.30		80. Actions et participations
81. Claims on non-residents	37.83	37.95	37.04	36.85	34.68	34.36	34.74	35.30	36.35	35.09		81. Créances sur des non résidents
82. Liabilities to non-residents	29.17	29.08	27.29	27.95	27.69	28.42	29.30	29.31	29.85	29.53		82. Engagements envers des non résidents

Notes

- All banks include Large commercial banks, Cantonal banks, Regional and savings banks, Loan associations and agricultural co-operative banks and Other Swiss and foreign commercial banks.

Notes

- L'Ensemble des banques comprend les Grandes banques commerciales, les Banques cantonales, les Banques régionales et caisses d'épargne, les Caisses de crédit mutuel et les banques mutualistes agricoles, et les Autres banques suisses et étrangères.

160

SWITZERLAND

Large commercial banks

Million Swiss francs

Grandes banques commerciales

Millions de francs suisses

	1985	1986	1987	1988	1989	1990	1991	1992	1993	1994	
INCOME STATEMENT											**COMPTE DE RESULTATS**
1. Interest income	21995	21157	22449	25335	33228	37805	39353	37330	34051	30069	1. Produits financiers
2. Interest expenses	16737	15530	16796	18894	26427	31374	31220	27990	22748	21186	2. Frais financiers
3. Net interest income	5258	5627	5653	6441	6801	6431	8133	9340	11303	8883	3. Produits financiers nets
4. Non-interest income (net)	4885	5571	5965	5800	6879	6676	8544	9394	11508	10678	4. Produits non financiers (nets)
5. Gross income	10143	11198	11618	12241	13680	13107	16677	18734	22811	19561	5. Résultat brut
6. Operating expenses	5368	5984	6509	7030	7849	8086	9023	9765	11168	11085	6. Frais d'exploitation
7. Net income	4775	5214	5109	5211	5831	5021	7654	8969	11643	8476	7. Résultat net
8. Provisions (net)	1972	2153	2128	2177	2447	2280	4402	5650	7384	5112	8. Provisions (nettes)
9. Profit before tax	2803	3061	2981	3034	3384	2741	3252	3319	4259	3364	9. Bénéfices avant impôt
10. Income tax	854	872	849	823	827	682	803	795	881	592	10. Impôt
11. Profit after tax	1949	2189	2132	2211	2557	2059	2449	2524	3378	2772	11. Bénéfices après impôt
12. Distributed profit	1257	1366	1423	1432	1623	1576	1585	1584	1959	1955	12. Bénéfices distribués
13. Retained profit	692	823	709	779	934	483	864	940	1419	817	13. Bénéfices mis en réserve
Memoranda											*Pour mémoire*
14. Staff costs	3611	3982	4340	4700	5242	5410	6060	6455	7506	7164	14. Frais de personnel
15. Provisions on loans	..	..	..	..	..	..	..	..	..	..	15. Provisions sur prêts
16. Provisions on securities	..	..	..	..	..	..	..	..	..	..	16. Provisions sur titres
BALANCE SHEET											**BILAN**
Assets											**Actif**
17. Cash & balance with Central bank	13836	14588	14774	5523	5468	5189	5123	4889	4635	4478	17. Caisse & solde auprès de la Banque centrale
18. Interbank deposits	112359	132805	135700	142738	117329	110780	100290	103289	105729	101679	18. Dépôts interbancaires
19. Loans	182383	197894	219954	255872	302566	319625	344106	353135	356268	362606	19. Prêts
20. Securities	51296	56863	55948	47052	52822	59255	64030	73671	105712	109562	20. Valeurs mobilières
21. Other assets	34753	34675	34377	32313	31528	28678	29637	32297	39496	43664	21. Autres actifs
Liabilities											**Passif**
22. Capital & reserves	23290	26260	28051	29619	33143	33196	34148	35187	39416	42294	22. Capital et réserves
23. Borrowing from Central bank	5043	7418	5408	3289	1203	1270	568	1107	1319	1406	23. Emprunts auprès de la Banque centrale
24. Interbank deposits	86610	105967	113804	112882	120732	125757	126306	127759	155908	146097	24. Dépôts interbancaires
25. Non-bank deposits	210121	220935	231597	247005	261719	271651	285212	303465	314050	335948	25. Dépôts non bancaires
26. Bonds	43374	48975	53041	57648	58710	58577	60272	59262	53765	52501	26. Obligations
27. Other liabilities	26189	27270	28852	33055	34206	33075	36682	40501	47383	43743	27. Autres engagements
Balance sheet total											**Total du bilan**
28. End-year total	394627	436825	460752	483497	509713	523526	543187	567281	611841	621989	28. En fin d'exercice
29. Average total	381428	415726	448788	472125	496605	516620	533357	555234	589561	616915	29. Moyen
Memoranda											*Pour mémoire*
30. Short-term securities	27284	26777	25097	16756	19541	26556	21777	26889	28279	30596	30. Titres à court terme
31. Bonds	17891	22105	22875	21059	22596	23619	30875	33756	53544	48148	31. Obligations
32. Shares and participations	6121	7981	7975	9237	10685	9080	11377	13026	23889	30819	32. Actions et participations
33. Claims on non-residents	205148	228827	237947	245803	242273	253852	267157	282046	308989	299813	33. Créances sur des non résidents
34. Liabilities to non-residents	160604	180068	179045	193070	201479	220536	240443	248042	266879	266182	34. Engagements envers des non résidents
SUPPLEMENTARY INFORMATION											**RENSEIGNEMENTS COMPLEMENTAIRES**
35. Number of institutions	5	5	5	5	5	4	4	4	4	4	35. Nombre d'institutions
36. Number of branches	1048	876	889	901	933	969	983	969	923	955	36. Nombre de succursales
37. Number of employees (x 1000)	52.7	56.6	59.9	60.8	62.9	62.4	62.5	61.9	61.2	62.0	37. Nombre de salariés (x 1000)

Large commercial banks

Grandes banques commerciales

Per cent

Pourcentage

INCOME STATEMENT ANALYSIS

ANALYSE DU COMPTE DE RESULTATS

	1985	1986	1987	1988	1989	1990	1991	1992	1993	1994		
% of average balance sheet total												**% du total moyen du bilan**
38. Interest income	5.77	5.09	5.00	5.37	6.69	7.32	7.38	6.72	5.78	4.87	38.	Produits financiers
39. Interest expenses	4.39	3.74	3.74	4.00	5.32	6.07	5.85	5.04	3.86	3.43	39.	Frais financiers
40. Net interest income	1.38	1.35	1.26	1.36	1.37	1.24	1.52	1.68	1.92	1.44	40.	Produits financiers nets
41. Non-interest income (net)	1.28	1.34	1.33	1.23	1.39	1.29	1.60	1.69	1.95	1.73	41.	Produits non financiers (nets)
42. Gross income	2.66	2.69	2.59	2.59	2.75	2.54	3.13	3.37	3.87	3.17	42.	Résultat brut
43. Operating expenses	1.41	1.44	1.45	1.49	1.58	1.57	1.69	1.76	1.89	1.80	43.	Frais d'exploitation
44. Net income	1.25	1.25	1.14	1.10	1.17	0.97	1.44	1.62	1.97	1.37	44.	Résultat net
45. Provisions (net)	0.52	0.52	0.47	0.46	0.49	0.44	0.83	1.02	1.25	0.83	45.	Provisions (nettes)
46. Profit before tax	0.73	0.74	0.66	0.64	0.68	0.53	0.61	0.60	0.72	0.55	46.	Bénéfices avant impôt
47. Income tax	0.22	0.21	0.19	0.17	0.17	0.13	0.15	0.14	0.15	0.10	47.	Impôt
48. Profit after tax	0.51	0.53	0.48	0.47	0.51	0.40	0.46	0.45	0.57	0.45	48.	Bénéfices après impôt
49. Distributed profit	0.33	0.33	0.32	0.30	0.33	0.31	0.30	0.29	0.33	0.32	49.	Bénéfices distribués
50. Retained profit	0.18	0.20	0.16	0.16	0.19	0.09	0.16	0.17	0.24	0.13	50.	Bénéfices mis en réserve
51. Staff costs	0.95	0.96	0.97	1.00	1.06	1.05	1.14	1.16	1.27	1.16	51.	Frais de personnel
52. Provisions on loans	..	..	..	..	..	..	..	..	..	..	52.	Provisions sur prêts
53. Provisions on securities	..	..	..	..	..	..	..	..	..	..	53.	Provisions sur titres
% of gross income												**% du total du résultat brut**
54. Net interest income	51.84	50.25	48.66	52.62	49.71	49.07	48.77	49.86	49.55	45.41	54.	Produits financiers nets
55. Non-interest income (net)	48.16	49.75	51.34	47.38	50.29	50.93	51.23	50.14	50.45	54.59	55.	Produits non financiers (nets)
56. Operating expenses	52.92	53.44	56.03	57.43	57.38	61.69	54.10	52.12	48.96	56.67	56.	Frais d'exploitation
57. Net income	47.08	46.56	43.97	42.57	42.62	38.31	45.90	47.88	51.04	43.33	57.	Résultat net
58. Provisions (net)	19.44	19.23	18.32	17.78	17.89	17.40	26.40	30.16	32.37	26.13	58.	Provisions (nettes)
59. Profit before tax	27.63	27.34	25.66	24.79	24.74	20.91	19.50	17.72	18.67	17.20	59.	Bénéfices avant impôt
60. Income tax	8.42	7.79	7.31	6.72	6.05	5.20	4.82	4.24	3.86	3.03	60.	Impôt
61. Profit after tax	19.22	19.55	18.35	18.06	18.69	15.71	14.68	13.47	14.81	14.17	61.	Bénéfices après impôt
62. Staff costs	35.60	35.56	37.36	38.40	38.32	41.28	36.34	34.46	32.91	36.62	62.	Frais de personnel
% of net income												**% du total du résultat net**
63. Provisions (net)	41.30	41.29	41.65	41.78	41.97	45.41	57.51	62.99	63.42	60.31	63.	Provisions (nettes)
64. Profit before tax	58.70	58.71	58.35	58.22	58.03	54.59	42.49	37.01	36.58	39.69	64.	Bénéfices avant impôt
65. Income tax	17.88	16.72	16.62	15.79	14.18	13.58	10.49	8.86	7.57	6.98	65.	Impôt
66. Profit after tax	40.82	41.98	41.73	42.43	43.85	41.01	32.00	28.14	29.01	32.70	66.	Bénéfices après impôt

SWITZERLAND

Large commercial banks

SUISSE

Grandes banques commerciales

Per cent / *Pourcentage*

BALANCE SHEET ANALYSIS / **ANALYSE DU BILAN**

% of year-end balance sheet total / % du total du bilan en fin d'exercice

	1985	1986	1987	1988	1989	1990	1991	1992	1993	1994	
Assets											**Actif**
67. Cash & balance with Central bank	3.51	3.34	3.21	1.14	1.07	0.99	0.94	0.86	0.76	0.72	67. Caisse & solde auprès de la Banque centrale
68. Interbank deposits	28.47	30.40	29.45	29.52	23.02	21.16	18.46	18.21	17.28	16.35	68. Dépôts interbancaires
69. Loans	46.22	45.30	47.74	52.92	59.36	61.05	63.35	62.25	58.23	58.30	69. Prêts
70. Securities	13.00	13.02	12.14	9.73	10.36	11.32	11.79	12.99	17.28	17.61	70. Valeurs mobilières
71. Other assets	8.81	7.94	7.46	6.68	6.19	5.48	5.46	5.69	6.46	7.02	71. Autres actifs
Liabilities											**Passif**
72. Capital & reserves	5.90	6.01	6.09	6.13	6.50	6.34	6.29	6.20	6.44	6.80	72. Capital et réserves
73. Borrowing from Central bank	1.28	1.70	1.17	0.68	0.24	0.24	0.10	0.20	0.22	0.23	73. Emprunts auprès de la Banque centrale
74. Interbank deposits	21.95	24.26	24.70	23.35	23.69	24.02	23.25	22.52	25.48	23.49	74. Dépôts interbancaires
75. Non-bank deposits	53.25	50.58	50.27	51.09	51.35	51.89	52.51	53.49	51.33	54.01	75. Dépôts non bancaires
76. Bonds	10.99	11.21	11.51	11.92	11.52	11.19	11.10	10.45	8.79	8.44	76. Obligations
77. Other liabilities	6.64	6.24	6.26	6.84	6.71	6.32	6.75	7.14	7.74	7.03	77. Autres engagements
Memoranda											*Pour mémoire*
78. Short-term securities	6.91	6.13	5.45	3.47	3.83	5.07	4.01	4.74	4.62	4.92	78. Titres à court terme
79. Bonds	4.53	5.06	4.96	4.36	4.43	4.51	5.68	5.95	8.75	7.74	79. Obligations
80. Shares and participations	1.55	1.83	1.73	1.91	2.10	1.73	2.09	2.30	3.90	4.95	80. Actions et participations
81. Claims on non-residents	51.99	52.38	51.64	50.84	47.53	48.49	49.18	49.72	50.50	48.20	81. Créances sur des non résidents
82. Liabilities to non-residents	40.70	41.22	38.86	39.93	39.53	42.13	44.27	43.72	43.62	42.80	82. Engagements envers des non résidents

SUISSE

Other Swiss and foreign commercial banks

Autres banques commerciales suisses et étrangères

Million Swiss francs / *Millions de francs suisses*

	1985	1986	1987	1988	1989	1990	1991	1992	1993	1994	
INCOME STATEMENT											**COMPTE DE RESULTATS**
1. Interest income	7139	6542	6725	7791	11134	13187	13228	12771	11989	9874	1. Produits financiers
2. Interest expenses	4947	4318	4470	5126	8100	9963	9633	9054	7480	6565	2. Frais financiers
3. Net interest income	2192	2224	2255	2665	3034	3224	3595	3717	4509	3309	3. Produits financiers nets
4. Non-interest income (net)	3179	3693	4268	4007	5579	5061	6113	5892	6637	6563	4. Produits non financiers (nets)
5. Gross income	5371	5917	6523	6672	8613	8285	9708	9609	11146	9872	5. Résultat brut
6. Operating expenses	2677	3068	3456	3762	4281	4728	4991	5135	5430	5394	6. Frais d'exploitation
7. Net income	2694	2849	3067	2910	4332	3557	4717	4474	5716	4478	7. Résultat net
8. Provisions (net)	1155	1158	1355	1236	1794	2034	3003	2624	2859	2285	8. Provisions (nettes)
9. Profit before tax	1539	1691	1712	1674	2538	1523	1714	1850	2857	2193	9. Bénéfices avant impôt
10. Income tax	468	501	516	487	542	407	410	454	723	536	10. Impôt
11. Profit after tax	1071	1190	1196	1187	1996	1116	1304	1396	2134	1657	11. Bénéfices après impôt
12. Distributed profit	445	540	573	571	1270	554	654	673	1018	862	12. Bénéfices distribués
13. Retained profit	626	650	623	616	726	562	650	723	1116	795	13. Bénéfices mis en réserve
Memoranda											*Pour mémoire*
14. Staff costs	*1727*	*1979*	*2239*	*2444*	*2732*	*3028*	*3180*	*3246*	*3415*	*3412*	14. Frais de personnel
15. Provisions on loans	..	..	..	..	..	..	..	..	..	..	15. Provisions sur prêts
16. Provisions on securities	..	..	..	..	..	..	..	..	..	..	16. Provisions sur titres
BALANCE SHEET											**BILAN**
Assets											**Actif**
17. Cash & balance with Central bank	5890	6096	6762	3201	3377	3135	2880	3046	3267	3150	17. Caisse & solde auprès de la Banque centrale
18. Interbank deposits	42497	44419	44826	51339	50703	57381	58495	61590	64281	63189	18. Dépôts interbancaires
19. Loans	46251	47683	49673	59906	67353	74007	76536	77108	80898	78090	19. Prêts
20. Securities	13945	16729	18828	20728	24400	24266	25062	26448	29945	31201	20. Valeurs mobilières
21. Other assets	5788	6091	6693	6918	7795	8947	9262	8532	8455	8486	21. Autres actifs
Liabilities											**Passif**
22. Capital & reserves	11836	13275	14376	15964	17112	19455	19965	21026	21892	21619	22. Capital et réserves
23. Borrowing from Central bank	207	486	215	3	40	68	-	16	2	153	23. Emprunts auprès de la Banque centrale
24. Interbank deposits	39359	42786	43419	50315	54071	57935	56446	59279	61615	60183	24. Dépôts interbancaires
25. Non-bank deposits	47128	46924	49903	55965	59633	63942	67664	69333	75551	76069	25. Dépôts non bancaires
26. Bonds	7781	8745	9476	10050	11307	14730	14675	13158	11853	10488	26. Obligations
27. Other liabilities	8060	8802	9392	9795	11464	11607	13485	13911	15933	15604	27. Autres engagements
Balance sheet total											**Total du bilan**
28. End-year total	114371	121018	126782	142091	153628	167737	172235	176723	186845	184116	28. En fin d'exercice
29. Average total	111047	117694	123900	134437	147860	160683	169986	174479	181784	185481	29. Moyen
Memoranda											*Pour mémoire*
30. Short-term securities	*2559*	*2765*	*3245*	*3471*	*5328*	*6501*	*6875*	*6420*	*4825*	*6331*	30. Titres à court terme
31. Bonds	*9904*	*11953*	*13420*	*14587*	*15957*	*15068*	*15694*	*16689*	*20368*	*19548*	31. Obligations
32. Shares and participations	*1482*	*2011*	*2163*	*2670*	*3115*	*2698*	*2493*	*3339*	*4752*	*5321*	32. Actions et participations
33. Claims on non-residents	*66850*	*68618*	*70288*	*82017*	*87395*	*90756*	*95500*	*99193*	*105648*	*102717*	33. Créances sur des non résidents
34. Liabilities to non-residents	*50228*	*49455*	*49847*	*57374*	*63889*	*66742*	*67487*	*71069*	*77797*	*76145*	34. Engagements envers des non résidents
SUPPLEMENTARY INFORMATION											**RENSEIGNEMENTS COMPLÉMENTAIRES**
35. Number of institutions	189	197	202	205	209	218	222	227	230	226	35. Nombre d'institutions
36. Number of branches	494	480	494	527	549	587	607	592	578	561	36. Nombre de succursales
37. Number of employees (x 1000)	20.2	22.4	25.0	25.9	27.0	28.9	28.1	26.8	26.7	26.6	37. Nombre de salariés (x 1000)

SWITZERLAND

Other Swiss and foreign commercial banks

SUISSE

Autres banques commerciales suisses et étrangères

Per cent	1985	1986	1987	1988	1989	1990	1991	1992	1993	1994	Pourcentage
INCOME STATEMENT ANALYSIS											**ANALYSE DU COMPTE DE RESULTATS**
% of average balance sheet total											**% du total moyen du bilan**
38. Interest income	6.43	5.56	5.43	5.80	7.53	8.21	7.78	7.32	6.60	5.32	38. Produits financiers
39. Interest expenses	4.45	3.67	3.61	3.81	5.48	6.20	5.67	5.19	4.11	3.54	39. Frais financiers
40. Net interest income	1.97	1.89	1.82	1.98	2.05	2.01	2.11	2.13	2.48	1.78	40. Produits financiers nets
41. Non-interest income (net)	2.86	3.14	3.44	2.98	3.77	3.15	3.60	3.38	3.65	3.54	41. Produits non financiers (nets)
42. Gross income	4.84	5.03	5.26	4.96	5.83	5.16	5.71	5.51	6.13	5.32	42. Résultat brut
43. Operating expenses	2.41	2.61	2.79	2.80	2.90	2.94	2.94	2.94	2.99	2.91	43. Frais d'exploitation
44. Net income	2.43	2.42	2.48	2.16	2.93	2.21	2.77	2.56	3.14	2.41	44. Résultat net
45. Provisions (net)	1.04	0.98	1.09	0.92	1.21	1.27	1.77	1.50	1.57	1.23	45. Provisions (nettes)
46. Profit before tax	1.39	1.44	1.38	1.25	1.72	0.95	1.01	1.06	1.57	1.18	46. Bénéfices avant impôt
47. Income tax	0.42	0.43	0.42	0.36	0.37	0.25	0.24	0.26	0.40	0.29	47. Impôt
48. Profit after tax	0.96	1.01	0.97	0.88	1.35	0.69	0.77	0.80	1.17	0.89	48. Bénéfices après impôt
49. Distributed profit	0.40	0.46	0.46	0.42	0.86	0.34	0.38	0.39	0.56	0.46	49. Bénéfices distribués
50. Retained profit	0.56	0.55	0.50	0.46	0.49	0.35	0.38	0.41	0.61	0.43	50. Bénéfices mis en réserve
51. Staff costs	1.56	1.68	1.81	1.82	1.85	1.88	1.87	1.86	1.88	1.84	51. Frais de personnel
52. Provisions on loans	..	..	..	..	..	..	..	..	..	..	52. Provisions sur prêts
53. Provisions on securities	..	..	..	..	..	..	..	..	..	..	53. Provisions sur titres
% of gross income											**% du total du résultat brut**
54. Net interest income	40.81	37.59	34.57	39.94	35.23	38.91	37.03	38.68	40.45	33.52	54. Produits financiers nets
55. Non-interest income (net)	59.19	62.41	65.43	60.06	64.77	61.09	62.97	61.32	59.55	66.48	55. Produits non financiers (nets)
56. Operating expenses	49.84	51.85	52.98	56.38	49.70	57.07	51.41	53.44	48.72	54.64	56. Frais d'exploitation
57. Net income	50.16	48.15	47.02	43.62	50.30	42.93	48.59	46.56	51.28	45.36	57. Résultat net
58. Provisions (net)	21.50	19.57	20.77	18.53	20.83	24.55	30.93	27.31	25.65	23.15	58. Provisions (nettes)
59. Profit before tax	28.65	28.58	26.25	25.09	29.47	18.38	17.66	19.25	25.63	22.21	59. Bénéfices avant impôt
60. Income tax	8.71	8.47	7.91	7.30	6.29	4.91	4.22	4.72	6.49	5.43	60. Impôt
61. Profit after tax	19.94	20.11	18.34	17.79	23.17	13.47	13.43	14.53	19.15	16.78	61. Bénéfices après impôt
62. Staff costs	32.15	33.45	34.32	36.63	31.72	36.55	32.76	33.78	30.64	34.56	62. Frais de personnel
% of net income											**% du total du résultat net**
63. Provisions (net)	42.87	40.65	44.18	42.47	41.41	57.18	63.66	58.65	50.02	51.03	63. Provisions (nettes)
64. Profit before tax	57.13	59.35	55.82	57.53	58.59	42.82	36.34	41.35	49.98	48.97	64. Bénéfices avant impôt
65. Income tax	17.37	17.59	16.82	16.74	12.51	11.44	8.69	10.15	12.65	11.97	65. Impôt
66. Profit after tax	39.76	41.77	39.00	40.79	46.08	31.37	27.64	31.20	37.33	37.00	66. Bénéfices après impôt

SWITZERLAND

Other Swiss and foreign commercial banks

SUISSE

Autres banques commerciales suisses et étrangères

Per cent / *Pourcentage*

BALANCE SHEET ANALYSIS / **ANALYSE DU BILAN**

% of year-end balance sheet total / % du total du bilan en fin d'exercice

	1985	1986	1987	1988	1989	1990	1991	1992	1993	1994	
Assets											**Actif**
67. Cash & balance with Central bank	5.15	5.04	5.33	2.25	2.20	1.87	1.67	1.72	1.75	1.71	67. Caisse & solde auprès de la Banque centrale
68. Interbank deposits	37.16	36.70	35.36	36.13	33.00	34.21	33.96	34.85	34.40	34.32	68. Dépôts interbancaires
69. Loans	40.44	39.40	39.18	42.16	43.84	44.12	44.44	43.63	43.30	42.41	69. Prêts
70. Securities	12.19	13.82	14.85	14.59	15.88	14.47	14.55	14.97	16.03	16.95	70. Valeurs mobilières
71. Other assets	5.06	5.03	5.28	4.87	5.07	5.33	5.38	4.83	4.53	4.61	71. Autres actifs
Liabilities											**Passif**
72. Capital & reserves	10.35	10.97	11.34	11.24	11.14	11.60	11.59	11.90	11.72	11.74	72. Capital et réserves
73. Borrowing from Central bank	0.18	0.40	0.17	0.00	0.03	0.04	-	0.01	-	0.08	73. Emprunts auprès de la Banque centrale
74. Interbank deposits	34.41	35.36	34.25	35.41	35.20	34.54	32.77	33.54	32.98	32.69	74. Dépôts interbancaires
75. Non-bank deposits	41.21	38.77	39.36	39.39	38.82	38.12	39.29	39.23	40.44	41.32	75. Dépôts non bancaires
76. Bonds	6.80	7.23	7.47	7.07	7.36	8.78	8.52	7.45	6.34	5.70	76. Obligations
77. Other liabilities	7.05	7.27	7.41	6.89	7.46	6.92	7.83	7.87	8.53	8.48	77. Autres engagements
Memoranda											*Pour mémoire*
78. Short-term securities	2.24	2.28	2.56	2.44	3.47	3.88	3.99	3.63	2.58	3.44	78. Titres à court terme
79. Bonds	8.66	9.88	10.59	10.27	10.39	8.98	9.11	9.44	10.90	10.62	79. Obligations
80. Shares and participations	1.30	1.66	1.71	1.88	2.03	1.61	1.45	1.89	2.54	2.89	80. Actions et participations
81. Claims on non-residents	58.45	56.70	55.44	57.72	56.89	54.11	55.45	56.13	56.54	55.79	81. Créances sur des non résidents
82. Liabilities to non-residents	43.92	40.87	39.32	40.38	41.59	39.79	39.18	40.21	41.64	41.36	82. Engagements envers des non résidents

SWITZERLAND

Other Swiss commercial banks

Million Swiss francs

SUISSE

Autres banques commerciales suisses

Millions de francs suisses

	1985	1986	1987	1988	1989	1990	1991	1992	1993	1994	
INCOME STATEMENT											**COMPTE DE RESULTATS**
1. Interest income	2022	2254	2343	2557	3527	5547	5908	5737	5548	4509	1. Produits financiers
2. Interest expenses	1199	1337	1406	1454	2214	3945	4055	3817	3189	2809	2. Frais financiers
3. Net interest income	823	917	937	1103	1313	1602	1853	1920	2359	1700	3. Produits financiers nets
4. Non-interest income (net)	1336	1677	1914	1667	2063	2328	2293	2655	2961	3068	4. Produits non financiers (nets)
5. Gross income	2159	2594	2851	2770	3376	3930	4146	4575	5320	4768	5. Résultat brut
6. Operating expenses	1192	1402	1555	1587	1860	2219	2329	2400	2467	2502	6. Frais d'exploitation
7. Net income	967	1192	1296	1183	1516	1711	1817	2175	2853	2266	7. Résultat net
8. Provisions (net)	407	474	537	467	683	957	983	1216	1351	1132	8. Provisions (nettes)
9. Profit before tax	560	718	759	716	833	754	834	959	1502	1134	9. Bénéfices avant impôt
10. Income tax	191	252	269	249	252	206	190	235	400	290	10. Impôt
11. Profit after tax	369	466	490	467	581	548	644	724	1102	844	11. Bénéfices après impôt
12. Distributed profit	173	213	229	231	270	290	369	390	608	539	12. Bénéfices distribués
13. Retained profit	196	253	261	236	311	258	275	334	494	305	13. Bénéfices mis en réserve
Memoranda											*Pour mémoire*
14. Staff costs	756	889	979	1000	1162	1407	1469	1510	1556	1573	14. Frais de personnel
15. Provisions on loans	..	..	..	..	..	..	..	..	..	..	15. Provisions sur prêts
16. Provisions on securities	..	..	..	..	..	..	..	..	..	..	16. Provisions sur titres
BALANCE SHEET											**BILAN**
Assets											**Actif**
17. Cash & balance with Central bank	2348	2591	2959	1351	1261	1296	1128	1083	1361	1341	17. Caisse & solde auprès de la Banque centrale
18. Interbank deposits	8558	12144	13064	12107	12697	20466	21116	22526	23528	23920	18. Dépôts interbancaires
19. Loans	20506	22518	24130	28666	32209	39791	42316	42436	44418	43969	19. Prêts
20. Securities	3826	4657	5002	5663	6629	11232	10817	12212	12010	12493	20. Valeurs mobilières
21. Other assets	2292	2549	2737	2777	3076	4518	4585	4343	4300	4283	21. Autres actifs
Liabilities											**Passif**
22. Capital & reserves	3913	4665	5285	5469	6070	8125	7893	8485	8526	8507	22. Capital et réserves
23. Borrowing from Central bank	78	118	113	-	40	68	-	16	2	153	23. Emprunts auprès de la Banque centrale
24. Interbank deposits	6846	8829	8844	10180	11126	16780	16001	17198	17086	16774	24. Dépôts interbancaires
25. Non-bank deposits	19231	22139	24172	24975	26768	36031	38948	40147	43370	44920	25. Dépôts non bancaires
26. Bonds	4557	5280	5709	6244	7654	11218	11433	10476	9512	8528	26. Obligations
27. Other liabilities	2905	3428	3766	3695	4215	5082	5688	6278	7120	7124	27. Autres engagements
Balance sheet total											**Total du bilan**
28. End-year total	37530	44459	47891	50564	55872	77304	79963	82600	85616	86007	28. En fin d'exercice
29. Average total	35720	40994	46175	49228	53218	66588	78634	81281	84108	85812	29. Moyen
Memoranda											*Pour mémoire*
30. Short-term securities	665	724	940	1254	1711	4667	4596	4315	2771	4056	30. Titres à court terme
31. Bonds	2487	2985	3086	3297	3403	5288	4955	5858	7110	6232	31. Obligations
32. Shares and participations	674	948	977	1111	1514	1277	1267	2039	2128	2205	32. Actions et participations
33. Claims on non-residents	11879	14957	15425	17047	19024	30140	32653	34826	36166	35054	33. Créances sur des non résidents
34. Liabilities to non-residents	9164	11834	12210	12759	14484	21644	25164	26160	27918	27093	34. Engagements envers des non résidents
SUPPLEMENTARY INFORMATION											**RENSEIGNEMENTS COMPLEMENTAIRES**
35. Number of institutions	85	88	91	89	91	92	92	93	87	86	35. Nombre d'institutions
36. Number of branches	277	266	273	287	301	327	333	317	289	277	36. Nombre de succursales
37. Number of employees (x 1000)	8.8	10.1	11.2	11.2	11.8	13.9	13.6	12.9	12.6	12.5	37. Nombre de salariés (x 1000)

SWITZERLAND

Other Swiss commercial banks

Per cent

INCOME STATEMENT ANALYSIS

SUISSE

Autres banques commerciales suisses

Pourcentage

ANALYSE DU COMPTE DE RESULTATS

	1985	1986	1987	1988	1989	1990	1991	1992	1993	1994	
% of average balance sheet total											**% du total moyen du bilan**
38. Interest income	5.66	5.50	5.07	5.19	6.63	8.33	7.51	7.06	6.60	5.25	38. Produits financiers
39. Interest expenses	3.36	3.26	3.04	2.95	4.16	5.92	5.16	4.70	3.79	3.27	39. Frais financiers
40. Net interest income	2.30	2.24	2.03	2.24	2.47	2.41	2.36	2.36	2.80	1.98	40. Produits financiers nets
41. Non-interest income (net)	3.74	4.09	4.15	3.39	3.88	3.50	2.92	3.27	3.52	3.58	41. Produits non financiers (nets)
42. Gross income	6.04	6.33	6.17	5.63	6.34	5.90	5.27	5.63	6.33	5.56	42. Résultat brut
43. Operating expenses	3.34	3.42	3.37	3.22	3.50	3.33	2.96	2.95	2.93	2.92	43. Frais d'exploitation
44. Net income	2.71	2.91	2.81	2.40	2.85	2.57	2.31	2.68	3.39	2.64	44. Résultat net
45. Provisions (net)	1.14	1.16	1.16	0.95	1.28	1.44	1.25	1.50	1.61	1.32	45. Provisions (nettes)
46. Profit before tax	1.57	1.75	1.64	1.45	1.57	1.13	1.06	1.18	1.79	1.32	46. Bénéfices avant impôt
47. Income tax	0.53	0.61	0.58	0.51	0.47	0.31	0.24	0.29	0.48	0.34	47. Impôt
48. Profit after tax	1.03	1.14	1.06	0.95	1.09	0.82	0.82	0.89	1.31	0.98	48. Bénéfices après impôt
49. Distributed profit	0.48	0.52	0.50	0.47	0.51	0.44	0.47	0.48	0.72	0.63	49. Bénéfices distribués
50. Retained profit	0.55	0.62	0.57	0.48	0.58	0.39	0.35	0.41	0.59	0.36	50. Bénéfices mis en réserve
51. Staff costs	2.12	2.17	2.12	2.03	2.18	2.11	1.87	1.86	1.85	1.83	51. Frais de personnel
52. Provisions on loans	..	..	..	..	..	..	..	..	..	..	52. Provisions sur prêts
53. Provisions on securities	..	..	..	..	..	..	..	..	..	..	53. Provisions sur titres
% of gross income											**% du total du résultat brut**
54. Net interest income	38.12	35.35	32.87	39.82	38.89	40.76	44.69	41.97	44.34	35.65	54. Produits financiers nets
55. Non-interest income (net)	61.88	64.65	67.13	60.18	61.11	59.24	55.31	58.03	55.66	64.35	55. Produits non financiers (nets)
56. Operating expenses	55.21	54.05	54.54	57.29	55.09	56.46	56.17	52.46	46.37	52.47	56. Frais d'exploitation
57. Net income	44.79	45.95	45.46	42.71	44.91	43.54	43.83	47.54	53.63	47.53	57. Résultat net
58. Provisions (net)	18.85	18.27	18.84	16.86	20.23	24.35	23.71	26.58	25.39	23.74	58. Provisions (nettes)
59. Profit before tax	25.94	27.68	26.62	25.85	24.67	19.19	20.12	20.96	28.23	23.78	59. Bénéfices avant impôt
60. Income tax	8.85	9.71	9.44	8.99	7.46	5.24	4.58	5.14	7.52	6.08	60. Impôt
61. Profit after tax	17.09	17.96	17.19	16.86	17.21	13.94	15.53	15.83	20.71	17.70	61. Bénéfices après impôt
62. Staff costs	35.02	34.27	34.34	36.10	34.42	35.80	35.43	33.01	29.25	32.99	62. Frais de personnel
% of net income											**% du total du résultat net**
63. Provisions (net)	42.09	39.77	41.44	39.48	45.05	55.93	54.10	55.91	47.35	49.96	63. Provisions (nettes)
64. Profit before tax	57.91	60.23	58.56	60.52	54.95	44.07	45.90	44.09	52.65	50.04	64. Bénéfices avant impôt
65. Income tax	19.75	21.14	20.76	21.05	16.62	12.04	10.46	10.80	14.02	12.80	65. Impôt
66. Profit after tax	38.16	39.09	37.81	39.48	38.32	32.03	35.44	33.29	38.63	37.25	66. Bénéfices après impôt

SWITZERLAND

Other Swiss commercial banks

SUISSE

Autres banques commerciales suisses

Per cent / *Pourcentage*

BALANCE SHEET ANALYSIS / **ANALYSE DU BILAN**

% of year-end balance sheet total / % du total du bilan en fin d'exercice

	1985	1986	1987	1988	1989	1990	1991	1992	1993	1994	
Assets											**Actif**
67. Cash & balance with Central bank	6.26	5.83	6.18	2.67	2.26	1.68	1.41	1.31	1.59	1.56	67. Caisse & solde auprès de la Banque centrale
68. Interbank deposits	22.80	27.32	27.28	23.94	22.73	26.47	26.41	27.27	27.48	27.81	68. Dépôts interbancaires
69. Loans	54.64	50.65	50.39	56.69	57.65	51.47	52.92	51.38	51.88	51.12	69. Prêts
70. Securities	10.19	10.47	10.44	11.20	11.86	14.53	13.53	14.78	14.03	14.53	70. Valeurs mobilières
71. Other assets	6.11	5.73	5.72	5.49	5.51	5.84	5.73	5.26	5.02	4.98	71. Autres actifs
Liabilities											**Passif**
72. Capital & reserves	10.43	10.49	11.04	10.82	10.86	10.51	9.87	10.27	9.96	9.89	72. Capital et réserves
73. Borrowing from Central bank	0.21	0.27	0.24	-	0.07	0.09	-	0.02	0.00	0.18	73. Emprunts auprès de la Banque centrale
74. Interbank deposits	18.24	19.86	18.47	20.13	19.91	21.71	20.01	20.82	19.96	19.50	74. Dépôts interbancaires
75. Non-bank deposits	51.24	49.80	50.47	49.39	47.91	46.61	48.71	48.60	50.66	52.23	75. Dépôts non bancaires
76. Bonds	12.14	11.88	11.92	12.35	13.70	14.51	14.30	12.68	11.11	9.92	76. Obligations
77. Other liabilities	7.74	7.71	7.86	7.31	7.54	6.57	7.11	7.60	8.32	8.28	77. Autres engagements
Memoranda											*Pour mémoire*
78. *Short-term securities*	*1.77*	*1.63*	*1.96*	*2.48*	*3.06*	*6.04*	*5.75*	*5.22*	*3.24*	*4.72*	78. *Titres à court terme*
79. *Bonds*	*6.63*	*6.71*	*6.44*	*6.52*	*6.09*	*6.84*	*6.20*	*7.09*	*8.30*	*7.25*	79. *Obligations*
80. *Shares and participations*	*1.80*	*2.13*	*2.04*	*2.20*	*2.71*	*1.65*	*1.58*	*2.47*	*2.49*	*2.56*	80. *Actions et participations*
81. *Claims on non-residents*	*31.65*	*33.64*	*32.21*	*33.71*	*34.05*	*38.99*	*40.84*	*42.16*	*42.24*	*40.76*	81. *Créances sur des non résidents*
82. *Liabilities to non-residents*	*24.42*	*26.62*	*25.50*	*25.23*	*25.92*	*28.00*	*31.47*	*31.67*	*32.61*	*31.50*	82. *Engagements envers des non résidents*

Notes

• Other Swiss commercial banks are a sub-group of Other Swiss and foreign commercial banks.

Notes

• Les Autres banques commerciales suisses sont un sous-groupe des Autres banques commerciales suisses et étrangères.

SWITZERLAND

Foreign commercial banks

Million Swiss francs

SUISSE

Banques commerciales étrangères

Millions de francs suisses

	1985	1986	1987	1988	1989	1990	1991	1992	1993	1994	
INCOME STATEMENT											**COMPTE DE RESULTATS**
1. Interest income	5117	4288	4382	5235	7607	7640	7320	7034	6442	5365	1. Produits financiers
2. Interest expenses	3748	2981	3064	3672	5886	6017	5578	5237	4291	3756	2. Frais financiers
3. Net interest income	1369	1307	1318	1563	1721	1623	1742	1797	2151	1609	3. Produits financiers nets
4. Non-interest income (net)	1843	2016	2354	2340	3516	2734	3820	3237	3677	3495	4. Produits non financiers (nets)
5. Gross income	3212	3323	3672	3903	5237	4357	5562	5034	5828	5104	5. Résultat brut
6. Operating expenses	1485	1666	1901	2175	2421	2509	2662	2734	2963	2891	6. Frais d'exploitation
7. Net income	1727	1657	1771	1728	2816	1848	2900	2300	2865	2213	7. Résultat net
8. Provisions (net)	748	684	818	769	1112	1077	2021	1408	1508	1153	8. Provisions (nettes)
9. Profit before tax	979	973	953	959	1704	771	879	892	1357	1060	9. Bénéfices avant impôt
10. Income tax	277	249	247	238	290	201	220	219	323	247	10. Impôt
11. Profit after tax	702	724	706	721	1414	570	659	673	1034	813	11. Bénéfices après impôt
12. Distributed profit	272	327	344	340	1000	264	285	283	409	323	12. Bénéfices distribués
13. Retained profit	430	397	362	381	414	306	374	390	625	490	13. Bénéfices mis en réserve
Memoranda											*Pour mémoire*
14. Staff costs	*971*	*1090*	*1260*	*1444*	*1569*	*1621*	*1712*	*1736*	*1859*	*1839*	14. Frais de personnel
15. Provisions on loans	..	..	..	..	..	..	..	..	..	..	15. Provisions sur prêts
16. Provisions on securities	..	..	..	..	..	..	..	..	..	..	16. Provisions sur titres
BALANCE SHEET											**BILAN**
Assets											**Actif**
17. Cash & balance with Central bank	3542	3505	3805	1850	2116	1839	1753	1963	1906	1809	17. Caisse & solde auprès de la Banque centrale
18. Interbank deposits	33939	32275	31762	39232	38006	36915	37379	39064	40752	39269	18. Dépôts interbancaires
19. Loans	25745	25165	25543	31239	35144	34215	34220	34672	36481	34121	19. Prêts
20. Securities	10119	12072	13826	15065	17771	13034	14244	14236	17935	18708	20. Valeurs mobilières
21. Other assets	3496	3542	3956	4141	4719	4429	4677	4189	4155	4203	21. Autres actifs
Liabilities											**Passif**
22. Capital & reserves	7923	8610	9091	10494	11042	11329	12072	12541	13366	13111	22. Capital et réserves
23. Borrowing from Central bank	129	368	102	3		-	-		-		23. Emprunts auprès de la Banque centrale
24. Interbank deposits	32513	33957	34575	40134	42946	41156	40444	42081	44529	43409	24. Dépôts interbancaires
25. Non-bank deposits	27897	24785	25731	30990	32865	27910	28716	29186	32181	31149	25. Dépôts non bancaires
26. Bonds	3224	3465	3767	3806	3653	3512	3243	2682	2340	1959	26. Obligations
27. Other liabilities	5155	5374	5626	6099	7249	6525	7797	7633	8812	8481	27. Autres engagements
Balance sheet total											**Total du bilan**
28. End-year total	76841	76559	78891	91527	97756	90433	92272	94124	101229	98109	28. En fin d'exercice
29. Average total	75328	76700	77725	85209	94642	94095	91353	93198	97677	99669	29. Moyen
Memoranda											*Pour mémoire*
30. Short-term securities	*1894*	*2041*	*2305*	*2217*	*3617*	*1834*	*2280*	*2105*	*2054*	*2275*	30. Titres à court terme
31. Bonds	*7417*	*8968*	*10334*	*11289*	*12554*	*9780*	*10739*	*10831*	*13257*	*13317*	31. Obligations
32. Shares and participations	*808*	*1063*	*1186*	*1559*	*1601*	*1421*	*1226*	*1300*	*2623*	*3116*	32. Actions et participations
33. Claims on non-residents	*54971*	*53661*	*54863*	*64970*	*68371*	*60616*	*62847*	*64367*	*69482*	*67663*	33. Créances sur des non résidents
34. Liabilities to non-residents	*41064*	*37621*	*37637*	*44614*	*49405*	*45098*	*42323*	*44909*	*49879*	*49052*	34. Engagements envers des non résidents
SUPPLEMENTARY INFORMATION											**RENSEIGNEMENTS COMPLEMENTAIRES**
35. Number of institutions	104	109	111	116	118	126	130	134	143	140	35. Nombre d'institutions
36. Number of branches	217	214	221	240	248	260	274	275	289	284	36. Nombre de succursales
37. Number of employees (x 1000)	11.5	12.3	13.9	14.7	15.2	15.0	14.5	13.9	14.2	14.2	37. Nombre de salariés (x 1000)

Foreign commercial banks

Banques commerciales étrangères

Per cent — *Pourcentage*

	1985	1986	1987	1988	1989	1990	1991	1992	1993	1994		
INCOME STATEMENT ANALYSIS												**ANALYSE DU COMPTE DE RESULTATS**
% of average balance sheet total												**% du total moyen du bilan**
38. Interest income	6.79	5.59	5.64	6.14	8.04	8.12	8.01	7.55	6.60	5.38	38.	Produits financiers
39. Interest expenses	4.98	3.89	3.94	4.31	6.22	6.39	6.11	5.62	4.39	3.77	39.	Frais financiers
40. Net interest income	1.82	1.70	1.70	1.83	1.82	1.72	1.91	1.93	2.20	1.61	40.	Produits financiers nets
41. Non-interest income (net)	2.45	2.63	3.03	2.75	3.72	2.91	4.18	3.47	3.76	3.51	41.	Produits non financiers (nets)
42. Gross income	4.26	4.33	4.72	4.58	5.53	4.63	6.09	5.40	5.97	5.12	42.	Résultat brut
43. Operating expenses	1.97	2.17	2.45	2.55	2.56	2.67	2.91	2.93	3.03	2.90	43.	Frais d'exploitation
44. Net income	2.29	2.16	2.28	2.03	2.98	1.96	3.17	2.47	2.93	2.22	44.	Résultat net
45. Provisions (net)	0.99	0.89	1.05	0.90	1.17	1.14	2.21	1.51	1.54	1.16	45.	Provisions (nettes)
46. Profit before tax	1.30	1.27	1.23	1.13	1.80	0.82	0.96	0.96	1.39	1.06	46.	Bénéfices avant impôt
47. Income tax	0.37	0.32	0.32	0.28	0.31	0.21	0.24	0.23	0.33	0.25	47.	Impôt
48. Profit after tax	0.93	0.94	0.91	0.85	1.49	0.61	0.72	0.72	1.06	0.82	48.	Bénéfices après impôt
49. Distributed profit	0.36	0.43	0.44	0.40	1.06	0.28	0.31	0.30	0.42	0.32	49.	Bénéfices distribués
50. Retained profit	0.57	0.52	0.47	0.45	0.44	0.33	0.41	0.42	0.64	0.49	50.	Bénéfices mis en réserve
51. Staff costs	1.29	1.42	1.62	1.69	1.66	1.72	1.87	1.86	1.90	1.85	51.	Frais de personnel
52. Provisions on loans	:	:	:	:	:	:	:	:	:	:	52.	Provisions sur prêts
53. Provisions on securities	:	:	:	:	:	:	:	:	:	:	53.	Provisions sur titres
% of gross income												**% du total du résultat brut**
54. Net interest income	42.62	39.33	35.89	40.05	32.86	37.25	31.32	35.70	36.91	31.52	54.	Produits financiers nets
55. Non-interest income (net)	57.38	60.67	64.11	59.95	67.14	62.75	68.68	64.30	63.09	68.48	55.	Produits non financiers (nets)
56. Operating expenses	46.23	50.14	51.77	55.73	46.23	57.59	47.86	54.31	50.84	56.64	56.	Frais d'exploitation
57. Net income	53.77	49.86	48.23	44.27	53.77	42.41	52.14	45.69	49.16	43.36	57.	Résultat net
58. Provisions (net)	23.29	20.58	22.28	19.70	21.23	24.72	36.34	27.97	25.88	22.59	58.	Provisions (nettes)
59. Profit before tax	30.48	29.28	25.95	24.57	32.54	17.70	15.80	17.72	23.28	20.77	59.	Bénéfices avant impôt
60. Income tax	8.62	7.49	6.73	6.10	5.54	4.61	3.96	4.35	5.54	4.84	60.	Impôt
61. Profit after tax	21.86	21.79	19.23	18.47	27.00	13.08	11.85	13.37	17.74	15.93	61.	Bénéfices après impôt
62. Staff costs	30.23	32.80	34.31	37.00	29.96	37.20	30.78	34.49	31.90	36.03	62.	Frais de personnel
% of net income												**% du total du résultat net**
63. Provisions (net)	43.31	41.28	46.19	44.50	39.49	58.28	69.69	61.22	52.64	52.10	63.	Provisions (nettes)
64. Profit before tax	56.69	58.72	53.81	55.50	60.51	41.72	30.31	38.78	47.36	47.90	64.	Bénéfices avant impôt
65. Income tax	16.04	15.03	13.95	13.77	10.30	10.88	7.59	9.52	11.27	11.16	65.	Impôt
66. Profit after tax	40.65	43.69	39.86	41.72	50.21	30.84	22.72	29.26	36.09	36.74	66.	Bénéfices après impôt

SWITZERLAND

Foreign commercial banks

Per cent / *Pourcentage*

BALANCE SHEET ANALYSIS / ANALYSE DU BILAN

% of year-end balance sheet total / *% du total du bilan en fin d'exercice*

	1985	1986	1987	1988	1989	1990	1991	1992	1993	1994	
Assets											**Actif**
67. Cash & balance with Central bank	4.61	4.58	4.82	2.02	2.16	2.03	1.90	2.09	1.88	1.84	67. Caisse & solde auprès de la Banque centrale
68. Interbank deposits	44.17	42.16	40.26	42.86	38.88	40.82	40.51	41.50	40.26	40.03	68. Dépôts interbancaires
69. Loans	33.50	32.87	32.38	34.13	35.95	37.83	37.09	36.84	36.04	34.78	69. Prêts
70. Securities	13.17	15.77	17.53	16.46	18.18	14.41	15.44	15.12	17.72	19.07	70. Valeurs mobilières
71. Other assets	4.55	4.63	5.01	4.52	4.83	4.90	5.07	4.45	4.10	4.28	71. Autres actifs
Liabilities											**Passif**
72. Capital & reserves	10.31	11.25	11.52	11.47	11.30	12.53	13.08	13.32	13.20	13.36	72. Capital et réserves
73. Borrowing from Central bank	0.17	0.48	0.13	0.00	-	-	-	-	-	-	73. Emprunts auprès de la Banque centrale
74. Interbank deposits	42.31	44.35	43.83	43.85	43.93	45.51	43.83	44.71	43.99	44.25	74. Dépôts interbancaires
75. Non-bank deposits	36.30	32.37	32.62	33.86	33.62	30.86	31.12	31.01	31.79	31.75	75. Dépôts non bancaires
76. Bonds	4.20	4.53	4.77	4.16	3.74	3.88	3.51	2.85	2.31	2.00	76. Obligations
77. Other liabilities	6.71	7.02	7.13	6.66	7.42	7.22	8.45	8.11	8.71	8.64	77. Autres engagements
Memoranda											*Pour mémoire*
78. Short-term securities	2.46	2.67	2.92	2.42	3.70	2.03	2.47	2.24	2.03	2.32	78. Titres à court terme
79. Bonds	9.65	11.71	13.10	12.33	12.84	10.81	11.64	11.51	13.10	13.57	79. Obligations
80. Shares and participations	1.05	1.39	1.50	1.70	1.64	1.57	1.33	1.38	2.59	3.18	80. Actions et participations
81. Claims on non-residents	71.54	70.09	69.54	70.98	69.94	67.03	68.11	68.39	68.64	68.97	81. Créances sur des non résidents
82. Liabilities to non-residents	53.44	49.14	47.71	48.74	50.54	49.87	45.87	47.71	49.27	50.00	82. Engagements envers des non résidents

Notes

- Foreign commercial banks are a sub-group of Other Swiss and foreign commercial banks.

Notes

- Les Banques commerciales étrangères sont un sous-groupe des Autres banques commerciales suisses et étrangères.

SWITZERLAND

Cantonal banks

Million Swiss francs

SUISSE

Banques cantonales

Millions de francs suisses

	1985	1986	1987	1988	1989	1990	1991	1992	1993	1994	
INCOME STATEMENT											**COMPTE DE RESULTATS**
1. Interest income	6825	7216	7470	7834	9504	12441	14496	15597	14889	13316	1. Produits financiers
2. Interest expenses	5246	5519	5704	5879	7387	9950	11531	12456	11241	10259	2. Frais financiers
3. Net interest income	1579	1697	1766	1955	2117	2491	2965	3141	3648	3057	3. Produits financiers nets
4. Non-interest income (net)	625	707	794	740	845	937	1794	1999	1640	1990	4. Produits non financiers (nets)
5. Gross income	2204	2404	2560	2695	2962	3428	4759	5140	5288	5047	5. Résultat brut
6. Operating expenses	1297	1422	1523	1636	1771	2006	2173	2312	2430	2594	6. Frais d'exploitation
7. Net income	907	982	1037	1059	1191	1422	2586	2828	2858	2453	7. Résultat net
8. Provisions (net)	417	458	482	468	546	732	1980	2236	2186	1779	8. Provisions (nettes)
9. Profit before tax	490	524	555	591	645	690	606	592	672	674	9. Bénéfices avant impôt
10. Income tax	49	52	60	60	60	114	64	46	42	39	10. Impôt
11. Profit after tax	441	472	495	531	585	576	542	546	630	635	11. Bénéfices après impôt
12. Distributed profit	321	338	360	379	413	427	406	418	468	484	12. Bénéfices distribués
13. Retained profit	120	134	135	152	172	149	136	128	162	151	13. Bénéfices mis en réserve
Memoranda											*Pour mémoire*
14. Staff costs	921	994	1053	1124	1210	1320	1455	1516	1576	1665	14. Frais de personnel
15. Provisions on loans	..	..	..	..	..	..	..	..	..	..	15. Provisions sur prêts
16. Provisions on securities	..	..	..	..	..	..	..	..	..	..	16. Provisions sur titres
BALANCE SHEET											**BILAN**
Assets											**Actif**
17. Cash & balance with Central bank	2439	2688	2942	2146	2024	2080	2203	2311	2500	2136	17. Caisse & solde auprès de la Banque centrale
18. Interbank deposits	19155	22901	24626	23943	20976	19885	20112	22311	25069	22802	18. Dépôts interbancaires
19. Loans	106569	112661	122697	134904	152419	170371	182581	189022	198362	205616	19. Prêts
20. Securities	10774	11251	12011	13218	13513	14639	15121	15414	17221	18212	20. Valeurs mobilières
21. Other assets	5070	5069	5205	5490	6241	6904	8265	9773	9928	10515	21. Autres actifs
Liabilities											**Passif**
22. Capital & reserves	6094	6582	7214	7603	8078	8838	9182	9827	10471	10825	22. Capital et réserves
23. Borrowing from Central bank	1303	1573	1396	691	199	338	213	246	249	331	23. Emprunts auprès de la Banque centrale
24. Interbank deposits	7160	7491	8854	9819	11736	15500	15821	16819	16921	17997	24. Dépôts interbancaires
25. Non-bank deposits	80065	85217	92911	100577	106657	109647	115245	117334	127706	131878	25. Dépôts non bancaires
26. Bonds	41656	45500	48334	51554	57677	66223	72846	77677	79506	78954	26. Obligations
27. Other liabilities	7729	8207	8772	9457	10831	13337	14978	16927	18226	19297	27. Autres engagements
Balance sheet total											**Total du bilan**
28. End-year total	144007	154570	167481	179701	195173	213879	228282	238830	253080	259281	28. En fin d'exercice
29. Average total	139172	149289	161025	173591	187437	204526	221081	233556	245955	256181	29. Moyen
Memoranda											*Pour mémoire*
30. Short-term securities	1002	974	941	932	712	660	588	992	1602	1896	30. Titres à court terme
31. Bonds	9240	9574	10215	11224	11396	12167	12653	12635	13480	14180	31. Obligations
32. Shares and participations	532	703	855	1062	1405	1812	1880	1786	2139	2136	32. Actions et participations
33. Claims on non-residents	6251	7051	7938	8632	8620	9208	9342	10673	12763	11780	33. Créances sur des non résidents
34. Liabilities to non-residents	3600	3684	3905	4475	4569	5283	5679	5854	5947	6139	34. Engagements envers des non résidents
SUPPLEMENTARY INFORMATION											**RENSEIGNEMENTS COMPLEMENTAIRES**
35. Number of institutions	29	29	29	29	29	29	28	28	28	27	35. Nombre d'institutions
36. Number of branches	1359	709	722	741	755	768	771	779	826	761	36. Nombre de succursales
37. Number of employees (x 1000)	15.3	16.1	16.9	17.3	18.0	18.8	19.5	19.3	19.8	19.6	37. Nombre de salariés (x 1000)

Cantonal banks

Banques cantonales

Per cent

Pourcentage

INCOME STATEMENT ANALYSIS

ANALYSE DU COMPTE DE RESULTATS

	1985	1986	1987	1988	1989	1990	1991	1992	1993	1994	
% of average balance sheet total											**% du total moyen du bilan**
38. Interest income	4.90	4.83	4.64	4.51	5.07	6.08	6.56	6.68	6.05	5.20	38. Produits financiers
39. Interest expenses	3.77	3.70	3.54	3.39	3.94	4.86	5.22	5.33	4.57	4.00	39. Frais financiers
40. Net interest income	1.13	1.14	1.10	1.13	1.13	1.22	1.34	1.34	1.48	1.19	40. Produits financiers nets
41. Non-interest income (net)	0.45	0.47	0.49	0.43	0.45	0.46	0.81	0.86	0.67	0.78	41. Produits non financiers (nets)
42. Gross income	1.58	1.61	1.59	1.55	1.58	1.68	2.15	2.20	2.15	1.97	42. Résultat brut
43. Operating expenses	0.93	0.95	0.95	0.94	0.94	0.98	0.98	0.99	0.99	1.01	43. Frais d'exploitation
44. Net income	0.65	0.66	0.64	0.61	0.64	0.70	1.17	1.21	1.16	0.96	44. Résultat net
45. Provisions (net)	0.30	0.31	0.30	0.27	0.29	0.36	0.90	0.96	0.89	0.69	45. Provisions (nettes)
46. Profit before tax	0.35	0.35	0.34	0.34	0.34	0.34	0.27	0.25	0.27	0.26	46. Bénéfices avant impôt
47. Income tax	0.04	0.03	0.04	0.03	0.03	0.06	0.03	0.02	0.02	0.02	47. Impôt
48. Profit after tax	0.32	0.32	0.31	0.31	0.31	0.28	0.25	0.23	0.26	0.25	48. Bénéfices après impôt
49. Distributed profit	0.23	0.23	0.22	0.22	0.22	0.21	0.18	0.18	0.19	0.19	49. Bénéfices distribués
50. Retained profit	0.09	0.09	0.08	0.09	0.09	0.07	0.06	0.05	0.07	0.06	50. Bénéfices mis en réserve
51. Staff costs	0.66	0.67	0.65	0.65	0.65	0.65	0.66	0.65	0.64	0.65	51. Frais de personnel
52. Provisions on loans	..	..	..	..	..	..	..	..	..	..	52. Provisions sur prêts
53. Provisions on securities	..	..	..	..	..	..	..	..	..	..	53. Provisions sur titres
% of gross income											**% du total du résultat brut**
54. Net interest income	71.64	70.59	68.98	72.54	71.47	72.67	62.30	61.11	68.99	60.57	54. Produits financiers nets
55. Non-interest income (net)	28.36	29.41	31.02	27.46	28.53	27.33	37.70	38.89	31.01	39.43	55. Produits non financiers (nets)
56. Operating expenses	58.85	59.15	59.49	60.71	59.79	58.52	45.66	44.98	45.95	51.40	56. Frais d'exploitation
57. Net income	41.15	40.85	40.51	39.29	40.21	41.48	54.34	55.02	54.05	48.60	57. Résultat net
58. Provisions (net)	18.92	19.05	18.83	17.37	18.43	21.35	41.61	43.50	41.34	35.25	58. Provisions (nettes)
59. Profit before tax	22.23	21.80	21.68	21.93	21.78	20.13	12.73	11.52	12.71	13.35	59. Bénéfices avant impôt
60. Income tax	2.22	2.16	2.34	2.23	2.03	3.33	1.34	0.89	0.79	0.77	60. Impôt
61. Profit after tax	20.01	19.63	19.34	19.70	19.75	16.80	11.39	10.62	11.91	12.58	61. Bénéfices après impôt
62. Staff costs	41.79	41.35	41.13	41.71	40.85	38.51	30.57	29.49	29.80	32.99	62. Frais de personnel
% of net income											**% du total du résultat net**
63. Provisions (net)	45.98	46.64	46.48	44.19	45.84	51.48	76.57	79.07	76.49	72.52	63. Provisions (nettes)
64. Profit before tax	54.02	53.36	53.52	55.81	54.16	48.52	23.43	20.93	23.51	27.48	64. Bénéfices avant impôt
65. Income tax	5.40	5.30	5.79	5.67	5.04	8.02	2.47	1.63	1.47	1.59	65. Impôt
66. Profit after tax	48.62	48.07	47.73	50.14	49.12	40.51	20.96	19.31	22.04	25.89	66. Bénéfices après impôt

Cantonal banks

Banques cantonales

Per cent / *Pourcentage*

BALANCE SHEET ANALYSIS / **ANALYSE DU BILAN**

% of year-end balance sheet total / % du total du bilan en fin d'exercice

	1985	1986	1987	1988	1989	1990	1991	1992	1993	1994	
Assets											**Actif**
67. Cash & balance with Central bank	1.69	1.74	1.76	1.19	1.04	0.97	0.97	0.97	0.99	0.82	67. Caisse & solde auprès de la Banque centrale
68. Interbank deposits	13.30	14.82	14.70	13.32	10.75	9.30	8.81	9.34	9.91	8.79	68. Dépôts interbancaires
69. Loans	74.00	72.89	73.26	75.07	78.09	79.66	79.98	79.14	78.38	79.30	69. Prêts
70. Securities	7.48	7.28	7.17	7.36	6.92	6.84	6.62	6.45	6.80	7.02	70. Valeurs mobilières
71. Other assets	3.52	3.28	3.11	3.06	3.20	3.23	3.62	4.09	3.92	4.06	71. Autres actifs
Liabilities											**Passif**
72. Capital & reserves	4.23	4.26	4.31	4.23	4.14	4.13	4.02	4.11	4.14	4.18	72. Capital et réserves
73. Borrowing from Central bank	0.90	1.02	0.83	0.38	0.10	0.16	0.09	0.10	0.10	0.13	73. Emprunts auprès de la Banque centrale
74. Interbank deposits	4.97	4.85	5.29	5.46	6.01	7.25	6.93	7.04	6.69	6.94	74. Dépôts interbancaires
75. Non-bank deposits	55.60	55.13	55.48	55.97	54.65	51.27	50.48	49.13	50.46	50.86	75. Dépôts non bancaires
76. Bonds	28.93	29.44	28.86	28.69	29.55	30.96	31.91	32.52	31.42	30.45	76. Obligations
77. Other liabilities	5.37	5.31	5.24	5.26	5.55	6.24	6.56	7.09	7.20	7.44	77. Autres engagements
Memoranda											*Pour mémoire*
78. Short-term securities	0.70	0.63	0.56	0.52	0.36	0.31	0.26	0.42	0.63	0.73	78. Titres à court terme
79. Bonds	6.42	6.19	6.10	6.25	5.84	5.69	5.54	5.29	5.33	5.47	79. Obligations
80. Shares and participations	0.37	0.45	0.51	0.59	0.72	0.85	0.82	0.75	0.85	0.82	80. Actions et participations
81. Claims on non-residents	4.34	4.56	4.74	4.80	4.42	4.31	4.09	4.47	5.04	4.54	81. Créances sur des non résidents
82. Liabilities to non-residents	2.50	2.38	2.33	2.49	2.34	2.47	2.49	2.45	2.35	2.37	82. Engagements envers des non résidents

SWITZERLAND

Regional and savings banks

SUISSE

Banques régionales et caisses d'épargne

Million Swiss francs / *Millions de francs suisses*

	1985	1986	1987	1988	1989	1990	1991	1992	1993	1994
INCOME STATEMENT / COMPTE DE RESULTATS										
1. Interest income / Produits financiers	3102	3319	3460	3666	4306	5606	6085	6053	5104	3761
2. Interest expenses / Frais financiers	2334	2494	2603	2708	3276	4402	4707	4677	3799	2828
3. Net interest income / Produits financiers nets	768	825	857	958	1030	1204	1378	1376	1305	933
4. Non-interest income (net) / Produits non financiers (nets)	272	303	386	327	370	418	446	549	474	721
5. Gross income / Résultat brut	1040	1128	1243	1285	1400	1622	1824	1925	1779	1654
6. Operating expenses / Frais d'exploitation	596	662	700	755	803	859	873	871	796	672
7. Net income / Résultat net	444	466	543	530	597	763	951	1054	983	982
8. Provisions (net) / Provisions (nettes)	152	163	230	201	252	411	596	704	662	726
9. Profit before tax / Bénéfices avant impôt	292	303	313	329	345	352	355	350	321	256
10. Income tax / Impôt	87	87	90	90	91	92	87	87	83	67
11. Profit after tax / Bénéfices après impôt	205	216	223	239	254	260	268	263	238	189
12. Distributed profit / Bénéfices distribués	114	122	128	137	149	153	155	149	128	88
13. Retained profit / Bénéfices mis en réserve	91	94	95	102	105	107	113	114	110	101
Memoranda / Pour mémoire										
14. Staff costs / Frais de personnel	399	435	456	489	519	553	566	558	500	424
15. Provisions on loans / Provisions sur prêts	:	:	:	:	:	:	:	:	:	:
16. Provisions on securities / Provisions sur titres	:	:	:	:	:	:	:	:	:	:
BALANCE SHEET / BILAN										
Assets / Actif										
17. Cash & balance with Central bank / Caisse & solde auprès de la Banque centrale	1370	1452	1543	1143	1108	1112	1119	1142	943	759
18. Interbank deposits / Dépôts interbancaires	3896	4384	4625	4141	4382	4303	3841	4185	5516	3723
19. Loans / Prêts	50924	55236	60738	67342	73364	78230	77898	75047	67931	59348
20. Securities / Valeurs mobilières	5921	6252	6628	7045	6725	6665	6464	6120	5938	5346
21. Other assets / Autres actifs	2277	2297	2548	2743	3028	3284	3418	3447	3132	2473
Liabilities / Passif										
22. Capital & reserves / Capital et réserves	3192	3499	3767	4000	4193	4369	4456	4435	4153	3631
23. Borrowing from Central bank / Emprunts auprès de la Banque centrale	455	616	586	236	143	111	439	50	87	66
24. Interbank deposits / Dépôts interbancaires	2350	2830	3622	4572	5376	6975	4868	3823	2659	2190
25. Non-bank deposits / Dépôts non bancaires	35909	38035	41198	44577	46076	45037	44756	43445	43414	38964
26. Bonds / Obligations	19903	22006	23963	25833	29091	32677	33547	33125	28362	22782
27. Other liabilities / Autres engagements	2579	2635	2946	3195	3727	4425	4675	5063	4786	4017
Balance sheet total / Total du bilan										
28. End-year total / En fin d'exercice	64388	69621	76082	82414	88607	93595	92741	89941	83460	71650
29. Average total / Moyen	62171	67004	72851	79248	85511	91101	93168	91341	86701	77555
Memoranda / Pour mémoire										
30. Short-term securities / Titres à court terme	241	203	167	152	172	152	142	109	90	76
31. Bonds / Obligations	5333	5664	6016	6425	5994	5953	5676	5359	5225	4731
32. Shares and participations / Actions et participations	347	385	446	468	559	560	646	652	623	539
33. Claims on non-residents / Créances sur des non résidents	1002	1051	1049	994	1018	1032	834	738	743	758
34. Liabilities to non-residents / Engagements envers des non résidents	862	885	971	1032	1013	963	892	990	903	808
SUPPLEMENTARY INFORMATION / RENSEIGNEMENTS COMPLEMENTAIRES										
35. Number of institutions / Nombre d'institutions	216	215	214	213	210	204	189	174	155	135
36. Number of branches / Nombre de succursales	1111	640	658	672	664	654	637	602	525	444
37. Number of employees (x 1000) / Nombre de salariés (x 1000)	7.4	7.7	8.0	8.2	8.4	8.5	8.2	7.9	6.7	5.5

SWITZERLAND

SUISSE

Regional and savings banks
Banques régionales et caisses d'épargne

Per cent / *Pourcentage*

	1985	1986	1987	1988	1989	1990	1991	1992	1993	1994		
INCOME STATEMENT ANALYSIS												**ANALYSE DU COMPTE DE RESULTATS**
% of average balance sheet total												**% du total moyen du bilan**
38. Interest income	4.99	4.95	4.75	4.63	5.04	6.15	6.53	6.63	5.89	4.85	38.	Produits financiers
39. Interest expenses	3.75	3.72	3.57	3.42	3.83	4.83	5.05	5.12	4.38	3.65	39.	Frais financiers
40. Net interest income	1.24	1.23	1.18	1.21	1.20	1.32	1.48	1.51	1.51	1.20	40.	Produits financiers nets
41. Non-interest income (net)	0.44	0.45	0.53	0.41	0.43	0.46	0.48	0.60	0.55	0.93	41.	Produits non financiers (nets)
42. Gross income	1.67	1.68	1.71	1.62	1.64	1.78	1.96	2.11	2.05	2.13	42.	Résultat brut
43. Operating expenses	0.96	0.99	0.96	0.95	0.94	0.94	0.94	0.95	0.92	0.87	43.	Frais d'exploitation
44. Net income	0.71	0.70	0.75	0.67	0.70	0.84	1.02	1.15	1.13	1.27	44.	Résultat net
45. Provisions (net)	0.24	0.24	0.32	0.25	0.29	0.45	0.64	0.77	0.76	0.94	45.	Provisions (nettes)
46. Profit before tax	0.47	0.45	0.43	0.42	0.40	0.39	0.38	0.38	0.37	0.33	46.	Bénéfices avant impôt
47. Income tax	0.14	0.13	0.12	0.11	0.11	0.10	0.09	0.10	0.10	0.09	47.	Impôt
48. Profit after tax	0.33	0.32	0.31	0.30	0.30	0.29	0.29	0.29	0.27	0.24	48.	Bénéfices après impôt
49. Distributed profit	0.18	0.18	0.18	0.17	0.17	0.17	0.17	0.16	0.15	0.11	49.	Bénéfices distribués
50. Retained profit	0.15	0.14	0.13	0.13	0.12	0.12	0.12	0.12	0.13	0.13	50.	Bénéfices mis en réserve
51. Staff costs	0.64	0.65	0.63	0.62	0.61	0.61	0.61	0.61	0.58	0.55	51.	Frais de personnel
52. Provisions on loans	:	:	:	:	:	:	:	:	:	:	52.	Provisions sur prêts
53. Provisions on securities	:	:	:	:	:	:	:	:	:	:	53.	Provisions sur titres
% of gross income												**% du total du résultat brut**
54. Net interest income	73.85	73.14	68.95	74.55	73.57	74.23	75.55	71.48	73.36	56.41	54.	Produits financiers nets
55. Non-interest income (net)	26.15	26.86	31.05	25.45	26.43	25.77	24.45	28.52	26.64	43.59	55.	Produits non financiers (nets)
56. Operating expenses	57.31	58.69	56.32	58.75	57.36	52.96	47.86	45.25	44.74	40.63	56.	Frais d'exploitation
57. Net income	42.69	41.31	43.68	41.25	42.64	47.04	52.14	54.75	55.26	59.37	57.	Résultat net
58. Provisions (net)	14.62	14.45	18.50	15.64	18.00	25.34	32.68	36.57	37.21	43.89	58.	Provisions (nettes)
59. Profit before tax	28.08	26.86	25.18	25.60	24.64	21.70	19.46	18.18	18.04	15.48	59.	Bénéfices avant impôt
60. Income tax	8.37	7.71	7.24	7.00	6.50	5.67	4.77	4.52	4.67	4.05	60.	Impôt
61. Profit after tax	19.71	19.15	17.94	18.60	18.14	16.03	14.69	13.66	13.38	11.43	61.	Bénéfices après impôt
62. Staff costs	38.37	38.56	36.69	38.05	37.07	34.09	31.03	28.99	28.11	25.63	62.	Frais de personnel
% of net income												**% du total du résultat net**
63. Provisions (net)	34.23	34.98	42.36	37.92	42.21	53.87	62.67	66.79	67.34	73.93	63.	Provisions (nettes)
64. Profit before tax	65.77	65.02	57.64	62.08	57.79	46.13	37.33	33.21	32.66	26.07	64.	Bénéfices avant impôt
65. Income tax	19.59	18.67	16.57	16.98	15.24	12.06	9.15	8.25	8.44	6.82	65.	Impôt
66. Profit after tax	46.17	46.35	41.07	45.09	42.55	34.08	28.18	24.95	24.21	19.25	66.	Bénéfices après impôt

SWITZERLAND

Regional and savings banks

Per cent

BALANCE SHEET ANALYSIS

% of year-end balance sheet total

SUISSE

Banques régionales et caisses d'épargne

Pourcentage

ANALYSE DU BILAN

% du total du bilan en fin d'exercice

	1985	1986	1987	1988	1989	1990	1991	1992	1993	1994	
Assets											**Actif**
67. Cash & balance with Central bank	2.13	2.09	2.03	1.39	1.25	1.19	1.21	1.27	1.13	1.06	67. Caisse & solde auprès de la Banque centrale
68. Interbank deposits	6.05	6.30	6.08	5.02	4.95	4.60	4.14	4.65	6.61	5.20	68. Dépôts interbancaires
69. Loans	79.09	79.34	79.83	81.71	82.80	83.58	84.00	83.44	81.39	82.83	69. Prêts
70. Securities	9.20	8.98	8.71	8.55	7.59	7.12	6.97	6.80	7.11	7.46	70. Valeurs mobilières
71. Other assets	3.54	3.30	3.35	3.33	3.42	3.51	3.69	3.83	3.75	3.45	71. Autres actifs
Liabilities											**Passif**
72. Capital & reserves	4.96	5.03	4.95	4.85	4.73	4.67	4.80	4.93	4.98	5.07	72. Capital et réserves
73. Borrowing from Central bank	0.71	0.88	0.77	0.29	0.16	0.12	0.47	0.06	0.10	0.09	73. Emprunts auprès de la Banque centrale
74. Interbank deposits	3.65	4.06	4.76	5.55	6.07	7.45	5.25	4.25	3.19	3.06	74. Dépôts interbancaires
75. Non-bank deposits	55.77	54.63	54.15	54.09	52.00	48.12	48.26	48.30	52.02	54.38	75. Dépôts non bancaires
76. Bonds	30.91	31.61	31.50	31.35	32.83	34.91	36.17	36.83	33.98	31.80	76. Obligations
77. Other liabilities	4.01	3.78	3.87	3.88	4.21	4.73	5.04	5.63	5.73	5.61	77. Autres engagements
Memoranda											***Pour mémoire***
78. Short-term securities	0.37	0.29	0.22	0.18	0.19	0.16	0.15	0.12	0.11	0.11	78. Titres à court terme
79. Bonds	8.28	8.14	7.91	7.80	6.76	6.36	6.12	5.96	6.26	6.60	79. Obligations
80. Shares and participations	0.54	0.55	0.59	0.57	0.63	0.60	0.70	0.72	0.75	0.75	80. Actions et participations
81. Claims on non-residents	1.56	1.51	1.38	1.21	1.15	1.10	0.90	0.82	0.89	1.06	81. Créances sur des non résidents
82. Liabilities to non-residents	1.34	1.27	1.28	1.25	1.14	1.03	0.96	1.10	1.08	1.13	82. Engagements envers des non résidents

SWITZERLAND

Loan associations and agricultural co-operative banks

SUISSE

Caisses de crédit mutuel et banques mutualistes agricoles

Million Swiss francs / Millions de francs suisses

	1985	1986	1987	1988	1989	1990	1991	1992	1993	1994	
INCOME STATEMENT											**COMPTE DE RESULTATS**
1. Interest income	960	1059	1129	1209	1422	1906	2280	2504	2466	2265	1. Produits financiers
2. Interest expenses	761	844	901	955	1137	1567	1878	2070	1978	1799	2. Frais financiers
3. Net interest income	199	215	228	254	285	339	402	434	488	466	3. Produits financiers nets
4. Non-interest income (net)	39	44	49	55	63	81	96	128	121	131	4. Produits non financiers (nets)
5. Gross income	238	259	277	309	348	420	498	562	609	597	5. Résultat brut
6. Operating expenses	146	166	183	203	230	259	291	325	359	380	6. Frais d'exploitation
7. Net income	92	93	94	106	118	161	207	237	250	217	7. Résultat net
8. Provisions (net)	36	40	42	53	64	106	146	172	179	143	8. Provisions (nettes)
9. Profit before tax	56	53	52	53	54	55	61	65	71	74	9. Bénéfices avant impôt
10. Income tax	16	16	15	16	15	18	18	21	24	27	10. Impôt
11. Profit after tax	40	37	37	37	39	37	43	44	47	47	11. Bénéfices après impôt
12. Distributed profit	4	4	4	4	5	5	5	5	6	6	12. Bénéfices distribués
13. Retained profit	36	33	33	33	34	32	38	39	41	41	13. Bénéfices mis en réserve
Memoranda											*Pour mémoire*
14. Staff costs	80	91	101	111	125	139	158	173	187	197	14. Frais de personnel
15. Provisions on loans	..	..	..	..	..	..	..	..	..	..	15. Provisions sur prêts
16. Provisions on securities	..	..	..	..	..	..	..	..	..	..	16. Provisions sur titres
BALANCE SHEET											**BILAN**
Assets											**Actif**
17. Cash & balance with Central bank	297	316	353	347	355	360	389	431	482	472	17. Caisse & solde auprès de la Banque centrale
18. Interbank deposits	2972	3305	3747	3907	3975	4266	4700	4967	5351	4817	18. Dépôts interbancaires
19. Loans	16668	18515	20310	22773	25672	28028	30286	32429	35145	38831	19. Prêts
20. Securities	143	166	168	204	223	229	229	244	244	257	20. Valeurs mobilières
21. Other assets	667	746	809	878	999	1159	1273	1368	1356	1369	21. Autres actifs
Liabilities											**Passif**
22. Capital & reserves	695	733	770	807	845	885	926	964	1019	1067	22. Capital et réserves
23. Borrowing from Central bank	-	-	-	-	-	18	20	13	13	22	23. Emprunts auprès de la Banque centrale
24. Interbank deposits	703	1153	1414	1627	2176	2352	2301	2260	2421	2794	24. Dépôts interbancaires
25. Non-bank deposits	14254	15460	17089	19034	19953	20386	21844	23487	27537	30919	25. Dépôts non bancaires
26. Bonds	4546	5121	5501	5968	7443	9301	10439	11229	10116	9584	26. Obligations
27. Other liabilities	549	581	612	674	808	1101	1347	1485	1474	1360	27. Autres engagements
Balance sheet total											**Total du bilan**
28. End-year total	20747	23048	25387	28109	31225	34042	36876	39438	42579	45747	28. En fin d'exercice
29. Average total	19805	21898	24217	26748	29667	32634	35459	38157	41009	44163	29. Moyen
Memoranda											*Pour mémoire*
30. Short-term securities	7	11	12	18	24	28	29	28	25	27	30. Titres à court terme
31. Bonds	21	20	21	18	18	20	17	20	16	11	31. Obligations
32. Shares and participations	115	135	135	167	181	181	183	197	203	219	32. Actions et participations
33. Claims on non-residents	..	..	..	..	..	..	..	..	..	..	33. Créances sur des non résidents
34. Liabilities to non-residents	..	..	..	..	..	..	..	..	..	..	34. Engagements envers des non résidents
SUPPLEMENTARY INFORMATION											**RENSEIGNEMENTS COMPLEMENTAIRES**
35. Number of institutions	2	2	2	2	2	2	2	2	2	1	35. Nombre d'institutions
36. Number of branches	1281	1243	1242	1241	1229	1213	1192	1169	1139	1086	36. Nombre de succursales
37. Number of employees (x 1000)	2.4	2.6	2.7	2.8	3.0	2.7	2.6	2.6	2.7	2.7	37. Nombre de salariés (x 1000)

SWITZERLAND

SUISSE

Loan associations and agricultural co-operative banks

Caisses de crédit mutuel et banques mutualistes agricoles

Per cent / *Pourcentage*

INCOME STATEMENT ANALYSIS / **ANALYSE DU COMPTE DE RESULTATS**

		1985	1986	1987	1988	1989	1990	1991	1992	1993	1994	
	% of average balance sheet total											**% du total moyen du bilan**
38.	Interest income	4.85	4.84	4.66	4.52	4.79	5.84	6.43	6.56	6.01	5.13	38. Produits financiers
39.	Interest expenses	3.84	3.85	3.72	3.57	3.83	4.80	5.30	5.42	4.82	4.07	39. Frais financiers
40.	Net interest income	1.00	0.98	0.94	0.95	0.96	1.04	1.13	1.14	1.19	1.06	40. Produits financiers nets
41.	Non-interest income (net)	0.20	0.20	0.20	0.21	0.21	0.25	0.27	0.34	0.30	0.30	41. Produits non financiers (nets)
42.	Gross income	1.20	1.18	1.14	1.16	1.17	1.29	1.40	1.47	1.49	1.35	42. Résultat brut
43.	Operating expenses	0.74	0.76	0.76	0.76	0.78	0.79	0.82	0.85	0.88	0.86	43. Frais d'exploitation
44.	Net income	0.46	0.42	0.39	0.40	0.40	0.49	0.58	0.62	0.61	0.49	44. Résultat net
45.	Provisions (net)	0.18	0.18	0.17	0.20	0.22	0.32	0.41	0.45	0.44	0.32	45. Provisions (nettes)
46.	Profit before tax	0.28	0.24	0.21	0.20	0.18	0.17	0.17	0.17	0.17	0.17	46. Bénéfices avant impôt
47.	Income tax	0.08	0.07	0.06	0.06	0.05	0.06	0.05	0.06	0.06	0.06	47. Impôt
48.	Profit after tax	0.20	0.17	0.15	0.14	0.13	0.11	0.12	0.12	0.11	0.11	48. Bénéfices après impôt
49.	Distributed profit	0.02	0.02	0.02	0.01	0.02	0.02	0.01	0.01	0.01	0.01	49. Bénéfices distribués
50.	Retained profit	0.18	0.15	0.14	0.12	0.11	0.10	0.11	0.10	0.10	0.09	50. Bénéfices mis en réserve
51.	Staff costs	0.40	0.42	0.42	0.41	0.42	0.43	0.45	0.45	0.46	0.45	51. Frais de personnel
52.	Provisions on loans	:	:	:	:	:	:	:	:	:	:	52. Provisions sur prêts
53.	Provisions on securities	:	:	:	:	:	:	:	:	:	:	53. Provisions sur titres
	% of gross income											**% du total du résultat brut**
54.	Net interest income	83.61	83.01	82.31	82.20	81.90	80.71	80.72	77.22	80.13	78.06	54. Produits financiers nets
55.	Non-interest income (net)	16.39	16.99	17.69	17.80	18.10	19.29	19.28	22.78	19.87	21.94	55. Produits non financiers (nets)
56.	Operating expenses	61.34	64.09	66.06	65.70	66.09	61.67	58.43	57.83	58.95	63.65	56. Frais d'exploitation
57.	Net income	38.66	35.91	33.94	34.30	33.91	38.33	41.57	42.17	41.05	36.35	57. Résultat net
58.	Provisions (net)	15.13	15.44	15.16	17.15	18.39	25.24	29.32	30.60	29.39	23.95	58. Provisions (nettes)
59.	Profit before tax	23.53	20.46	18.77	17.15	15.52	13.10	12.25	11.57	11.66	12.40	59. Bénéfices avant impôt
60.	Income tax	6.72	6.18	5.42	5.18	4.31	4.29	3.61	3.74	3.94	4.52	60. Impôt
61.	Profit after tax	16.81	14.29	13.36	11.97	11.21	8.81	8.63	7.83	7.72	7.87	61. Bénéfices après impôt
62.	Staff costs	33.61	35.14	36.46	35.92	35.92	33.10	31.73	30.78	30.71	33.00	62. Frais de personnel
	% of net income											**% du total du résultat net**
63.	Provisions (net)	39.13	43.01	44.68	50.00	54.24	65.84	70.53	72.57	71.60	65.90	63. Provisions (nettes)
64.	Profit before tax	60.87	56.99	55.32	50.00	45.76	34.16	29.47	27.43	28.40	34.10	64. Bénéfices avant impôt
65.	Income tax	17.39	17.20	15.96	15.09	12.71	11.18	8.70	8.86	9.60	12.44	65. Impôt
66.	Profit after tax	43.48	39.78	39.36	34.91	33.05	22.98	20.77	18.57	18.80	21.66	66. Bénéfices après impôt

SWITZERLAND

Loan associations and agricultural co-operative banks

SUISSE

Caisses de crédit mutuel et banques mutualistes agricoles

Per cent	1985	1986	1987	1988	1989	1990	1991	1992	1993	1994		Pourcentage
BALANCE SHEET ANALYSIS												**ANALYSE DU BILAN**
% of year-end balance sheet total												**% du total du bilan en fin d'exercice**
Assets												**Actif**
67. Cash & balance with Central bank	1.43	1.37	1.39	1.23	1.14	1.06	1.05	1.09	1.13	1.03	67.	Caisse & solde auprès de la Banque centrale
68. Interbank deposits	14.32	14.34	14.76	13.90	12.73	12.53	12.75	12.59	12.57	10.53	68.	Dépôts interbancaires
69. Loans	80.34	80.33	80.00	81.02	82.22	82.33	82.13	82.23	82.54	84.88	69.	Prêts
70. Securities	0.69	0.72	0.66	0.73	0.71	0.67	0.62	0.62	0.57	0.56	70.	Valeurs mobilières
71. Other assets	3.21	3.24	3.19	3.12	3.20	3.40	3.45	3.47	3.18	2.99	71.	Autres actifs
Liabilities												**Passif**
72. Capital & reserves	3.35	3.18	3.03	2.87	2.71	2.60	2.51	2.44	2.39	2.33	72.	Capital et réserves
73. Borrowing from Central bank	-	-	-	-	-	0.05	0.05	0.03	0.03	0.05	73.	Emprunts auprès de la Banque centrale
74. Interbank deposits	3.39	5.00	5.57	5.79	6.97	6.91	6.24	5.73	5.69	6.11	74.	Dépôts interbancaires
75. Non-bank deposits	68.70	67.08	67.31	67.71	63.90	59.88	59.24	59.55	64.67	67.59	75.	Dépôts non bancaires
76. Bonds	21.91	22.22	21.67	21.23	23.84	27.32	28.31	28.47	23.76	20.95	76.	Obligations
77. Other liabilities	2.65	2.52	2.41	2.40	2.59	3.23	3.65	3.77	3.46	2.97	77.	Autres engagements
Memoranda												*Pour mémoire*
78. Short-term securities	*0.03*	*0.05*	*0.05*	*0.06*	*0.08*	*0.08*	*0.08*	*0.07*	*0.06*	*0.06*	*78.*	*Titres à court terme*
79. Bonds	*0.10*	*0.09*	*0.08*	*0.06*	*0.06*	*0.06*	*0.05*	*0.05*	*0.04*	*0.02*	*79.*	*Obligations*
80. Shares and participations	*0.55*	*0.59*	*0.53*	*0.59*	*0.58*	*0.53*	*0.50*	*0.50*	*0.48*	*0.48*	*80.*	*Actions et participations*
81. Claims on non-residents	*..*	*..*	*..*	*..*	*..*	*..*	*..*	*..*	*..*	*..*	*81.*	*Créances sur des non résidents*
82. Liabilities to non-residents	*..*	*..*	*..*	*..*	*..*	*..*	*..*	*..*	*..*	*..*	*82.*	*Engagements envers des non résidents*

181

TURKEY

Commercial banks

Billion Turkish liras

TURQUIE

Banques commerciales

Milliards de livres turques

English	1985	1986	1987	1988	1989	1990	1991	1992	1993	1994	Français
INCOME STATEMENT											**COMPTE DE RESULTATS**
1. Interest income	2609	4317	6314	12165	20232	33243	63597	117540	207330	514052	1. Produits financiers
2. Interest expenses	2386	3437	4482	9177	17250	23803	42282	78163	121951	339317	2. Frais financiers
3. Net interest income	223	880	1832	2988	2982	9440	21315	39377	85379	174735	3. Produits financiers nets
4. Non-interest income (net)	229	185	417	1098	2854	1963	-1956	-2471	-14022	-50508	4. Produits non financiers (nets)
5. Gross income	452	1065	2249	4086	5836	11403	19359	36906	71357	124227	5. Résultat brut
6. Operating expenses	346	534	855	1658	3014	5943	10896	20146	34504	60869	6. Frais d'exploitation
7. Net income	106	531	1394	2428	2822	5460	8463	16760	36853	63358	7. Résultat net
8. Provisions (net)	39	128	498	841	947	1341	2430	2073	6785	21187	8. Provisions (nettes)
9. Profit before tax	67	403	896	1587	1875	4119	6033	14687	30068	42171	9. Bénéfices avant impôt
10. Income tax	24	50	81	185	406	637	804	2134	6254	8765	10. Impôt
11. Profit after tax	43	353	815	1402	1469	3482	5229	12553	23814	33406	11. Bénéfices après impôt
12. Distributed profit	54	163	321	695	762	1788	2399	3848	9907	17719	12. Bénéfices distribués
13. Retained profit	-11	190	494	707	707	1694	2830	8705	13907	15687	13. Bénéfices mis en réserve
Memoranda											*Pour mémoire*
14. Staff costs	286	433	684	1313	2420	4820	8353	15507	24943	42159	14. Frais de personnel
15. Provisions on loans	-	119	438	654	671	861	1772	1438	3647	10954	15. Provisions sur prêts
16. Provisions on securities	-	-	-	-	-	7	142	40	331	92	16. Provisions sur titres
BALANCE SHEET											**BILAN**
Assets											**Actif**
17. Cash & balance with Central bank	1317	2143	3984	5331	7340	10349	16911	29766	54533	104892	17. Caisse & solde auprès de la Banque centrale
18. Interbank deposits	1615	2415	3375	8037	9733	14701	32039	85047	201809	316511	18. Dépôts interbancaires
19. Loans	6080	10378	16989	24496	38904	68887	111813	206434	388218	693028	19. Prêts
20. Securities	1458	2279	4180	6987	12476	17111	34283	60357	112829	218776	20. Valeurs mobilières
21. Other assets	4395	6042	9702	16701	28229	41544	74912	128810	216203	521056	21. Autres actifs
Liabilities											**Passif**
22. Capital & reserves	677	726	1407	2793	4517	6999	13635	23960	46326	83617	22. Capital et réserves
23. Borrowing from Central bank	450	657	2033	2538	3088	3129	4013	8003	16969	12319	23. Emprunts auprès de la Banque centrale
24. Interbank deposits	244	1375	1984	3222	4262	6837	8259	20435	78412	50306	24. Dépôts interbancaires
25. Non-bank deposits	8627	14452	22128	35111	58141	88726	160595	285234	466751	1224806	25. Dépôts non bancaires
26. Bonds	7	7	7	54	389	413	704	6187	24525	16615	26. Obligations
27. Other liabilities	4859	6040	10671	17834	26285	46488	82752	166595	340609	466600	27. Autres engagements
Balance sheet total											**Total du bilan**
28. End-year total	14865	23257	38230	61552	96682	152592	269958	510414	973592	1854263	28. En fin d'exercice
29. Average total	11947	19061	30744	49891	79117	124637	211275	390186	742003	1413928	29. Moyen
Memoranda											*Pour mémoire*
30. Short-term securities	1073	1627	2611	3961	9417	12579	19296	41965	90302	106754	30. Titres à court terme
31. Bonds	257	355	706	1305	2666	4081	6370	11096	18116	34325	31. Obligations
32. Shares and participations	26	1635	2351	6848	9208	13931	36108	81980	162573	393540	32. Actions et participations
33. Claims on non-residents	36	1015	2192	3578	5040	12821	22428	55466	144014	126322	33. Créances sur des non résidents
34. Liabilities to non-residents											34. Engagements envers des non résidents
SUPPLEMENTARY INFORMATION											**RENSEIGNEMENTS COMPLÉMENTAIRES**
35. Number of institutions	48	50	51	53	53	56	56	58	59	55	35. Nombre d'institutions
36. Number of branches	6259	6338	6407	6517	6579	6543	6463	6188	6208	6085	36. Nombre de succursales
37. Number of employees (x 1000)	136.3	141.8	147.3	149.4	151.1	152.0	150.8	144.6	141.7	136.8	37. Nombre de salariés (x 1000)

TURKEY

Commercial banks

TURQUIE

Banques commerciales

Per cent	1985	1986	1987	1988	1989	1990	1991	1992	1993	1994	*Pourcentage*	
INCOME STATEMENT ANALYSIS											**ANALYSE DU COMPTE DE RESULTATS**	
% of average balance sheet total											**% du total moyen du bilan**	
38. Interest income	21.84	22.65	20.54	24.38	25.57	26.67	30.10	30.12	27.94	36.36	38. Produits financiers	
39. Interest expenses	19.97	18.03	14.58	18.39	21.80	19.10	20.01	20.03	16.44	24.00	39. Frais financiers	
40. Net interest income	1.87	4.62	5.96	5.99	3.77	7.57	10.09	10.09	11.51	12.36	40. Produits financiers nets	
41. Non-interest income (net)	1.92	0.97	1.36	2.20	3.61	1.57	-0.93	-0.63	-1.89	-3.57	41. Produits non financiers (nets)	
42. Gross income	3.78	5.59	7.32	8.19	7.38	9.15	9.16	9.46	9.62	8.79	42. Résultat brut	
43. Operating expenses	2.90	2.80	2.78	3.32	3.81	4.77	5.16	5.16	4.65	4.30	43. Frais d'exploitation	
44. Net income	0.89	2.79	4.53	4.87	3.57	4.38	4.01	4.30	4.97	4.48	44. Résultat net	
45. Provisions (net)	0.33	0.67	1.62	1.69	1.20	1.08	1.15	0.53	0.91	1.50	45. Provisions (nettes)	
46. Profit before tax	0.56	2.11	2.91	3.18	2.37	3.30	2.86	3.76	4.05	2.98	46. Bénéfices avant impôt	
47. Income tax	0.20	0.26	0.26	0.37	0.51	0.51	0.38	0.55	0.84	0.62	47. Impôt	
48. Profit after tax	0.36	1.85	2.65	2.81	1.86	2.79	2.47	3.22	3.21	2.36	48. Bénéfices après impôt	
49. Distributed profit	0.45	0.86	1.04	1.39	0.96	1.43	1.14	0.99	1.34	1.25	49. Bénéfices distribués	
50. Retained profit	-0.09	1.00	1.61	1.42	0.89	1.36	1.34	2.23	1.87	1.11	50. Bénéfices mis en réserve	
51. Staff costs	2.39	2.27	2.22	2.63	3.06	3.87	3.95	3.97	3.36	2.98	51. Frais de personnel	
52. Provisions on loans	.	0.62	1.42	1.31	0.85	0.69	0.84	0.37	0.49	0.77	52. Provisions sur prêts	
53. Provisions on securities	.	.	.	.	.	0.01	0.07	0.01	0.04	0.01	53. Provisions sur titres	
% of gross income											**% du total du résultat brut**	
54. Net interest income	49.34	82.63	81.46	73.13	51.10	82.79	110.10	106.70	119.65	140.66	54. Produits financiers nets	
55. Non-interest income (net)	50.66	17.37	18.54	26.87	48.90	17.21	-10.10	-6.70	-19.65	-40.66	55. Produits non financiers (nets)	
56. Operating expenses	76.55	50.14	38.02	40.58	51.64	52.12	56.28	54.59	48.35	49.00	56. Frais d'exploitation	
57. Net income	23.45	49.86	61.98	59.42	48.36	47.88	43.72	45.41	51.65	51.00	57. Résultat net	
58. Provisions (net)	8.63	12.02	22.14	20.58	16.23	11.76	12.55	5.62	9.51	17.06	58. Provisions (nettes)	
59. Profit before tax	14.82	37.84	39.84	38.84	32.13	36.12	31.16	39.80	42.14	33.95	59. Bénéfices avant impôt	
60. Income tax	5.31	4.69	3.60	4.53	6.96	5.59	4.15	5.78	8.76	7.06	60. Impôt	
61. Profit after tax	9.51	33.15	36.24	34.31	25.17	30.54	27.01	34.01	33.37	26.89	61. Bénéfices après impôt	
62. Staff costs	63.27	40.66	30.41	32.13	41.47	42.27	43.15	42.02	34.96	33.94	62. Frais de personnel	
% of net income											**% du total du résultat net**	
63. Provisions (net)	36.79	24.11	35.72	34.64	33.56	24.56	28.71	12.37	18.41	33.44	63. Provisions (nettes)	
64. Profit before tax	63.21	75.89	64.28	65.36	66.44	75.44	71.29	87.63	81.59	66.56	64. Bénéfices avant impôt	
65. Income tax	22.64	9.42	5.81	7.62	14.39	11.67	9.50	12.73	16.97	13.83	65. Impôt	
66. Profit after tax	40.57	66.48	58.46	57.74	52.06	63.77	61.79	74.90	64.62	52.73	66. Bénéfices après impôt	

TURKEY

Commercial banks

Per cent

BALANCE SHEET ANALYSIS

% of year-end balance sheet total

	1985	1986	1987	1988	1989	1990	1991	1992	1993	1994
Assets										
67. Cash & balance with Central bank	8.86	9.21	10.42	8.66	7.59	6.78	6.26	5.83	5.60	5.66
68. Interbank deposits	10.86	10.38	8.83	13.06	10.07	9.63	11.87	16.66	20.73	17.07
69. Loans	40.90	44.62	44.44	39.80	40.24	45.14	41.42	40.44	39.87	37.37
70. Securities	9.81	9.80	10.93	11.35	12.90	11.21	12.70	11.83	11.59	11.80
71. Other assets	29.57	25.98	25.38	27.13	29.20	27.23	27.75	25.24	22.21	28.10
Liabilities										
72. Capital & reserves	4.55	3.12	3.68	4.54	4.67	4.59	5.05	4.69	4.76	4.51
73. Borrowing from Central bank	3.03	2.82	5.32	4.12	3.19	2.05	1.49	1.57	1.74	0.66
74. Interbank deposits	1.64	5.91	5.19	5.23	4.41	4.48	3.06	4.00	8.05	2.71
75. Non-bank deposits	58.04	62.14	57.88	57.04	60.14	58.15	59.49	55.88	47.94	66.05
76. Bonds	0.05	0.03	0.02	0.09	0.40	0.27	0.26	1.21	2.52	0.90
77. Other liabilities	32.69	25.97	27.91	28.97	27.19	30.47	30.65	32.64	34.98	25.16
Memoranda										
78. Short-term securities	*..*	*..*	*..*	*..*	*..*	*..*	*..*	*..*	*..*	*..*
79. Bonds	*7.22*	*7.00*	*6.83*	*6.44*	*9.74*	*8.24*	*7.15*	*8.22*	*9.28*	*5.76*
80. Shares and participations	*1.73*	*1.53*	*1.85*	*2.12*	*2.76*	*2.67*	*2.36*	*2.17*	*1.86*	*1.85*
81. Claims on non-residents	*0.17*	*7.03*	*6.15*	*11.13*	*9.52*	*9.13*	*13.38*	*16.06*	*16.70*	*21.22*
82. Liabilities to non-residents	*0.24*	*4.36*	*5.73*	*5.81*	*5.21*	*8.40*	*8.31*	*10.87*	*14.79*	*6.81*

TURQUIE

Banques commerciales

Pourcentage

ANALYSE DU BILAN

% du total du bilan en fin d'exercice

Actif
67. Caisse & solde auprès de la Banque centrale
68. Dépôts interbancaires
69. Prêts
70. Valeurs mobilières
71. Autres actifs

Passif
72. Capital et réserves
73. Emprunts auprès de la Banque centrale
74. Dépôts interbancaires
75. Dépôts non bancaires
76. Obligations
77. Autres engagements

Pour mémoire
78. Titres à court terme
79. Obligations
80. Actions et participations
81. Créances sur des non résidents
82. Engagements envers des non résidents

Notes

- The category Commercial banks covers all commercial banks operating in Turkey including branches of foreign banks and foreign banks established in Turkey, and, since 1986, foreign branches of domestic banks.

Change in methodology

- Iller Bankasi, although not being a full commercial bank, is included in the data until end-1988.
- Until 1986, "Interest income" (item 1) includes interest paid by the Central bank on required reserves for Turkish lira denominated deposits.
- "Operating expenses" (item 6) do not include rents for the year 1985.

Notes

- La catégorie "Banques commerciales" regroupe toutes les banques commerciales en activité en Turquie y compris les filiales de banques étrangères ainsi que les banques étrangères basées en Turquie, et, depuis 1986, les filiales étrangères des banques domestiques.

Changement méthodologique :

- Jusqu'en fin 1988, Iller Bankasi, bien que celle-ci ne soit pas à tous égards une banque commerciale, est incluse dans les données.
- Jusqu'en 1986 les "Produits financiers" (poste 1) couvrent la rémunération par la Banque centrale des réserves obligatoires assises sur les dépôts en livres turques.
- Les "Frais d'exploitation" (poste 6) ne comprennent pas les loyers pour l'année 1985.

UNITED KINGDOM / ROYAUME-UNI

Commercial banks / Banques commerciales

Million pounds sterling / Millions de livres sterling

	Item (EN)	Item (FR)	1985	1986	1987	1988	1989	1990	1991	1992	1993	1994
	INCOME STATEMENT	**COMPTE DE RESULTATS**										
1.	Interest income	Produits financiers	31941	31684	34363	39998	56101	63140	57737	52004	44836	43005
2.	Interest expenses	Frais financiers	22544	21607	23124	27121	41736	48286	42199	36550	28463	26490
3.	Net interest income	Produits financiers nets	9397	10077	11239	12877	14365	14854	15538	15454	16373	16515
4.	Non-interest income (net)	Produits non financiers (nets)	4951	5750	6710	7300	8772	9474	10645	11407	13113	12539
5.	Gross income	Résultat brut	14348	15827	17949	20177	23137	24328	26183	26861	29486	29054
6.	Operating expenses	Frais d'exploitation	9378	10319	11583	13159	14977	16021	17197	17761	18622	18619
7.	Net income	Résultat net	4970	5508	6366	7018	8160	8307	8986	9100	10864	10435
8.	Provisions (net)	Provisions (nettes)	1676	1733	5382	1228	7325	4766	6885	7298	5814	2349
9.	Profit before tax	Bénéfices avant impôt	3294	3775	984	5790	835	3541	2101	1802	5050	8086
10.	Income tax	Impôt	1488	1345	763	2113	550	1630	872	997	1847	2709
11.	Profit after tax	Bénéfices après impôt	1806	2430	221	3677	285	1911	1229	805	3203	5377
12.	Distributed profit	Bénéfices distribués	450	576	710	949	1201	1262	1273	1238	1838	2188
13.	Retained profit	Bénéfices mis en réserve	1356	1854	-489	2728	-916	649	-44	-433	1365	3189
	Memoranda	*Pour mémoire*										
14.	*Staff costs*	*Frais de personnel*	*5612*	*6167*	*6749*	*7719*	*8658*	*9114*	*9519*	*9704*	*10272*	*10434*
15.	*Provisions on loans*	*Provisions sur prêts*	..	..	..	..	..	..	..	..	..	..
16.	*Provisions on securities*	*Provisions sur titres*	..	..	..	..	..	..	..	..	..	..
	BALANCE SHEET	**BILAN**										
	Assets	**Actif**										
17.	Cash & balance with Central bank	Caisse & solde auprès de la Banque centrale	5879	6091	5864	6107	7433	7249	7057	5191	5252	5152
18.	Interbank deposits	Dépôts interbancaires	62873	70466	72308	77191	79191	80039	79774	87921	102950	113393
19.	Loans	Prêts	179618	191201	219420	257865	306456	319817	322240	376505	376115	375285
20.	Securities	Valeurs mobilières	20347	23878	28987	27986	34189	38401	45448	84290	110735	126055
21.	Other assets	Autres actifs	33133	42994	43463	52112	65416	69913	77832	92946	95074	102008
	Liabilities	**Passif**										
22.	Capital & reserves	Capital et réserves	13632	17506	19791	23833	24728	24614	24440	24518	26228	29520
23.	Borrowing from Central bank	Emprunts auprès de la Banque centrale	-	-	-	-	-	-	-	-	-	-
24.	Interbank deposits (1)	Dépôts interbancaires (1)										
25.	Non-bank deposits	Dépôts non bancaires	269036	290594	326047	366372	429820	453145	465404	476173	493912	502948
26.	Bonds	Obligations	10495	12677	11230	13941	16778	15077	16616	62101	75112	82619
27.	Other liabilities	Autres engagements	8687	13853	12974	17115	21359	22583	25891	84062	94875	106806
	Balance sheet total	**Total du bilan**										
28.	End-year total	En fin d'exercice	301850	334630	370042	421261	492685	515419	532351	646854	690127	721892
29.	Average total	Moyen	302233	318240	352336	395652	456973	504052	523885	589603	668491	706010
	Memoranda	*Pour mémoire*										
30.	*Short-term securities*	*Titres à court terme*	*5639*	*5993*	*8709*	*10718*	*15405*	*16403*	*17458*	*16519*	*21699*	*25498*
31.	*Bonds*	*Obligations*	..	..	..	..	..	..	..	..	..	..
32.	*Shares and participations*	*Actions et participations*	..	..	..	..	..	..	..	..	..	..
33.	*Claims on non-residents*	*Créances sur des non résidents*	..	..	..	..	..	..	..	..	..	..
34.	*Liabilities to non-residents*	*Engagements envers des non résidents*	..	..	..	..	..	..	..	..	..	..
	SUPPLEMENTARY INFORMATION	**RENSEIGNEMENTS COMPLEMENTAIRES**										
35.	Number of institutions	Nombre d'institutions	54	53	53	52	49	47	41	39	37	37
36.	Number of branches	Nombre de succursales	13615	13332	13813	13702	13467	12994	12306	11751	11445	11075
37.	Number of employees (x 1000)	Nombre de salariés (x 1000)	340.0	350.0	374.6	402.6	414.2	411.5	399.9	401.2	371.7	359.4

Per cent / *Pourcentage*

INCOME STATEMENT ANALYSIS / **ANALYSE DU COMPTE DE RESULTATS**

	1985	1986	1987	1988	1989	1990	1991	1992	1993	1994		
% of average balance sheet total												**% du total moyen du bilan**
38. Interest income	10.57	9.96	9.75	10.11	12.28	12.53	11.02	8.82	6.71	6.09	38.	Produits financiers
39. Interest expenses	7.46	6.79	6.56	6.85	9.13	9.58	8.06	6.20	4.26	3.75	39.	Frais financiers
40. Net interest income	3.11	3.17	3.19	3.25	3.14	2.95	2.97	2.62	2.45	2.34	40.	Produits financiers nets
41. Non-interest income (net)	1.64	1.81	1.90	1.85	1.92	1.88	2.03	1.93	1.96	1.78	41.	Produits non financiers (nets)
42. Gross income	4.75	4.97	5.09	5.10	5.06	4.83	5.00	4.56	4.41	4.12	42.	Résultat brut
43. Operating expenses	3.10	3.24	3.29	3.33	3.28	3.18	3.28	3.01	2.79	2.64	43.	Frais d'exploitation
44. Net income	1.64	1.73	1.81	1.77	1.79	1.65	1.72	1.54	1.63	1.48	44.	Résultat net
45. Provisions (net)	0.55	0.54	1.53	0.31	1.60	0.95	1.31	1.24	0.87	0.33	45.	Provisions (nettes)
46. Profit before tax	1.09	1.19	0.28	1.46	0.18	0.70	0.40	0.31	0.76	1.15	46.	Bénéfices avant impôt
47. Income tax	0.49	0.42	0.22	0.53	0.12	0.32	0.17	0.17	0.28	0.38	47.	Impôt
48. Profit after tax	0.60	0.76	0.06	0.93	0.06	0.38	0.23	0.14	0.48	0.76	48.	Bénéfices après impôt
49. Distributed profit	0.15	0.18	0.20	0.24	0.26	0.25	0.24	0.21	0.27	0.31	49.	Bénéfices distribués
50. Retained profit	0.45	0.58	-0.14	0.69	-0.20	0.13	-0.01	-0.07	0.20	0.45	50.	Bénéfices mis en réserve
51. Staff costs	1.86	1.94	1.92	1.95	1.89	1.81	1.82	1.65	1.54	1.48	51.	Frais de personnel
52. Provisions on loans	:	:	:	:	:	:	:	:	:	:	52.	Provisions sur prêts
53. Provisions on securities	:	:	:	:	:	:	:	:	:	:	53.	Provisions sur titres
% of gross income												**% du total du résultat brut**
54. Net interest income	65.49	63.67	62.62	63.82	62.09	61.06	59.34	57.53	55.53	56.84	54.	Produits financiers nets
55. Non-interest income (net)	34.51	36.33	37.38	36.18	37.91	38.94	40.66	42.47	44.47	43.16	55.	Produits non financiers (nets)
56. Operating expenses	65.36	65.20	64.53	65.22	64.73	65.85	65.68	66.12	63.16	64.08	56.	Frais d'exploitation
57. Net income	34.64	34.80	35.47	34.78	35.27	34.15	34.32	33.88	36.84	35.92	57.	Résultat net
58. Provisions (net)	11.68	10.95	29.98	6.09	31.66	19.59	26.30	27.17	19.72	8.08	58.	Provisions (nettes)
59. Profit before tax	22.96	23.85	5.48	28.70	3.61	14.56	8.02	6.71	17.13	27.83	59.	Bénéfices avant impôt
60. Income tax	10.37	8.50	4.25	10.47	2.38	6.70	3.33	3.71	6.26	9.32	60.	Impôt
61. Profit after tax	12.59	15.35	1.23	18.22	1.23	7.86	4.69	3.00	10.86	18.51	61.	Bénéfices après impôt
62. Staff costs	39.11	38.97	37.60	38.26	37.42	37.46	36.36	36.13	34.84	35.91	62.	Frais de personnel
% of net income												**% du total du résultat net**
63. Provisions (net)	33.72	31.46	84.54	17.50	89.77	57.37	76.62	80.20	53.52	22.51	63.	Provisions (nettes)
64. Profit before tax	66.28	68.54	15.46	82.50	10.23	42.63	23.38	19.80	46.48	77.49	64.	Bénéfices avant impôt
65. Income tax	29.94	24.42	11.99	30.11	6.74	19.62	9.70	10.96	17.00	25.96	65.	Impôt
66. Profit after tax	36.34	44.12	3.47	52.39	3.49	23.00	13.68	8.85	29.48	51.53	66.	Bénéfices après impôt

UNITED KINGDOM

Commercial banks

ROYAUME-UNI

Banques commerciales

Per cent — *Pourcentage*

BALANCE SHEET ANALYSIS — **ANALYSE DU BILAN**

% of year-end balance sheet total — % du total du bilan en fin d'exercice

	1985	1986	1987	1988	1989	1990	1991	1992	1993	1994	
Assets											**Actif**
67. Cash & balance with Central bank	1.95	1.82	1.58	1.45	1.51	1.41	1.33	0.80	0.76	0.71	67. Caisse & solde auprès de la Banque centrale
68. Interbank deposits	20.83	21.06	19.54	18.32	16.07	15.53	14.99	13.59	14.92	15.71	68. Dépôts interbancaires
69. Loans	59.51	57.14	59.30	61.21	62.20	62.05	60.53	58.21	54.50	51.99	69. Prêts
70. Securities	6.74	7.14	7.83	6.64	6.94	7.45	8.54	13.03	16.05	17.46	70. Valeurs mobilières
71. Other assets	10.98	12.85	11.75	12.37	13.28	13.56	14.62	14.37	13.78	14.13	71. Autres actifs
Liabilities											**Passif**
72. Capital & reserves	4.52	5.23	5.35	5.66	5.02	4.78	4.59	3.79	3.80	4.09	72. Capital et réserves
73. Borrowing from Central bank	-	-	-	..	-	-	-	-	-	-	73. Emprunts auprès de la Banque centrale
74. Interbank deposits (1)	..	..	..	..	..	..	..	..	..	..	74. Dépôts interbancaires (1)
75. Non-bank deposits	89.13	86.84	88.11	86.97	87.24	87.92	87.42	73.61	71.57	69.67	75. Dépôts non bancaires
76. Bonds	3.48	3.79	3.03	3.31	3.41	2.93	3.12	9.60	10.88	11.44	76. Obligations
77. Other liabilities	2.88	4.14	3.51	4.06	4.34	4.38	4.86	13.00	13.75	14.80	77. Autres engagements
Memoranda											*Pour mémoire*
78. Short-term securities	*1.87*	*1.79*	*2.35*	*2.54*	*3.13*	*3.18*	*3.28*	*2.55*	*3.14*	*3.53*	*78. Titres à court terme*
79. Bonds	*..*	*..*	*..*	*..*	*..*	*..*	*..*	*..*	*..*	*..*	*79. Obligations*
80. Shares and participations	*..*	*..*	*..*	*..*	*..*	*..*	*..*	*..*	*..*	*..*	*80. Actions et participations*
81. Claims on non-residents	*..*	*..*	*..*	*..*	*..*	*..*	*..*	*..*	*..*	*..*	*81. Créances sur des non résidents*
82. Liabilities to non-residents	*..*	*..*	*..*	*..*	*..*	*..*	*..*	*..*	*..*	*..*	*82. Engagements envers des non résidents*

1. Included under "Non-bank deposits" (item 25 or item 75).

1. Inclus sous "Dépôts non bancaires" (poste 25 ou poste 75).

Change in methodology:

• As from 1987 data include Abbey National Plc.
• As from 1992, due to revised reporting requirements, balance-sheet data include long-term assurance funds.

Changement méthodologique :

• A compter de 1987 les données incluent Abbey National Plc.
• A compter de 1992, suite aux révisions du règlement en vigueur, les données de bilan comprennent les fonds d'assurance à long terme.

UNITED STATES

Commercial banks (1)

Million US dollars

	1985	1986	1987	1988	1989	1990	1991	1992	1993	1994	
INCOME STATEMENT											**COMPTE DE RESULTATS**
1. Interest income	248388	239084	245089	274144	317075	320185	289853	257037	244892	257419	1. Produits financiers
2. Interest expenses	157451	143741	145166	166345	205094	204822	167848	122788	105671	110963	2. Frais financiers
3. Net interest income	90937	95343	99923	107799	111981	115363	122005	134249	139221	146456	3. Produits financiers nets
4. Non-interest income (net)	33093	40660	43581	46822	52737	56868	64790	71367	80740	76616	4. Produits non financiers (nets)
5. Gross income	124030	136003	143504	154621	164718	172231	186795	205616	219961	223072	5. Résultat brut
6. Operating expenses	82644	91096	97857	103062	108995	116559	126050	133143	140602	145051	6. Frais d'exploitation
7. Net income	41386	44907	45647	51559	55723	55672	60745	72473	79359	78021	7. Résultat net
8. Provisions (net)	17857	22356	37891	19777	31304	32275	34868	26866	16843	10972	8. Provisions (nettes)
9. Profit before tax	23529	22551	7756	31782	24419	23397	25877	45607	62516	67049	9. Bénéfices avant impôt
10. Income tax	5667	5333	5431	10009	9577	7811	8506	14320	19574	22435	10. Impôt
11. Profit after tax	17862	17218	2325	21773	14842	15586	17371	31287	42942	44614	11. Bénéfices après impôt
12. Distributed profit	8530	9224	10659	13275	14113	13944	15080	14235	22069	28178	12. Bénéfices distribués
13. Retained profit	9332	7994	-8334	8498	729	1642	2291	17052	20873	16436	13. Bénéfices mis en réserve
Memoranda											*Pour mémoire*
14. Staff costs	*40128*	*43327*	*45405*	*47134*	*49414*	*52082*	*53597*	*55625*	*58538*	*60988*	14. Frais de personnel
15. Provisions on loans	*17857*	*22356*	*37891*	*19777*	*31304*	*32275*	*34868*	*26866*	*16843*	*10972*	15. Provisions sur prêts
16. Provisions on securities	*:*	*:*	*:*	*:*	*:*	*:*	*:*	*:*	*:*	*:*	16. Provisions sur titres
BALANCE SHEET											**BILAN**
Assets											**Actif**
17. Cash & balance with Central bank	156101	179367	154880	167862	174867	176071	162506	161666	153820	172987	17. Caisse & solde auprès de la Banque centrale
18. Interbank deposits	181394	197332	200667	185022	172718	139029	140460	135538	118416	129661	18. Dépôts interbancaires
19. Loans	1737530	1861879	1904215	2006638	2143235	2191118	2139564	2130386	2241077	2443469	19. Prêts
20. Securities	477907	525310	551286	569295	598208	648779	754068	846730	950561	911270	20. Valeurs mobilières
21. Other assets	169785	167379	178878	190705	197382	217963	221387	218966	227321	332033	21. Autres actifs
Liabilities											**Passif**
22. Capital & reserves	168481	181342	180158	195938	204128	217681	230709	262502	295481	311025	22. Capital et réserves
23. Borrowing from Central bank	:	:	:	:	:	:	:	:	:	:	23. Emprunts auprès de la Banque centrale
24. Interbank deposits	181102	184033	185356	161736	157303	134022	148140	134277	141268	170826	24. Dépôts interbancaires
25. Non-bank deposits	1928691	2088617	2139784	2258365	2377617	2498605	2525507	2548592	2596838	2683208	25. Dépôts non bancaires
26. Bonds	14585	16886	17515	16769	19618	23737	24850	33521	37148	40580	26. Obligations
27. Other liabilities	429858	460390	467114	486714	527743	498915	488779	514395	620460	783781	27. Autres engagements
Balance sheet total											**Total du bilan**
28. End-year total	2722717	2931267	2988926	3119522	3286410	3372960	3417985	3493286	3691195	3989420	28. En fin d'exercice
29. Average total	2572329	2775382	2921866	3047722	3186517	3338084	3379166	3441968	3566580	3863454	29. Moyen
Memoranda											*Pour mémoire*
30. Short-term securities	*:*	*:*	*:*	*:*	*:*	*:*	*:*	*:*	*:*	*:*	30. Titres à court terme
31. Bonds	*:*	*:*	*:*	*:*	*:*	*:*	*:*	*:*	*:*	*:*	31. Obligations
32. Shares and participations	*:*	*:*	*:*	*:*	*:*	*:*	*:*	*:*	*:*	*:*	32. Actions et participations
33. Claims on non-residents	*:*	*:*	*:*	*:*	*:*	*:*	*:*	*:*	*:*	*:*	33. Créances sur des non résidents
34. Liabilities to non-residents	*:*	*:*	*:*	*:*	*:*	*:*	*:*	*:*	*:*	*:*	34. Engagements envers des non résidents
SUPPLEMENTARY INFORMATION											**RENSEIGNEMENTS COMPLEMENTAIRES**
35. Number of institutions	14393	14191	13705	13130	12727	12369	11949	11496	11001	10489	35. Nombre d'institutions
36. Number of branches	42620	43637	44753	45878	47390	49885	51514	52290	53123	55573	36. Nombre de succursales
37. Number of employees (x 1000)	1558	1558	1543	1525	1529	1513	1484	1475	1490	1482	37. Nombre de salariés (x 1000)

UNITED STATES

Commercial banks (1)

ETATS-UNIS

Banques commerciales (1)

Per cent / Pourcentage

	1985	1986	1987	1988	1989	1990	1991	1992	1993	1994	
INCOME STATEMENT ANALYSIS											**ANALYSE DU COMPTE DE RESULTATS**
% of average balance sheet total											**% du total moyen du bilan**
38. Interest income	9.66	8.61	8.39	9.00	9.95	9.59	8.58	7.47	6.87	6.66	38. Produits financiers
39. Interest expenses	6.12	5.18	4.97	5.46	6.44	6.14	4.97	3.57	2.96	2.87	39. Frais financiers
40. Net interest income	3.54	3.44	3.42	3.54	3.51	3.46	3.61	3.90	3.90	3.79	40. Produits financiers nets
41. Non-interest income (net)	1.29	1.47	1.49	1.54	1.66	1.70	1.92	2.07	2.26	1.98	41. Produits non financiers (nets)
42. Gross income	4.82	4.90	4.91	5.07	5.17	5.16	5.53	5.97	6.17	5.77	42. Résultat brut
43. Operating expenses	3.21	3.28	3.35	3.38	3.42	3.49	3.73	3.87	3.94	3.75	43. Frais d'exploitation
44. Net income	1.61	1.62	1.56	1.69	1.75	1.67	1.80	2.11	2.23	2.02	44. Résultat net
45. Provisions (net)	0.69	0.81	1.30	0.65	0.98	0.97	1.03	0.78	0.47	0.28	45. Provisions (nettes)
46. Profit before tax	0.91	0.81	0.27	1.04	0.77	0.70	0.77	1.33	1.75	1.74	46. Bénéfices avant impôt
47. Income tax	0.22	0.19	0.19	0.33	0.30	0.23	0.25	0.42	0.55	0.58	47. Impôt
48. Profit after tax	0.69	0.62	0.08	0.71	0.47	0.47	0.51	0.91	1.20	1.15	48. Bénéfices après impôt
49. Distributed profit	0.33	0.33	0.36	0.44	0.44	0.42	0.45	0.41	0.62	0.73	49. Bénéfices distribués
50. Retained profit	0.36	0.29	-0.29	0.28	0.02	0.05	0.07	0.50	0.59	0.43	50. Bénéfices mis en réserve
51. Staff costs	1.56	1.56	1.55	1.55	1.55	1.56	1.59	1.62	1.64	1.58	51. Frais de personnel
52. Provisions on loans	0.69	0.81	1.30	0.65	0.98	0.97	1.03	0.78	0.47	0.28	52. Provisions sur prêts
53. Provisions on securities	:	:	:	:	:	:	:	:	:	:	53. Provisions sur titres
% of gross income											**% du total du résultat brut**
54. Net interest income	73.32	70.10	69.63	69.72	67.98	66.98	65.31	65.29	63.29	65.65	54. Produits financiers nets
55. Non-interest income (net)	26.68	29.90	30.37	30.28	32.02	33.02	34.69	34.71	36.71	34.35	55. Produits non financiers (nets)
56. Operating expenses	66.63	66.98	68.19	66.65	66.17	67.68	67.48	64.75	63.92	65.02	56. Frais d'exploitation
57. Net income	33.37	33.02	31.81	33.35	33.83	32.32	32.52	35.25	36.08	34.98	57. Résultat net
58. Provisions (net)	14.40	16.44	26.40	12.79	19.00	18.74	18.67	13.07	7.66	4.92	58. Provisions (nettes)
59. Profit before tax	18.97	16.58	5.40	20.55	14.82	13.58	13.85	22.18	28.42	30.06	59. Bénéfices avant impôt
60. Income tax	4.57	3.92	3.78	6.47	5.81	4.54	4.55	6.96	8.90	10.06	60. Impôt
61. Profit after tax	14.40	12.66	1.62	14.08	9.01	9.05	9.30	15.22	19.52	20.00	61. Bénéfices après impôt
62. Staff costs	32.35	31.86	31.64	30.48	30.00	30.24	28.69	27.05	26.61	27.34	62. Frais de personnel
% of net income											**% du total du résultat net**
63. Provisions (net)	43.15	49.78	83.01	38.36	56.18	57.97	57.40	37.07	21.22	14.06	63. Provisions (nettes)
64. Profit before tax	56.85	50.22	16.99	61.64	43.82	42.03	42.60	62.93	78.78	85.94	64. Bénéfices avant impôt
65. Income tax	13.69	11.88	11.90	19.41	17.19	14.03	14.00	19.76	24.67	28.76	65. Impôt
66. Profit after tax	43.16	38.34	5.09	42.23	26.64	28.00	28.60	43.17	54.11	57.18	66. Bénéfices après impôt

ETATS-UNIS

Commercial banks (1)

Banques commerciales (1)

Per cent

Pourcentage

BALANCE SHEET ANALYSIS

ANALYSE DU BILAN

% of year-end balance sheet total

% du total du bilan en fin d'exercice

	1985	1986	1987	1988	1989	1990	1991	1992	1993	1994	
Assets											**Actif**
67. Cash & balance with Central bank	5.73	6.12	5.18	5.38	5.32	5.22	4.75	4.63	4.17	4.34	67. Caisse & solde auprès de la Banque centrale
68. Interbank deposits	6.66	6.73	6.71	5.93	5.26	4.12	4.11	3.88	3.21	3.25	68. Dépôts interbancaires
69. Loans	63.82	63.52	63.69	64.33	65.22	64.96	62.60	60.99	60.71	61.25	69. Prêts
70. Securities	17.55	17.92	18.44	18.25	18.20	19.23	22.06	24.24	25.75	22.84	70. Valeurs mobilières
71. Other assets	6.24	5.71	5.98	6.11	6.01	6.46	6.48	6.27	6.16	8.32	71. Autres actifs
Liabilities											**Passif**
72. Capital & reserves	6.19	6.19	6.03	6.28	6.21	6.45	6.75	7.51	8.01	7.80	72. Capital et réserves
73. Borrowing from Central bank	..	..	..	..	..	..	..	..	..	..	73. Emprunts auprès de la Banque centrale
74. Interbank deposits	6.65	6.28	6.20	5.18	4.79	3.97	4.33	3.84	3.83	4.28	74. Dépôts interbancaires
75. Non-bank deposits	70.84	71.25	71.57	72.39	72.35	74.08	73.89	72.96	70.35	67.26	75. Dépôts non bancaires
76. Bonds	0.54	0.58	0.59	0.54	0.60	0.70	0.73	0.96	1.01	1.02	76. Obligations
77. Other liabilities	15.79	15.71	15.62	15.60	16.06	14.79	14.30	14.73	16.81	19.65	77. Autres engagements
Memoranda											**Pour mémoire**
78. Short-term securities	..	..	..	..	..	..	..	..	..	..	78. Titres à court terme
79. Bonds	..	..	..	..	..	..	..	..	..	..	79. Obligations
80. Shares and participations	..	..	..	..	..	..	..	..	..	..	80. Actions et participations
81. Claims on non-residents	..	..	..	..	..	..	..	..	..	..	81. Créances sur des non résidents
82. Liabilities to non-residents	..	..	..	..	..	..	..	..	..	..	82. Engagements envers des non résidents

1. The coverage of Commercial banks was modified to bring the data into line with those published in the *Federal Reserve Bulletin*.

Notes

- Income data have been adjusted to account for the effects of mergers on reported earnings.
- "Non-interest income" (item 4 or 41 or 55) includes extraordinary items and realized gains on investment account securities.
- "Loans" (item 19 or 69) are reported net of loss reserves and include federal funds sold and reverse repurchase agreements.
- "Bonds" (item 26 or 76) include subordinated notes and debentures and exclude senior debt.
- Average balance sheet totals (item 29) are based on the quarterly average levels.

1. Le champ couvert par les banques commerciales a été modifié afin d'accorder les données à celles publiées dans le *Federal Reserve Bulletin*.

Notes

- Les données sur le revenu ont été ajustées pour rendre compte des effets de fusion en ce qui concerne les gains rapportés.
- La rubrique "Produits non-financiers" (item 4 ou 41 ou 55) comprend les profits exceptionnels et les revenus provenant des ventes de titres de placement.
- Les données publiées dans la rubrique "Prêts" (items 19 ou 69) sont nettes de réserves pour pertes et comprennent le solde des fonds fédéraux et les opérations de mise en pension.
- La rubrique "Obligations" (item 26 ou 76) regroupe les créances et les certificats de dettes subordonnés et ne comprend pas la dette de premier rang.
- Le total moyen du bilan (item 29) est basé sur les moyennes trimestrielles.

UNITED STATES

Large commercial banks (1)

ETATS-UNIS

Grandes banques commerciales (1)

Million US dollars / *Millions de dollars des EU*

		1985	1986	1987	1988	1989	1990	1991	1992	1993	1994		
INCOME STATEMENT													**COMPTE DE RESULTATS**
1.	Interest income	122996	116861	122871	141128	166876	167378	145040	131250	130427	138294	1.	Produits financiers
2.	Interest expenses	83112	74367	78736	92052	116580	115763	89444	68030	62901	65537	2.	Frais financiers
3.	Net interest income	39884	42494	44135	49076	50296	51615	55596	63220	67526	72757	3.	Produits financiers nets
4.	Non-interest income (net)	18774	23869	26579	29166	33509	35715	39736	45241	52395	49292	4.	Produits non financiers (nets)
5.	Gross income	58658	66363	70714	78242	83805	87330	95332	108461	119921	122049	5.	Résultat brut
6.	Operating expenses	38622	43680	48003	51155	55139	59872	64919	69955	76535	80290	6.	Frais d'exploitation
7.	Net income	20036	22683	22711	27087	28666	27458	30413	38506	43386	41759	7.	Résultat net
8.	Provisions (net)	8964	11203	27711	9896	21278	18211	21023	16470	10329	6328	8.	Provisions (nettes)
9.	Profit before tax	11072	11480	-4559	17191	7388	9247	9390	22036	33057	35431	9.	Bénéfices avant impôt
10.	Income tax	3082	3019	1710	5453	4330	3501	3156	6850	10176	12023	10.	Impôt
11.	Profit after tax	7990	8461	-6269	11738	3058	5746	6234	15186	22881	23408	11.	Bénéfices après impôt
12.	Distributed profit	3338	3830	4640	6189	6373	5613	6186	6005	10555	15908	12.	Bénéfices distribués
13.	Retained profit	4652	4631	-10909	5549	-3315	133	48	9181	12326	7500	13.	Bénéfices mis en réserve
Memoranda													*Pour mémoire*
14.	*Staff costs*	*19178*	*21417*	*22867*	*24068*	*25331*	*27135*	*27969*	*29232*	*31870*	*33727*	14.	*Frais de personnel*
15.	*Provisions on loans*	*8964*	*11203*	*27270*	*9896*	*21278*	*18211*	*21023*	*16470*	*10329*	*6328*	15.	*Provisions sur prêts*
16.	*Provisions on securities*	..	..	..	..	..	..	..	..	..	..	16.	*Provisions sur titres*
BALANCE SHEET													**BILAN**
Assets													*Actif*
17.	Cash & balance with Central bank	94366	106117	88304	95835	101996	103545	94222	93742	91737	104555	17.	Caisse & solde auprès de la Banque centrale
18.	Interbank deposits	108794	113185	124893	113928	108129	83432	86832	87829	77928	91907	18.	Dépôts interbancaires
19.	Loans	901140	953791	966987	1020859	1092996	1124969	1096605	1109360	1201840	1346936	19.	Prêts
20.	Securities	168604	204544	218360	222965	244293	261258	315286	375440	458419	438566	20.	Valeurs mobilières
21.	Other assets	110811	107375	116409	124741	126865	139182	139783	141105	153695	252433	21.	Autres actifs
Liabilities													*Passif*
22.	Capital & reserves	71190	78035	71573	83527	85072	92661	99831	123521	147034	158240	22.	Capital et réserves
23.	Borrowing from Central bank	..	..	..	..	..	..	..	..	..	..	23.	Emprunts auprès de la Banque centrale
24.	Interbank deposits	148751	147791	152166	129535	127770	109827	119573	106540	114230	145986	24.	Dépôts interbancaires
25.	Non-bank deposits	833334	902926	937826	1009189	1071453	1139366	1145959	1172636	1237383	1325701	25.	Dépôts non bancaires
26.	Bonds	12067	13883	14469	14483	16666	21027	22412	30722	33887	36889	26.	Obligations
27.	Other liabilities	318373	342377	338919	341595	373318	349507	344953	374057	451085	567581	27.	Autres engagements
Balance sheet total													*Total du bilan*
28.	End-year total	1383715	1485012	1514953	1578328	1674279	1712386	1732728	1807476	1983619	2234397	28.	En fin d'exercice
29.	Average total	1314148	1416574	1492652	1555275	1632951	1720137	1722974	1777490	1900719	2152895	29.	Moyen
Memoranda													*Pour mémoire*
30.	*Short-term securities*	..	..	..	..	..	..	..	..	..	..	30.	*Titres à court terme*
31.	*Bonds*	..	..	..	..	..	..	..	..	..	..	31.	*Obligations*
32.	*Shares and participations*	..	..	..	..	..	..	..	..	..	..	32.	*Actions et participations*
33.	*Claims on non-residents*	..	..	..	..	..	..	..	..	..	..	33.	*Créances sur des non résidents*
34.	*Liabilities to non-residents*	..	..	..	..	..	..	..	..	..	..	34.	*Engagements envers des non résidents*
SUPPLEMENTARY INFORMATION													**RENSEIGNEMENTS COMPLEMENTAIRES**
35.	Number of institutions	100	100	100	100	100	100	100	100	100	100	35.	Nombre d'institutions
36.	Number of branches	NA	NA	NA	NA	NA	NA	NA	NA	NA	NA	36.	Nombre de succursales
37.	Number of employees (x 1000)	648	653	646	648	661	659	646	668	693	696	37.	Nombre de salariés (x 1000)

Large commercial banks (1)

Grandes banques commerciales (1)

Per cent

Pourcentage

	1985	1986	1987	1988	1989	1990	1991	1992	1993	1994	
INCOME STATEMENT ANALYSIS											**ANALYSE DU COMPTE DE RESULTATS**
% of average balance sheet total											**% du total moyen du bilan**
38. Interest income	9.36	8.25	8.23	9.07	10.22	9.73	8.42	7.38	6.86	6.42	38. Produits financiers
39. Interest expenses	6.32	5.25	5.27	5.92	7.14	6.73	5.19	3.83	3.31	3.04	39. Frais financiers
40. Net interest income	3.03	3.00	2.96	3.16	3.08	3.00	3.23	3.56	3.55	3.38	40. Produits financiers nets
41. Non-interest income (net)	1.43	1.68	1.78	1.88	2.05	2.08	2.31	2.55	2.76	2.29	41. Produits non financiers (nets)
42. Gross income	4.46	4.68	4.74	5.03	5.13	5.08	5.53	6.10	6.31	5.67	42. Résultat brut
43. Operating expenses	2.94	3.08	3.22	3.29	3.38	3.48	3.77	3.94	4.03	3.73	43. Frais d'exploitation
44. Net income	1.52	1.60	1.52	1.74	1.76	1.60	1.77	2.17	2.28	1.94	44. Résultat net
45. Provisions (net)	0.68	0.79	1.83	0.64	1.30	1.06	1.22	0.93	0.54	0.29	45. Provisions (nettes)
46. Profit before tax	0.84	0.81	-0.31	1.11	0.45	0.54	0.54	1.24	1.74	1.65	46. Bénéfices avant impôt
47. Income tax	0.23	0.21	0.11	0.35	0.27	0.20	0.18	0.39	0.54	0.56	47. Impôt
48. Profit after tax	0.61	0.60	-0.42	0.75	0.19	0.33	0.36	0.85	1.20	1.09	48. Bénéfices après impôt
49. Distributed profit	0.25	0.27	0.31	0.40	0.39	0.33	0.36	0.34	0.56	0.74	49. Bénéfices distribués
50. Retained profit	0.35	0.33	-0.73	0.36	-0.20	0.01	0.00	0.52	0.65	0.35	50. Bénéfices mis en réserve
51. Staff costs	1.46	1.51	1.53	1.55	1.55	1.58	1.62	1.64	1.68	1.57	51. Frais de personnel
52. Provisions on loans	0.68	0.79	1.83	0.64	1.30	1.06	1.22	0.93	0.54	0.29	52. Provisions sur prêts
53. Provisions on securities	:	:	:	:	:	:	:	:	:	:	53. Provisions sur titres
% of gross income											**% du total du résultat brut**
54. Net interest income	67.99	64.03	62.41	62.72	60.02	59.10	58.32	58.29	56.31	59.61	54. Produits financiers nets
55. Non-interest income (net)	32.01	35.97	37.59	37.28	39.98	40.90	41.68	41.71	43.69	40.39	55. Produits non financiers (nets)
56. Operating expenses	65.84	65.82	67.88	65.38	65.79	68.56	68.10	64.50	63.82	65.79	56. Frais d'exploitation
57. Net income	34.16	34.18	32.12	34.62	34.21	31.44	31.90	35.50	36.18	34.21	57. Résultat net
58. Provisions (net)	15.28	16.88	38.56	12.65	25.39	20.85	22.05	15.19	8.61	5.18	58. Provisions (nettes)
59. Profit before tax	18.88	17.30	-6.45	21.97	8.82	10.59	9.85	20.32	27.57	29.03	59. Bénéfices avant impôt
60. Income tax	5.25	4.55	2.42	6.97	5.17	4.01	3.31	6.32	8.49	9.85	60. Impôt
61. Profit after tax	13.62	12.75	-8.87	15.00	3.65	6.58	6.54	14.00	19.08	19.18	61. Bénéfices après impôt
62. Staff costs	32.69	32.27	32.34	30.76	30.23	31.07	29.34	26.95	26.58	27.63	62. Frais de personnel
% of net income											**% du total du résultat net**
63. Provisions (net)	44.74	49.39	120.07	36.53	74.23	66.32	69.13	42.77	23.81	15.15	63. Provisions (nettes)
64. Profit before tax	55.26	50.61	-20.07	63.47	25.77	33.68	30.87	57.23	76.19	84.85	64. Bénéfices avant impôt
65. Income tax	15.38	13.31	7.53	20.13	15.11	12.75	10.38	17.79	23.45	28.79	65. Impôt
66. Profit after tax	39.88	37.30	-27.60	43.33	10.67	20.93	20.50	39.44	52.74	56.05	66. Bénéfices après impôt

UNITED STATES

Large commercial banks (1)

ETATS-UNIS

Grandes banques commerciales (1)

Per cent — *Pourcentage*

BALANCE SHEET ANALYSIS — **ANALYSE DU BILAN**

% of year-end balance sheet total — **% du total du bilan en fin d'exercice**

		1985	1986	1987	1988	1989	1990	1991	1992	1993	1994	
	Assets											**Actif**
67.	Cash & balance with Central bank	6.82	7.15	5.83	6.07	6.09	6.05	5.44	5.19	4.62	4.68	Caisse & solde auprès de la Banque centrale
68.	Interbank deposits	7.86	7.62	8.24	7.22	6.46	4.87	5.01	4.86	3.93	4.11	Dépôts interbancaires
69.	Loans	65.12	64.23	63.83	64.68	65.28	65.70	63.29	61.38	60.59	60.28	Prêts
70.	Securities	12.18	13.77	14.41	14.13	14.59	15.26	18.20	20.77	23.11	19.63	Valeurs mobilières
71.	Other assets	8.01	7.23	7.68	7.90	7.58	8.13	8.07	7.81	7.75	11.30	Autres actifs
	Liabilities											**Passif**
72.	Capital & reserves	5.14	5.25	4.72	5.29	5.08	5.41	5.76	6.83	7.41	7.08	Capital et réserves
73.	Borrowing from Central bank	..	..	..	..	..	..	..	..	..	..	Emprunts auprès de la Banque centrale
74.	Interbank deposits	10.75	9.95	10.04	8.21	7.63	6.41	6.90	5.89	5.76	6.53	Dépôts interbancaires
75.	Non-bank deposits	60.22	60.80	61.90	63.94	63.99	66.54	66.14	64.88	62.38	59.33	Dépôts non bancaires
76.	Bonds	0.87	0.93	0.96	0.92	1.00	1.23	1.29	1.70	1.71	1.65	Obligations
77.	Other liabilities	23.01	23.06	22.37	21.64	22.30	20.41	19.91	20.69	22.74	25.40	Autres engagements
	Memoranda											***Pour mémoire***
78.	*Short-term securities*	..	..	..	..	..	..	..	..	..	..	*Titres à court terme*
79.	*Bonds*	..	..	..	..	..	..	..	..	..	..	*Obligations*
80.	*Shares and participations*	..	..	..	..	..	..	..	..	..	..	*Actions et participations*
81.	*Claims on non-residents*	..	..	..	..	..	..	..	..	..	..	*Créances sur des non résidents*
82.	*Liabilities to non-residents*	..	..	..	..	..	..	..	..	..	..	*Engagements envers des non résidents*

1. "Large commercial banks" refer to the 100 largest Commercial banks. The coverage was modified to bring the data into line with those published in the *Federal Reserve Bulletin*.

Notes

* Income data have been adjusted to account for the effects of mergers on reported earnings.

* "Non-interest income" (item 4 or 41 or 55) includes extraordinary items and realized gains on investment account securities.

* "Loans" (item 19 or 69) are reported net of loss reserves and include federal funds sold and reverse repurchase agreements.

* "Bonds" (item 26 or 76) include subordinated notes and debentures and exclude senior debt.

* Average balance sheet totals (item 29) are based on the quarterly average levels.

1. Les " Grandes banques commerciales" font référence aux 100 plus grandes Banques commerciales. Le champ couvert a été modifié afin d'accorder les données à celles publiées dans le *Federal Reserve Bulletin*.

Notes

* Les données sur le revenu ont été ajustées pour rendre compte des effets de fusion en ce qui concerne les gains rapportés.

* La rubrique "Produits non-financiers" (item 4 ou 41 ou 55) comprend les profits exceptionnels et les revenus provenant des ventes de titres de placement.

* Les données publiées dans la rubrique "Prêts" (items 19 ou 69) sont nettes de réserves pour pertes et comprennent le solde des fonds fédéraux et les opérations de mise en pension.

* La rubrique "Obligations" (item 26 ou 76) regroupe les créances et les certificats de dettes subordonnés et ne comprend pas la dette de premier rang.

* Le total moyen du bilan (item 29) est basé sur les moyennes trimestrielles.

UNITED STATES

Saving institutions (1)

Million US dollars

ETATS-UNIS

Institutions d'épargne (1)

Millions de dollars des EU

#	Item (English)	Rubrique (Français)	1991	1992	1993	1994
	INCOME STATEMENT	**COMPTE DE RESULTATS**				
1.	Interest income	Produits financiers	94428	75419	65803	67502
2.	Interest expenses	Frais financiers	66018	43441	34710	37745
3.	Net interest income	Produits financiers nets	28410	31978	31093	29757
4.	Non-interest income (net)	Produits non financiers (nets)	9769	8408	8488	5129
5.	Gross income	Résultat brut	38179	40386	39581	34886
6.	Operating expenses	Frais d'exploitation	25387	24678	24227	23687
7.	Net income	Résultat net	12792	15708	15354	11199
8.	Provisions (net)	Provisions (nettes)	10727	7877	4738	2790
9.	Profit before tax	Bénéfices avant impôt	2065	7831	10616	8409
10.	Income tax	Impôt	3106	3211	4264	3577
11.	Profit after tax	Bénéfices après impôt	-1041	4620	6352	4832
12.	Distributed profit	Bénéfices distribués	..	2106	2293	2598
13.	Retained profit	Bénéfices mis en réserve	-1041	2514	4059	2234
	Memoranda	***Pour mémoire***				
14.	*Staff costs*	*Frais de personnel*	*9897*	*10014*	*10477*	*9867*
15.	*Provisions on loans*	*Provisions sur prêts*	*2065*	*7831*	*10616*	*8409*
16.	*Provisions on securities*	*Provisions sur titres*	..	..	..	..
	BALANCE SHEET	**BILAN**				
	Assets	**Actif**				
17.	Cash & balance with Central bank	Caisse & solde auprès de la Banque centrale	17922	..	..	16714
18.	Interbank deposits	Dépôts interbancaires	..	17796	18067	..
19.	Loans	Prêts	734848	657739	632030	640825
20.	Securities	Valeurs mobilières	288755	300063	303201	307317
21.	Other assets	Autres actifs	78834	62560	52337	45722
	Liabilities	**Passif**				
22.	Capital & reserves	Capital et réserves	68461	74010	77972	79032
23.	Borrowing from Central bank	Emprunts auprès de la Banque centrale	..	..	..	..
24.	Interbank deposits (2)	Dépôts interbancaires (2)	..	..	..	..
25.	Non-bank deposits	Dépôts non bancaires	901612	825727	768884	733608
26.	Bonds	Obligations	3524	3056	2534	2395
27.	Other liabilities	Autres engagements	146762	135364	156245	195544
	Balance sheet total	**Total du bilan**				
28.	End-year total	En fin d'exercice	1120359	1038157	1005634	1010579
29.	Average total	Moyen	1196666	1079258	1021896	1008107
	Memoranda	***Pour mémoire***				
30.	*Short-term securities*	*Titres à court terme*	..	..	..	..
31.	*Bonds*	*Obligations*	..	..	..	..
32.	*Shares and participations*	*Actions et participations*	..	..	..	..
33.	*Claims on non-residents*	*Créances sur des non résidents*	..	..	..	..
34.	*Liabilities to non-residents*	*Engagements envers des non résidents*	..	..	..	..
	SUPPLEMENTARY INFORMATION	**RENSEIGNEMENTS COMPLEMENTAIRES**				
35.	Number of institutions	Nombre d'institutions	2561	2394	2269	2155
36.	Number of branches	Nombre de succursales	NA	NA	NA	NA
37.	Number of employees (x 1000)	Nombre de salariés (x 1000)	303.0	294.2	284.9	260.3

UNITED STATES

Saving institutions (1)

Per cent

ETATS-UNIS

Institutions d'épargne (1)

Pourcentage

	1991	1992	1993	1994	
INCOME STATEMENT ANALYSIS					**ANALYSE DU COMPTE DE RESULTATS**
% of average balance sheet total					**% du total moyen du bilan**
38. Interest income	7.89	6.99	6.44	6.70	38. Produits financiers
39. Interest expenses	5.52	4.03	3.40	3.74	39. Frais financiers
40. Net interest income	2.37	2.96	3.04	2.95	40. Produits financiers nets
41. Non-interest income (net)	0.82	0.78	0.83	0.51	41. Produits non financiers (nets)
42. Gross income	3.19	3.74	3.87	3.46	42. Résultat brut
43. Operating expenses	2.12	2.29	2.37	2.35	43. Frais d'exploitation
44. Net income	1.07	1.46	1.50	1.11	44. Résultat net
45. Provisions (net)	0.90	0.73	0.46	0.28	45. Provisions (nettes)
46. Profit before tax	0.17	0.73	1.04	0.83	46. Bénéfices avant impôt
47. Income tax	0.26	0.30	0.42	0.35	47. Impôt
48. Profit after tax	-0.09	0.43	0.62	0.48	48. Bénéfices après impôt
49. Distributed profit	..	0.20	0.22	0.26	49. Bénéfices distribués
50. Retained profit	-0.09	0.23	0.40	0.22	50. Bénéfices mis en réserve
51. Staff costs	0.83	0.93	1.03	0.98	51. Frais de personnel
52. Provisions on loans	0.17	0.73	1.04	0.83	52. Provisions sur prêts
53. Provisions on securities	..	..	..		53. Provisions sur titres
% of gross income					**% du total du résultat brut**
54. Net interest income	74.41	79.18	78.56	85.30	54. Produits financiers nets
55. Non-interest income (net)	25.59	20.82	21.44	14.70	55. Produits non financiers (nets)
56. Operating expenses	66.49	61.11	61.21	67.90	56. Frais d'exploitation
57. Net income	33.51	38.89	38.79	32.10	57. Résultat net
58. Provisions (net)	28.10	19.50	11.97	8.00	58. Provisions (nettes)
59. Profit before tax	5.41	19.39	26.82	24.10	59. Bénéfices avant impôt
60. Income tax	8.14	7.95	10.77	10.25	60. Impôt
61. Profit after tax	-2.73	11.44	16.05	13.85	61. Bénéfices après impôt
62. Staff costs	25.92	24.80	26.47	28.28	62. Frais de personnel
% of net income					**% du total du résultat net**
63. Provisions (net)	83.86	50.15	30.86	24.91	63. Provisions (nettes)
64. Profit before tax	16.14	49.85	69.14	75.09	64. Bénéfices avant impôt
65. Income tax	24.28	20.44	27.77	31.94	65. Impôt
66. Profit after tax	-8.14	29.41	41.37	43.15	66. Bénéfices après impôt

UNITED STATES

Saving institutions (1)

ETATS-UNIS

Institutions d'épargne (1)

Per cent

Pourcentage

BALANCE SHEET ANALYSIS

ANALYSE DU BILAN

	1991	1992	1993	1994	
% of year-end balance sheet total					**% du total du bilan en fin d'exercice**
Assets					**Actif**
67. Cash & balance with Central bank	1.60	1.71	1.80	1.65	67. Caisse & solde auprès de la Banque centrale
68. Interbank deposits	65.59	63.36	62.85	63.41	68. Dépôts interbancaires
69. Loans	25.77	28.90	30.15	30.41	69. Prêts
70. Securities	7.04	6.03	5.20	4.52	70. Valeurs mobilières
71. Other assets					71. Autres actifs
Liabilities					**Passif**
72. Capital & reserves	6.11	7.13	7.75	7.82	72. Capital et réserves
73. Borrowing from Central bank					73. Emprunts auprès de la Banque centrale
74. Interbank deposits (2)					74. Dépôts interbancaires (2)
75. Non-bank deposits	80.48	79.54	76.46	72.59	75. Dépôts non bancaires
76. Bonds	0.31	0.29	0.25	0.24	76. Obligations
77. Other liabilities	13.10	13.04	15.54	19.35	77. Autres engagements
Memoranda					*Pour mémoire*
78. Short-term securities					78. Titres à court terme
79. Bonds					79. Obligations
80. Shares and participations					80. Actions et participations
81. Claims on non-residents					81. Créances sur des non résidents
82. Liabilities to non-residents					82. Engagements envers des non résidents

1. Savings institutions include Savings banks and Savings and loan associations,

2. Included under "Non-bank deposits" (item 25 or item 75).

1. Institutions d'épargne comprennent les Caisses d'épargne et les Associations d'épargne et de prêts.

2. Inclus sous "Dépôts non bancaires" (poste 25 ou poste 75).

MAIN SALES OUTLETS OF OECD PUBLICATIONS
PRINCIPAUX POINTS DE VENTE DES PUBLICATIONS DE L'OCDE

ARGENTINA – ARGENTINE
Carlos Hirsch S.R.L.
Galería Güemes, Florida 165, 4° Piso
1333 Buenos Aires   Tel. (1) 331.1787 y 331.2391
Telefax: (1) 331.1787

AUSTRALIA – AUSTRALIE
D.A. Information Services
648 Whitehorse Road, P.O.B 163
Mitcham, Victoria 3132   Tel. (03) 9210.7777
Telefax: (03) 9210.7788

AUSTRIA – AUTRICHE
Gerold & Co.
Graben 31
Wien I   Tel. (0222) 533.50.14
Telefax: (0222) 512.47.31.29

BELGIUM – BELGIQUE
Jean De Lannoy
Avenue du Roi 202 Koningslaan
B-1060 Bruxelles   Tel. (02) 538.51.69/538.08.41
Telefax: (02) 538.08.41

CANADA
Renouf Publishing Company Ltd.
1294 Algoma Road
Ottawa, ON K1B 3W8   Tel. (613) 741.4333
Telefax: (613) 741.5439
Stores:
61 Sparks Street
Ottawa, ON K1P 5R1   Tel. (613) 238.8985
12 Adelaide Street West
Toronto, ON M5H 1L6   Tel. (416) 363.3171
Telefax: (416)363.59.63

Les Éditions La Liberté Inc.
3020 Chemin Sainte-Foy
Sainte-Foy, PQ G1X 3V6   Tel. (418) 658.3763
Telefax: (418) 658.3763

Federal Publications Inc.
165 University Avenue, Suite 701
Toronto, ON M5H 3B8   Tel. (416) 860.1611
Telefax: (416) 860.1608

Les Publications Fédérales
1185 Université
Montréal, QC H3B 3A7   Tel. (514) 954.1633
Telefax: (514) 954.1635

CHINA – CHINE
China National Publications Import
Export Corporation (CNPIEC)
16 Gongti E. Road, Chaoyang District
P.O. Box 88 or 50
Beijing 100704 PR   Tel. (01) 506.6688
Telefax: (01) 506.3101

CHINESE TAIPEI – TAIPEI CHINOIS
Good Faith Worldwide Int'l. Co. Ltd.
9th Floor, No. 118, Sec. 2
Chung Hsiao E. Road
Taipei   Tel. (02) 391.7396/391.7397
Telefax: (02) 394.9176

**CZECH REPUBLIC –
RÉPUBLIQUE TCHÈQUE**
Artia Pegas Press Ltd.
Narodni Trida 25
POB 825
111 21 Praha 1   Tel. (2) 242 246 04
Telefax: (2) 242 278 72

DENMARK – DANEMARK
Munksgaard Book and Subscription Service
35, Nørre Søgade, P.O. Box 2148
DK-1016 København K   Tel. (33) 12.85.70
Telefax: (33) 12.93.87

EGYPT – ÉGYPTE
Middle East Observer
41 Sherif Street
Cairo   Tel. 392.6919
Telefax: 360-6804

FINLAND – FINLANDE
Akateeminen Kirjakauppa
Keskuskatu 1, P.O. Box 128
00100 Helsinki
Subscription Services/Agence d'abonnements :
P.O. Box 23
00371 Helsinki   Tel. (358 0) 121 4416
Telefax: (358 0) 121.4450

FRANCE
OECD/OCDE
Mail Orders/Commandes par correspondance :
2, rue André-Pascal
75775 Paris Cedex 16   Tel. (33-1) 45.24.82.00
Telefax: (33-1) 49.10.42.76
Telex: 640048 OCDE
Internet: Compte.PUBSINQ @ oecd.org
Orders via Minitel, France only/
Commandes par Minitel, France exclusivement :
36 15 OCDE
OECD Bookshop/Librairie de l'OCDE :
33, rue Octave-Feuillet
75016 Paris   Tel. (33-1) 45.24.81.81
(33-1) 45.24.81.67
Dawson
B.P. 40
91121 Palaiseau Cedex   Tel. 69.10.47.00
Telefax: 64.54.83.26
Documentation Française
29, quai Voltaire
75007 Paris   Tel. 40.15.70.00
Economica
49, rue Héricart
75015 Paris   Tel. 45.78.12.92
Telefax: 40.58.15.70
Gibert Jeune (Droit-Économie)
6, place Saint-Michel
75006 Paris   Tel. 43.25.91.19
Librairie du Commerce International
10, avenue d'Iéna
75016 Paris   Tel. 40.73.34.60
Librairie Dunod
Université Paris-Dauphine
Place du Maréchal-de-Lattre-de-Tassigny
75016 Paris   Tel. 44.05.40.13
Librairie Lavoisier
11, rue Lavoisier
75008 Paris   Tel. 42.65.39.95
Librairie des Sciences Politiques
30, rue Saint-Guillaume
75007 Paris   Tel. 45.48.36.02
P.U.F.
49, boulevard Saint-Michel
75005 Paris   Tel. 43.25.83.40
Librairie de l'Université
12a, rue Nazareth
13100 Aix-en-Provence   Tel. (16) 42.26.18.08
Documentation Française
165, rue Garibaldi
69003 Lyon   Tel. (16) 78.63.32.23
Librairie Decitre
29, place Bellecour
69002 Lyon   Tel. (16) 72.40.54.54
Librairie Sauramps
Le Triangle
34967 Montpellier Cedex 2   Tel. (16) 67.58.85.15
Telefax: (16) 67.58.27.36

A la Sorbonne Actual
23, rue de l'Hôtel-des-Postes
06000 Nice   Tel. (16) 93.13.77.75
Telefax: (16) 93.80.75.69

GERMANY – ALLEMAGNE
OECD Publications and Information Centre
August-Bebel-Allee 6
D-53175 Bonn   Tel. (0228) 959.120
Telefax: (0228) 959.12.17

GREECE – GRÈCE
Librairie Kauffmann
Mavrokordatou 9
106 78 Athens   Tel. (01) 32.55.321
Telefax: (01) 32.30.320

HONG-KONG
Swindon Book Co. Ltd.
Astoria Bldg. 3F
34 Ashley Road, Tsimshatsui
Kowloon, Hong Kong   Tel. 2376.2062
Telefax: 2376.0685

HUNGARY – HONGRIE
Euro Info Service
Margitsziget, Európa Ház
1138 Budapest   Tel. (1) 111.62.16
Telefax: (1) 111.60.61

ICELAND – ISLANDE
Mál Mog Menning
Laugavegi 18, Pósthólf 392
121 Reykjavik   Tel. (1) 552.4240
Telefax: (1) 562.3523

INDIA – INDE
Oxford Book and Stationery Co.
Scindia House
New Delhi 110001   Tel. (11) 331.5896/5308
Telefax: (11) 332.5993
17 Park Street
Calcutta 700016   Tel. 240832

INDONESIA – INDONÉSIE
Pdii-Lipi
P.O. Box 4298
Jakarta 12042   Tel. (21) 573.34.67
Telefax: (21) 573.34.67

IRELAND – IRLANDE
Government Supplies Agency
Publications Section
4/5 Harcourt Road
Dublin 2   Tel. 661.31.11
Telefax: 475.27.60

ISRAEL – ISRAËL
Praedicta
5 Shatner Street
P.O. Box 34030
Jerusalem 91430   Tel. (2) 52.84.90/1/2
Telefax: (2) 52.84.93
R.O.Y. International
P.O. Box 13056
Tel Aviv 61130   Tel. (3) 546 1423
Telefax: (3) 546 1442
Palestinian Authority/Middle East:
INDEX Information Services
P.O.B. 19502
Jerusalem   Tel. (2) 27.12.19
Telefax: (2) 27.16.34

ITALY – ITALIE
Libreria Commissionaria Sansoni
Via Duca di Calabria 1/1
50125 Firenze   Tel. (055) 64.54.15
Telefax: (055) 64.12.57
Via Bartolini 29
20155 Milano   Tel. (02) 36.50.83

Editrice e Libreria Herder
Piazza Montecitorio 120
00186 Roma   Tel. 679.46.28
                               Telefax: 678.47.51

Libreria Hoepli
Via Hoepli 5
20121 Milano   Tel. (02) 86.54.46
                               Telefax: (02) 805.28.86

Libreria Scientifica
Dott. Lucio de Biasio 'Aeiou'
Via Coronelli, 6
20146 Milano   Tel. (02) 48.95.45.52
                               Telefax: (02) 48.95.45.48

JAPAN – JAPON
OECD Publications and Information Centre
Landic Akasaka Building
2-3-4 Akasaka, Minato-ku
Tokyo 107   Tel. (81.3) 3586.2016
                               Telefax: (81.3) 3584.7929

KOREA – CORÉE
Kyobo Book Centre Co. Ltd.
P.O. Box 1658, Kwang Hwa Moon
Seoul   Tel. 730.78.91
                               Telefax: 735.00.30

MALAYSIA – MALAISIE
University of Malaya Bookshop
University of Malaya
P.O. Box 1127, Jalan Pantai Baru
59700 Kuala Lumpur
Malaysia   Tel. 756.5000/756.5425
                               Telefax: 756.3246

MEXICO – MEXIQUE
OECD Publications and Information Centre
Edificio INFOTEC
Av. San Fernando no. 37
Col. Toriello Guerra
Tlalpan C.P. 14050
Mexico D.F.
              Tel. (525) 606 00 11 Extension 100
                               Fax: (525) 606 13 07

Revistas y Periodicos Internacionales S.A. de C.V.
Florencia 57 - 1004
Mexico, D.F. 06600   Tel. 207.81.00
                               Telefax: 208.39.79

NETHERLANDS – PAYS-BAS
SDU Uitgeverij Plantijnstraat
Externe Fondsen
Postbus 20014
2500 EA's-Gravenhage   Tel. (070) 37.89.880
Voor bestellingen: Telefax: (070) 34.75.778

**NEW ZEALAND –
NOUVELLE-ZÉLANDE**
GPLegislation Services
P.O. Box 12418
Thorndon, Wellington   Tel. (04) 496.5655
                               Telefax: (04) 496.5698

NORWAY – NORVÈGE
NIC INFO A/S
Bertrand Narvesens vei 2
P.O. Box 6512 Etterstad
0606 Oslo 6   Tel. (022) 57.33.00
                               Telefax: (022) 68.19.01

PAKISTAN
Mirza Book Agency
65 Shahrah Quaid-E-Azam
Lahore 54000   Tel. (42) 353.601
                               Telefax: (42) 231.730

PHILIPPINE – PHILIPPINES
International Booksource Center Inc.
Rm 179/920 Cityland 10 Condo Tower 2
HV dela Costa Ext cor Valero St.
Makati Metro Manila   Tel. (632) 817 9676
                               Telefax: (632) 817 1741

POLAND – POLOGNE
Ars Polona
00-950 Warszawa
Krakowskie Przedmieácie 7   Tel. (22) 264760
                               Telefax: (22) 268673

PORTUGAL
Livraria Portugal
Rua do Carmo 70-74
Apart. 2681
1200 Lisboa   Tel. (01) 347.49.82/5
                               Telefax: (01) 347.02.64

SINGAPORE – SINGAPOUR
Gower Asia Pacific Pte Ltd.
Golden Wheel Building
41, Kallang Pudding Road, No. 04-03
Singapore 1334   Tel. 741.5166
                               Telefax: 742.9356

SPAIN – ESPAGNE
Mundi-Prensa Libros S.A.
Castelló 37, Apartado 1223
Madrid 28001   Tel. (91) 431.33.99
                               Telefax: (91) 575.39.98

Mundi-Prensa Barcelona
Consell de Cent No. 391
08009 – Barcelona   Tel. (93) 488.34.92
                               Telefax: (93) 487.76.59

Llibreria de la Generalitat
Palau Moja
Rambla dels Estudis, 118
08002 – Barcelona
              (Subscripcions) Tel. (93) 318.80.12
              (Publicacions) Tel. (93) 302.67.23
                               Telefax: (93) 412.18.54

SRI LANKA
Centre for Policy Research
c/o Colombo Agencies Ltd.
No. 300-304, Galle Road
Colombo 3   Tel. (1) 574240, 573551-2
                    Telefax: (1) 575394, 510711

SWEDEN – SUÈDE
CE Fritzes AB
S–106 47 Stockholm   Tel. (08) 690.90.90
                               Telefax: (08) 20.50.21

Subscription Agency/Agence d'abonnements :
Wennergren-Williams Info AB
P.O. Box 1305
171 25 Solna   Tel. (08) 705.97.50
                               Telefax: (08) 27.00.71

SWITZERLAND – SUISSE
Maditec S.A. (Books and Periodicals - Livres
et périodiques)
Chemin des Palettes 4
Case postale 266
1020 Renens VD 1   Tel. (021) 635.08.65
                               Telefax: (021) 635.07.80

Librairie Payot S.A.
4, place Pépinet
CP 3212
1002 Lausanne   Tel. (021) 320.25.11
                               Telefax: (021) 320.25.14

Librairie Unilivres
6, rue de Candolle
1205 Genève   Tel. (022) 320.26.23
                               Telefax: (022) 329.73.18

Subscription Agency/Agence d'abonnements :
Dynapresse Marketing S.A.
38, avenue Vibert
1227 Carouge   Tel. (022) 308.07.89
                               Telefax: (022) 308.07.99

See also – Voir aussi :
OECD Publications and Information Centre
August-Bebel-Allee 6
D-53175 Bonn (Germany)   Tel. (0228) 959.120
                          Telefax: (0228) 959.12.17

THAILAND – THAÏLANDE
Suksit Siam Co. Ltd.
113, 115 Fuang Nakhon Rd.
Opp. Wat Rajbopith
Bangkok 10200   Tel. (662) 225.9531/2
                               Telefax: (662) 222.5188

TUNISIA – TUNISIE
Grande Librairie Spécialisée
Fendri Ali
Avenue Haffouz Imm El-Intilaka
Bloc B 1 Sfax 3000   Tel. (216-4) 296 855
                               Telefax: (216-4) 298.270

TURKEY – TURQUIE
Kültür Yayinlari Is-Türk Ltd. Sti.
Atatürk Bulvari No. 191/Kat 13
Kavaklidere/Ankara
                    Tel. (312) 428.11.40 Ext. 2458
                         Telefax: (312) 417 24 90
Dolmabahce Cad. No. 29
Besiktas/Istanbul   Tel. (212) 260 7188

UNITED KINGDOM – ROYAUME-UNI
HMSO
Gen. enquiries   Tel. (171) 873 8242
Postal orders only:
P.O. Box 276, London SW8 5DT
Personal Callers HMSO Bookshop
49 High Holborn, London WC1V 6HB
                               Telefax: (171) 873 8416
Branches at: Belfast, Birmingham, Bristol,
Edinburgh, Manchester

UNITED STATES – ÉTATS-UNIS
OECD Publications and Information Center
2001 L Street N.W., Suite 650
Washington, D.C. 20036-4922 Tel. (202) 785.6323
                               Telefax: (202) 785.0350

Subscriptions to OECD periodicals may also be
placed through main subscription agencies.

Les abonnements aux publications périodiques de
l'OCDE peuvent être souscrits auprès des
principales agences d'abonnement.

Orders and inquiries from countries where Distribu-
tors have not yet been appointed should be sent to:
OECD Publications Service, 2, rue André-Pascal,
75775 Paris Cedex 16, France.

Les commandes provenant de pays où l'OCDE n'a
pas encore désigné de distributeur peuvent être
adressées à : OCDE, Service des Publications,
2, rue André-Pascal, 75775 Paris Cedex 16, France.

1-1996

OECD PUBLICATIONS, 2, rue André-Pascal, 75775 PARIS CEDEX 16
PRINTED IN FRANCE
(21 96 05 3) ISBN 92-64-04837-5 – No. 48740 1996